Praise for *Something for N[...]*

"Lears leads us on a grand tour of American [...] magic bags, voodoo and bibliomancy to lotterie[s...] ulation. This is the most playful book Lears has written. His prose is brisk and often funny; in many cases, he illuminates complex theory with winking double entendres. Invigorating."   —*Chicago Tribune*

"[A] rich and complex study . . . Lears performs a species of intellectual wizardry himself, assembling disparate cultural fragments—from riverboat gamblers to Wall Street brokers, from Cotton Mather to William James to Bill Gates, from Mark Twain to Ralph Ellison to Jackson Pollock—into a persuasive model of the rambling mansion of American thought. *Something for Nothing* looks largely backward in analyzing this peculiarly American antithesis between the belief in virtuous management and the belief in chance, but not without provoking in the reader intriguing speculation about where we stand today, susceptible as we seem to be to those who talk the managerial talk but walk the walk of fortunate sons kissed in the cradle by Lady Luck."   —*The Boston Globe*

"For some twenty years now, Jackson Lears, myriad-minded professor of cultural history at Rutgers, has been hammering out the details to a single story about the hidden costs of modern life. . . . Lears has now produced the third volume in this story. Put most dryly, *Something for Nothing* is a cultural history of American attitudes toward gambling. But it is also a Lears book through and through, a fevered dream encyclopedia filled with sharpers, grifters, conjurers, diviners and a kind of shadow companion to Nicholas Lemann's *The Big Test: The Secret History of the American Meritocracy*, tracing out lines of resistance . . . to the high Protestant myth that would yoke grace to social status."   —*Los Angeles Times*

"Distinctions in styles of wooing luck pop from the pages of Jackson Lears's *Something for Nothing: Luck in America*. Lears weds an astonishing erudition to a beguiling writing style. *Something for Nothing* is invaluably lavish in cultural observation and record."   —*The Times Literary Supplement*

"A . . . brief, stark summary . . . does not do justice to the subtlety, density, and intelligence of [Lears's] argument. This book has a serious, even a moral purpose. In examining the interplay between gambling and the wider culture in America, Mr. Lears, a humane man, seeks to underline how fitfully and unpredictably people get what they deserve in life."   —*The Economist* (London)

"A narrative so sweeping that there is a fresh example in nearly every paragraph." —*The New Yorker*

"Eclectic, provocative . . . Lears's admiration for gamblers, shamans, and tricksters inspires the wide-ranging curiosity that makes *Something for Nothing* fascinating to read. Like Louis Menand's *The Metaphysical Club*, Mr. Lears's book is a brimming tub of histories, biographies, and revealing anecdotes." —*The New York Sun*

"In his wide-ranging, big-hearted, and brilliant new book, Lears probes the ambivalence Americans have shown toward the masterless world of chance, from sacred bundles and faro banks to atonal music and abstract expressionism. But *Something for Nothing* is much more than a capacious piece of scholarship. . . . Lears beckons toward and occasionally enters an uncharted realm of cultural criticism. In every roll of the dice, he sees a question posed to the unknown—and maybe beneficent—forces of the universe. It's a view we'd do well to consider as we face a future in which imperial violence is a cruel terrestrial certainty." —*In These Times*

"Provocative . . . ambitious . . . a work that takes a chance—and succeeds—in presenting a new paradigm for understanding American culture." —*Business History Review*

"Lears thoughtfully reviews the American reverence for grace, fortune, and luck all the way from provincial casting of lots down to last week's bingo in the church basement. Fresh from the dust of antique books and obscure magazines, our author has clearly done a great deal more than adequate research in an attempt to encompass all of our national civilization under one mysterious rubric." —*Kirkus Reviews*

"It may seem unlikely that there is still something original to say about deep America; so many brilliant minds, starting with Tocqueville, have been at work deciphering the paradoxes of our all too mythic, all too preponderant country. But if anyone can, it is likely to be the author of *Something for Nothing*. Nobody is thinking with more spiritedness and subtlety about the roots (and ethical tangle) of American culture and the distinctive American pursuit of happiness than Jackson Lears." —Susan Sontag

PENGUIN BOOKS

SOMETHING FOR NOTHING

Jackson Lears is a Board of Governors Professor of History at Rutgers University and the editor of the distinguished journal *Raritan*. His previous books include *No Place of Grace* and *Fables of Abundance: A Cultural History of Advertising in America*, which won the *Los Angeles Times* Book Prize for history. He writes regularly for *The New Republic, The Washington Post, The New York Times,* and the *Los Angeles Times Book Review* and lives in the Delaware valley of western New Jersey.

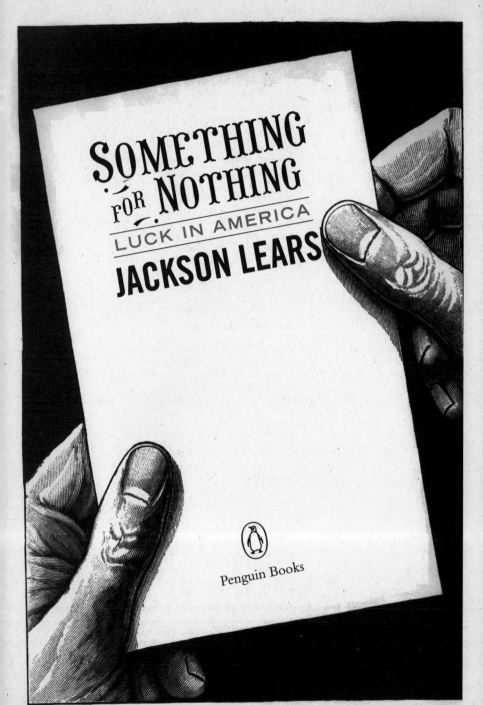

SOMETHING FOR NOTHING

LUCK IN AMERICA

JACKSON LEARS

Penguin Books

PENGUIN BOOKS

Published by the Penguin Group
Penguin Group (USA) Inc., 375 Hudson Street, New York, New York 10014, U.S.A.
Penguin Books Ltd, 80 Strand, London WC2R 0RL, England
Penguin Books Australia Ltd, 250 Camberwell Road, Camberwell, Victoria 3124, Australia
Penguin Books Canada Ltd, 10 Alcorn Avenue, Toronto, Ontario, Canada M4V 3B2
Penguin Books India (P) Ltd, 11 Community Centre,
Panchsheel Park, New Delhi – 110 017, India
Penguin Group (NZ), cnr Airborne and Rosedale Roads,
Albany, Auckland 1310, New Zealand
Penguin Books (South Africa) (Pty) Ltd, 24 Sturdee Avenue,
Rosebank, Johannesburg 2196, South Africa

Penguin Books Ltd, Registered Offices:
80 Strand, London WC2R 0RL, England

First published in the United States of America by Viking Penguin,
a member of Penguin Putnam Inc. 2003
Published in Penguin Books 2004

1 3 5 7 9 10 8 6 4 2

Portions of this book first appeared in different form in *The New Republic*

THE LIBRARY OF CONGRESS HAS CATALOGED THE HARDCOVER EDITION AS FOLLOWS:
Lears, T. J. Jackson, 1947–
Something for nothing : luck in America / Jackson Lears.
p. cm.
ISBN 0-670-03173-9 (hc.)
ISBN 0 14 20.0387 5 (pbk.)
1. Gambling—Social aspects—United States.   2. Gambling—United States—
Public opinion—History.   3. United States—Moral conditions—History.
4. Fortune.   I. Title.
HV6715.L415   2003
363.4'2—dc21   2002069196

Printed in the United States of America
Set in Bembo
Designed by Jaye Zimet

For K. P. L.

M. Fortuna

Il faut parier.

—PASCAL

{ACKNOWLEDGMENTS}

In writing this book, I have been the beneficiary of more generosity than anyone could deserve. Institutions and individuals have repeatedly demonstrated that the gift economy is alive and well in contemporary intellectual life. Besides financial and emotional support, they have provided constructive criticism and encouragement as well as a rich array of specific sources and leads. This book is heavily dependent on the work of scholars in various disciplines, but it is even more indebted to the kindness of my family, friends, and colleagues. I have been lucky.

My research was supported by fellowships from the National Endowment for the Humanities, The Winterthur Museum, and the Smithsonian Institution. At Winterthur, Gretchen Buggeln and the students in her advanced studies seminar created a stimulating atmosphere for the development of my ideas while Neville Thompson guided me through an extraordinary trove of sources and Karen Rege provided much useful advice. At the Smithsonian, as always, the staff of the National Museum of American History offered superb research assistance. I am especially grateful to Barbara Clark Smith, John Fleckner, Larry Bird, Charles McGovern, Fath Ruffins, and Annie Kuebler. The staffs of Alexander Library at Rutgers, Firestone Library at Princeton, and the Library of Congress all contributed dependable and essential support.

The participants in my National Endowment for the Humanities Summer Seminar at Rutgers University in 1996 deserve special mention. Carol Colatrella, Ruth Crocker, Chuck Bishop, Paul Vincent, Alexis McCrossen, Stephen Sylvester, Ed Zukowski, Fred Blevens, John Recchiuti, Ken Gutwein, Ralph Watkins, and Tim Killikelly brought many illuminating perspectives to the subject of "Grace, Luck, and Fortune," helping me to strengthen my conceptual framework as well as broaden my empirical range. They collaborated to make that seminar a deeply rewarding intellectual experience.

Rutgers University once again provided generous research support as well as a lively environment for thinking and writing. Among my colleagues, Richard Foley, Rudolph Bell, Matt Matsuda, John Whiteclay Chambers, and Michael Adas offered well-timed observations. Ann Fabian opened up the topic of gambling in provocative and stimulating ways. David Oshinsky read several chapters with perception and precision. John Gillis gave me an exceptionally thoughtful reading of the entire manuscript. Jill Anderson, Finis Dunaway, Neil Miller, Karen Balcom, James Levy, Ameer Sohrawardy, and Rachel Lears provided outstanding research assistance.

Many other generous people supplied advice and criticism along the way. Michael Laskawy, Gene McCarraher, and Sam Elworthy read the entire manuscript and commented helpfully on it. Ed Tenner, Scott Sandage, Christine Skwiot, and Gadi Taub offered fruitful leads and reflections. Colleagues at other universities invited me to try out my interpretations and engaged imaginatively with my work: these included Amy Dru Stanley, Tom Chappelear, James Curtis, Tony LaVopa, John Kasson, Charles Capper, Todd Gitlin, Rick Teichgraeber, Chris Rasmussen, Lois Banner, Steven Ross, Mauricio Mazon, Jill Fields, Walter Adamson, Jonathan Prude, Lizabeth Cohen, Joan Ockman, Richard Pells, Robert Abzug, and Nell Irvin Painter. Leon Weiseltier gave me a superb venue for working out the implications of my ideas as well as a steady stream of books, ideas, and encouragement.

En route to publication, two figures in particular deserve thanks: Loretta Barrett, my agent, for her enthusiasm and expertise; and Wendy Wolf, my editor, for her uncommon combination of skills. She has a lively wit, a sharp eye for academic verbiage, an impatience with abstract formulas, a keen sense of how to move an argument forward—and a host of other talents that make her one of the best editors in the business. Having a chance to work with her has been an extraordinary stroke of good fortune.

Family members have backed me in various essential ways. Robbie Parker, my nephew, kindly allowed me to use a picture of his Lucky Box. His dad, Rob Parker, explained how it worked and took a terrific photograph of it. My mother, Margaret Lears, and my brother, Lee Lears, both kept up a substantial interest in this project and supplied me with a number of invaluable sources, including some of the stories I like best. My daughters, Rachel and Adin, sustained me with shrewd observations and inspired suggestions. They have been a constantly revivifying influence on my work—and my life.

My greatest debt of gratitude is implied in the dedication. Karen Parker Lears has played a central role in the birth and development of this book. In her artistic work, she has been imaginatively exploring the implications of chance and accident (among other things) for years. It was she who first suggested I write a book on luck, and—as always—she urged me to push beyond stale formulations toward fresh ideas and insights. She provided many of those ideas and insights herself. Her presence in my life is the most astonishing gift of all.

Furman's Corner, New Jersey
May 2002

{CONTENTS}

{SOMETHING FOR NOTHING}

GAMBLING FOR GRACE

[I]

The impulse to gamble is mysterious and powerful. Anyone who doubts it might consider a few scenes from the recent casino revival: In Connecticut, a couple leaves a nine-year-old boy in a car overnight in freezing weather while they gamble at Foxwoods Casino. In Mississippi, parents also leave their twelve-year-old son in a vehicle, but with a revolver for protection. In Niagara Falls, casino operators complain that slot machine players are urinating into the plastic coin cups supplied by the casino or onto the floor beside the machines. Some wear adult diapers. All are reluctant to leave a machine they are hoping will soon pay off. And in Louisiana, video poker players report trancelike out-of-body experiences, the feeling of "being sucked into oblivion."[1]

What is going on here? For many public moralists, the answer is simple. According to Walter Cronkite, the legalization of gambling means that "a nation once built on a work ethic embraces the belief that it's possible to get something for nothing." Similar sentiments have sparked nationwide campaigns against casinos, one led by a Methodist minister and Vietnam veteran named Thomas Grey. He calls his recruits "Gideon's Army" and claims to be "fighting a battle for the soul of America."[2]

This struggle is not uniquely American. Gambling is provoking ferocious controversy in other countries as well. In 1992 Chinese Communist officials in Shanghai unleashed a campaign against mah-jongg that included mass self-criticisms by 4300 party members who had sworn off gambling, the public burning of 400 mah-jongg sets, and the commissioning of 5000 antigambling squads. None of this stemmed the Chinese obsession with the game. The modern conflict over gambling is part of a global war that has erupted periodically for several centuries—the clash between revolutionary virtue and reactionary vice. That struggle has sur-

faced whenever the righteous declare their intention to remake the licentious, to create a systematically disciplined "new man." As Michael
Walzer once observed, there is a direct lineage from Cromwell to Lenin.
And rectitudinous modernizers, whether Puritans or Communists, have
never had much truck with gambling.[3]

From the modernizers' view, gambling was a relic of a decadent old
regime—a vice that epitomized the European haut monde evoked by
Dostoevsky in *The Gambler* (1866). Dostoevsky's Roulettenburg is a society powered by feverish, erotic obsession—with money, status, romantic
attachment. Whatever the object, what is crucial is the desire to be always
in pursuit, on the edge, whether at the roulette tables or in a lady's cham-
ber. The only constraints on this quest for intense experience are the
remnants of a creaking caste tradition, a set of musty principles and rituals that easily can be counterfeited. In Roulettenburg, it is always an open
question whether this marquis or that countess is the genuine article or
not. In contrast, the revolutionary "new man"—bourgeois or socialist—
was an icon of authenticity.

Still, despite the international dimensions of controversy over gambling, the recurrent furor has a peculiarly American resonance. Debate
about gambling reveals fundamental fault lines in American character,
sharp tensions between an impulse toward risk and a zeal for control.
Those tensions may be universal, but seldom have they been so sharply
opposed as in the United States, where longings for a lucky strike have
been counterbalanced by a secular Protestant Ethic that has questioned
the very existence of luck. That conflict is the subject of this book. It is
not a history of gambling per se, but a history of conflicting attitudes
toward luck. Contemporary gambling games recall ancient rituals—attempts to divine the decrees of fate, and conjure the wayward force of
luck. Those rituals were (and are) rooted in a distinctive world view,
based on a certain respect—even reverence—for chance. This outlook
contrasted sharply with what became an American creed: the faith that
we can master chance through force of will, and that rewards will match
merits in this world as well as the next. For me, writing about luck is a
way of eavesdropping on a contentious conversation at the core of our
culture—a conversation that raises fundamental ethical, philosophical,
and even religious issues.

What makes the conversation so revealing is that it counterposes two
distinct accounts of American character. One narrative puts the big gam-

ble at the center of American life: from the earliest English settlements at Jamestown and Massachusetts Bay, risky ventures in real estate (and other less palpable commodities) power the progress of a fluid, mobile democracy. The speculative confidence man is the hero of this tale—the man (almost always he is male) with his eye on the Main Chance rather than the Moral Imperative. The other narrative exalts a different sort of hero—a disciplined self-made man, whose success comes through careful cultivation of (implicitly Protestant) virtues in cooperation with a Providential plan. The first account implies a contingent universe where luck matters and admits that net worth may have nothing to do with moral worth. The second assumes a coherent universe where earthly rewards match ethical merits and suggests that Providence has ordered this world as well as the next.

The self-made man has proven to be a far more influential culture hero than the confidence man. The secular version of Providence has resonated with some characteristically American presumptions. A providential sense of destiny could be expanded from individuals to groups and ultimately to nations—and to none more easily than the United States. Even before there was a United States, colonial orators assumed their settlements would play a redemptive role in the sacred drama of world history. As the Puritan John Winthrop declared in 1630, the holy commonwealth at Massachusetts Bay would be a "Citty on a Hille," a beacon of inspiration for all Christendom. By the revolutionary era, the city on a hill had spread to the whole society: America became "God's New Israel." As the new nation grew richer and more powerful during the nineteenth century, the profounder religious meanings of Providence began to fall away. Prosperity itself came to seem a sign of God's blessing—at least to the more affluent, who have always felt drawn to secular notions of Providence. Like the Rockefellers and other prominent pewholders in Protestant churches, America was rich because it deserved to be. For the deserving nation as for the deserving individual, progress was inevitable. Or so the more fortunate have assumed, from the first Gilded Age to our own more recent one.

A providentially ordered society contained little space for gamblers— at least in its conventional morality. Yet it was precisely the pervasiveness of social uncertainty that made the insistence on moral certainty so necessary. The salience of secular providence rose in response to the comparative openness of American society. Fortunate people have always

wanted to believe that they deserved their good fortune, but fortunate
Americans were in especially urgent need of reassurance. Compared to
the Old World, the United States was a riot of shape-shifting status
strivers. Beginning in colonial times, the abolition of hereditary privilege
broadened opportunities for counterfeiting profitable selves. Main Chances
multiplied with the emergence of unregulated market society in the early
nineteenth century. As in Dostoevsky's Roulettenburg, impostors proliferated, and the very boundlessness of American possibility demanded a
stricter set of internal prohibitions than were available in aristocratic old
Europe. The exorcism of the confidence man required the invocation of
his double, the self-made man.

As the apotheosis of plodding diligence, the cult of self-made manhood has posed severe challenges to American gamblers. For more than
two centuries, our moralists and success mythologists have disdained
gambling and denied chance, arguing that "you make your own luck"
and insisting on a solid link between merit and reward. The *New York
Times* columnist William Safire echoes generations of clerical critics in
his bitter condemnations of legalized gambling. "The truth is that nothing is for nothing," he writes. "Hard work, talent, merit, will win you
something. Reliance on luck, playing the sucker, will make you a loser all
your life."[4] In a competitive society, few apparitions are more terrifying
than the specter of "the loser"—the poor sap who never really grasps
how to play the game.

Yet the defenders of diligence have never entirely vanquished the
devotees of chance. At least since Tocqueville compared American society to "a vast lottery," our business mythology has celebrated risk-taking,
knowing when to hold and when to fold, taking advantage of "the
breaks."[5] Especially in flush times, it has not always been easy to distinguish gambling from speculation or investment, and even Horatio Alger
knew that luck was as important as pluck in achieving success. The gambler, endlessly starting over with every hand of cards, has embodied the
American metaphysic of reinventing the self, reawakening possibilities
from one moment to the next. The gambler and the entrepreneur have
been twinned.

Still it has been crucial to tell them apart. For those who believed that
the American economic system was part of a providential order, the respectable businessman could never be reduced to merely a fortunate gambler. Illicit gambling had to be distinguished from shrewd investing and

successful entrepreneurship. Historically, Safire and other moralists have played a crucial role in legitimating market culture, explaining away random or rigged inequalities by incantatory references to hard work and just desserts.

For a while, in recent years, it looked as if the bull market of the 1990s had posed a fundamental challenge to this rhetorical tradition. The sorcerers of the dot-com economy temporarily severed stock prices from the ballast of company earnings—the product of disciplined achievement over time. By banishing that vestige of the Protestant Ethic, they also helped to create new models of legitimate gambling. The best-known were day traders—sitting entranced at their computer consoles, dodging bullets, riding momentum, selling out just in time (they hoped), and feeling drawn inexorably to the frisson of danger. Their solitary, obsessive existence bore a striking resemblance to the life of the compulsive gambler.

Yet descriptions of day trading remained largely untainted by the language of pathology. It was a risky business, economic pundits agreed, but at the same time merely a distilled version of the game we were all constantly being urged to play. When money seemed magically to beget more money—or make it disappear—with no more apparent rhyme or reason than the arrangement of numbers on a screen, the hallowed distinction between gambling and investment became more difficult than ever to sustain.

All the more reason, then, to legitimate the new, on-line gamblers by stigmatizing the old, off-line ones, who tend to be grayer, paunchier, and poorer than the young whippets of Wall Street and Silicon Valley. Stock trading may breed pathological or destructive behavior, but it is seldom subjected to the clinical gaze of psychiatry—and even more rarely, in recent years, to the baleful stare of moralists. Even now, when we know that much of the bull market prosperity was based on fraud, moral outrage tends to focus on the confidence men who rigged the game rather than the game itself. As official thought leaders squirm to protect investor confidence, stock trading preserves a precarious legitimacy. Gambling, in contrast, remains a perfect target for dissection, disapproval, and oversimplification.

Though attitudes toward gambling reveal complexities at the core of our culture, inquiry into its significance has remained largely within the censorious boundaries suggested by a *New York Times* headline: "Fervid Debate on Gambling: Disease or Moral Weakness?"[6] This puritanism has long framed American discussion of personal habits that undermine the (implicitly Protestant) ethos of systematic self-control: cigarettes, alcohol, drugs, idiosyncratic sexual tastes. With respect to gambling, as with other guilty pleasures, we are offered a nonchoice between moral and medical idioms of disapproval.

The tendency to view gambling only in the context of other associated vices (alcoholism, drug addiction, prostitution) has clouded our understanding of its larger cultural meanings. A reformist agenda of social control provides a lens too limited to capture the complexity of practices rooted in venerable traditions. The problem with the critique of gambling is not that it is mistaken—without question, compulsive gamblers have ruined legions of lives, not least their own—but that it is too narrowly circumscribed. By reducing gambling to a collection of psychiatric symptoms or a sign of political corruption, critics have overlooked its wider web of connections to ancient, multifaceted rituals that have addressed profound human needs and purposes.

Debate about gambling is never just about gambling: it is about different ways of being in the world. That is a major assumption behind this book. It is not the sort of claim that can be comprehensively demonstrated, but comprehensiveness is not what this book intends. I aim to suggest persuasively, not prove conclusively. The main narrative concerns the constantly shifting tensions between rivalrous American cultures of chance and control. At its most familiar moments, this tale involves the face-off between the confidence man, the devotee of Fortuna, and the self-made man, the herald of Providence. But the story raises more serious philosophical issues than that confrontation suggests. It also ranges more widely, including women as well as men, conjurers and their clients as well as faro dealers and their dupes.

The confidence man is only a recent and commercial representative of an ancient, capacious culture of chance—a culture more at ease with randomness and irrationality, more doubtful that diligence is the only path to success, than our dominant culture of control. The culture of chance acquired special significance in the American setting, where it met unprecedented opposition from Protestant and later managerial apostles of self-discipline. But its origins can be traced into the dim past, to the person who first cast stones or shells to read in their chance array the will of the cosmos—and perhaps to conjure its power in his own or his clients' behalf. Runes are the ancestors of cards and dice. The conjurer and the gambler are kinfolk under the skin.

Cultures of chance and control are ideals that overlap and intermingle. They rarely exist in pure form. While both seek patterns of meaning in the random chaos of human events, what varies is the role of chance in this project. Cultures of control—as in the American Protestant or managerial tradition—dismiss chance as a demon to be denied or a difficulty to be minimized; while cultures of chance treat it as a source of knowledge and a portal of possibility. Cultures of chance have their own rituals, beliefs, even gods (though ones largely unacknowledged). They also have their own fetishes. A glance at the baroque extravagance of slot machine design leaves little doubt that the one-armed bandit is a fetish object refashioned for a modern industrial age.

Whatever their forms and rituals, cultures of chance encourage reverence for grace, luck, and fortune—powers beyond human mastery whose favor may nonetheless be courted. Since these three words will be frequently mentioned in the text that follows, they deserve some preliminary clarification here. By luck or fortune, I mean the force at the core of the cosmos that governs chance events, that can be sometimes conjured but never coerced. Grace is even more elusive. It is what happens when openness to chance yields a deeper awareness of the cosmos or one's place in it—when luck leads to spiritual insight.

The gods of the culture of chance survive in the contemporary American setting. The woman who consults a dream book to interpret her unconscious life (and learn what number to play) may be participating in an ancient tradition of divination. The man who buys a lottery ticket may be paying homage to Fortuna, a deity long discredited by devotees of self-help. However futile, his gesture still loosens the keystone of the dominant culture of control: our quasi-official faith (evangelical or managerial) in the human capac-

American slot machine, 1890.

ity to master fate. Apparently trivial games can
become ways of raising ultimate questions—of connecting numbers running
and cosmology, gambling and grace.

Outside Christian tradition, grace
could appear in many secular forms. It
could serve as a term for that ever-
elusive sense of oneness with the cosmos that athletes experience when they
are "in the zone," artists when they are
compelled by inspiration, or gamblers
when they are on a hot streak. If we are
lucky, grace could be what happens
when we take a chance, when we
cease trying to control events and simply play.

American slot machine, 1935.

In *Homo Ludens* (1938), the Dutch historian Johan Huizinga identified "the play element in culture," demonstrating how a spirit of serious
play animated religion, philosophy, law, war, and a host of other human
activities—a spirit obscured but not obliterated by the modern obsession
with systematic work.[7] The spirit of serious play preserves a critical edge,
despite its alarming resemblance to pop-psychological cant about the
wisdom of recovering our "inner child." The key to its complexity is the
constant possibility (and perhaps the ultimate certainty) of loss.

For the gambler as for the believer, grace can be born of losing as
well as of winning. According to the fictional female gambler in Peter
Carey's *Oscar and Lucinda*, there was always the chance that "one could
experience that lovely, lightheaded feeling of loss, the knowledge that
one had abandoned one more brick from the foundation of one's fortune, that one's purse was quite, quite empty . . . and no matter what
panic and remorse all this would produce on the morrow, one had in
those moments of loss such an immense feeling of relief—there was no
responsibility, no choice."[8]

In a society such as ours, where responsibility and choice are exalted,
where capital accumulation is a duty and cash a sacred cow, what could
be more subversive than the readiness to reduce money to mere counters
in a game? The gambler's willingness to throw it all away with merely a
shrug of the shoulders could embody a challenge, implicit but powerful,

to the modern utopian fantasy of the systematically productive life. The idea that loss is not only inescapeable but perhaps even liberating does not sit well with our success mythology, which assumes at least implicitly that "winning is the only thing."

What is sorely missing from American public debate is a sense, historical and spiritual, of this connection between gambling and grace. How could it not be? Urgent policy decisions regarding the prohibition of video poker or the providing of tax breaks for casino owners can hardly await the outcome of metaphysical speculation. Still the larger questions—the ultimate questions—demand consideration. Occasionally they have received it. The maverick psychoanalyst Theodor Reik, for example, called gambling "a kind of question addressed to destiny"—aptly catching the religious motives behind the wagering impulse.[9] But the crucial, clarifying connection between casinos and churches is the link between gambling and grace. The notion of grace as a kind of spiritual luck, a free gift from God, lies at the heart of gambling's larger cultural significance.

To some readers, the attempt to associate the sordid scenes of gambling with the exalted aspirations of religion may seem sentimental at best. Yet religious people themselves acknowledge the link. The Episcopal Reverend Jeffrey Black of Kansas City, Missouri, likens the wagering impulse to a yearning for redemption: "The whole hope of a human being is that somehow, in spite of the things I've done wrong, there will be an episode when grace and fate shower down on me and an unearned blessing will come to me—that I'll be the one."[10]

The most profound meditations on grace, from Blaise Pascal to Jonathan Edwards and Paul Tillich, have all led toward a refusal of anxious striving, a recognition that the dream of mastery over fate was a delusion. In this tradition, a sense of grace could not be produced predictably or earned systematically (though schoolmen sought to formulate methods); it could be courted only obliquely and experienced fleetingly. It was a gift, "something for nothing."

But even without referring to grace, thinkers who have given chance its due have raised fundamental philosophical issues. From William James to Ralph Ellison, the most thoughtful meditations on chance have been rooted in a willingness to live with unresolved conflicts—to embrace accident while affirming the possibility of transcending it, to acknowledge absurdity while sustaining a vision of cosmic coherence. This acceptance of paradox and contradiction undergirds a tragic sense of life: a capacity for hope in the face of inevitable, pointless loss—a state of grace where the cultures of chance and control can somehow come together.

Such speculations may be a long stretch from the bleary-eyed slot players, pissing in their change cups. I do not mean to dignify compulsive gambling or to deny its damaging effects. Lotteries are not in my view a fair way to raise public revenue, nor are casinos a good solution to the economic redevelopment of depressed areas. But this book is not about the contemporary public policy debate surrounding the legalization of gambling, nor indeed about gambling at all as an isolated subject. It uses gambling as a port of entry into a broader territory of contending cosmologies. Gamblers and their critics will appear often in these pages, but so will fortune-tellers, fabulists, philosophers, and theologians.

Participants in the culture of chance share a common indebtedness to a primary figure in Western myth—the shape-shifting Greek god Hermes. Patron of herdsmen and artisans and musicians, tradesmen and travelers and thieves, he was above all trickster-god and "bringer of luck"—hence patron of the Athenian lottery as well. Hermes presided over crossroads, places of uncertainty where chance and choice merged. His earliest monuments were piles of phallic-shaped stones often used as boundary markers. They set off the line between the known and the unknown, embodying a primal erotic energy for tradesmen and other itinerants.[11] Hermes captured connections between gambling and divination, between the desire to comprehend the cosmos and the longing for luck. In this he resembled other tricksters: the North American Coyote, the West Central African Eshu. By tracing Hermes' ties to the trickster tradition, we can begin to see the largest meanings of the culture of chance—its resistance to intellectual system, its openness to ambiguity and accident.

[II]

Toward the end of the Homeric hymn to Hermes [c. 535–512 B.C.E.], the lordly rationalist Apollo lectures the trickster Hermes on divination. "Only the mind of Zeus knows the future," he announces, and only Apollo himself has access to that knowledge. Human beings will be free to consult auguries but must somehow learn to distinguish between the genuine omens ("the flight of ominous birds") from mere mumbo-jumbo ("birds that chatter idly"). Like his father, Apollo will destroy some men and help others, without any apparent rhyme or reason from the human point of view.[12]

Apollo intends that Hermes will not know much more of divine purpose than human beings do. But he does bestow some divinatory power on Hermes, giving him three virgin sisters with swift wings, who live on Parnassus. "They teach their own kind of fortune telling," says Apollo, who practiced it himself as a boy. His father had no objection, apparently viewing this form of divination as a harmless amusement.[13]

Apollo's gift suggests a demotion of divination by lots from a sacred to a profane sphere of knowledge. As Norman O. Brown wrote in *Hermes the Thief,* the shape-shifting god "had no such oligarchic principles [as Apollo]. He was the patron of lottery—of which the mantic dice are one species—and lottery was one of the characteristic institutions of Greek democracy; the extensive use of lottery in the selection of Athenian public officials was the supreme expression of the democratic principle of the absolute equality of all citizens."[14] But Hermes is less a democrat than a diviner, who finds significance in randomness and prophecy in contingency. He epitomizes the central role played by tricksters in cultures of chance as finite but fitfully powerful deities. Like other tricksters, Hermes can conjure significance from apparent accident by deploying the appropriate rituals.

Divinatory rituals involve serious play with sacred artifacts—cowrie shells, palm nuts, smooth stones, soothsayers' bones, dice, or lots or coins. These apparently trivial objects can be charged with the force anthropologists call *mana*—the spiritual power that pervades, sustains, and rules the cosmos. *Mana* is morally neutral; it can be conjured for good or evil. It is a kind of first principle of potentiality, suffused with hope and foreboding. It is, in short, another word for luck, and like luck, it can serve as the raw material for grace. Divination ceremonies are attempts to conjure *mana*—to discern fate but also, perhaps, to alter it.[15] In nearly all cultures where such rituals are found, the trickster-god is their presiding deity, and chance plays a decisive role.

To understand cultures of chance and the ceremonies at their core, we need to question some familiar habits of mind. In particular, we need to abandon the linear, progressive framework that has often framed inquiry into "magical thinking." Divination and magical rites in general do not constitute merely "failed technology," as the anthropologist Bronislaw Malinowski put it in an influential formulation. Nor are they expressions of a "prelogical" or "prescientific" world view. They represent a different kind of thinking altogether, not an earlier station on an evolutionary commuter line. As a number of anthropologists have suggested,

the kind of "speech act" embodied in divinatory and other magical rites is "performative" rather than empirical.[16]

To compare divination to a scientific experiment is to make what philosophers call a category mistake. Divination offers solutions to existential problems, not by verifying or falsifying hypotheses, but by symbolizing hidden truths in ways that resonate with normative traditions. Though the process is symbolic rather than scientific, it can still have practical

Fecund inconstant Fortune . . .

results; magical rituals can be therapeutically effective—at least from time to time. As anthropological and psychological literature demonstrates, in cultures that mingle matter and

spirit, belief alone can sometimes create an extraordinary sense of physical strength and even foster apparently miraculous recoveries from organic disease.[17]

Still there are no guarantees. The divination process is far more subject to the play of uncertainty than its rationalist critics have acknowledged. The truths revealed by the ritual courting of chance are fragmentary and paradoxical—"an accidental glimpse of the divine," the poet Lewis Hyde writes, "and no sure way to know what it means." What is glimpsed is often less a static, timeless cosmic order

**. . . and sterile Misfortune;
English prints, 1779.**

than a primal plenitude that underlies and overflows all conventional forms. Fortune has traditionally been linked to material abundance and earthly well-being. The goddess Fortuna has often been pictured with a cornucopia, and good fortune has taken fleshly form in the traditional German use of the pig as a symbol for luck.[18]

Yet luck has never been reducible to a simple superabundance of worldly goods; it has
remained a basic principle of potentiality. Hermes and other trickster-diviners make appropriate emissaries between an imaginary
world of endless possibility and the everyday

German lottery sign, 1907.

world of imperfection and frustration. The diviner's clients hope to turn
the formless energy of pure potential into a benign, transfigurative
force—to transform *mana,* in effect, into what Christians call grace. But
there is nothing foreordained about the outcome of their efforts. Magical
thinking does not preclude uncertainty.[19]

Cultures of chance, far from constituting closed systems, are extraordinarily fluid. The symbols of divination themselves are polyvalent, beginning with the trickster gods, who all have shape-shifting multiple
identities. In cultures of chance, even apparently straightforward symbols
bear multiple meanings. Amulets, charms, mojos, "hands," sorcerers' bottles, and other vessels of *mana* can contain strong countercurrents of ambiguous possibility. Among the Luba of West Central Africa, for example,
a blind man's stick can serve as both an activating agent for visionary
powers and a conceptually meaningful object that concentrates knowledge, perception, imagery, and experience into one metaphorical location.[20]

If a single stick could be bursting with meanings, imagine the complexity of sacred bundles. Common in African, Native American, and
African American traditions, the sacred bundle is a bag, basket, or hollow
gourd containing miscellaneous things, ranging from glass beads, rocks,
and bits of wood to elegantly carved figures. These objects can be shaken
in their container and tossed in significant patterns.

There is something primordial and universal about the impulse to
make little bags or bundles of special things—special, that is to the maker;
to the observer they may still look like a pile of junk. Children are among
the most avid and inspired finders of fetish pieces and, in effect, creators
of sacred bundles. When they were small, my daughters made "lucky
bags" and other containers filled with fragments of *mana,* quite on their
own initiative. At age five, my nephew, Robbie Parker, made a lucky box
by filling an old metal moneybox with shiny beads, buttons, and bits of
glass. When a sports team he had decided to back (on whatever obscure
basis) fell behind in a particular game, Robbie pointed the box at the

players on the television screen. (More often than not, the chosen team turned things around.) The play-world of childhood is an animated universe, where *mana* can be conjured from stuff that appears worthless to adult eyes.

My point is not to resurrect the mistaken evolutionary equation between children and "savages," but to suggest that the impulse to create sacred bundles can take a variety of cultural forms. It is not merely a feature of remote tribal life. Consider the gentleman's cup and dice, which became a standard accoutrement of aristocracy in Europe and North America during the eighteenth century. Like every toss of the diviner's gourd, every roll of the dice created a new configuration of meanings, depending on the rules of the game. But those meanings were more limited in number and range than the soothsayer's. The sacred bundle may be less mechanically refined than the cup and dice, but more ambitious metaphorically.

African divination gourd and power figure, 20th century.

Divination hides as well as clarifies; it offers a fleeting glance at hidden truths but often leaves them obscure. Oracular language can be notoriously opaque, and even attempts to codify ritual meanings end by leaving much to interpretation. Whether one is casting sacred palm nuts or posing questions to the I Ching, numerology coexists with ambiguity. As in William James's pluralistic universe, truth remains enigmatic—a matter of "ever not quite!" There is something very Jamesian about cultures of chance.[21]

In cultures of chance, indeterminacy of meaning is paralleled by indeterminacy of form, such as the interrupted patterns of textiles made by Senegambians in West Africa and African

Robbie Parker's lucky box.

Americans in Ohio and Alabama or the aggregate of distinct shapes on the Yoruba diviner's bag. According to the art historian Robert Farris Thompson, such irregularities are meant to confuse and repel evil spirits for, as the Senegambians believe, "evil travels in straight lines." Their artistic decisions have philosophical significance as well. "The discretionary irregularities of design," Thompson writes, indicate "resistance to the closure of the Western technocratic way." This aesthetic parallels pluralistic philosophy in its openness to accident. Play is the bridge between sacred bundle or diviner's bag and modern collage or assemblage. The diviner and the artist are tricksters with the wit to make music from noise.[22]

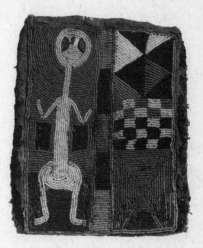

Yoruba diviner's bag;
Nigeria, 20th century.

Rather than elevating accident over design, cultures of chance tend to acknowledge their complementarity, in personal character as well as in the wider cosmos. Neither passive resignation to fate nor futile attempts to master it make sense in a culture of chance. Better to mix *alea* with *agon*— "chance" with "skill"—like a good poker player, who makes the best of the hands he is dealt. Better to emulate the trickster, to see contingency as a chance for creative improvisation—serious play—rather than to see it as a fatal loss of control. Better to live, as Sophocles said, on "the razor's edge of luck," than to succumb to the hubris of demanding certain outcomes.[23]

The largest significance of the culture of chance, then, is the opposite of the modernizer's dismissive view. Far from imprisonment in a closed system of rigid tradition, the culture of chance offers the ever-present possibility of springing the trap that keeps us shackled to routine—escaping from the narrow confines of alleged necessity (law, custom, circumstance, fate). Tricksters are adept at springing traps; diviners emulate them metaphorically. The typical diviner offers assistance to people who are "*caught*"—in a run of bad luck at hunting, in reproductive disorders, in illness of any kind. For diviners and their clients, the ritual courting of chance promises at least a fleeting opportunity to contact a realm where hope is alive.[24]

Luck is a gift from the gods, but an ambiguous one. Its meanings never stand still; like the trickster himself they zigzag and reverse their direction, revealing themselves obliquely and obscurely. An apparent "big break" can lead into a slough of misfortune; a bitter disappointment can open a path of possibility. The only good is "so far, so good."

For centuries, human beings have tried to bring chance to heel, by instituting a reign of religious or scientific certainty. In many ways, this impulse has been understandable and laudable—and responsible for extraordinary human achievement. Who can blame people for wanting to break the bonds of misfortune, mobilizing human mastery to alleviate suffering and to end injustice? Who can dismiss the desire for a universe that makes sense? Yet reality stubbornly resists intellectual regimes of control. To be sure, much misfortune can be explained empirically, traced to systemic inequalities of wealth and power, within the United States as well as the rest of the world. Yet loss and pain enter life at all economic levels. Among the privileged as well as the poor, events can seem opaque, suffering senseless, the universe inscrutable. Life itself still seems dependent on the mysterious power of luck.

No wonder amulets and other charms have preserved a fetishlike charge in a variety of settings, including the modern United States. Even in Western cultures, committed to economic and technical rationality, the lucky piece can preserve a transfiguring power. Think of the humble lottery ticket. An American sociologist summarized its magical significance in 1949: "The lottery ticket represents a tiny hole in the closed system of toil and budgeting, a 'safety valve' through which the repressed wishes crowd for escape."[25] Translated from psychoanalytic sociology into a more capacious idiom, the observation reinforces the affinity between gambling and divination. It suggests the common longing that animates the lottery ticket, the prophetic palm nuts, and the sacred bundle—the desire to connect with a force of pure potentiality and turn it to liberating ends, to conjure grace from *mana*. The lottery player and the diviner have more in common than they may suspect.

[III]

Yet it would be a mistake to overemphasize the similarities in cultures of chance or the continuities in their history. The American culture of chance, as it developed over several centuries, became a thing unto itself. It was largely a product of African, Native American, and European Catholic traditions confronting and commingling with a dominant culture of British-American Protestantism—a culture that (at least officially) exalted systematic achievement and allowed little space for spontaneity: a culture of control. Though Anglo-American conduct was often far more spontaneous and playful than official norms suggested, the dominant values' emphasis on *system* was subtle and far-reaching. It structured economic as well as spiritual life. In religious and later managerial idioms, this modern culture of control has shaped our public discourse for more than two hundred years—leading most educated Americans to dismiss the culture of chance as little more than a superstitious muddle.

Like the culture of chance, the American culture of control stemmed from profound and ancient religious longings. The most potent force in its development was Christianity—in particular its monotheistic impulse to sanctify a single, sovereign God, a *mysterium tremendum* whose powers transcended human efforts to influence or even comprehend them. There was a supreme irony here: what became an ethic of human mastery over fate was rooted in a Christian tradition that began by emphasizing human helplessness in the face of divine omnipotence.

In early Christianity, the rejection of pagan polytheism was the centerpiece of a broad theological agenda. At the heart of the emerging orthodoxy was a radical dualism, a denial of any intermediaries between God and man, or of any interpenetration between matter and spirit. *Mana* was no longer materialized in objects or conjured by divination it was etherealized into grace and dispensed solely by God. Or so theologians claimed, as they sought to centralize spiritual authority in a sovereign deity.

During late antiquity and the Middle Ages, orthodox Christianity was an attempt to assert the authority of an eternal order of things over the apparent chaos of everyday life. Trickster-gods were banished, along with the rest of the polytheistic horde. This was a cosmos that *made sense,* at least ultimately. In this providential design, there was no room for chance or for the glimpses of its significance provided by diviners. Indeed, theologians from Augustine to Aquinas consigned divination to the devil.

But popular Christianity was a different matter. Despite orthodox adherence to dualism, the untutored populace still inhabited a world where matter and spirit were one. The persistence of an animistic frame of mind meant that grace could not be entirely etherealized. It still preserved the properties of *mana;* it could still be conjured by performing the proper ritual or invoking the appropriate intermediary. And, despite the official triumph of monotheism, intermediaries survived and flourished—saints and angels and other embodiments of spirit in the developing worldview of medieval Christianity. Their proliferation suggested that for medieval Christians, revelation remained continuous and the world an enchanted place, alive with signs and portents.[26]

The merger of magic and religion flourished among ordinary folk (if not theologians) for centuries, well into the era of the Protestant Reformation. But eventually the Reformation created real problems for popular animism. The Puritan effort to recover an Augustinian strain of piety—a direct relationship with the deity—posed an especially sharp challenge to familiar habits of mind and sources of social authority. The denial of sacramental mediation between natural and supernatural worlds; the reassertion of an all-embracing Providence; the insistence that the experience of grace must be an inner transformation, divorced from all material artifacts and external observances—these impulses were rooted in the compelling conviction that God was too great to be cajoled by merely human hocus-pocus. Protestant reformers (and Puritans in particular) assaulted the European culture of chance at its foundation, undermining vestigial structures of magical belief.

Yet as Max Weber brilliantly observed, a Protestant theology of human helplessness coexisted paradoxically with a Protestant ethic of self-help. Eventually the ethic displaced the theology, as Puritans found themselves facing a strange New World that demanded and (sometimes) rewarded disciplined achievement. What remained constant in Protestant (and especially Puritan) tradition was what William James called "the sentiment of rationality"—the desire to make the detritus of life fit into a single, orderly scheme. Aquinas and Calvin shared that sentiment, but Calvin and the Puritans he inspired wanted to bring rigorous order into the rhythms of common experience. Life became, for many Puritans, a constant struggle for control of the inner self and the outer environment, not through magical ritual but through technical mastery. There was no room for divination—and none for its near relation, gambling—on this Puritan quest. What Weber called the disenchantment of the world had begun to pick up speed. As early as the seventeenth century, a modern culture of control had begun to emerge in Europe and North America, challenging the culture of chance at every turn.[27]

But never entirely suppressing it. The American culture of chance was constantly reinforced and enriched by infusions of energy from non-European sources—Native American, African, later Asian—as well as from European Catholic traditions. Nor was the culture of control entirely dominant among the Anglo-Protestant majority, many of whom consulted conjurers, carried lucky charms, and engaged in the recreational divination of gambling. Sometimes local circumstances—frontier conditions, superstitious immigrants, a Southern code of honor—preserved the popularity of the culture of chance. And throughout the nineteenth century, a continent full of opportunities combined with an unregulated market economy to underwrite a commercial culture of chance, with a variety of participants: gold diggers and oil drillers looking for a lucky strike, real estate speculators and three-card monte players looking for a gullible investor. Risky business remained the mainspring of entrepreneurial expansion.

It was not until the early twentieth century that the American culture of control acquired real dominance, and then in a secular rather than a religious idiom. A managerial ideal of productivity, dedicated to the systematic organization of just about everything, emerged in tandem with a more systematically regulated economy, dominated by a partnership between big business and big government. During the first two-thirds of the twentieth century, tolerance for gambling hit a low ebb. Laws long on the books began finally to be enforced; new prohibitions proliferated. A managerial consensus developed during the Second World War and dominated public discourse for several decades, until its social basis—an economically secure working population—began to fall apart during the 1970s. The post–World War II decades were the high point of the culture of control. That midcentury moment, for all its inequalities and exclusions, still constituted an era of unprecedented comfort and security for a large part of the population.

But even as the culture of control rose to unprecedented power in the twentieth century, it faced serious challenges—not only from the usual suspects in the gambling community (which survived well in private if only marginally in public), but also from artists and intellectuals. Gambling, suppressed as a social fact by the 1910s, made a comeback as a metaphor and a technique. Since the 1890s, an aesthetic of accident had been seeping into European avant-garde art and thought; by the 1910s it had spread to the United States. As older notions of Providence waned among the educated classes, the centrality of chance in human life became harder to deny. From the 1920s through the 1960s, as folklorists and anthropologists cataloged divinatory rituals, avant-garde artists rediscovered the role of chance in creativity. Happy accidents and lucky finds, they discovered, might well open new dimensions of meaning.

Then again, they might not. The very notion of meaning was under suspicion in avant-garde circles during the early and midtwentieth century. Religious and secular ideas of cosmic order were crumbling, and there was nothing in particular to replace them—though Paul Tillich and other idiosyncratic believers did succeed in revitalizing the spiritual meanings of chance. Artists who courted chance often hoped for illumination through accident, just as the early abstract expressionists used apparently random gestures as a way of releasing meaning from the painterly or collective unconscious. Yet chance artists faced the constant possibility that randomness might become an end in itself—another source of avant-garde high-jinks meant to shock an ever-shockable bourgeoisie. The specter of nihilism haunted the aesthetic of accident. Still, quite a few artists—Joseph Cornell, Louise Nevelson, Robert Motherwell, and others—kept that specter at bay by combining randomness and craft, lucky finds with larger intentions.

Different difficulties characterized the philosophical outlook fostered by the rediscovery of chance, the pragmatic tradition. Pragmatism began in William James's protest against the "'block universe" of Herbert Spencer and other mechanistic determinists, who denied chance by asserting that natural law governed all. But after James's death, pragmatism gradually became adjusted to the managerial ethos. The contrast between James and his successors underscores the accommodation. James's rehabilitation of chance as a philosophical concept foreshadowed his fascination with the realm of "pure experience"—a notion luminous with *mana,* remarkably similar to the idea of plenitude that underlies and animates the culture of chance. For James, chance could be a gift from the gods, a form of grace; for many of his successors in the pragmatic tradition, beginning with John Dewey, it was little more than a problem to be solved. Particularly when pragmatism was brought into the public sphere, it faced the constant threat of assimilation by social science and social engineering. The post-Jamesian pragmatists' uncritical (and unpragmatic) reverence for a timeless "scientific method," existing beyond history, politics, and power, opened the way for the positivist absorption of pragmatism and accelerated its transformation into a managerial tool. It was left to Tillich and other existentialists to keep the Jamesian legacy alive.

Thus, while the culture of chance began to spread into some new areas of American thought in the twentieth century, the managerial culture of control found new ways to contain it. The emergence of probabilistic thought was the paradigmatic example: in market research, risk assessment, and other forms of knowledge based on statistical surveys, the random occurrence became part of the standard deviation, the unpredictable exception that proved the predictable rule. After acknowledging the existence of chance, statistical thinking aimed to rob it of its power.

During the last third of the century, a meaner version of the managerial ethos developed. It lacked the sense of public responsibility in the midcentury version, and the secure working-class social base. (By the 1970s, a large part of the labor force was being fragmented and sorted into a "contingent labor market.") As economic insecurities and inequalities proliferated, so did the prospects of immense wealth for the privileged few. In the new Gilded Age of the late-twentieth-century United States, subcultures of chance resurfaced in the revival of legalized casinos and the entrepreneurial rhetoric of risk, as well as in the importation of magical beliefs by many recent immigrants.

But the culture of control still shapes our success ethic. Despite fresh evidence that hardworking people can easily lose everything to corporate confidence men, the insistence that "you make your own luck"—that you are personally responsible for your own economic fate—remains a keystone of our public life. There is of course a core of truth to this idea: disciplined effort is essential to success at most endeavours. But that does not mean that people necessarily get what they deserve. In recent decades, that notion has been repeated so often and so simplemindedly that it has become part of the general buzz of background noise in our society. By probing the historical origin of contemporary moral clichés and by playing them off against neglected alternatives, I hope to illuminate the philosophical outlook embedded within them—to make them seem less a part of the natural order of things and more a creation of fallible human beings.

In a public discourse dominated by the culture of control, this book is in part an attempt to redress the rhetorical balance by resurrecting the culture of chance, taking it seriously but not uncritically, reasserting the claims of luck against the hubris of human will. A culture less intent on the individual's responsibility to master destiny might be more capacious, more generous, more gracious. A recognition of the power of luck might encourage fortunate people to imagine their own misfortune and transcend the arrogance of the meritocratic myth—to acknowledge how fitfully and unpredictably people get what they deserve. So at least we can hope.

But that sort of openness is in short supply in the contemporary United States. Ideals of order and system, productivity and predictability, dominate our daily lives. In private affairs, the culture of control has made the harried look a sign of success—or at least of full participation in society. Sensible strivers and their children compete for an empty (and unattainable) goal of "peak performance" in everything from sports and sex to standardized testing. Genuine leisure languishes. Possibilities for play evaporate in a utilitarian atmosphere.

The culture of control continues to sustain the smug, secular version of Christian providentialism that has framed American morality for two centuries, though the favored idiom is now technocratic rather than religious. The hubris of the providential view lies in its tendency to sanctify the secular; in its glib assurance not merely that we are all part of a divine—or "evolutionary"—plan, but also that we can actually see that plan at work in prevailing social and economic arrangements, even in the outcomes of global power struggles. A more chastened (and realistic) perspective might grant a greater role to chance, if only as a counterpoint to the arrogance of ultimate explanation. That perspective is tricky to reconstruct, but it can be located in the speculations of artists and intellectuals, the assumptions of idiosyncratic believers and marginal subcultures, and the vernacular philosophy of gamblers.

All these groups are well positioned to challenge the central dogma of our time: the idea that money is an indicator of fundamental value. But none is better positioned than gamblers. "Great gamblers have seen the grim absurdities in capital and its accumulation," David Thomson reports from Nevada. "They know money is merely a game (like 10,000 on the Dow) and they insist on being playful with it. There is ease and even transcendence in that feeling." Viewed from Thomson's angle of vision, Las Vegas might lay claim to a more than metaphorically religious significance. The city is, he writes, "that rare thing: a city built in the spirit that knows its days are numbered. That's the eerie spirit of its profound casualness. The house itself knows that it is only there by the grace of God."[28] An emphasis on the pracariousness of wealth, the impermanence of life, and the arbitrariness of money as a measure of worth—if these are tenets of a gambler's worldview, it may be a perspective worth cultivating.

Even among gamblers, the desire for something for nothing is more than mere laziness and greed; it often involves a longing to transcend the realm of money-worship altogether. In his *Memoir of a Gambler* (1979), the playwright Jack Richardson acknowledged that the gambler (or at least the one he knew best) was engaged in a theodicy—in an effort to glimpse some coherence in the cosmos. To the "old voices" in his head demanding that he justify his life as a gambler, Richardson replied: "I want to know. . . . I want finally to know. . . . Whether I am to have any grace in this life."[29]

Such vast longings may well remain unfulfilled, at the gaming table as well as at the Communion table. Usually the best the gambler can hope for is a reminder that in spite of all the talk about making your own luck, good luck still happens on its own terms—obeying its own mysterious (or nonexistent) laws, without regard for the merits or demerits of the lucky person. But it does happen, at least from time to time. And when it does, it brings a dizzying sense of release from the grip of moral convention. As Frederick and Steven Barthelme recall in their remarkable memoir of gambling and loss, a big win at the casino was "a victory over money, the tyrant that has been pushing you around your whole life," and it was also something more. "There is a perfect alignment or echo between our experience in gambling and our experience in the world, and it is in the big win . . . that the echo is most apparent. All the disorder, illogic, injustice, and pointlessness that we have spent our ordinary days ignoring or denying, pretending to see the same world our fellow citizens insist on seeing, trying to go along to get along, trying not to think too much about the implications, all of it flows forth in this confirmation of pointlessness—by luck."

Watching those funny little symbols fall into place, the ones that resemble turtles and that represent a thousand dollars each, the jackpot
winner knows better than any Sartrean the absurdity of life. "It's about
beating *logic,*" the Barthelmes observe. "It's about chance confirming
everything you knew but could make no place for in your life."[30] To
court grace, luck, and fortune through serious play is to circumvent what
passes for common sense and seek to spring the trap of the predictable.
What happens next remains to be seen.

CHAPTER ONE

THE DANCE OF DIVINATION

A man grief-stricken by the loss of his son persuades some friends to join him on a journey to the underworld, the Land of Souls. They are delighted at first to find the same game animals, the same sorts of dogs even, as they knew in their life at home; but then they are accosted by the giant Papkoutparout, guardian of the Land of Souls, who threatens to kill them all. The mourning man flings himself on Papkoutparout's mercy, pouring out his tale of loss. Papkoutparout is moved; he decides to spare the father and restore the son. But first, he insists on playing a game of chance.

Since this is an Iroquois legend, Papkoutparout chooses the sacred bowl game, with caribou-bone counters that are tumbled from a dish or bowl and function as dice—six black, six white. (This is godlike elegance; mere mortals generally use peach pits.) During the game, the soul of the of the dead son returns invisibly to the wigwam. Papkoutparout turns it into the size of a nut, pops it in a bag, and tells the father to replace it in the son's body—but not to open it or to look into it. (The animated bag is a key artifact in the culture of chance, reappearing elsewhere as grisgris, mojo, sacred bundle, or voodoo bag.) If the bag is opened the soul will fly back to the Land of Souls. Arriving home, the father capers with joy, drinking and dancing with his friends; while he celebrates, his wife (or some other woman, in various versions of this misogynist tale) peeks into the bag, and the boy's soul flees.[1]

The role of gambling in this Orpheus-narrative is not entirely clear. The sacred bowl game was a form of serious play: it was associated with a weighty transaction between man and the supernatural; its ritual may have affected or at least ratified a crucial divine judgment regarding human affairs. The sacred bowl game was also played at the green corn and harvest festivals, as propitiation and thanksgiving and a means of keeping evil spirits at bay. It was a means of summoning *mana* for beneficent purposes.[2]

This was the essence of divination. The Iroquois tale reveals that gambling and divination are blood kin, though their relationship may sometimes be obscure. By exploring divinatory rituals in various early modern settings—European, West African, North American—it is possible to piece together the cultures of chance that coalesced to shape early American attitudes toward luck. What all shared was a common fascination with the mysterious power of *mana*.

CONJURING MANA

Wherever the culture of chance appears, at its center is the force anthropologists call *mana*. It is essentially luck, but it takes a more powerful and concrete form. It is a palpable energy that can be mobilized through ritual for good or ill. Multiform and mobile, it can reside in sticks and stones, rocks and trees, sacred springs and holy wells, serpents, birds, and swine—not to mention human beings and their products, material and immaterial: urine, blood, hair, words, thoughts, dreams, icons and images, amulets, talismans, and charms. A first principle of potentiality, it is suffused with hope and foreboding. It is luck made material, palpable, and accessible.[3]

Mana epitomizes the animistic world view that pervades most cultures of chance. From this perspective, there are no clear boundaries between matter and spirit, body and mind. The world is an enchanted place, alive with signs and portents, saturated with spiritual significance. The fluidity of *mana* means that it can be materialized in almost any form. Spirit does not inhabit a remote, transcendant realm; it can inhere in apparently trivial events (the flight of wild geese, the arrival of an unexpected guest) as well as in the basest bodily effluvia, the most mundane detritus of life—glass beads, chicken feathers, graveyard dirt, cowrie shells. In cultures of chance, humble things can be exalted; in the right ritual combination, almost anything can become a potent fetish, part of a sacred bundle or a voodoo bag. But these things remain mere trash unless they are charged with *mana*.

How does that transformation occur? The conjurer's methods are often mysterious and obscure. Gestures are made, formulas pronounced, gongs sounded—all in an effort to make material objects into instruments of revelation. Some forms of soothsaying do not require the use of fetishes: oracular inspiration, prophetic frenzy. But all cultures of chance at least occasionally endow material things with the power to mediate between the natural and the supernatural. Through the ritual use of artifacts, the diviner conjures *mana*—sometimes seeking to direct its power, sometimes simply trying to interpret its significance.

Methods of divination vary endlessly, but one of the most widespread (and one that most resembles gambling) is sortilege: the casting of lots to decide difficult questions, to discern the will of the universe. The most avid practitioners of sortilege in early modern North America—rivaled only by the aboriginal inhabitants—were the Africans who were brought there as slaves. In 1705 a Dutch trader in what is now Ghana noted that the natives there consulted their gods "by a sort of Wild Nuts, which they pretend to take up by guess and let fall again"; the actual procedures were probably much more complicated. Twentieth-century anthropologists have found that the Yoruba of contemporary Nigeria practice divination by (among other methods) throwing kola nuts or cowrie shells on the ground. For the most important occasions, they save the sixteen sacred palm nuts, which were given by the high god Ifa to his children as the concentrated essence of his healing wisdom, a means of renewing order and life in the world. In a rough parallel to the ancient Chinese use of the I Ching, specific arrangements of randomly thrown palm nuts correspond to specific verses memorized by disciplined diviners.[4]

The links between the sacred palm nuts and the gambler's dice are elusive but essential. Similarities between gambling and divination involve more than mere outward form; the gambler and the diviner both seek to conjure *mana* with the ritualized use of objects; both enact fundamental beliefs at the heart of the culture of chance. In trying to reconstruct that culture, often all we have are the objects themselves—or remnants or reports of them.

This sort of evidence is fragmentary but widespread. At Poplar Forest and Monticello (Thomas Jefferson's plantations) and at the Hermitage (Andrew Jackson's home in Tennessee) as well as in tidewater Maryland and Virginia, recent archaeological excavations have uncovered a variety of potentially significant objects in the vicinity of the slave quarters: quartz crystals, polygonal counters decorated with stars, cowrie shells, bone and ebony rings, and bright blue beads. "At Garrison plantation in Maryland," a cultural historian reports, "a worked tumbler base, decanter finials, and a polished stone were found in connection with a number of worked gaming pieces in a variety of materials." Such elaborate "gaming pieces" may well have had divinatory significance as well.[5]

The boundary between gambling and divination has always been shifting and loosely patroled, with different roles in different territories. Often the difference is difficult to verify. Consider the four cowrie shells of the Igbo of West Africa, who threw them to divine the future: four shells with the openings down were a good omen; three and one signified calamity and ruin. In the eighteenth century, Igbos were enslaved and dragged off to North America, where they were observed on the wharves of New England ports, playing a game with cowrie shells. They shook four and cast them: even combinations won, odd ones lost.[6]

What was at stake in this game? It seems reasonable to suppose that, for the Igbo, cowrie shells carried their divinatory powers to the New World. Old magical beliefs survived in a radically new setting, though we can never know their full significance for the believers themselves. What we do know is that the Europeans who encountered such rituals in America (or discovered their remains) came from a very different tradition. The elite sources of Western thought—classical, Jewish, Christian—were ambivalent and often overtly hostile toward magical thinking and divination while vernacular opinion remained more consistently sympathetic. This made for ambiguities from the outset in the Western culture of chance.

MAGIC AND LUCK IN THE WESTERN TRADITION

In the classical world, notions of cosmic order jostled uneasily with awareness of chance. Apollo and Hermes remained constantly at odds. As the Homeric hymn to Hermes implied, the apparent triumph of Apollo concealed the complex actuality of Hermes' power. Despite the authority of reason among the elite, the trickster continued to vindicate the irrational force of luck among ordinary people. The popular Roman dice game *alea* not only provided opportunities for testing one's *fortuna;* it also constituted a vernacular form of divination, providing insight into a hidden cosmic order where rich and poor could meet on equal terms. No wonder classical philosophers aimed to discredit reliance on divination by fostering an ethic of autonomy. "A man is the origin of his actions," Aristotle announced in the *Nicomachean Ethics* (c. 322 B.C.E.), and Sallust told the Roman senate that "every man is the author of his own fortune." This emphasis on making your own luck, which would become a centerpiece of modern liberal individualism, was carried forward in the writings of such protoliberals as Cicero. Yet even among men of affairs, belief in signs and portents was pervasive. Most Romans were unwilling to place their faith in human abilities alone; all sorts sought to propitiate Fortuna with ritual offerings at her shrine.[7]

The ancient Jews had no use for such practices. As monotheists, they distrusted intermediaries and emphasized direct revelation; Yahweh alone was the source of spiritual power. Divinatory rites were mostly confined to the mysterious Urim and Thummim, which may have been two stones or other objects used by the high priests to divine the will of God in crisis situations.[8] Early Christians shared the Hebrew suspicion of magic and divination. Like the Jews, the Christians were concerned to emphasize God's majesty, remoteness, and omnipotence. Dualistic divisions between matter and spirit, nature and the supernatural, flowed from that concern and rendered *mana* problematic. It could no longer reside in the fallen, earthly realm; to call up the oracular powers of rivers, rocks, and trees was to risk summoning demons, disturbers of the lower air.[9]

In lieu of a principle of luck, embedded in the workings of the natural order, Christians embraced a transcendent Providence. Its unfolding was as mysterious as the movements of luck, but however remote its creator or apparently perverse his decrees, Christians believed he was orchestrating everything in accordance with a benevolent plan. Everything was under control. Boethius made this clear in *The Consolation of Philosophy* (c. 524), which became a major basis of elite apologetics for a thousand years. The author, after a distinguished public-service career, had fallen out of favor in the corridors of power and, due to his own unbending rectitude, had been imprisoned. "Well here am I, stripped of my possessions and honors, my reputation ruined, punished because I tried to do good," he lamented. "Why should uncertain Fortune control our lives?" Lady Philosophy appeared and upbraided him. Behind the apparent caprices of Fortune, she said, God is governing all things with "the rudder of goodness." This was Providence. What we thought of as whims of fate were part of the divine plan; our inability to discern it was merely a result of human frailty: "divine wisdom does what the ignorant cannot understand."[10]

As for chance—it was merely "an empty word," said Lady Philosophy. "Nothing in the realm of Providence is left to chance." After all, "what room can there be for random events since God keeps all things in order?"[11] This was the orthodox Christian argument that would be repeated for centuries. There was little room for divination in such a cosmos. The Christian God was too abstract, distant, and powerful to be conjured through ritual play. *Mana* was etherealized into divine grace, no longer dispersed in streams and stones. That remained the orthodox Christian view for centuries, from the decline of the Roman Empire to the European settlement of North America. From Augustine and Aquinas to Calvin and Edwards, theologians embraced this view.

Yet we should take care not to confuse elite orthodoxy with vernacular belief. On the ground, the old animistic tendencies continued to flourish. As early as Boethius's time, canonical authorities began to realize that compromise with popular magic was more effective than opposition to it. Early medieval Catholicism made its peace with paganism; syncretism sustained magical thinking.

Well into the era of the Reformation, most Christian believers had difficulty distinguishing prayers and rituals from charms and spells. Popular Catholicism fostered the belief that the mere act of repeating Latin words and phrases according to formula constituted a mechanically effective means of protection against plague, storm, fire, or other misfortune. Material objects continued to possess a fetishlike power in the popular imagination. Altarcloths and tombcloths, for example, were known as *Godwebbe* and were used in sortilege as well as in curing cattle of lung disease. The *Godwebbe* were part of a burned mixture that supposedly produced therapeutic smoke; spirit and matter mingled in this *mana*. It could be conjured through the use of amulets and talismans, altarpieces and chalices and holy wells, not to mention the bread and wine of the Eucharistic sacrifice.[12]

Some magic had to be confronted head-on, but even then there were contradictions and compromises. Astrology grew in strength through the early Middle Ages because Christian commentators realized it could be assimilated to their doctrines far more easily than other more alarming forms of divination, such as witchcraft or necromancy (contacting the dead). But the clearest example of successful religious magic was the adaptation of sortilege to Christian purposes. The ritual persisted from ancient Rome and barbarian Germany into the late sixth and early seventh centuries: the Frisians practiced what might be called extreme sortilege, human sacrifice by lot (the subject, incidentally, of Shirley Jackson's famous story "The Lottery"). A milder version was the *Sortes Sangallenses,* a written lottery, operated by dice, that answered questions about the future. Christians condemned it, then went into competition by resorting to the *Sortes Sanctorum*—the use of the Bible as a means of divination, either by opening it to a random passage or rolling dice to choose chapter and verse.[13]

This bibliomancy was never completely orthodox but almost always tolerated by canny Christian clerics who knew a way to accommodate popular magic when they saw one. And, indeed, there were sound psychological reasons for encouraging the practice—deep affinities between *sortes* and hope. As the historian Valerie Flint remarks: "It is hard to perpetuate a joyous belief in Divine Providence and yet totally to deny to that Providence all possibility of interventions of this kind. Lotteries could (and can) keep hope alive, and a faith in the conceivably beneficial effects of chance can do much to lift the spirits." Like Fortune, Providence could be courted through sortilege—sacred play. It is of course possible to see elite-sponsored lotteries (religious or secular) as cynical strategies for social control, but they evoke sentiments too complex to be reducible to mere sociological meaning. In fact, the Christian adoption of magic marked a major shift in intercessory rituals, a change in their emotional tone from fear to hope.[14]

This transition was part of a broad and powerful but implicit redefinition of *mana* as grace—a beneficent force, a free gift from God, spiritual luck. According to the Augustinian tradition, grace was entirely supernatural, a product of conversion, a precondition for salvation. But the emerging medieval synthesis—dualism for the few, animism for the many—sanctioned a drift toward sacramental instruments of grace. While the orthodox emphasized the worthlessness of the sacrament without the proper disposition of the soul, the popular tradition attached magical powers to the things themselves: crucifixes, medals, and icons became, in effect, good luck charms, containers for *mana* with the capacity to ward off earthly calamity. The vernacular version of grace, like *mana,* mingled natural and supernatural powers.

Despite the efforts of Thomas Aquinas and other theologians to equate divination with demon worship, the merger of magic and religion flourished among ordinary folk for centuries, well into the era of the Protestant Reformation. Reformers assaulted the animistic core of magical belief, but their project remained incomplete. Old beliefs died hard, and sometimes did not die at all. Despite the seriousness of the Protestant challenge, the culture of chance persisted, even among Protestants themselves. On the eve of the Virginia Company's landing at Jamestown, the English population's worldview was a patchwork of animism and dualism, of medieval magic, Renaissance science, and varieties of Protestant religion.[15] This was the intellectual baggage the colonists would bring to the New World.

THE LIMITS OF DISENCHANTMENT

Luther's idea that salvation came through faith rather than works occurred to him while he sat astride the privy. This coincidence of circumstances was theologically significant: It sharpened Luther's polemic against Catholic ritual. He came to believe that all of humankind's puny efforts to placate or cajole divine favor were as so much dung in the eyes of the Almighty (or, as later evangelicals would have it, a stench in the nostrils of Jehovah). What Catholics and other practitioners of magic thought was *mana,* in Luther's view, was little more than shit.[16] His scatological imagination embodied the founding faith of Protestantism: that grace came not through outer observance, but through inner conviction. And for at least some of his successors, a state of grace could be achieved only through protracted psychic torment.

Few Protestants yearned for grace more intensely than the English Puritans, and no English document expresses their longings more eloquently than John Bunyan's *Grace Abounding to the Chief of Sinners* (1666). Despite its title, *Grace Abounding* is not a rapturous account of delight in the presence of the deity. On the contrary, the experience of grace occurs almost imperceptibly, while Bunyan is silently repeating the biblical incantation: "My grace is sufficient [for thee]"—and only after long passages of "sorrow and affliction." Bunyan worries constantly that he missed his opportunity: "How if the day of grace be past and gone?" he asks. As his conviction of his own worthlessness becomes almost overwhelming, he writes, "the very stones in the street and tiles upon the houses, did bend themselves against me." And at last, when he does experience what he believes is a genuine conversion, he has "such strange apprehensions of the grace of God, that I could hardly bear up under it, it was so out of measure amazing . . . if that sense of it had abode long upon me, it would have made me incapable for business."[17] The impact of amazing grace could sometimes run afoul of commitments to disciplined achievement; Protestant theology and Protestant ethics could be at odds.

But they came together in distrust of gambling. For Luther, Bunyan, and other early Protestants, gambling was not only a frivolous waste of precious time, it was a port of entry into a rival cosmology. "Any way of grappling with the unknowable, any potential animistic path which explained the inexplicable and sought favors of an all-powerful exterior being became heretical," writes the psychoanalyst Peter Fuller. "Gambling was just such a diabolic phenomenon."[18] Protestant critics of gambling were shrewd enough to recognize a rival religion—or at least an alternative worldview. The gambler's quest was directed to a different sort of God and situated in a different sort of economy—one based on conjuring rather than calculating, interpreting rather than accumulating, play rather than work.

Early Protestant pronouncements on gambling recognized its religious basis. "I say all lots are religious," the American Puritan John Cotton asserted in 1656. "In all kinds of lottery, whatsoever it bee about, wee appeal to God, who is disposer of all things." To gamble was to "play with the Judgments of God." As God's will was involved in the minutiae of everyday life, down to and including the roll of a die, gambling was a blasphemous attempt to attract divine attention to frivolous matters.[19]

The capaciousness of the Puritan notion of Providence left only one conclusion possible regarding the existence of chance. "*There is no such thing as fortune or chance,*" John Calvin had announced in 1561, and generations of his followers embraced that view. Every unfolding event, no matter how tiny or trivial, was governed by "a new, a special providence of God." The doctrine of special providences meant that even "things seemingly most fortuitous are subject to him"—a branch breaking off a tree and killing a passing traveler; an apparently random casting of pebbles (or dice); even wildly unequal divisions of wealth and poverty. Indeed, it is only by God's "secret plan," Calvin wrote, "that some distinguish themselves, while others remain contemptible." This was the ultimate deterministic universe.[20]

As long as predestination was coupled with the Calvinist stress on innate depravity, it preserved a sort of spiritual democracy: everyone was equally base in the sight of God. But when liberalizing theologians began to emphasize human beings' ability to save themselves, success began to signify a convergence of personal merit and providential plan. Gradually and haltingly but unmistakably, the Protestant belief in Providence (and the parallel disbelief in chance) became a way of providing spiritual sanctions for the economic status quo—rather than providing insight, as gambling sometimes did, into a hidden order of things in which rich and poor alike were subject to the whims of fortune. Providence implicitly underwrote inequalities of wealth. "A female sectary confessed [in 1653] that she fell into a religious depression when she saw her neighbors prosper more in the world than she, for it could only mean that they prayed at home more than she did," Keith Thomas reports. Providence surrounded prosperity with an aura of sanctity.[21]

Summarized thus quickly and baldly, the impact of the Reformation on the culture of chance seems devastating. The effort to conjure *mana* was etherealized and internalized into a psychological struggle for grace; the early Christian cleavage between body and soul, matter and spirit, was restored; the material world was deprived of sanctity, turned to (rhetorical) shit. Everyday life became the inner struggle of the autonomous soul, scrutinizing itself for evidence of election and later—as liberal optimism spread—seeking systematic self-improvement in accordance with providential plan. The idea that God was revealing himself continuously, the basis for the survival of magic in the Church, began to give way to a notion of discontinuous revelation—the belief that God had revealed himself in the Bible, once and for all. If that were true, then divination was pointless at best, demonic at worst.

The problem with this summary is not that it is fundamentally wrong. Max Weber was onto something: Protestantism, and especially its more Puritanical forms, really did help to inaugurate a profound disenchantment of the world and to promote the emergence of a modern culture of control.[22] The problem is that the emphasis on the decline of magic takes the Puritan mind as somehow typical of early modern thought. If we step back a little from the Atlantic world of the sixteenth and seventeenth centuries, we can see that the orthodox Puritan mentality was the exception that proves the rule. The Puritans were a tiny (though eventually influential) minority, and they were far outnumbered on both sides of the Atlantic by people who still inhabited an enchanted universe. Most English people—not to mention other Europeans, Africans, and Native Americans—were not Puritans, and most Puritans were more attached to *mana* than their leaders let on.

There were good reasons for the persistence of the culture of chance. The arbitrariness of fate continued to haunt the English imagination. Despite the dramatic changes wrought by the Reformation, the scientific revolution, and the exploration of the New World, everyday life remained full of unpredictable disaster. Indeed the acceleration of change may well have heightened sensitivity to the precariousness of existence. Cities were in many ways more dangerous than the countryside, breeding grounds of plague and the proliferation of accidents. In London, the incidence of fire caused calamitous reversals of fortune every day. As one chronicler observed: "He which at one o'clock was worth five thousand pounds and, as the prophet saith, drank his wine in bowls of fine silver plate, had not by two o'clock so much as a wooden dish left to eat his meat in, nor a house to cover his sorrowful head." Science and social insurance had not yet softened the pain of unprovoked peril.[23]

Despite the Christian insistence that Fortuna was subservient to Providence, the capricious goddess continued to assert her claims through the violent tenor of life—the prospect of military misadventure as well as the constant threat of disease, injury, and accidental death. Small wonder that the profoundest literature of the age peered into an abyss of nothingness. Amid an officially Christian culture, Shakespeare's Gloucester could cry out: "As flies to wanton boys are we to the gods; / They kill us for their sport."[24] The gods had no plan for human beings, let alone an exalted one.

To those for whom orthodox notions of Providence were too abstract and remote, a culture of chance offered alternatives to despair. Against the specter of a meaningless void, animistic beliefs posed a universe teeming with spiritual significance. Early modern Europe, like Africa and North America, remained a world of signs and wonders. England was no exception. Anglicans, Puritans, and pagans believed dreams were a form of occult knowledge in need of interpretation—or divination. For the English, as for the Igbo, to dream of a serpent was to dream of death or the coming of an enemy. English and Igbo also shared the belief that a dead tree falling in no wind was a sign of approaching death. In Yorkshire as in Senegambia, omens and portents were an inescapable part of life.[25]

Mana inhered in materials and rituals and helped English people navigate a sea of spirits. Houses were built with crooked chimneys and doorposts carved with Saxon fertility icons to keep the devil at bay; a crooked sixpence could serve the same purpose. These practices recall the Senegambian belief that evil travels in straight lines. Some similar assumption may have underlain the English attachment to crookedness, which may have also signified resistance to technocratic closure and which had therapeutic as well as spiritual significance. A crooked sixpence could also be used to lance teething babies' gums and help them generally "get along better"—though coral (also in irregular shapes) was the favored material for such purposes among the English elite.[26]

Despite the Church of England's official injunctions against magic, forbidden practices persisted even in godly circles. Clerics themselves used magic: in 1583, the churchwardens of Thatcham, Berkshire, consulted a cunning woman in an attempt

Coral rattle; Philadelphia, 18th century.

to find out who had stolen the cloth from their Communion table—no longer *Godwebbe,* maybe, but still an artifact possessing *mana*. Even educated people resorted to divination in their attempts to recover lost property, locate straying spouses, or peer into the future. Bibliomancy not only survived; in some ways it became more acceptable, given the emerging Protestant insistence on the Bible as the single sacred text of Christianity. Less exalted forms of sortilege flourished in the increasingly popular lotteries of London and in the spreading mania for cockfighting, cards, and dice among the elite as well as the poor. A culture of chance dramatized the uncertainties of existence in Elizabethan England.[27]

In many English minds, the prospect of grace continued to promise relief from those uncertainties—to offer a feeling, however fleeting, of oneness with the will or force that rules the cosmos. Catholics and some

Anglicans believed that experience was available through the sacraments; reformed Protestants rejected that view as a covenant of works. Few Protestants believed that grace could be earned through human effort; that idea did not emerge until the eighteenth century, when the mainstream denominations began to drift from piety to moralism—creating, in effect, a Protestant covenant of works. But early Puritans did believe that even though human beings could never make grace appear, they could prepare themselves to make its advent more likely. Preparation could be grueling; grace only came after a protracted inner struggle—you paid your spiritual dues, in a sense.[28]

Outside Puritan circles, among idiosyncratic believers in various traditions, grace remained a free gift. It might be conjured but more likely it would appear miraculous and unbidden, an unexpected benefice. Grace was still synonymous with spiritual luck. The melding of grace and luck was implicit but apparent in Robert Herrick's poem, "The Coming of Good Luck" (1648).

> So good luck came, and on my roof did light
> Like noiseless snow, or as the dew of night;
> Not all at once, but gently, as the trees
> Are by the sunbeams tickled by degrees.[29]

The coming of good luck, like the coming of grace, was no more humanly controllable than the coming of snow, dew, or sun; the imagery of nature surrounded the experience of grace in Christian devotional literature, from medieval Catholicism to romantic liberal Protestantism. Herrick redirected that imagery from one form of *mana* to another, from grace to luck.

This move was consistent with Herrick's animistic worldview, which refused any distinction between sacred and secular, nature and the supernatural. He was an Anglican divine for social rather than religious reasons, yet he was also a genuinely religious man. His poetry revealed his faith to be a "personal paganism," as Robert Adams writes. Like Emily Dickinson's two centuries later, it was full of "private sacrifices to household gods, tiny rituals and allusions to ancient creeds only half-seriously taken." Herrick believed "life was a sacrament" and that nature was pervaded by the presence of God. Though he was a target of the Puritans, who deprived him of his profession for twelve years, Herrick never took his faith solemnly. He was a celebrant of ritual and festival, of erotic courtship and fantasy—a poet of sacred play. Maybe that is why Herrick seems an appropriate laureate for the early modern culture of chance and why, as Adams says, despite his misfortunes "he is the happiest of English poets."[30]

The etymological connection between happiness and chance is worth examining. The thirteenth-century English substantive "*hap*" derives from the Old Norse "*happ,*" meaning "chance" or "good luck." The verb "happen" and the adverb "haply" (by chance) emerged from this root in the fourteenth century, as did "happy"—which originally meant "prosperous" and by the sixteenth century had acquired the connotation of contentment. In the seventeenth century, the phrase "happy-go-lucky" appeared.[31]

Happiness, in short, has long been linguistically dependent on chance. In traditional English usage, at least down to the era of Robert Herrick, happiness is something that happens to you; it cannot be manufactured or controlled. That is the insight at the heart of the culture of chance, and that (perhaps) is why it has survived so long—a counterweight to the powerful modern faith in the systematic pursuit of happiness. Certainly it flourished among the men and women who settled British North America. They shared and traded mental furniture with Native Americans and African Americans, as well as with other European settlers. Together these groups began unwittingly to create a distinctive new culture of chance.

RED, WHITE, AND BLACK: THE AMERICAN CULTURE OF CHANCE

Most of what we know about the cosmology of the Eastern Woodland Indians of North America comes from the French Jesuits, who observed Iroquois games and rituals with a bemused (if condescending) tolerance that contrasted sharply with the Puritans' general horror. According to one priest, writing from Seneca country in 1639, "The Iroquois have, properly speaking, only a single divinity—the dream. To it they render their submission, and follow its orders with the utmost exactness." Even discounting for Christian hyperbole and misunderstanding, it seems reasonable to accept the scholarly consensus that the Woodland Indians regarded dream as a school for life. The Iroquois expression *Kateraswas*—"I dream as a habit"—can also be translated as "I bring myself luck [or good fortune, or prosperity]." The expression *Warera'swo*—"dream"—means "it endows with luck, fortune, prosperity, chance." Dreams were a source of *mana*.[32]

They were also messages from the soul. A Jesuit reported from Huron country in 1649 that the Indians there believed the soul made its desires known through dreams; if its desires were denied, the soul became angry and withdrew from the body, producing disease or even death. "Soul-loss" was the gravest diagnosis any shaman could present.[33]

The remedies for soul-loss involved ritual play. Either the sick person or the physician could dream up a cure, as the Jesuit Father Lalemant observed in 1639: "A sick man of a neighboring village . . . for his health, dreamed, or received the order from the physician of the country, that a game of dish [the sacred bowl game] should be played for him." The players' preparation for the game involved a trial shaking of the dish to see who had the luckiest hand, displaying and exhorting their good luck charms, fasting and abstaining from intercourse with their wives, tossing fine tobacco into the fire to placate the spirits, and—the night before the game—sleeping all together in the same cabin in the hope of having some auspicious dream, which they must relate to the others the next morning. "Finally, they collect all the things which they have dreamed can bring good luck, and fill pouches with them in order to carry them. They search everywhere, besides, for those who have charms suitable to the game, or ascwandics or familiar demons, that these may assist the one who holds the dish, and be nearest to him when he shakes it."[34]

The game begins; the two individuals chosen as luckiest from each side take turns casting six bicolored counters from the bowl; all white or black is the highest throw; five and six of a kind are the only winning throws. Stakes can range from beans to tobacco pouches, robes, shoes, leggings—"in a word, all they have," said Lalemant, up to and including their wives' or their own personal liberty. (Iroquois women gambled too, and sometimes staked their own services—domestic or sexual.) Their tendency to risk all was proverbial. Edward Winslow, one of the founding settlers at Plymouth, Massachusetts, observed the Indians "will play away all, even their skin from their backe, yea their wives' skin also." In the big ceremonial games, losses and gains could be spread more communally, and villages could sacrifice huge amounts of valuable property: glass beads, porcelain collars, and other trade goods as well as clothes, weapons, and tools.[35]

During the contests, Lalemant wrote, "every one begins to pray or mutter, I know not what words, with gestures and eager motions of the hands, eyes, and the whole face, all to attract to himself good luck and to exhort their daimons to take courage and not let themselves be tormented. Some are deputed to utter execrations and to make precisely contrary gestures, with the purpose of driving ill luck back to the other side and of imparting fear to the demon of their opponent." When one side has lost all it has, or cares to lose, the game is over. The patient, for whom this ritual has been arranged, thanks them for aiding his recovery, "always professing himself cured at the end of these fine ceremonies, although frequently he does not do this long afterward in this world." Whether he survives or not, he has been bathed in the knowledge that many people had come together to call for his soul's return.[36]

.The sacred bowl game reveals enormously complex cultural meanings. At bottom it was an instrument of divination through sacred play—a sortilege ritual that unveiled the decrees of luck, or fate. It was also an elaborate means of conjuring *mana* for therapeutic purposes, using various fetishes, such as sacred bundles (the pouches filled with good luck charms) and bicolored counters. Matter and spirit merged in the cure; the ailment expressed itself bodily, but its origin was soul-loss. To heal the physical illness, the spiritual power of the soul had to be appeased and restored. The healing process possessed social dimensions: the game brought the community together in behalf of an individual, and when it was played at green corn and harvest ceremonies, it was a ritual protection of the community food supply. Like other Native American gambling games, this one was a way of circulating goods without using money and a way of competing for booty without resorting to war. Here as elsewhere, gambling evoked an alternative economy as well as an alternative cosmology.[37]

If the mark of a true gambler is his indifference to material gain, Eastern Woodlands Indian people were the genuine article. Europeans marveled at their insouciant disregard for calculating advantage. "They wager a new gun against an old one which is not worth anything, as readily as if it were good, and they give as a reason that if they are going to win they will as well against a bad article as against a good one, and that they would rather bet against something than not bet at all," wrote Father LeClercq. The play was the thing.[38]

The distinction between Indian gambling and avarice is underscored by the virtually complete absence of cheating among native North American gamblers. One hostile French observer claimed some Hurons cheated at straws (a guessing game), but also observed that the cheaters were shunned by the community. The disapproval of cheating is consistent with the notion of gambling as sacred play.[39] Cheating would, in effect, have been an antisocial and faintly blasphemous attempt to undermine the ritual meaning of the game and circumvent the judgment of fate.

What can we provisionally conclude about Native American cultures of chance? For early America east of the Mississippi, the written sources on the sacred bowl game are richest with respect to the Hurons and Seneca in the Northeast, the Lenape in the middle colonies, and the Cherokee in the South. But there is also abundant corroboration of comparable beliefs and practices among other tribes in other regions. The most authoritative survey found a dice game of some sort "existing among 130 tribes belonging to 30 linguistic stocks, and from no one tribe does it appear to be absent." In nearly every case, methods and materials used in gambling overlapped with those employed in divination; play was embedded in larger rituals and narratives. From the sacred bundles carried by the Sac and Fox on the Great Plains, to the beaver teeth thrown by the Makah of the Pacific Northwest, fetishes played dual roles in Native American cultures—mere counters in a game, they could also be a potent means of plumbing fate.[40]

For European Protestants in North America, the use of fetishes was more problematic, and the attempt to read the will of the cosmos more fraught with moral danger. The New World, like the Old, remained alive with supernatural powers. But, in accordance with the tenets of Christian dualism, there were only two possible sources for those powers: God and the Devil. The Devil's power was pervasive in the vigor and omnipresence of evil; it also could be summoned from the natural world in more palpable forms, through sorcery. Yet Satan was ultimately subordinate to God's will, which infused all creation down to its tiniest details; its divinity shaped our ends. As one theologian put it: "That which seems chance to us, is as a word of God acquainting us with his will." This was the core of the doctrine of special providences—the idea that the hand of God could be discerned not only in major historical events (the discovery of America, the Reformation) but in the most apparently trivial happenstance. The belief in special providences put an acceptably Christian gloss on older ideas of a universe suffused with signs.[41]

Special providences opened the possibility for Protestant divination. Even among orthodox Puritans, a magical frame of mind continued to inform perceptions of reality. Though they attacked divination, Puritans preserved their own forms of it—through dream interpretation, biblical sortilege, or simply seeing the will of God at work in every detail of their lives. No less an authority than Cotton Mather believed that God spoke to us in dreams, and many Puritans opened the Bible at random to discover if their sick child would live or if God approved an action they were contemplating. Decisions to emigrate to America were often based on bibliomancy.[42]

Intellect and magic mingled in Puritan conceptions of education. The impeccably orthodox founders of Yale College devised a seal in 1701 that contained the Hebrew words "*Urim and Thummim*" and the Latin "*Lux et Veritas.*" The implication was that the college would provide not merely human truth, but also divine light—as the Urim and Thummim had done. It was not coincidental that the founding generations at Yale liked to think of it as the "school of the prophets"—a place where interpretation melded with illumination, where biblical study might become a form of divination.[43]

But the ability to divine God's purpose was not confined to specialists. Special providences were known to ordinary Puritans as well as ministers. Consider John Dane's experience one fine fall morning in 1649 as he left his home in Andover, Massachusetts, to hunt for food for his family. The cupboard was bare and he was eager for success. Yet his prize pig began to follow him; this had never happened before. Dane took it as a sign from God that he should turn around and head for home. He did, "and when I cam within less than forty Rod of my house, a company of great grey geese cam over me, and I shot and brout down a galant goose in the very nick of time." The family was fed and Providence was vindicated. The doctrine proved capacious and elastic under severe tests. When Mary Rowlandson was held captive by Indians, she considered her "afflictions" a sign of God's concern for her; when she was released, that was a sign of his Providence, too. For believers there were no holes in this self-confirming system.[44]

But even orthodox belief could waver. Mary Rowlandson herself, after being rescued and returned to her community, lay awake "in the night season" and wondered—at the fragility of apparently settled society, the ease with which even the righteous could be dragged from their comfortable ways and subjected (as she was) to hunger and other privations that reduced her to stealing food from a child. She had drunk "the wine of astonishment," she said, and everyday life would never look quite so secure again.[45]

The pervasive insecurities of life were spiritual as well as physical. According to Puritan doctrine, one could prepare for grace but never be certain of it. The uncertainty and instability of grace created a climate of fear for the future. The persistence of divination and other forms of magical practice reduced anxiety about what might happen next week, if not about one's ultimate destiny. Magic may not have been an alternative means of grace, but it was at least a source of solace.

In part, the attachment to magic was simply pragmatic. If *mana* still pervaded the material world, then why not harness some of it to therapeutic purposes? Folk remedies preserved hints of older Catholic rituals and artifacts. A toothache remedy mentioned by Increase Mather in 1687 consisted of a "Sealed Paper . . . wherein were drawn several confused characters, and these words written, In Nomine Patris, Filii, et Spiritus Sancti, Preserve Thy Servant, such an one." This was a sacred bundle for a literate society; it resituated *mana* from wonder-stuff to words and marks on paper, verbal formulas and "confused characters."[46]

Apart from therapeutic pragmatism, there was a more compelling reason for the persistence of magic among Puritans: the need to keep Satan's minions at bay. The pervasive possibility that one might be victimized by diabolic manipulation of *mana* intensified the temptation to try countermagic. It was possible, for example, to heal a victim of magic by putting her urine in a bottle with some needles and pins. The problem with this sort of countermagic from the orthodox point of view, as Richard Godbeer has suggested, is that it constituted a sort of "spiritual vigilantism"—a more activist response to misfortune than the doctrine of Providence prescribed. God's power could not be manipulated by human beings, only supplicated: that was the difference between conjuring and praying. But many Puritans (and probably a majority of New Englanders) did not observe that distinction closely. Many rituals and materials preserved a trace of *mana*.[47]

Compromises with paganism were possible, even for Puritans. The Reverend Samuel Sewall had cherubim carved into the doorposts of his house in Northampton, Massachusetts, Christianizing the old Saxon fertility figures. Still, contact with enchanted things could court catastrophe. Any apparently innocent homemade representation of a person could be a "poppet," suitable for use in witchcraft—an instrument for storing and transmitting diabolical power. The historian Karin Calvert writes, "a poppet was as dangerous as a loaded gun, and, in the wrong hands, it could be just as deadly." Discovery of a poppet played a major role in convicting a defendant at the Salem witch trials. Increase Mather was certain that the use of "Sieves, and Keys, and Glasses" for fortune-telling helped explain why God had "let loose evil Angels upon New England" in the Salem witchcraft troubles of 1692. Popular belief in divination, for benign or diabolical purposes, survived and even flourished well into the eighteenth century.[48]

As for recreational divination—gambling—the pattern was similar: official disapproval, unofficial popularity. Increase Mather reasserted the doctrine articulated by John Cotton in 1653 that gambling verged on blasphemy. "Now a Lot is a serious thing not to be trifled with; the scripture saith not only (as some would have it) of *Extraordinary Lots,* but of a Lot in general, that *the whole disposing* (or Judgment) *thereof is of the Lord.*" The Massachusetts Bay Colony passed laws against gambling in 1646, 1651, and 1670. A Plymouth law of 1674 fined anyone caught racing horses in the street five shillings or one hour in the stocks. Horse racing (and breeding stock) declined, but gambling continued to flourish in the taverns of the Bay Colony. Elite leaders often reasserted their determination to enforce laws against gambling. But nothing could entirely extinguish the appeal of traditional popular culture or the desire of male gamblers to use wagering as a form of competitive rivalry. When Sewall preached against gambling one cold sabbath eve in 1699, he awoke the next morning to find a pack of playing cards strewn about his front yard—a ritual reassertion of reactionary leisure against the Puritan modernizers' attempt to suppress it.[49]

But the Puritans' influence in British North America, however disproportionate to their numbers, was nevertheless limited geographically and demographically. In New England itself (let alone the rest of the country) the Puritans' cultural hegemony was contested, as the work of many recent scholars has made clear. Most European settlers remained attached to various forms of the culture of chance.

Like Native Americans, colonists were capable of playing for keeps. Well into the eighteenth century, the very notion of play was far less restricted than it became in the Victorian era (and has remained to our own time). Adults and children played at the same games and sports, whether leapfrog or horse racing. Among the Virginia gentry, there was no attempt to keep young boys away from the nefarious influence of the racetrack (girls may have been another matter), and even the Puritans, who opposed idle sport, opposed it with equal fervor for children and adults. Like modern carnival games, colonial Americans' play was not age-specific.[50]

Play could serve serious purposes, for children as well as adults. Toys could provide pleasure but also (at least implicitly) conjure *mana*. The sinister poppet was a case in point, but so—more benignly—was the infant's coral rattle. English colonials brought their reverence for coral to the New World; and despite the Puritans' distrust, the custom of giving coral at christenings survived for centuries in America. (As late as 1851, Catherine Havens, an eleven-year-old girl from New York City, reported of one her friends that "Constance wears a string of coral beads, and says she takes cold if she takes them off.")[51]

Non-Puritan Christians openly revealed their attachments to old beliefs and practices, especially the use of material artifacts in rituals that blended magical and sacramental elements. The German farmers who settled east central Pennsylvania were formally Protestant but preserved strong connections with Anglo-Saxon pagan folklore, including animal sacrifice as well as more familiar (to us) rituals involving the distribution of Easter eggs and the sanctification of boundary stones. Prayers and spells were still occasionally confused—as among the Swedes of Delaware, who believed that saying the Lord's Prayer backward would prevent rain during the harvest.[52]

Farther south, the culture of chance flourished among the English plantations that emerged in the rich bottom lands around the Chesapeake Bay. This swampy tidewater region produced more than its share of typhoid and malaria; the "demi-paradise" envisioned by early explorers soon revealed the death at its core. All colonial ventures contained major elements of risk, yet conditions in Virginia and Maryland—volatile markets, uncertain weather, suspicious aborigines, and frequent "dying times"—reinforced the colonists' belief in their Elizabethan symbolic universe of signs and portents. Like most early modern Europeans, the Jamestown settlers had little faith in the power of systematic labor to master fate. Much to the consternation of their governors, they preferred "bowling in the streets" and betting on horses to planting corn, even when they were close to starvation.[53] This moral background helped make the Chesapeake colonists more respectful of randomness than the Puritans, less willing to attribute all misadventure to providential design.

Everyday pastimes paid homage to Fortuna. The Tidewater elites' passion for betting was legendary. Provided the thing was done gracefully, winning and losing were each ways of demonstrating one's masculine honor, gaining the esteem of one's peers, and reasserting one's elite credentials. The relation of gambling to warfare was not lost on the players: "Did I not tell you that ours is a sort of military business?" asks a participant in a late-seventeenth-century English dialogue on gaming. "Play is fighting for money and dominion."[54]

Virginia laws reflected the values of a raw, new, and uncertain plantation elite, fighting to demonstrate its power to those it sought to dominate. Horse racing and betting were prohibited, but not (as in Massachusetts) to everyone—only to people of "lower estate." In York County, Virginia, in 1674, an unfortunate artisan was punished for failing to keep his station: "James Bullock, a Taylor, having made a race for his mare to run with a horse belonging to Mr. Matthew Slader for two thousand pounds of tobacco and cask, it being contrary to law for a laborer to make a race, being a sport only for gentlemen, is fined for the same one hundred pounds of tobacco and cask." Only the gentry—and often not even they—could afford the ruinously high-stakes betting that the dominant ethos demanded.[55]

Yet gambling was more than a ritual of elite affirmation. The planters' constant, ritualized repetition of risk may well have been an entryway to a larger cosmology. "A gentleman's dice were like the soothsayer's bones from which they had descended," writes the historian David Hackett Fischer, "a clue to the cosmos, and a token of each individual's place in it." Dice, cocks, cards, horses—all these instruments of luck became animated with fetishlike power as magical extensions of the self. What began as mere status rivalry acquired a more exalted, nearly supernatural charge. As Johan Huizinga observed, luck can acquire "a sacred significance; the fall of the dice may signify and determine divine workings; by it we may move the gods as efficiently as by any other form of contest."[56]

The Virginia gentry were devotees of the Renaissance cult of Fortuna; though they paid rhetorical respects to Providence, they were far less inclined than the Puritans to stress God's omnipresence. They were also less inclined to stress Satan's omnipresence: resisting rigid dualism, they avoided any protracted witchcraft hysteria of the sort that arose in Salem in 1692. There were scattered accusations in Virginia, but they lacked clerical or other elite legitimation and never led to conviction. Often the accusers themselves risked trial for slander.[57]

Inhabiting the murky territory between Renaissance science and medieval magic, the planters were eager to puzzle out the portents of their own particular fortune. More zealously and overtly than the New England Puritans, they consulted cunning persons for news about the future of a current romantic infatuation; they searched the heavens for hints of how their crops would turn out; they kept "fortune books" full of magical and astrological lore regarding the means of assuring luck in love, marriage, sex, health, and travel. *Mana* was holding its own in the New World.[58]

The prominent planter William Byrd (1674–1744) provides a nice illustration of how the gentry kept one foot in the Middle Ages and another in the emerging Enlightenment. Byrd strove to be au courant with the science of his day and even wrote an essay satirizing the prevalence of English superstition. Yet he believed in the prophetic power of dreams and omens, fortune-tellers and witches. While in London as a middle-aged man, he repeatedly consulted a Negro conjurer, Old Abram, to keep him informed about the future progress of one of his amours. If even the educated elite were consulting cunning folk in London, we can be sure that the Virginia rustics were as well.[59]

The key to the continuing vitality of the American culture of chance, North and South, was the African presence in the population—and the receptivity of Europeans to African beliefs. What one historian has said of New England could be said of the colonies as a whole: "Most of the African American supernatural ideas that remained active in early New England survived because they were not particularly alien to local whites."[60] Nor were they particularly alien to the aboriginal North Americans. The American culture of chance involved a melding of red, white, and black.

There were probably a dozen or more distinct West African cultures whose people were decimated, uprooted, enslaved, and shipped off to America. Those cultures differed profoundly in certain ways, their family structures and tendencies toward war or peace, their means of livelihood, their foodways and folkways. Nevertheless, it is possible to suggest certain points of overarching contact—particularly with respect to the discourse of *mana*. Despite the inroads made by Islamic monotheism, the peoples of West Africa still largely inhabited a cosmos where spirit was myriad, multiform, and suffused throughout the material world.

For many Africans and African Americans alike, supernatural power was neither good nor evil; those two categories were merely different ways of using the same force. This neutrality also characterized luck, fate, fortune—or, in the largest sense, *mana*. Hence the Dahomean *gbo* or fetish could be used for good or ill; one variant of *gbo*, the *njuneme* charm, could protect one's property and at the same time doom interlopers to impotence, barrenness, or (in the next generation) death. In West African societies, the taxonomy of charms was functional, not moral. Though details of belief varied, similar assumptions and structures characterized nearly all the cultures that supplied slaves to the New World.[61]

The Igbo of the river Niger delta and the Akan of the Gold Coast, who were brought mostly to Virginia and Maryland, embraced roughly similar cosmologies. Both contained multiple spirits and possibilities for intercession. Chineke, the Igbo high god, combined male and female principles. S/he created spiritual forces (*alusi*), including the sun, associated with good fortune, and the sky, associated with ancestors and land. Each Igbo had a kind of "personalized providence" (to use the historian Michael Gomez's phrase) or guardian angel, called a *chi*. Igbo melded luck and effort in *Ikenga*, the cult of the right hand, which was a symbol of good luck but also of individual ability.[62]

The Akan were equally committed to mediation. Their highest god, *Onyame*, created the visible world with the earth mother, *Asase Yaa*. Beneath them were hundreds of lesser spirits, known as *abosom*, which inhabited rocks, trees, and, most of all, bodies of water. (The centrality of river gods in African fertility rites and other religious ceremonies later

helped ease slaves' assimilation to the evangelical Christian ritual of bap-
tism by total immersion.) Like other African cultures, the Akan emphasized the continuity of spiritual life between the dead and the living.
Those ties were embodied not only in their attachment to the same land
over generations but also in their sacred stools, which were passed on
from parents to children and which embodied the supernatural power of
the ancestors. When the Akan were uprooted from their land and deprived of their stools, they lost the foundations of a coherent cosmos. No
wonder they were known in the New World for their tendency to suicide.[63]

Belief in the multiplicity and mobility of the soul was central to
African *mana*. The Ewe people, for example, lived near the Bight of
Benin and were uprooted to Louisiana, Georgia, and South Carolina;
they believed in an immortal soul that leaves the body temporarily in
trance and permanently in death; but they also believed in a dream soul
or indwelling spirit they called *Kra*. What the sleeping person experienced or "saw" in a dream were the adventures of the *Kra* during its absence. Sleepers had to be awakened slowly and gently to give the dream
soul time to return. For Africans as for early modern Europeans, dreams
were palpable, meaningful events in the life of the soul.[64]

Senegambians shared similar beliefs. From the region around what is
now Senegal and Sierra Leone, they were also brought to the lower
South, largely because of their skills in rice cultivation. They included the
Bambara of the upper Niger, who believed in three elements of the
soul—the *dya,* the *ni,* and the *tere*—which separated at death. The *dya* enters the water, the *ni* an ancestral altar, and the *tere* becomes a *nyama,*
which roams about freely, choosing to reside in animals, plants, or insects.
Like other forms of *mana, nyama* could be dangerous—especially if its
host creature has been killed. So the Bambara wore distinctive amulets, or
gris-gris, which became common among the African Americans of the
Mississippi Delta, the Sea Islands of Georgia, and much of the lower
South.[65]

To Louisiana also came the Yoruba, who lived (and live) in what is
now Nigeria, around the eastern part of the Bight of Benin. Their beliefs, like those of the Bambara, combine conjuring and intercession. The
Yoruba version of *mana* is a vital spiritual force that they call *ashe,* manifested in prophecy and grace. And it is available through (or from) many

orisha, or mediators, who occupy the boundaries between natural and supernatural worlds. (These powerful but approachable figures resembled Catholic saints; this made formal adherence to Christianity easier for the Yoruba in Louisiana and the French Caribbean.) One *orisha* is Eshu (sometimes called Elegba), the messenger at the crossroads, who is mischievous but full of creative grace—"the ultimate master of potentiality," according to Robert Farris Thompson. Like Hermes, Eshu is an appropriate deity for a culture of chance.[66]

Despite the trauma of displacement and enslavement, evidence is overwhelming that African beliefs persisted with remarkable resilience in the New World—even into the twentieth century, let alone the eighteenth. As late as the 1780s, according to a recent estimate, a minimum of 92 percent of blacks in North America were still practicing African religions.[67] To be sure, the specific forms might change; indeed, syncretic beliefs might coalesce into new, more coherent synthetic versions. The most dramatic example of this process was the New World belief system known as voodoo, vodou, or vodun.

Voodoo was a complex synthesis of Bambara, Yoruba, and other African beliefs combined with a tincture of French Catholicism—all traditions that used fetishes to connect the natural and supernatural worlds. Practitioners of voodoo shared animistic assumptions with most other participants in the culture of chance: they believed in the interpenetration of mind and body, the cohabitation of matter and spirit. What seemed like the merest rubbish (to the outsider) could possess *mana,* could become an instrument for creating harmony—or disharmony— between nature and the supernatural.

The names for those instruments varied as voodoo survived and spread (albeit often in diluted form)—*gris-gris, hand, goopher, mojo, toby.* Meanings could change as objects migrated and their people were enslaved: a Bambara amulet, intended to promote comity between phenomenal and noumenal realms, was transformed in New Orleans—under sadder, harder conditions—to a dangerous revenge charm, called a *wanga.* But other sorts of meanings remained attached to the same sorts of objects, despite the disintegrative impact of slavery. A mideighteenth-century slave trader noted the ubiquity among West Africans of "charms"—objects worn on the body for protection or wish-fulfillment. The most common were "leather bags," which they called "spirit bundles." These might contain polished rocks, mirror fragments, bones, nails, river sand, graveyard dirt (an especially potent *goopher*). "Voodoo bags," as whites tended to call them, became potent sources of *mana* in North America as in Africa.[68]

All the odd items in a voodoo bag were apparently worthless but potentially powerful; indeed, it was their potentiality that gave them their spiritual charge. In the right hands, in the right rituals, they might become alive with the capacity to heal the sick, protect the fearful, avenge the aggrieved, or reveal the inner workings of fate. Under special, benign circumstances, anything from "a little dry up ole dead turtle" to a pair of perfectly matched, white smooth stones might be transfigured into a material embodiment of luck or a means of grace.[69]

The voodoo synthesis flourished in Louisiana and the Mississippi Delta, especially in the region around New Orleans. By the early 1700s, conjuring lore had become an important ingredient in the city's multiracial cultural stew. (So was high-stakes gambling.) But New Orleans was not British North America. What is most significant for the American culture of chance is not the tenacity of voodoo in New Orleans, but the appearance of voodoo-like beliefs—in diluted form—as far north as New Hampshire.[70]

Outside New Orleans and the Delta, voodoo was more likely to be hoodoo, or conjuration—less a coherent belief system than a loosely held set of attitudes and assumptions that resembled the magical worldview of early modern Europe. Indeed, a mere listing of the similarities between African American and European conjuring lore could fill an encyclopedia. Consider just a few examples. Similar settings possessed the same occult fascination: the crossroads, in particular, produced a comparable lore (which would later show up in the Delta Blues). In Europe as in Africa, the crossroads was a place freighted with hope and foreboding—a threshold to an ambiguous future, guarded by ambiguous gods: Hermes the trickster in Europe, eponymous inspiration for the "hermetic tradition" of Renaissance magic; and Eshu-Elegba, the Yoruba "master of potentiality" in Africa.[71]

Fetish-beliefs were similar as well. To ensure a normal birth, pregnant Yoruba women wore a single shell bracelet—a parallel to the English use of coral. African Americans, like British Americans, used pierced or bent coins as charms; slave narratives refer to coins strung with beads or shells as "charm strings." Pins were good luck for both English and African Americans, and both groups used plants in matrimonial divination ("He loves me, he loves me not. . . .").[72]

On both sides of the Atlantic, herbal remedies were available for heartsickness as well as more visceral distempers; anxious lovers turned to the forest and garden for potions, powders, and charms—hemp seed in New London and Cornwall, lemon verbena in New Orleans and Biskara.[73] Though the particular plants and procedures varied in accordance with climate, the intentions were the same: to find or keep a mate, to ensure his or her devotion, to bring the cosmos into conformity with one's dearest wish.

Sometimes the disconnections were as puzzling as the connections. Ponder the ordinary household sieve: in Europe and British America witches sailed through the air on it; in Africa and African America they had to count all the holes in it before they could enter the house.[74] In the end, though, the point is not to catalog an endless list of oddly matched or mismatched details; it is, instead, to underscore the centrality of African beliefs in sustaining and spreading the American culture of chance, not as an exotic import but as a taken-for-granted fact of everyday life. When one of William Byrd's "people"—even, perhaps, one of his own family—was sick, he was as likely to call a black herb-doctor as a white one, and the difference between the doctor's methods and those of the local "cunning person" (or conjurer) might not be all that apparent to contemporary eyes. Well into the early eighteenth century, occult lore was a part of every educated person's library and, long after that, a part of ordinary people's common assumptions about life.

The attempt to conjure *mana*—to envision and perhaps influence the playing out of luck—was clearly far more than a mere excrescence of primitive thought patterns. It enacted a coherent worldview, as distinct from Calvinist determinism as from modern liberal notions of autonomy. Conjuring epitomized what the anthropologist Claude Lévi-Strauss called "the science of the concrete."[75] The tendency to make mojos out of just about anything, to try to catch somebody's spirit in glass beads or graveyard dirt, was a form of spiritual *bricolage*. It depended on a notion of selfhood that was more fluid and dissociated than the Western concept of the individual. From the conjurer's view, the self is *in* special objects—or at least a portion of the self, indeed its spiritual essence. Personhood permeates the world. This was one important philosophical implication of the culture of chance.

But that implication was increasingly problematic for European Americans. Despite their immersion in a transatlantic culture of chance, many became more reluctant to embrace it unambivalently. By the mideighteenth century, occult books were no longer de rigueur in gentlemen's libraries. A rationalist emphasis on scientific law, a religious preoccupation with Providence, and a liberal faith in human ability combined in various ways to accelerate the legitimacy of an emerging culture of control.

Gradually, the American culture of chance became more concentrated on the poorer, darker margins of the social order. Magic became a little less quotidian, a little more exotic—especially as it became more associated with Native American or African American practitioners. The link was double-edged. It paved the way for dismissal of the culture of chance as an expression of backward or even savage beliefs: as early as 1709, the Bristol county court in Massachusetts recorded a complaint lodged against practioners of "negromancy"—a racial play on "necromancy," the conjuring of the dead.[76]

Yet the blackening (and reddening) of magic also implied that darkskinned outsiders possessed a secret knowledge unavailable to whites. This ambivalence would characterize race relations in America for decades if not centuries: the despised Other would exert a powerful, magnetic fascination among the dominant whites—a complex blend of admiration and contempt, envy and fear. The poet John Greenleaf Whittier would pose the awkward question in 1847: "Is it not strange that the desire to lift the great veil of the mystery before us should overcome, in some degree, our peculiar and most republican prejudice against color, and reconcile us to the necessity of looking at Futurity through a black medium?"[77] It is clear from this question that, despite decades of Jacksonian democracy and liberal individualism, even in the 1840s white Northerners were still seeking mana, still trying to lift the veil of mystery from the future with the help of a colored conjurer.

Enlightenment had failed to banish the shadow of chance, but for many Europeans at least, it had secularized some of the philosophical questions. Through the eighteenth century and beyond, gambling would carry the baggage of divination implicitly; it would not be a mysterious

ritual, but only a game. So it would seem to educated elites. But to less
fortunate folk the questions were not so neatly categorized. We might recall the Igbo on the wharves of Colonial New England, tossing cowrie
shells in odd and even combinations. And we might plausibly conclude
that more was at stake than mere money.

{CHAPTER TWO}

THE AMUSEMENTS OF THE ALEHOUSE

A hundred years after the first settlements in Virginia and Massachusetts, a raw colonial society had established itself east of the Alleghenies. British settlers inspired by rectitude and ambition, restlessness and greed, had begun the conquest of a continent: subduing and nearly exterminating the aboriginal inhabitants, searching single-mindedly for the blackest soil, the clearest streams. Often they had to settle for clay and shale or swampland, but still they wrested a living from this inhospitable place. What interest could such independent, practical people have in the hocus-pocus of conjuring up luck? Or in the thrill of risking hard-won resources at the gaming tables?

A great deal, it turns out. From the Great Awakening of the 1740s through the ferment of the American Revolution and the evangelical revivals of the early 1800s, Americans remained attached to the culture of chance—though they refashioned its rituals to meet their changing circumstances. The broadest social change was just picking up steam during this period and was dramatically accelerated by the movement for national independence: the shift from a society where everyone was supposed to know his place to one where everyone was supposed to pull himself up by his bootstraps. As inherited habits of deference collided with emerging individualist ideals, the culture of chance preserved its appeal. Conjuring coexisted with striving in the name of self-help. Divination became a product in the embryonic market economy: dream books appeared in the bookstalls of the bustling port cities. Despite frequent clerical condemnation, bibliomancy survived among Protestants and Catholics, white and black. Sensible folk still consulted fortune-tellers, deployed charms to sustain physical or psychic health, and in general conjured *mana* as a means of satisfying their deepest desires.

Yet there were subtle social changes all the time. As secular rationality and Protestant Christianity made headway among the literate population, the practice of magic (though not necessarily the resort to it) lost legitimacy. Compare Samuel Wardwell of late-seventeenth-century Andover, Massachusetts, with Luman Walter of early-nineteenth-century Boscawen, New Hampshire; both men were arrested for "knowledge, of magic, conjuration, and palmistry"—Wardwell in 1690, Walter in 1818—but Wardwell was a substantial citizen, Walter a transient and messianic treasure seeker.[1] By the early nineteenth century, specialists in conjuring were more likely to be itinerant, economically insecure, dark-skinned, and female than they had been a century earlier. Still, they attracted a steady clientele. Fortune-telling became less respectable for whites to practice but not necessarily to seek out.

Recreational conjuring, in contrast, flourished more flagrantly and widely than before. Gambling remained a ritual of status display and masculine self-assertion among all sorts of people—down-at-heel sailors in Gloucester as well as high-rolling planters in Williamsburg. In a society still clinging to deferential social forms, horse races and cockfights and late-night rounds of loo at the local tavern all offered occasions for promiscuous mingling of men and women, blacks and whites, rich boys and ruffians. Such carnivals of vice dramatized the link between gambling and other forms of sensual self-indulgence, provoking the ire of moralists bent on defending social hierarchy or promoting self-control.

Yet the solution to problems created by gambling was often more gambling. Land-poor planters who had bet themselves neck deep into debt used lotteries to liquidate their assets and keep creditors at bay. And the lottery could serve public good as well as private gain. During and after the revolution, lotteries acquired legitimacy as a means of pooling capital for civic purposes—clearing roads, building courthouses, founding universities. Gambling remained a feature of everyday life in the early republic.

What might be called a gambler's worldview survived as well. From the mideighteenth to the early nineteenth century, the American culture of chance became more secular and commercial, more attuned to the embryonic stirrings of an entrepreneurial society—and more openly challenged by a developing culture of control. The conflict between chance and control was played out in a variety of venues, from public house to meeting house. At bottom it involved a struggle between rival moral and philosophical perspectives.

THE ETHIC OF FORTUNE
AND THE ETHIC OF MASTERY

The ethic of fortune involved a willingness to grant the ancient goddess some mysterious power in human affairs—hazardous but potentially benign, ineffable but ultimately significant. The gambler had ambivalent faith in magic—he dreamed of conjuring *mana* but also realized that the fetish might not work, the faith might not be strong enough. Or good luck just might not be in the cards. In the gambler's mental universe, chance was powerful and real, not a mere optical illusion caused by human ignorance of Providence. In a cosmos where Fortuna still held sway, one must be willing to cultivate ease with ambiguity.

Yet, even as gamblers preserved a faith in Fortuna, the American culture of chance became detached from other traditional moorings. Sortilege became secularized. The casting of dice and lots gradually lost its vestigial associations with divinatory ritual; it became an aleatory amusement, conducted in the numerous public houses that became the focus for community life in the American colonies. In Virginia the law allowed one tavern per county; it usually stood near the courthouse, attracting defendants, attornies, judges, and juries along with miscellaneous local citizens. In New England the taverns adjoined the unheated meetinghouses, providing a warm refuge from a chilly sermon.[2]

The tavern was predominantly but not exclusively a male preserve. One can imagine similar scenes enacted many times: a cavelike interior of rough-hewn timbers, lit by an enormous fire along with a few candles or oil lamps, filled with knots of men in conversation or at play with cards and dice—a convivial but unstable community, given to frequent toasts and occasional eruptions of hilarity or violence.

A few artifacts survive that convey the character of the earliest alehouse amusements. One is a worn wooden box in the Winterthur Museum labeled "Bell at the Bar," which was in use in a New England tavern in the later eighteenth century. Players tossed marbles into an entry hole; the marbles traveled through a series of nails concealed inside the box and finally emerged from one of the numbered holes below. The player with the highest point total no doubt won drinks or money from his fellows. There was no skill involved; players submitted responsibility for the game's outcome to a force hidden from view, the nails.[3] In Bell at the Bar, as in other tavern amusements, an apparently trivial pastime modeled the mysterious contingencies of fate. The structure of ancient ritual remained (the players manipulated material artifacts to discover the decrees of fortune), but the game became a form of mundane leisure—another step in the removal of the culture of chance to an apparently secular realm.

By the later 1700s, the gambler's worldview began to blend more thoroughly with secular and individualistic currents, and especially with the stream of Enlightenment thought that resurrected the classical wisdom of stoical resignation. Generations of literate Americans avidly imbibed the lessons of ancient authors, who often emphasized the arbitrariness of fate. Herodotus (c. 485–425 B.C.E.) summarized the ethic of "so far, so good": "Until he is dead, do not yet call a man happy, but only lucky."[4] An ethic of Fortune remained strong among the literate elite as well as less articulate folk—a conviction that misfortune fell upon the worthy as well as the licentious, that there was no necessary link between merit and reward.

Gambling, even at its most apparently frivolous, ritualized and enacted those insights. Playing the hand one was dealt, one learned resignation but also hope. "Patience, and shuffle the cards," Cervantes wrote in *Don Quixote,* and the phrase became a colloquial English expression, referring to the uses of loss. Gambling modeled the quintessential American myth, the reinvention of the self, but it also resonated with religious longings for what Martin Buber called "the grace of beginning again and ever again."[5]

Indeed, the ethic of Fortune remained consistent with much in the

The secularization of chance—a tavern game; late 18th century.

Jewish and Christian traditions, in particular the worldview expressed in Ecclesiastes:

> I returned, and saw under the sun, that the race is not to the swift, nor the battle to the strong, neither yet bread to the wise, nor yet riches to men of understanding, nor yet favour to men of skill; but time and chance happeneth to them all.
> For man also knoweth not his time; as the fishes that are taken in an evil net, and as the birds are caught in the snare; so are the sons of men snared in an evil time, when it falleth suddenly upon them. (9:11–12)

It is probably safe to say that, during the middle and later 1700s, much of the British American population knew this passage and endorsed the worldview it articulated. The ethic of fortune encompassed farmers and artisans, goodwives and tavern wenches, orthodox Christians and Enlightened stoics; it included the barely literate as well as a sizable portion of the classically educated elite. Whatever their differences, they agreed that God's ways were not our ways and that those who prospered in this world might well fry in the next. Indeed, there was a subversive strain of Christianity that declared one should take no thought for the morrow, for raiment or shelter, and should lose all in this world to gain all in the next—advice that could resonate remarkably well with the gambler's insouciant disregard for security. What the ethic of fortune challenged was not Christianity per se, and certainly not the teachings of Jesus, but the secular providentialist framework that sanctioned the developing culture of control.

The origins of that framework can be traced to the educated Protestant ministers, mostly in the urban Northeast, who sought to create a "rational religion" by making Christianity compatible with Newtonian science and focusing on moral conduct rather than spiritual introspection. They ranged from the conservative Congregationalist Timothy Dwight to the liberal Unitarian William Ellery Channing. Many reacted against the psychological demands of Calvinism by emphasizing the role of human will in the process of conversion. The anguished wait for a conversion experience that never came led many a Christian believer to a more liberal position—what Calvinists called the Arminian heresy, after the sixteenth-century Dutch theologian Jacobus Arminius. Arminians turned away from the endless self-scrutiny required by Puritanism; instead they emphasized the individual's capacity to choose his or her own salvation and to demonstrate that choice by living a moral life. This was appealing doctrine to middle and upper sorts especially. To upwardly mobile artisans and clerks as well as more established elites, the new emphasis on spiritual self-help resonated with new opportunities and demands for economic self-help: a fluid social milieu, a new continent to exploit and subdue. Changes in material life reinforced religious aspirations, and vice versa, accelerating the drift in Protestant emphasis from piety to moralism.[6]

This liberalizing trend, though rooted in powerful religious convictions, nevertheless led to a secularization of Providence. Most devotees of "rational religion" were comparatively affluent; then as now, pastors who ministered to comfortable congregations tended to equate morality with conformity to dominant norms. So the Arminian trend allowed more and more Protestants to muddle faith and works, to confuse mere worldly respectability with an outward sign of grace, and to discern the workings of Providence in the economic status quo as well as the laws of nature.

From time to time, evangelical revivalists challenged this complacency head-on. During the Great Awakening of the 1730s and 1740s, Jonathan Edwards and other preachers used what one historian has called a "rhetoric of fortune." They wanted to assert the spontaneity and unpredictability of God's grace against the arrogance of those who claimed they could see God's purpose at work in the everyday workings of society. Decades later, in the next great wave of revivals during the early nineteenth century, backcountry Methodists and Baptists made grace a more fluid, visceral, and ecstatic experience than Bunyan or the Mathers could ever have imagined it. But the revivalists themselves realized (as Bunyan had) that prolonged ecstasy could make one "incapable for business." Even for evangelicals, moralism ultimately trumped piety: the fruits of a true conversion could be seen only in adherence to a strict moral code, one that demonized magic and denied gambling.[7]

Evangelical preachers became a key force for popularizing a culture of control, a force that put human choice at the center of the spiritual order. As evangelicalism suffused Protestant Christianity, an Arminian emphasis on will played a greater and greater role in the process of con-

version; by the 1820s, for most Protestants, one chose salvation or rejected it.

Faith in human ability was also intensified by a broad transformation
in scientific and political thought—a shift that would eventually sanction
the creation of the American republic. The scientific revolution of the
seventeenth century had reshaped notions of causality in human affairs as
well as in the natural order. Looking back from the 1730s to the Revolution of 1688, Lord Bolingbroke observed that recent English history was
"not the effect of ignorance, mistakes, or what we call chance, but of design and scheme in those who had the sway at that time." One could see
that there were no accidents in history, if one viewed historical events "as
they produced one another, causes or effects, immediate or remote."[8]

History from Bolingbroke's perspective was made by rational, autonomous individuals "who had the sway at that time." Power mattered.
This was the Enlightenment worldview shared by British and American
republicans (Bolingbroke was one of their favorite authors); it lay behind
the Revolutionaries' faith in their capacity to direct the course of human
events—as well as their tendency to see conspiracies everywhere. In the
republican imagination, deliberate (often secret) plans lurked behind historical occurrences. Though George Washington still claimed to "trace
the finger of Providence" through the events of the Revolution, neither
he nor his contemporaries discounted the significance of human power
and will.[9]

In some Enlightenment circles, chance was being subordinated to
statistical law as well as to human will. By the mid-1700s, a demystifica-
tion of randomness was under way—at least among a select group of
mathematicians. The process began with the development of probability
theory, which reflected the growing preoccupation with managing risk in
a market economy. The emergence of probabilistic thought encouraged
scientists to shift their emphasis from the specific and strange to the general and recurring—from wonders to averages.[10]

By the early 1800s, the foundations of an emergent culture of control were in place. Its strength lay in its capacity to meld Enlightenment
ideals of rationality and liberal ideals of individual autonomy with an increasingly evangelical rhetoric of Providence. Moralists deployed that
strength skillfully, attacking and undermining the culture of chance at
every opportunity. The intellectual consequence was a new consensus

about why the world makes sense, a synthesis of science and religion that can be characterized as evangelical rationality. This outlook became the philosophical common sense of American society for much of the nineteenth century.

For believers as well as skeptics, a world full of oddly significant occurrences began to seem more regular and predictable. Belief in special providences yielded to a faith in a more remote and general Providence—still a personal God, to be sure, but one who allowed more scope for the exercise of human will in everyday life. For many Americans, science and religion were increasingly joined in opposition to magic, a culture of control arrayed against a culture of chance.

Both Enlightenment rationality and evangelical Christianity placed the freely choosing, self-controled individual at the center of the cosmos. Though their idioms varied, both discourses sanctioned an ethic of mastery through disciplined achievement. The growing emphasis on choice meant that human beings could, in effect, become partners with Providence (or if one preferred a more secular idiom, with Progress). As evangelical rationality spread, an appeal to Providence became a means of legitimating worldly developments: the emergence of a new nation, the westward course of empire, the steady ascent of a successful entrepreneur.

Evangelical rationality fostered an ethic of mastery to challenge the ethic of fortune and reshaped public debate about gambling and its cultural meanings. In a society officially dedicated to success through self-control, the gambler became an antiself. Yet despite the didactic barrage of moralists, gambling survived. It supplied an animistic perspective on the universe—a perspective that remained satisfying and necessary to many Americans. It became the characteristic expression of a culture of chance, embedded in vernacular consciousness and the rhythms of everyday life, but increasingly confined to the fringes of respectable society.

THE MARGINALIZING OF MAGIC

On February 14, 1795, John Francis, for years a fortune-teller in Charlestown, Massachusetts, published an important business announcement in a local newspaper.

JOHN FRANCIS respectfully informs the public, that he would thank them kindly not to call on him after this public notice, for any explanations in Astronomy, Physiognomy, &c, commonly called Fortune Telling, as he [is] now engaged in a line of mercantile business that will require his whole attention.[11]

Like many cunning persons in New England, Francis was African American. But as the historian Peter Benes has discovered, Francis was more respectable by far than the typical black (or white) fortune-teller. He was a permanent resident of the sizable black community in Charlestown, a husband and father who was married in the First Church and had his children baptized there. Unlike many fortune-tellers, Francis was settled, literate, and articulate. And after some time in the conjuring business, he was getting out of it.[12]

It is tempting to see Francis's advertisement as one of those apparently insignificant historical documents that captures a momentous change: the shift from magic to rationality, tradition to modernity. The temptation is understandable: there is no question that, by 1795 in some colonial settings, a disenchantment of the world was under way.

The effort to suppress the culture of chance had been in the works for almost a century, with only fitful success. Ministers denounced divination repeatedly, in private and in public—sometimes with catastrophic results for the diviners, as at the Salem witchcraft trials in 1692. Civil authorities were equally hostile. In 1718 New Hampshire passed a law jailing anyone "pretending that they can tell Destinies, Fortunes, or discover where lost or stolen Goods can be found."[13] But in 1795, as Francis's advertisement indicates, a practice that was against both civil and ecclesiastical law was still being patronized by the public. The discrepancy between legality and popularity intensified through the eighteenth century: the culture of chance increasingly provoked the disapproval of moralists—secular or religious—while it continued to inspire the loyalty of the general population.

Magic did not disappear; it moved to the margins. Francis had left the fortune-telling business, but he had clearly established a clientele that would want to go somewhere else—maybe to another black conjurer in the neighborhood, one perhaps poorer, less educated, and less rooted in the community than Francis. Certainly African slaves and their descendants were still wedded to a magical worldview. Writing in 1801, a Connecticut judge recalled blacks worshiping "many gods, mostly unkind"; this (allegedly) harsh polytheism, he claimed, made "fetish worship . . . almost inherent" in their way of life.[14] For New England Protestants, few practices could be stranger, more redolent of cultural otherness, than this materialization of *mana* in statues, amulets, and charms.

Among whites, African conjuring practices no longer evoked fear of diabolism (as they had at Salem in 1692), but rather a range of emotions from dismissive amusement to anxiety, fascination, and respect. In certain communities, African American fortune-tellers acquired white clients as well as black. Francis was probably one of these crossover conjurers; so, one suspects, was Tuggie Bannock, a slave woman of Narragansett who protected herself from rivals by wearing a bag of eggshells around her neck and who set complicated revenge projects in motion for her customers. Her tools included sprigs of wood from the intended victim's yard, grave dirt, a rabbit's foot, bits of red flannel, rusty nails, a herring's tail—all the sort of flotsam and jetsam traditionally found in African conjurers' bags.[15]

Well after the Revolution, belief in the efficacy of amulets was still common among whites. The use of coral to ensure children's health remained common through the 1820s. Alongside that ancient practice arose the use of ceramic cradles, given as wedding presents to encourage fertility, and lucky spoons with coffin-shaped handles, which were hung from babies' cradles and used for teething. According to the artifactual evidence, coffin spoons were widespread until at least 1830. And the white peoples' culture of chance involved belief in conjuring as well as in charms. A minister named Paul Coffin recalled that during the 1790s in New Hampshire, "A man in Gilmanton lost a bar of iron and suspecting such a neighbor, a negro quack gave him directions to find it. These [the aggrieved man] followed, tormented the suspected man, and his brother paid for the iron." Coffin's dismissive use of "quack" overlooked the uncomfortable fact

Coffin spoon; c. 1790.

that the magic apparently worked—at least psychologically. As the historian William Piersen observes, "What is interesting about Coffin's tale is that in backcountry New England a white thief took African-American supernatural power so seriously that he believed himself physically suffering the torments of punitive black magic, and his brother had to make amends to cure him."[16]

Despite the growing influence of African Americans on conjuring practice, white people still embarked on careers in magic. Henry Tufts of New Hampshire was one. Born in 1748, Tufts began his fortune-telling career on a walking tour of Vermont, after deserting from the Continental Army in 1776. Using a lobster claw as a talisman, he persuaded occupants of the houses where he stopped that he was a celebrated conjurer with the power to predict the future. He earned eight shillings an evening and a reputation as a "Salem wizard." For a while he lived in an Abenaki village; he married an Abenaki woman and added Indian medicines to his repertoire. Like many of his conjuring contemporaries, Tufts was an itinerant and faintly disreputable figure.[17]

It is hard to make generalizations about the clientele for conjuring. Literacy was no barrier to belief in divination; as more colonists learned to read and more booksellers set up shop, the trade in dream books prospered. By the 1820s, various versions of the genre were being published in New York, Boston, Philadelphia, Baltimore, and as far west as Cincinnati. Many included other systems of fortune-telling besides dream interpretation. A dream book published in Haverhill, Massachusetts, in 1816, supposedly authored by Madam Connoisseur ("First of the Seven Wise Mistresses of Rome"), promised "a new and regular system for Foretelling Future Events by Astrology, Physiognomy, Palmistry, Moles, Cards, Dreams, &c." This eclecticism constituted what stock speculators would term diversification and gamblers would call hedging your bets. And the promise of a "new and regular system" played to enlightened taste; the rhetoric of scientific predictability made divination seem intellectually respectable.[18]

Many Americans had no need of such respectability. Uncertain conditions of life promoted an unembarrassed resort to divination. Those involved in hazardous occupations—sailors, for example—felt no need to be furtive when visiting Fortuna's shrines. When the fortune-teller Molly Pitcher of Boston died in 1813 at seventy-five, the local police records reported that "her fame as a fortune-teller was known throughout the world. No vessel arrived on the coast, but some of the hardy crew visited Molly." She lived on a lonely road near High Rock, with the bleached bones of a beached whale washed up at the gate of her cottage. She peered into teacups and read the leaves, but also eavesdropped on her clients' conversations with her servant-girl, as they waited in her ante-room. No conjurer worth the name would pass up relevant information from any source.[19]

The practice of divination persisted most tenaciously among the "lower sorts," the people most exposed to fortune's slings and arrows—and hence most resistant to secular providentialism. In Colonial North America as in early modern England, willingness to grant chance a major role in human affairs tended to increase as one moved down the social ladder.[20] Traditionally even the wealthy bent the knee to Fortuna (as in the cautionary tales collected in *A Mirror for Magistrates*); everyone feared losing her favor. But as the ideology of self-help spread, successful people were more likely to see their worldly condition as part of an unfolding divine plan; poor folk continued to grant the potency of accident.

African Americans were a significant part of the poor population, especially in the South. In some parts of the low country, by the early 1700s, they were a sizable majority. Instead of isolated and scattered communities, they constituted a large and growing alternative culture, uprooted but still attached to traditional African beliefs. Well into the nineteenth century, Christian attempts to proselytize among the enslaved were only sporadically successful. In 1724, when the Church of England's Society for the Propagation of the Gospel in Foreign Parts inquired about the condition of the "infidel" in James City Parish, Virginia, the local representative reported: "My Lord, I can't say we have any freemen infidels, but our Negroe [*sic*] slaves imported daily, are, altogether ignorant of God and religion, and in truth have so little Docility in them that they scarce ever become capable of instruction."[21] A century later an ex-slave provided a comparable account of black religion:

There is, in general, very little sense of religious obligation, or duty, amongst the slaves on the cotton plantations; and Christianity cannot be, with propriety, called the religion of these people. They are universally subject to the grossest and most abject superstition; and uniformly believe in witchcraft, conjuration, and the agency of evil spirits in the affairs of human life. Far the greater part of them are either natives of Africa, or the descendants of those who have always, from generation to generation, lived in the south, since their superstition, since it does not deserve the name of religion, is no better, nor is it less ferocious, than that which oppresses the inhabitants of the wildest regions of Negro-Land.[22]

As in any effort to reconstruct discredited worldviews, one must depend on the perspectives provided by skeptical observers. It is a tricky business, studying the unconverted through the eyes of the converted. Yet certain conclusions can reasonably be drawn from recent scholarly investigations. Through the eighteenth and early nineteenth centuries, African gods and rites receded from slaves' consciousness, but African views on causality and the means of making contact with the spiritual world remained essential to the structure of their emerging mentality.[23] Core beliefs and practices survived and centered on the conjuring of *mana*. This was what came to be called "hoodoo."

So amulets were everywhere among the slave population, as were shamans who claimed to conjure with them. Nearly all agreed on fundamentals: the potency of graveyard dirt; the value of bundled objects as charms and remedies for soul loss; the danger of staring into such a bundle (as in the Iroquois version of the Orpheus myth). We can glimpse this culture of chance fitfully in stray bits of evidence, such as the advertisement placed in a Georgia newspaper in 1788 for the return of a runaway slave called "Long Hercules, otherwise known as Doctor Hercules, from his remarkable conjurations of pigs feet, rattlesnakes teeth, and from the feet and legs of several sick people, many of whom still believe him in reality to have performed miracles."[24]

It is easy to see how such a powerful figure might haunt the slaveholders' midnight hours, and historians have repeatedly demonstrated the importance of African beliefs in fostering rebellious impulses among slave populations from South Carolina to Haiti. More typically, though, hoodoo offered opportunities for resistance to everyday indignities and cruelties—promising slaves the chance, for example, to take revenge on a master for a whipping. A conjurer might claim to make a master's wife feel every cut the victim had received, or even to make an evil master sicken and die. Such remedies were not always possible to test, but if it became clear that the conjure had failed, the shaman had recourse to the common belief that the white man's magic and the black man's were not the same.[25]

But the conjure was not simply a failed technology. Conjuring expressed truths through ritual performance rather than scientific demonstration—truths that could serve therapeutic purposes, though not in replicable forms. Everything depended on the unpredictable interaction between mind and body. Belief in the efficacy of the ritual could some-

times lead to psychological and even physiological cures. In any case, neither white physicians nor black conjurers could claim reliable results. As
in earlier times, the biological ground of life and death remained shrouded
in uncertainty. North American colonists (black and white) looked for
reassurance in religion, in magic, and in other, more secular versions of
serious play.

THE SPINNING OF FORTUNE'S WHEEL

Like other forms of divination, gambling offered the opportunity to confront and (with luck) overcome uncertainty—however fleetingly. It was a
powerful rite of reassurance. Horse racing, cockfighting, playing cards
and dice at taverns: all these were occasions for men (and sometimes
women) in risky conditions to play at conjuring destiny—and perhaps
even shaping it, if they won or lost at high enough odds. This was true
throughout the British colonies, but especially in the South.

From the Chesapeake to the low country of Carolina and Louisiana,
gambling ritually embodied the hazards of everyday existence in malarial
backwaters where one's basic security seemed to hang by the slenderest of
threads. Though the cruelties of fate were most acutely present in the
lives of African slaves, unexpected illness or accident could afflict the
most fortunate among the master class as well. And while there were
many canny businessmen among the planter elite, there were also many
overextended debtors who constantly confronted ruin, depending on the
vagaries of markets and weather. Neither whiteness nor wealth guaranteed escape from the snares of Fortuna. Her caprices were experienced
universally.

Small wonder, then, that more than any other public ritual, homage
to Fortuna brought everyone together, mixing classes and races without
regard for social distance. Though gambling was officially declared illegal
and immoral by legislators and churchmen, it flourished among all sorts.
Elkanah Watson, a North Carolina planter, decribed a typical Southern
gambling scene in 1787, after a trip to a cockfight in Southampton
County, Virginia:

> The roads, as we approached the scene, were alive with carriages,
> horses, and pedestrians, black and white, hastening to the point of

attraction. Several houses formed a spacious square, in the center of which was arranged a large cock-pit; surrounded by many genteel people, promiscuously mingled with the vulgar and debased. Exceedingly beautiful cocks were produced, armed with long, steel-pointed gaffs, which were firmly attached to their natural spurs. The moment the birds were dropped, bets ran high.[26]

Once the gaffs began their bloody work, Watson turned in disgust from the "barbarous sport," but his revulsion was apparently the exception rather than the rule. Indeed, other travelers reported on the astonishing excitement of bettors and spectators at cockfights. The Marquis de Chastellux, one of Rochambeau's officers, attended a cockfight in 1780 at a little tavern in the pinewoods near Richmond, a place called Willis's Ordinary: "I know not which is the most astonishing, the insipidity of such diversion, or the stupid interest with which it animates the parties," he wrote. "Whilst the interested parties animated the cocks to battle, a child of fifteen, who was near me, kept leaping for joy, and crying, Oh! It is a *charming diversion!*"[27]

Despite its broad popularity, though, gambling preserved a peculiar significance for the gentry. High-stakes wagering remained central to elite definitions of masculinity and status. A French traveler, visiting Jane Vobe's tavern in Williamsburg in 1765, met William Byrd III—the son of the famous diarist—and some of his friends; they were "all professed gamesters," the Frenchman wrote, "especially Col. Byrd, who is never happy but when he has the box and dices in hand." Twelve years later, the aptly named Ebenezer Hazard reported that "[H]orse-racing and cock-fighting seem to be the principle objects of attention between Williamsburg and Smithfield at present." For much of the eighteenth century, the sporting man, who cared not a fig for money matters, was still the beau ideal of the plantation gentry.[28]

Other sorts of people may not have embraced that ideal uncritically but they apparently found it fascinating, as they flocked to the impromptu race courses to watch the horses flash by and the planters place their bets. They also placed their own, on their own games in taverns and slave quarters. Money was beside the point—slaves played marbles for rum, peanuts, and cantaloupes—the play was the thing.[29]

The emphasis on play revealed itself in elite antiprofessionalism, the disdain for calculation that supposedly characterized the gentleman-amateur.

To the gentleman, the game was not a struggle for success but an elegant amusement. Reading Blount of North Carolina considered "a [professional] gamester of all things the most detestable," but "joining four or more jentlement [*sic*] for an hour or so" at the table, he decided, "cant be any disgrace." The true sportsman was a thorough-going amateur: unlike the professional, who depended on the game for his livelihood, the gentleman gambler could remain serenely indifferent to sordid pecuniary details.[30]

Still, indifference to money could have serious consequences, even for grandees like Byrd. The diaries of George Washington are full of references to lotteries staged by cash-strapped members of the planter elite. On 4 November 1768, for example, Washington reported: "Colo. Byrds Lottery began drawing." William Byrd III was raffling off most of his property, including "the entire towns of Rocky Ridge and Shockoe, lying at the falls of the James River"—all in a desperate attempt to pay off debts incurred from gambling. On the eve of the revolution, the Virginia gentry remained entangled in an ethos of recklessness and risk.[31]

Lottery sales proliferated in Northern cities as well. Real estate developers used lotteries to bid up the price on property, far beyond the level a single buyer could afford—but only the price of a lottery ticket for the lucky winner. Cities strapped for cash by stringent rural legislatures turned to lotteries for fiscal relief. By the mideighteenth century, Philadelphia was in such dire straits that the city government itself began speculating in lottery tickets. Both before and after the Revolution, lotteries served not only as private strategies for debt relief but also as public instruments for pooling investment capital for civic ends—roads, bridges, schools. Depending on its auspices, gambling could be essential to the survival of the republic. Fortune's wheel spun busily throughout the colonies and the young republic.[32]

Though gambling was never as central to upper-class cultural hegemony in the North as it was among the Virginia gentry, its history in New England and the Middle Colonies revealed comparable patterns of official disapproval and popular approval, and comparable opportunities for social mingling across class and race lines. By the mid-1700s, organized horse racing with sizable stakes was well established in the streets of Boston, New York, and Philadelphia. Puritan and Quaker dreams of a Holy Commonwealth faded with the growth of commercial prosperity. In Philadelphia, despite official prohibition of the sport, citizens took to racing horses on Sassafras Street so regularly (as one Philadelphian lamented) that "the sweet name Sassafras" was discarded in favor of "Race Street"—a place name one still finds in the older sections of Eastern cities down to the present. Racing attracted boisterous crowds of gentlemen and street urchins, prostitutes and genteel ladies. More than a few—especially among the men—were reeling with drink. Moralists fretted; crowds thronged.[33]

Gambling became woven into the fabric of everyday life. From seaport cities to frontier villages, American colonists took to betting on horse races and cockfights, card games and billiards—or such ingenious tavern games as Bell at the Bar. Sometimes sodden with alcohol, they frequently fell to fighting over the outcome of these contests.[34]

All of this suggests the secularization—and maybe the degradation—of the American culture of chance. It is difficult to argue that a drunken gambler was enacting a divinatory ritual; surely only the husk of religious significance survived in the amusements of the alehouse. Yet it is also nearly impossible to know what was inside the gambler's mind. Most of the evidence we have comes from the outside, from disapproving critics and other defenders of public order. We can only speculate about the mentality of the gamblers themselves. Still, we can safely suggest that secularization was not always the same as degradation, nor was it a simple or linear process.

We can see its complexity in the contradictory currents of vernacular philosophy and religion during the middle and later eighteenth century. Even as some Americans grew more skeptical regarding the efficacy of magic, they continued to pose old questions about the apparent arbitrariness of fate. The answers they embraced were provisional and various, expressed in idioms that ranged from classical stoicism to evangelical Christianity.

THE DECREES OF DESTINY

From the 1740s to the 1820s, traditional attitudes toward fortune flourished in a variety of American forms. Everyday life in the New World sustained the lessons of Ecclesiastes among everyone from Pennsylvania German potters to the cultivated editors of literary magazines. The earthenware known as *fraktur,* from the Lancaster Valley, carried inscriptions articulating the *ubi sunt* theme: Where are the snows of yesteryear? The question underscored the transiency and fragility of existence—a theme of equal concern to literary men in seaboard cities.[35]

Gentlemen authors in Philadelphia and Boston, men with some money and at least a modicum of classical education, mused often on the mutability of fortune and the need to cultivate resignation in the face of unpredictable loss. Those who defended this ethic of fortune sometimes felt forced to refute the emergent emphasis on the power of human will. Away with the fashionable doctrine that denies luck and fortune by calling them only names for good and bad management, an "honest country farmer" wrote in the *American Magazine* in 1745. What nonsense! Look at the Stuart family, look at any farm (no matter how well managed), look at the man who said his fortune had been told, that he would die that day by drowning. He laughed at this, as he had just successfully completed a long sea voyage, but late that night, far advanced in drink, he fell into a well and drowned![36]

As the eighteenth century advanced, fewer literary devotees of fortune were willing to defend divination even indirectly. But they continued to insist on the ever-present possibility of sudden reversals and the impossibility of matching merit and reward. They marshaled innumerable examples to show that blockheads grew rich, that fools and fops were dear to women; while men of wit and spirit, virtue and skill, languished and failed. "Wisdom is often found guilty of folly, and ingenuity of error," as a writer in the *New York Weekly Magazine* observed in 1796. Good fortune, from this view, remained as inscrutable as God's grace.[37]

In 1813 an anonymous contributor to a magazine called *Olio* recalled the language of Robert Herrick in a paean to "the Power of Fortune," which emphasized her mysterious capacity to transform beauty and talent into real distinction. "The freshest flowers, the most verdant meadows, the most beautiful gardens, and the most cultivated fields lose their various charms at the approach of night. The first dawn of the sun restores them to their former splendor. The most honorable birth, the most eminent merit, and the most useful virtues, strike not the eye, nor attract the attention of the world, till fortune brings these qualities to light by her fostering rays, and every spectator is dazzled on a sudden with their effulgence."[38] We could no more control the whims of fortune than we could force the sun to shine; good fortune—like Herrick's good luck—was an unbidden beneficence.

Rather than viewing earthly rewards as a sign of one's intrinsic worth, as liberal providentialists tended to do, defenders of the ethic of fortune counseled a stoic indifference to the things of this world. "The Gifts of Fortune [Are] Incapable of Making Us Happy," the *American Magazine* announced in 1745—bad news, one would think, but the obverse was true, too. If we had become immune to the vanities of wealth, honors, and titles we might better endure disappointment and even disaster. The pursuit of earthly good fortune, which in the Declaration of Independence would become the pursuit of happiness, was from this stoical point of view a fool's errand. Happiness was fleeting and beyond human control. Satisfaction came from the cultivation of wisdom and virtue. As the *New Hampshire Magazine* announced in 1793: "A Wise and Good Man is a Proof Against All Accidents of Fate."[39]

This sort of stoicism was rooted in classical models but susceptible to Christian interpretation. Literary devotees of fortune often quoted Ecclesiastes in reference to dethroned monarchs, deaths by misadventure, and maidens left waiting at the altar. A self-conscious articulation of a vernacular point of view, the ethic of fortune could foster an agnostic resignation to fate or a chastened faith in Providence. Protestant preachers still sanctioned some respect for the awesome power of accident, even as they framed it in a divine plan beyond human control or understanding. During the early and mideighteenth century, untimely deaths in Puritan communities inspired their ministers to preach on Ecclesiastes, reminding congregations that "we know not the Hour" when the Lord will take us.[40] A Christian ethic of fortune could be built on such sentiments.

Traditional conjuring rituals survived in some circles as well. Throughout the eighteenth century, Pietist sects continued to use sortilege as a means of making decisions. The Moravian brethren, whose settlements were scattered in pockets from North Carolina to Pennsylvania, wrote down two opposing statements expressing "the Saviour's Will" on separate pieces of paper, such as "the Saviour approves (or does not approve) the elevation of brother Heinz to the Elder's Conference," then drew one from a container. Luther had insisted that "God is so beneficent and just that he will not allow the lot to err." Human will and reason were fallible and must be subordinated to divine judgment. Faith required the relinquishing of any effort to control outcomes; it was, in that sense, a gamble.[41]

Count von Zinzendorf, the founder of the Brethren, connected gaming, play, and spiritual insight as he likened faithful believers to children. "The lot is a game of truth among us, in the sense of Proverbs 8:31," he wrote. The passage cited is spoken by wisdom, in a female persona; she recalls "rejoicing in the habitable part of [God's] earth; and my delights were with the sons of men." Wisdom, in other words, is not something pronounced from on high, but is available in the everyday pastimes of ordinary people. As Zinzendorf wrote, "wisdom plays on their ground, and indeed [plays] a game that is truthful and reliable if we are children and allow it to play with us."[42] The resonance of these words with Pascal—and Jesus—is striking. Receptiveness to saving grace required a childlike willingness to play.

Outside the Pietist sects, sortilege persisted among Protestants even while it provoked clerical disapproval. "Many professing people make a lottery-book of the Bible. They open it at random, and think the first passage they cast their eyes upon to be designed of God for them," a minister observed in 1816. Literate Christians (black and white) used bibliomancy to discover "whether their deceased friend is gone to heaven; whether they themselves are Christians; and whether it is lawful for them to undertake a certain proposed work, or join in certain amusements."[43] Like gambling, bibliomancy defied official disdain and remained popular.

But perhaps the subtlest and most pervasive penetration of chance in American Protestantism was the spread of a rhetoric of fortune in evangelical revivals. In Jonathan Edwards's account of the "surprising conversions" at Northampton, Massachusetts, in 1734–35, the historian Jon Pahl observes, "Edwards used the striking images of caprice, fortune, and change to balance the usual Calvinist emphasis on the order of predestination." A conversion could appear "like a flash of lightning," then multiply into an "endless variety" of reappearances. The "shower of divine blessings"—ecstatic religious paroxysms—was wholly unexpected; it made "those that were wont to be the vainest and loosest . . . now generally subject to great awakenings." Edwards could only conclude that the Northampton revival was "a very extraordinary dispensation of Providence: God has in many respects gone out of, and much beyond his usual and ordinary way." To say the conversions were "wonderful," as Edwards did, was to say far more than we would mean by that word. It was, for Edwards, a harking back (albeit with a new, evangelical inflection) to the Puritan folk culture of chance—the world of signs and wonders and remarkable providences that the colonists had brought in their baggage from Britain. Loss of "controul" became a feature of revivals, well into the nineteenth century. Edwards noted (and approved) "tears, tremblings, groans, loud outcries, agonies of body," all coming together in "a kind of ecstacy." Grace was a rush of spiritual luck, a melding of body and soul in communion with God.[44]

Ecstatic religion provided African American slaves with a path into Christianity. Revivals sanctioned and even celebrated behavior that the more conventionally orthodox condemned as mere "enthusiasm." The resemblance between revivalistic fervor and trance or spirit-possession, the echo of ancient river cults in the baptismal ritual of immersion, the revivalists' greater willingness to acknowledge the spiritual significance of bodily and emotional experience—all these characteristics made evangelical Protestantism a bridge between white and black cultures.[45]

But it was a narrow and rickety bridge. Despite all the ecstasy—indeed, one could argue, because of it—evangelical revivalists placed an unprecedented emphasis on the ultimate containment of emotional excitement through a strict regimen of self-discipline. However "wonderful" the workings of grace may have seemed when the Dove descended, the fruits of a true conversion could only be found in a systematically moral life.[46] Evangelical morality blended with liberal individualism and enlightened reason to create a worldview that can be called evangelical rationality. At its core was an outlook that disdained gambling as indiscipline and the culture of chance as superstition—an ethic of mastery for a culture of control.

THE MASTERY OF FATE

The rise of the ethic of mastery depended on the gradual (if halting) transformation of Calvinist theology. The growth of an Arminian emphasis on human beings' individual ability to save themselves sanctioned self-help in secular as well as religious matters. Benjamin Franklin's aphorisms in *Poor Richard's Almanac* (1733–1758) caught the new spirit of enterprise.[47] An expanding commercial society offered new rewards for self-reliance. But what made these changes emotionally compelling, what made the opportunities seem heaven-sent, was a transformation of religious consciousness.

By the early nineteenth century, even among evangelical revivalists, conversion itself came increasingly to be seen as a matter of will and choice—not that one could pinpoint exactly when the spirit would fill one with transports of joy (the spirit would still bloweth where it listeth), but that one could choose whether or not to embrace that joy and put it to Christian purposes. Grace was simply "a liberty or power to accept of proffered salvation," announced the *Evangelical Record* in 1812.[48]

The blandness of that definition was symptomatic. No matter how intense at their inception, transports of religious ecstasy were impossible to sustain. This meant that revivalism was fated to fall into the recurring pattern of Protestant history: white-hot ardor flames through entire populations, creating a host of conversions; the ardor cools as believers are organized into a church; new prophets arise, lamenting the backslide from pristine belief and fomenting a new revival. The pattern repeated itself so often in western New York during the first half of the nineteenth century that the region became known as "the burned-over district."[49]

Yet the history of evangelical Protestantism from the 1740s to the 1820s was not merely a series of recurring cycles. There was a linear development as well. The rise of Arminian tendencies accelerated the shift from piety to moralism, from a covenant of grace to what Luther had reviled, a covenant of works. Only by the mideighteenth century, the works in question were not sacred rituals (as in traditional Catholicism), but secular moral strivings. Protestantism, as Weber aptly said, "turned the world into a monastery." Any ambition could be a calling, if it were pursued honestly and diligently. What Weber called "worldly asceticism" sanctioned an ethic of self-controlled mastery. Human will acquired new powers and new scope, in evangelical as well as liberal discourse.[50]

The expansion of will had consequences for Providence. A general Providence still governed all, according to Protestant belief: God had ordained every event; there was no such thing as chance. But human beings could freely choose to participate in the unfolding of God's plan, could somehow align themselves with God's purpose. Evangelical rationality balanced belief in an overarching providence with an unprecedented celebration of human effort. Special providences receded; "wonders" yielded to regularities. Most Protestants, and certainly the more educated and affluent among them, were less inclined to look for spiritual significance in unusual events, more inclined to see Providence working hand-in-hand with human effort. Providence and will could work in partnership.

Those who had striven successfully, from this view, were the beneficiaries of God's will as well as their own; the transfigurative powers of grace were scaled down to meld more easily with a culture of control. Among evangelicals, the concept of "restraining grace" emerged: instead of inflaming believers with longings for union with Christ, it merely prevented them from doing evil, fostered their calm acceptance of catastrophe, kept them from raging at fate. The ethic of mastery began with the mastery of the self.[51]

We can see the growing primacy of personal autonomy in the Moravians' abandonment of sortilege as a means of discovering God's will. The American Brethren in particular bridled at the practice of casting lots for decision-making purposes, especially its use in matrimony. By 1789 they were already requesting exemptions to the regulations on the basis of "the American freedom." Ideals of human reason, individual liberty, and romantic love combined to make the holy lot intolerable to younger Brethren. In 1801 Gottlieb Schober of Salem, North Carolina, complained bitterly of his expulsion from the local community after a quarrel with another administrator (who was also expelled); the decision had been made by lot, and Schober fumed: "I said it, and I continue to say that no God can act in such a way and therefore it is a card game and the work of man." To call the lot a "card game" was a serious insult from a Pietist for whom gambling was the work of Satan.[52]

The Moravians' rejection of lots signified their participation in a seismic cultural shift—a transformation in the basic understanding of cosmic order. Older cosmologies contained an enduring, mysterious realm of the sacred that manifested its power in the most apparently trivial accidents of mundane life—and that could be reached through ritual play. Newer notions of the cosmos were less mysterious, more predictable, and more manipulable by human will. The older cosmologies fostered an ethic of fortune, the newer ones an ethic of mastery.

The faint afterglow of an older cosmology persisted in American politics as late as 1809. In that year, a United States senator from Connecticut named James Hillhouse proposed an amendment to the Constitution that would require the president to be appointed by the casting of lots in the senate. Hillhouse was a conservative Federalist who envisioned a deferential society governed by cultivated gentlemen of talent and decency, men (he assumed) like himself and his senate colleagues. Since the president would be chosen from among this select group, the apparent randomness of the lottery was contained within an elite, homogenous political universe—one where God and Fortuna were allied, in Hill-house's mind. What this selection procedure would avoid, Hillhouse maintained, was the election of corrupt public officials animated by party spirit and personal ambition. A careful appeal to Fortuna (and God) would keep roistering factions at bay. But politicians of both parties wanted opportunities for self-help through intrigue and manipulation. Hillhouse's proposal went nowhere. His Federalist colleagues (to say nothing of their Jeffersonian opponents) were baffled by it. The fate of the presidential lottery was an indication of how far the ethic of mastery had penetrated politics, how thoroughly even conservatives were imbued with individualist ideals.[53]

In vernacular religious practice, the decline of sortilege was less complete. The practice of bibliomancy survived into the early nineteenth century, but it came under intensifying assault. To evangelicals and liberals alike, it seemed too much like "making a lottery-book of the Bible." However innocent the ritual seemed, the *Panoplist* opined in 1816, in actuality it was "really tempting God." To the anonymous editorialist, this was an outrage: "I know of no rite," he wrote, "termed religious in a Christian country, [that is] more profane, more dishonorary to God, and more dangerous to their souls, than this solemn, deliberate abuse of the Holy Scriptures." The *Panoplist* was outraged on traditional grounds: bibliomancy blasphemed Providence.[54]

The orthodox notion of Providence remained strong in many American minds well into the nineteenth century. In fact, even such unimpeachably Protestant poets as John Milton provoked annoyance from an author in the *Philadelphia Repository* in 1803. Milton had used "Chance Governs All" as an epigraph; according to the *Repository,* this would never do. "It is to be regretted that ever a Christian poet called to his aid the heathen Mythology, to give dignity to his productions," the author complained. There was no such thing as chance: a painter throws his sponge at the canvas and "by chance" produces precisely the effect he was striving unsuccessfully to create, foam at the horse's mouth. But the sponge acts in accordance with natural laws, which express the will of Providence, the *Repository* author concluded. Our unawareness of those laws doesn't mean they don't exist. This would become the central doctrine of evangelical rationality through the nineteenth century and well into the twentieth: Providence worked in partnership with Natural Law.[55]

But for many American Protestants, this sort of abstract reassurance was insufficient; they yearned for a more convincing demonstration that God was engaged with their lives. That longing, rooted as it was in religious aspiration, nevertheless eased the assimilation of Providence to secular ideologies of nationalism and progress. As early as 1735, Jonathan Edwards himself had come to believe that there was scriptural warrant to expect that the Second Coming of Christ would occur in America. Millennialism fed the embryonic notion of a "redeemer nation," before the nation was even officially formed.[56]

Millennial dreams made sacred and profane events increasingly difficult to distinguish. In many colonists' minds, Providence gradually merged with events in human history—in particular the development of "the American freedom," as the younger Moravian Brethren called it in 1789. As their critique of the holy lot suggested, it was not always easy to distinguish religious from secular motives in the assault on the culture of chance. As Providence became confused with Progress, the culture of chance became reflexively associated with backwardness, ignorance, and passivity. During the second half of the eighteenth century, a broad spectrum of respectable opinion, from evangelicals to rationalists, began to deploy the word "superstition" as a weapon against the culture of chance.

Faith in progress led critics to locate superstition in the dim past or its remnants. Religious and secular journalists dredged up instances of delusions from the annals of Roman Catholicism and even early Protestantism; sacred relics and special providences alike came in for a beating. Occasionally the author took a trip into the backcountry to detail "the follies of superstition" that survived there, such as the contributor to *The Rural Magazine, or Vermont Repository* who returned in 1795 from a visit to "an old aunt in the north" to provide a bemused account of old wives' tales and young girls' fancies. The moral of these stories was frequently self-congratulatory: thank God we have left such foolishness behind us.[57]

The idea of progress toward an ideal of rational autonomy was central to the culture of control. As in *The Rural Magazine,* men were often assumed to be putting that ideal into practice while women clung to superstitious ways. But whatever the gender of its proponents, the culture of chance was dialectically related to dependency, ignorance, and anxiety about the unknown. Rooted in irrationality, superstition reinforced it—

or so the critics charged. Thomas Paine's critique of dream interpretation succinctly summarized the rationalist case. To him it made no sense to grant special powers to the mind when it is least subject to the discipline of consciousness, when "the master of the school is gone and the boys are in an uproar." Why choose childish confusion over disciplined clarity? Dreams, from this view, were not a form of knowledge but an escape from it.[58]

The ethic of mastery asserted that older ethics and beliefs were products of impotence and fear. In 1806 the *Literary Tablet* traced superstition to an ideal type, the poor savage at the dawn of the human race. He faces a world "where no extensive or complicated union has taken place for mutual defense and protection." His life is so perilous that that he naturally invents a mythology based on "the wanderings of a terrified imagination" and influenced by the climate and geography where he lives—and this creed remains in place as long as he is "unacquainted with any rational system of religion." Ascent from the tyranny of chance allowed one to transcend "weakness, fear, melancholy, together with ignorance," which were (according to David Hume's frequently quoted formulation) "the true sources of superstition." Rational religion brought strength to the fainthearted. [59]

It was easy for advocates of rational religion to dismiss vestigial occultism as superstition but harder when suspicious behavior claimed the sanction of Protestant piety. The rise of revivalistic enthusiasm posed especially complicated problems for critics of superstition. Clearly the ecstatic evangelical was a different figure from the Catholic peasant crossing herself or the savage conjuring *mana*. But there were similarities as well, rationalist critics were convinced. During the first Great Awakening, in 1743, the *American Magazine* tried to sort things out, noting "A Parallel Between Superstition and Enthusiasm, Commonly Mistaken for Religion." To be sure, the author admitted, there were differences: superstition "debases the soul below [Reason]," while enthusiasm "exalts it above Reason"; superstitious man was a slave to his terrors, enthusiastic man was "superior to all men in his own conceit." But the fundamental resemblance was that both misrepresent God as "a cruel, fantastical, arbitrary Master; and make his Government of the world to be conducted not by the Rules of Reason, but by the uncertain determination of his mere positive Will." Both superstition and enthusiasm, by stressing the capricious fluidity of grace (or *mana*), flouted Providence and overvalued chance.[60]

Similar arguments appeared throughout the next half century and beyond. The specter of chance continued to haunt the devotees of control, whether they used religious or secular idioms—or resorted to heavy-handed satire, as the Congregational minister Timothy Dwight did in seeking to refute the Epicurean doctrines of Ethan Allan's *Oracles of Reason*. According to "the Epicurean or atomic philosophers," Dwight wrote in 1787, "the mighty frame, which we call creation, resulted from mere casualty. . . ." In Dwight's view, Allen and other Epicureans regarded "her ladyship [Fortuna] with such high respect, as to think her the most proper person to fill the throne of the universe, which they have conceived to be vacant of any other incumbent." Dwight feigned respect for this doctrine, based on his discovery of animals that (he pretended) could only have been produced by chance: the angleworms and toads that appeared after thunderstorms, and the "chance-colts" borne by mares whose owners had allowed them to forage for food in the woods. The "genuine effects of mere chance" could be seen from "the characteristics of every species of chance product." The shabbiness and awkwardness of the chance-colt, "the deformity, ill-nature, and venom of the toad . . . the reptility and insignificance of the angleworm—are the real characteristics of the children of chance," Dwight wrote. He concluded that Allen's *Oracles of Reason* displayed all these qualities, demonstrating that Epicurean philosophers, too, belonged among the children of chance.[61]

Ethan Allen was an idiosyncratic village atheist; Dwight, in contrast, was a quintessential product of the American Enlightenment. Like many of his contemporaries, Dwight saw no conflict between Providence and Natural Law. In his effort to bring them together he embodied a fundamental impulse of evangelical rationality. He succinctly summarized what would be the key philosophical doctrines of the culture of control: "[e]vents are contingent only because we discern not the connexion between them and the causes by which they are produced. In the eye of the Creator, [reasonable men] have supposed chance a nihility [*sic*]: and the connexion between cause and effect, they have conceived to be indispensably necessary, and uniformly actual, in all things." Religion and science collaborated in Dwight's scheme of cosmic order; neither perspective could tolerate the inconstancy of Fortuna.[62]

Most American critics of chance followed Dwight's example: they proceeded by assertion rather than argument. They were unaware that mathematicians were beginning to formulate procedures that might systematically reduce the scientific significance of chance to near-nonexistence. This was the accomplishment ultimately claimed by the statistical thinkers who pioneered probabilistic thought in European intellectual circles during the eighteenth and early nineteenth century. From Jacob Bernoulli to Adolphe Quételet, early statisticians provided the intellectual tools to demystify chance and make a methodological cornerstone for modern capitalism. They created a scientific rationale for the ethic of mastery—a rationale that would bring secular determinists and religious providentialists into unprecedented if precarious agreement.[63]

Statistics would come to constitute a modern form of numerology. Even if only a few evangelical rationalists followed Florence Nightingale in seeing statistics as "messages from God," many more embraced the systematic gathering of numbers as the key to social salvation. (The fullfillment of this trend awaited the rise of opinion polling in the midtwentieth century, and with it a growing tendency to treat poll results as runic mysteries to be interpreted as guides to policy.) The alliance of Protestantism and probability accelerated the shift from a respectful and even fearful Renaissance view of Fortuna to an evangelical rationalist perspective that was far more confident of the human ability to manage chance.[64]

Probabilistic thought focused on regularities rather than wonders. This was the drift of science generally in the eighteenth century: Linnaeus and other natural philosophers began by cataloging curiosities and ended by creating taxonomies that fit strange and familiar creatures alike into predictable structural categories. The organization of oddity became the order of the day.

The laws of statistics gave the new categorical emphasis a method and a rationale—and also imported it into the study of the human. The psychological consequences of this were incalculable: nothing less than a new conception of selfhood. As the historian Theodore Porter writes, statistics were an effort "to evade the unpredictability of human subjects by aggregating people and their acts into collective wholes"—the unique individual became a social type, what Porter calls a "statistical subject." The key to finding regularities among people and events was "the law of large numbers," which was articulated by Bernoulli in his *Ars Conjectandi* (1713). It stated that an increasing number of coin tosses would raise the probability that the ratio of heads thrown to total throws will vary from 50 percent by less than some stated amount (the standard deviation). The greater the number of tosses, the closer the number of heads and tails would come to dividing evenly. The larger the sample, the more closely it would resemble the population it was meant to represent.[65]

As the law of large numbers suggested, for statistical concepts (such as the standard deviation) to have any meaning or use, one had to work with large aggregates of data. Mastery of circumstances depended on access to huge quantities of information. Gamblers generally lacked that access, and statistical theorists tended to distrust gambling. "Nature's admonition is to avoid the dice altogether," Bernoulli wrote. "Everyone who bets any part of his fortune, however small, on a mathematically fair game of chance acts irrationally."[66]

Bernoulli epitomized the calculating cast of mind that we associate with economic rationality. In the economic rationalist's version of the ethic of mastery, nearly all forms of gambling were chumps' games. Adam Smith provided the classic critique of lotteries in *The Wealth of Nations* (1776): "The world neither ever saw, nor ever will see, a perfectly fair lottery; or one in which the whole gain compensated the whole loss; because the undertaker could make nothing by it. In the state lotteries the tickets are really not worth the price which is paid by the original subscribers, and yet commonly sell in the market for twenty, thirty, and sometimes forty per cent advance. The vain hope of gaining some of the great prizes is the sole cause of this demand." Nor did it make any sense to buy more than one ticket in the hope of increasing one's chances. "There is not," Smith wrote, " a more certain proposition in mathematics, than that the more tickets you adventure upon, the more likely you are to be a loser. Adventure upon all the tickets in the lottery, and you lose for certain; and the greater the number of your tickets the nearer you approach to this certainty." The universal success of lotteries suggested, to Smith, how common was the tendency to overvalue one's chances of gain.[67]

Success in the market required a mentality more calculating than the lottery player's, and sometimes the calculator and the free-spending risk-taker confronted each other in open conflict. When William Byrd III of Virginia attempted to liquidate his debts by holding a lottery, he discovered that the more prudent members of the mercantile class refused to buy tickets. His agent Thomas Adams decried "a narrowness of soul that does not exist in any other mortal save a Virginia tobacco merchant." But what seemed narrowness of soul to some spelled success for others. Prudence paid, at least some of the time.[68]

The language of commerce seeped into the realm of luck and grace. What had been words for an ineffable experience began to refer to more measurable entities, at least under market circumstances. As early as 1732, in Daniel Defoe's *The English Tradesman,* one finds the expression "days of grace" used with respect to the period allowed a debtor to meet his obligations without fear of interest payments. Grace became a halycon moment when market discipline was suspended—a place in time outside the calculus of money. Yet many an entrepreneur who depended on sales for his livelihood was naturally inclined to equate money and luck. Jacob Joder, a Pennsylvania German potter, was one example. In 1800 Joder produced a decorative plate, now housed in the Winterthur Museum. The German inscription translates as: "Out of clay such skill he brings, the potter makes all kings of things, luck, glass, and earth, are all their money's worth." Money was the new, more rationalized form of *mana*— a universal standard of value that united "luck, glass, and earth."[69]

Wherever the market spread, one found an arbitrary measure of worth—money—concealed by an appearance of order and system. The spread of statistical thinking reinforced this pattern. Consider the complications of statistically based rationality. It was particularly well suited—at least in principle—to stock trading. In the complex systems of speculation that began to appear in major European cities during the 1700s, the ablest risk-takers were not the brave loners, but those who were most finely attuned to what other traders were thinking and doing. Stock speculators, in a sense, were the ultimate "statistical subjects." Their profits depended on accurately anticipating aggregate movements of capital—which may have been accelerated by rumor, fantasy, or other irrational forces—on staying a half-step ahead of the crowd of investors, but never falling entirely out of step. This habit of mind would become the major conceptual strategy for managing monetary risk in the modern capitalist economy.[70]

But the concepts of risk management would only gradually be articulated. Even among educated Americans, the probabilistic

A decorative plate, Jacob Joden; Pennsylvania, 1800.

revolution went largely unnoticed until the later nineteenth century. The real significance of statistical thought for the colonies and early republic was that it expressed with special clarity a fundamental impulse of Enlightenment rationalism: to see the universe as an orderly and predictable mechanism, wherein chance was a mere illusion and human intelligence conquered the accidents of fate. Now ministers, businessmen, and farmers—as well as scientists—searched for regularity rather than singularity, averages rather than wonders.

Yet the Enlightenment's taming of chance remained incomplete, abstract, and unsatisfying. For the law of large numbers to apply, each observation had to be independent from all the others—as in the repeated tossing of a coin. It was impossible to find many real situations where this was the case; life was less a loose collocation of atomized events than an interdependent web of contingencies. Nor were many people (even stock traders) likely to think of themselves as statistical subjects. In the eighteenth century as in our own time, human beings experienced life as individuals, not as aggregates. No matter how similar they may have seemed to the statistician, their aspirations and anxieties remained unique—at least to themselves. Regularities and predictablities appeared only from an Olympian vantage point; life on the ground remained irreducibly idiosyncratic, full of unbidden beneficences and unforeseen calamities.

To make sense of this muddle, the culture of control had to blend Christian Providence with Enlightenment rationalism. This was accomplished, not only by such devotees of "rational religion" as Timothy Dwight, but also by the Scottish philosophers of "common sense"—a group that included Adam Smith. The Scottish Enlightenment thinkers melded economic rationality with "moral sentiment." By postulating an innate "moral sense" in every human being, Smith and his colleagues provided a internal counterweight to the amoral anarchy produced by the unimpeded pursuit of self interest (unless one accepted Bernard Mandeville's formula: "Private vices, public benefits"; few Americans did). The moral sense was a benign, personal Providence, internalized and individualized in every human heart. It would be a central feature of American moral philosophy throughout the nineteenth century—an ideal reconfiguring of Providence for a romantic, liberal age, and a key source of legitimacy for the culture of control.[71]

Despite the reassurances of common sense philosophy, though, the culture of control remained vulnerable. The facts of everyday life subverted its power and limited its influence. The universe did not always fit into a seamless pattern of significance. The culture of chance survived and continued to pose an alternative to the mythos of regularity. But it was an alternative that increasingly lacked legitimacy among political, moral, and intellectual elites. It tended to flourish most openly on street corners, in slave cabins, in taverns and other places where ordinary people gathered for fun. As the alehouse came to be the most visible venue for paying homage to Fortuna, the critique of gambling acquired a sharper emotional edge. Critics shifted their focus from the social to the personal consequences of the vice.

THE CRITIQUE OF GAMBLING: FROM PROMISCUOUS MINGLING TO LOST SELF-CONTROL

Gambling was never a big hit with custodians of public order. Beginning in 1621, when King James I told Governor Francis Wyatt of Virginia that the drunkenness and gambling at Jamestown must be suppressed, colonial officials fretted about the impact of gambling on the social fabric and attempted to control it with legislation. After prohibiting cards, dice, shuffleboard, and bowling in the 1600s, Massachusetts extended the ban in 1719 to private lotteries. But this was not simply a Puritan impulse. North Carolina, Virginia, and even French Louisiana all tried repeatedly to regulate or even prohibit gambling in the course of the first two-thirds of the eighteenth century. Virginia, for example, moved from a 1705 law that forbade gaming on Sunday to a 1727 statute that made money lost at gambling recoverable by law to a series of laws in the 1740s that forbade gambling outright.[72]

Though none of these laws dimmed the enthusiasm for gaming, they are nonetheless culturally significant. They show the persistent suspicion of gambling among public moralists, even in the South where the practice was firmly embedded in gentry ritual. The growing complexity of the moral critique reveals the beginnings of a subtle social change, from a deferential to an individualistic society. As disciplined morality came to seem essential to success, moralists devoted less attention to gambling's corrosion of social hierarchy and more to its corruption of personal character.

One can see some straws in the wind in a remarkable sermon against gambling preached in 1752 by the Reverend William Stith, rector of Henrico Parish, to the General Assembly of Virginia in Williamsburg. "Gaming is of a growing and encroaching nature," Stith warned. It is therefore prudent "carefully to guard against, or even wholly to avoid, such a dangerous contagion, lest it gains insensibly upon the mind, and at last totally engrosses and enslaves us." Here was the enlightened fear of threats to rational autonomy, the worry that one's mind could become "enslaved" by an overmastering passion. (The metaphor of enslavement came naturally to eighteenth-century Virginians: the planter Landon Carter, who fretted constantly about his son's obsessive gambling, confided to his diary that "no affrican [sic] is so great a Slave" as a man with a "passion for gaming.") This concern was a portent of critiques to come: the fear of lost autonomy would resonate as powerfully with evangelical and liberal moralists as with Anglican rationalists.[73]

Unlike later critics, though, Stith was more preoccupied with public than with private virtue. He lamented the tendency of gambling to distract men from useful callings: Who could be so deceived, he asked, "as to promise themselves more Profit from one Hour's Play, than from a year's Labour[?]" But there was not much we could do about the fallible human individual. Human Nature was naturally self-indulgent and prone "joyfully to embrace the Scheme of much Money and little Trouble."[74]

The real problems arose when one considered the social consequences of gambling. It created no wealth for the community but only transferred it from one wastrel to another. Worse: by distracting laborers from their divinely ordained duties, it tempted them "to run counter to God's Providence and to contradict his Divine Will in alloting them their Rank and Condition." Gambling scrambled the social hierarchy, Stith warned: "Persons, who by their fortune and Figure in Life are marked out for Labor, have to desert their Post at the Plow and the Hoe, where they may do their Country good Service by increasing the public Export and riches, and betake themselves to the more easy and idle, but less honest Employment of Gaming." For elite churchmen like Stith, the promiscuous social mingling of gamblers on public occasions evoked a democratic mélee where the old constraints of rank had melted away. It was not a pretty sight.[75]

But it was not only the lower orders who were corrupted by gambling. The pastime also undermined "Persons of Distinction," distracting them from their paternalistic duties to employ the lower orders and promote the betterment of the country. Far from distinguishing a gentleman, Stith said, gambling disgraced him. "It degrades and brings him down to the level of every Scoundrel; who, if he has the Rashness and Resolution to venture a large Sum of Money on the cast of a Dye, immediately commences a Man of Spirit; and without any other good Quality to recommend him, is admitted as a fit Companion among Persons of the highest Dignity and most conspicuous Fortune." Stith challenged the deeply held belief of the planter elite that there was a link between ritualized risk and true manhood.[76]

Yet the questions he raised transcended gender issues. Gambling, according to Stith, threatened the stoical inner calm and deep sense of personal moral responsibility that should be the marks of every Christian. The danger was that "by committing ourselves to the blind Arbitrement of Chance, to the cast of a Dye or the turn of a card, we give the reins quite out of our own Hands, and lose all Power and Authority over our spirits. We are tossed to and fro by every Wind of Passion, and are enslaved to wild desires, excessive Hopes, impotent Joys, and groundless Griefs." Given such consequences, Stith said, we can only conclude that "a State of Grace, and a State of Gaming, seem hardly compatible with each other."[77]

Stith stood on the threshold of the modern culture of control. On the one hand, his social critique depended largely on a traditional view of society, in which the gulf between high and low was bridged by an ethic of mutual responsibility. That criticism of gambling survived in England—William Blackstone gave it classic expression in his *Commentaries on the English Common Law* (1761–1765)—but it tended to languish in the American colonies. On the other hand, Stith's concern about the effects of gambling on the individual psyche (or soul) prefigured the pattern of the emerging evangelical-rational critique. So did his redefinition of manhood as self-mastery rather than reckless exuberance.

During the second half of the eighteenth century, these new emphases gained greater legitimacy. The ferment of revolution accelerated that development. Ideologies of republican virtue associated gambling with luxury, as was shown in the boycott of goods affected by the Stamp Act. They included playing cards, which advocates of the boycott assailed as "baubles of Britain," emblems of aristocratic vice. In the 1770s, legislatures in North Carolina and Virginia banned public gaming with cards and dice, and the Continental Congress of 1774 required Virginians to "discourage every species of extravagance and dissipation, especially all horse-racing, and all kinds of gaming, cockfighting, and other extensive diversions and entertainments." Revolution was a serious matter.[78]

Yet the war for independence had a contradictory impact on gambling. The "itching disease" was a threat to revolutionary virtue but also, through public lotteries, a means of pooling scarce capital. Further: even while revolutionary ideology demanded more uniform adherence to norms of self-control, the social upheaval generated by the war itself led to a loosening of moral constraints. And that change was sanctioned by the new rhetoric of freedom. After the revolution, the growing popularity of billiards provided new opportunities, while authorities raged at the spread of this perfidious "French custom" and even (in Virginia in 1798) ordered the public burning of billiard tables. Desperate times called for desperate measures.[79]

Postrevolutionary gamblers pushed the boundaries of permissible counduct in small-town settings, provoking the hostility of antigambling zealots. Consider the situation in Farmington, Connecticut. Before the Revolution, the justice of the peace there was empowered to arrest "all night-walkers, jugglers, and fortunetellers," as well as other itinerants and idle and dissolute persons. There were no arrests for gambling before the Revolution; apparently it did not occur often enough to be an issue. By 1784, though, the town saw fit to ban cardplaying outright; in 1786, billiards; and in 1808, "immoral books." Moralists feared an increase in gambling might signify a broader decline in public probity.[80]

For some critics, gambling was just another form of "the speculating spirit," the mania for sudden wealth that was sweeping the young republic. But according to Benjamin Austin, writing in 1785, speculation was the more dangerous practice: "though [the] independent gentleman may claim this right [to gamble], within his *private sphere*, yet a public amusement may with propriety prove fatal to a community, and may with propriety be *supprest* [sic] *as such*." Speculation was gambling gone public, an individual vice turned social. In *Political Arithmetic* (1798), Thomas Cooper summarized the republican case: "the commercial speculator often gets rich by accident, by unfair venturing, by sudden exertions.

Wealth thus suddenly obtained is in many respects detrimental to the community. It operates as a lottery; it tempts capital into trade beyond prudent bounds; it entices to unjustifiable boldness; it introduces ostentation, luxury and pride, and manners out of harmony with republican principles."[81]

Gradually this emphasis on the public consequences of risky business began to fade; gambling and speculation diverged in the public imagination, and speculation acquired greater legitimacy. But only slightly greater. The republican moral tradition survived and fostered recurrent critiques of speculation throughout the nineteenth century. Still the critique of gambling became steadily privatized. Concerns about gambling became increasingly focused on its threat to self-mastery. For women the wagering impulse was associated with erotic passion and sexual surrender; for men, with the reckless squandering of wealth—and perhaps as well with the wasting of their very substance in some more fundamental sense. As early as the revolutionary era, the critique of gambling began to show a psychological dimension.

The link between gambling and pathology appeared in a didactic drama called *Red and Black; or, the Fates at Faro* (1796). Two honest republicans, Adolphus and Camillus, confront the scene at the faro bank with horror. "Do you note the amazement on every countenance, ghastly visages, and paralytic nerves? Does not your heart, Camillus, recoil from this scene with unconquerable disgust? Every discordant passion here rages in the extreme—unhappy mortals, each joy is poisoned by insatiable desire, and every bountiful remuneration of Heaven, is converted into a self-tormenting engine." Gambling fostered the agony of incessant, unfulfilled desire. Indeed, Camillus replies, even "reasonable men" can be sucked into a "vortex of infamy" by the seductions of gaming. "Expectation is here buoyed up to the very zenith, and plunged as suddenly into an abyss. Such rapid alternate hopes and fears sap the vital springs of the constitution. To such a height is the frenzied imagination carried, that every faculty of the soul is strained almost to bursting." Here we see in embryo the Victorian scarcity psychology of the nineteenth century. It was based on the assumption that there was only so much psychic energy available to any individual, and that the lurching of "discordant passion" from zenith to abyss was a waste of precious personal resources—a prescription for nervous exhaustion, and by implication, failure to meet one's manly responsibilities, financial and otherwise.[82]

The concern about women gamblers was expressed in a different idiom, a compound of economic realism and sexual anxiety. In 1777 an
English writer named L. M. Stretch observed correctly that the losing
lady gambler had fewer resources to depend on than the man: "the husband has his lands to dispose of; the wife her person. Now when the female body is once dipped, if the creditor be very importunate, I leave my
reader to consider the consequences." Stretch told the story of Dorinda,
in heroic couplets: she loses her brilliant necklace, her miniature, her
watch, her diamond buckles, and finally her virtue to "a son of Mars,
with brazen face." The moral was clear:

> *Ye fair, if happiness ye prize,*
> *Be warn'd, shun gaming, and be wise.*[83]

The successful lady gambler was as disturbing to men as the vulnerable loser. Mrs. P——, for example, was a character from *Red and Black*. A
big winner at the faro bank, she steps into the street (*solus*) and ponders
what to do next:

> In the actual possession of so much money, strangely and fortu-
> nately won at the Bank, ought I not to enjoy it in a manner most
> congenial to my feelings? Without doubt, fancy already points the
> way, pleasure conducts my steps, and love, all facinating [*sic*] emo-
> tion of the sentimental mind, promises full fruition. I have a hus-
> band at home it is true, but what then? he would do very well for a
> mechanical mind, but to me he is wretchedly insipid—A woman of
> spirit confined to a cold insensible—Indeed I will follow my incli-
> nation!
> 'For what is gold compar'd to love?' (*Sings.*) (*Exit.*)[84]

Mrs. P—— embodied the nightmare vision of the evangelical-rational
moralist: a free-spending woman on her own, indifferent to conventional
morality, in pursuit of sexual pleasure, justifying her self-indulgence with
romantic slogans about sensibility and spirit. Gambling, in the moralists'
view, fed this undisciplined way of life in men as well as women, tempting men from their financial responsibilities and women from their domestic duties.

Such anxieties surfaced during the 1790s, when cardplaying came
into vogue among among elite young adults in the urban Northeast; it

was, according to its critics, of a piece with other permissive tendencies in this postrevolutionary generation. Aimless gilded youth (as their critics saw them), in the shadow of their heroic forebears; boys and girls together, in foppish and revealing dress—these Federalist elites made gambling an occasion for erotic as well as social display. Women "got loo'd [lewd]" (as the popular phrase had it) while they played in public; republican ideologues, fuming at the double entendre, lamented the decay of revolutionary virtue. There was little they could do about private parties, but they managed to ban horse racing in Massachusetts in 1802 and in New York in 1803. Republican fervor remained at high tide.[85]

Gradually, after the turn of the nineteenth century, the arguments against gambling increasingly focused on its menace to the very existence of a self. In 1804 the *Boston Weekly Magazine* deployed the new science of statistics in a report on the fate of six hundred gamblers in Hamburg: "nearly one half not only lost considerable sums, but were finally stript of all means of subsistence, and ended their days by self-murder . . . not less than a hundred finished their careers by becoming swindlers, or robbers on the highway. The remnant of this unfortunate group perished, some by apoplexy, but the greater number by chagrin and despair." This was an early example of what has become a staple of contemporary journalism and social science: the statistical survey. Its point was less to indicate the impact of gambling on society than to underscore its destruction of the individual self. Suicide would be a leitmotif in nineteenth-century gambling tales, a reminder that, far from being a hell of a fellow, the gambler was really the ultimate loser.[86]

By the early decades of the nineteenth century, evangelical rationality defined the culture of control and with it the critique of gambling. In 1812 the Reverend Eli Hyde of Oxford, New York, delivered a sermon on the doctrine of the lot that repeated most of the old Puritan arguments against "fitfully trifling" with Providence, then upped the rhetorical ante by condemning mere cardplaying as well as wagering for money.[87]

This was a characteristic evangelical move. It depended on the assumption that there was a slippery slope between playing for amusement and playing for money; it treated cards as a gateway drug. The language is not altogether anachronistic; much of Hyde's critique pivoted on assumptions (often plausible) about gambling's psychological effects. Those who embraced "the great and fruitful tree of iniquity, called gambling" were victims of self-delusion. "They feel strong; they think they are able to manage their hand well; they hope they shall have good *luck;* they have learned to venture cents and sixpences in the fashionable circles: this with their other accomplishments gives them courage to venture more, according to what they have, which they can stake."[88]

The cardplayers' "progress toward sin" was inexorable, given the seductive nature of games of chance. Healthy recreations were easy to leave off when one had to return to "the business of life." Not so gambling: "there is in the very nature of the game of chance a perpetual and increasing incitement. It tempts, fascinates, absorbs. The glass runs out unheeded: hour is added to hour, and the party rises fatigued and exhausted." In this overwrought but perceptive observation, as in *Red and Black,* one can again see the elements of the scarcity psychology that dominated the American discourse of health throughout much of the nineteenth century. According to this view, the human body and mind had a limited supply of nervous energy that had to be carefully husbanded, stored up in a psychic savings account. The connections between assumptions of psychic scarcity and assumptions of economic scarcity are inescapable: both promoted an ethos of systematic labor and accumulation, well suited to the early stages of an expanding market society. And as if to underscore his anticipation of later success literature, Hyde concluded his sermon with the warning that "amusing yourselves with cards is a mispense [*sic*], a sinful mispense of time."[89]

By the 1810s, a new and sharper critique of gambling pervaded the culture of control, a critique that reflected the hegemony of evangelical rationality. Mason Locke Weems, the hagiographer of George Washington, epitomized the moral perspective of this emerging worldview: the melding of Providence and will. In his *Life of Washington* (1814), Weems told how Washington's father planted seeds in a pattern that would spell out the boy's name. When his father attributed the pattern to "chance," the boy cries, "Oh Pa, you must not say *chance!*" The satisfied father turns the conversation into a sermon about the partnership of human and divine design.[90]

Weems's denial of chance coexisted with his horror of gambling. "It is not easy to conceive any vice more hateful than Gambling," he wrote in 1816, "because none can be conceived MORE DIAMETRICALLY

OPPOSITE TO THE VERY END OF OUR CREATION! God cre-
ated the human family to be as one great *social body . . .* but alas! The
gambler is blind to all such beautiful ideas. . . . Himself, himself, is all that
he cares for; provided he swims no matter who sinks."[91]

Weems articulated a communitarian concern with gambling's effect
on the "social body." But the cautionary tales he told all focused on the
gambler's destruction of his family and himself. Like the fictitious Tom
Tittles of Culpeper County, Virginia, who squandered all the money his
parents had given him and then hanged himself, Weems's exemplary
gamblers refused to toil, pissed away their patrimony, courted public scorn,
and commited suicide. Gamblers risked a slide to self-murder, or at least
economic failure. Weems challenged his readers to show him "one single
gambler, who *has lived and died rich.*" Weems was both an old-fashioned
republican and a man of the new entrepreneurial age.[92]

By the time Weems was writing, few critics emphasized gambling's
corrosion of social comity; instead they stressed its dangers to individual
morality and autonomy. The most apparent of these was the temptation
to laziness, as a Baltimore poet suggested in *The Lottery* (1815):

> She seems to give to all who ask
> Without imposing labour's task
> The idle as the busy bask
> Alike in the sunshine of her mask.[93]

But there were more disturbing dangers as well. They involved gambling's capacity to inflame the passions, for hours and even days on end,
until the gambler had wasted his vital force, destroying himself and those
around him. As a new emphasis on the sanctity of the domestic sphere
began to enter the culture of control, gambling—like alcohol—became
an enemy of the family. Men resort to gambling as relaxation, the *Saturday Evening Post* observed in 1821, but "led on as it were by an *ignis fatuus,*
they soon immerse families in distress and themselves in ruin." The wagering impulse posed a mortal threat to the only sources of stability in the
developing entrepreneurial society: the self-controlled individual and the
bourgeois family.[94]

The culture of control was poised on the brink of widespread influence, but the language of the antigambling critique suggested how powerful the adversary remained. No critic could satisfactorily explain the

gambler's motivation; there was something ineffable or magical about the appeal of cards and dice. Was it merely an *ignis fatuus* or something more substantial? Maybe the new century would hold some clues. As more and more Americans submitted to the discipline of the market, the culture of control acquired unprecedented legitimacy. But it was never the only game in town.

CHAPTER THREE

CONFIDENCE GAMES

rederick Douglass was desperate. It was 1834, and his master had
sent the young slave to spend a year on the Maryland farm of Edward Covey, a cruel man well known for breaking the spirits of
troublesome bondsmen. For six months, Covey worked Douglass relentlessly, beating him weekly with cowhide straps and heavy sticks. Then
Douglass met a wizened slave named Sandy Jenkins.

> He was not only a religious man [Douglass recalled], but he pro-
> fessed to believe in a system for which I have no name. He was a
> genuine African, and had inherited some of the so-called magical
> powers said to be possessed by the eastern nations. He told me that
> he could help me, that in those very woods there was an herb which
> in the morning might be found, possessing all the powers required
> for my protection . . . and that if I would take his advice he would
> procure me the root of the herb of which he spoke. He told me,
> further, that if I would take that root and wear it on my right side it
> would be impossible for Covey to strike me a blow, and that with
> this root about my person, no white man could whip me. He said
> he had carried it for years, and that he had fully tested its virtues. He
> had never received a blow from a slaveholder since he he carried it,
> and he never expected to receive one, for he always meant to carry
> that root for protection.

Douglass, a Christian and one of the few literate slaves in the neighborhood, at first recoiled from Sandy's suggestion. "I had a positive aver-
sion to all pretenders to 'divination,'" he said. "It was beneath one of my
intelligence to countenance such dealings with the devil as this power
implied." Jenkins reminded him that neither book learning nor anything

else had so far protected him from Hovey's wrath; the root couldn't make things any worse than they were already. So Douglass agreed to the plan.

What happened next was remarkable. Douglass carried the root on his right side, tied to his thigh. When the master tried to beat him, the slave struck back. Douglass had never done this before; indeed, it was virtually unthinkable—the penalty was public whipping or worse. The men struggled for two hours; Douglass gave at least as good as he got, and finally Covey backed down. He never laid a finger on Douglass again. Nor did he call on the authorities to punish the rebellious slave.

In his autobiography, Douglass considered this confrontation the crucial catalyst in his stride toward freedom. He wondered "whence came the daring spirit necessary to grapple with a man who, eight and forty hours before, could, with his slightest word, have made me tremble like a leaf in a storm?" And he admitted "that the easy manner in which I got off was always a surprise to me." Douglass acknowledged that "a slight gleam or shadow of [Jenkins's] superstition had fallen on me," but he never really discussed what role the root might have played in this revitalization of spirit and reversal of fortune—he was writing, after all, for an educated white Protestant audience who had little patience for magic. We can be sure, though, that Sandy Jenkins was not surprised by how things turned out.[1]

What can be made of this incident? Clearly more than Douglass made of it. The story of Sandy and the root suggests not merely the continued existence of the culture of chance, but also some of the reasons for it. Even the skeptical Douglass felt a "slight gleam or shadow" of belief in the power of the root. This gave him confidence in his own capacity to resist the master. As for Covey's failure to call in the authorities, who knows? Maybe he was embarrassed by his own failure to whip an uppity slave; maybe he sensed and feared the confidence in Douglass. In any case, it is easy to understand how Sandy and other slaves would have assumed that the root had successfully conjured *mana*. The magic had worked.

For Douglass the situation was not so simple. Yet even his ambivalent half-belief may have provided him access to a kind of *mana*. As Johan Huizinga observed, self-conscious play-acting was perfectly consistent with participation in magical rites: "the mental attitude in which the great religious feasts of savages are celebrated and witnessed is not one of complete illusion. There is an underlying consciousness of things 'not being real.'" But for the participants, the theatricality of the ritual does not undermine its capacity to command assent. Among the Loango of West Africa, Huizinga wrote, "belief in the sanctities is a sort of half-belief, and goes with scoffing and pretended indifference. The really important thing is the *mood*," he wrote. In conjuring situations, "Whether one is sorcerer or sorcerized, one is always knower and dupe at once. But one chooses to be the dupe."[2]

Douglass chose to be what his rational self (and certainly his audience) would dismiss as a dupe, yet he acquired a preternatural feeling of power from his decision to play along with an apparently meaningless ritual. Magic did not always demand complete credulity; like child's play, it could coexist with the awareness that there was something unreal about the proceedings. But that did not necessarily destroy the efficacy of the ritual. Conjurers and their clients could be excellent actors, and their performances profited from their absorption in the play. Even scoffers like Douglass could be persuaded to suspend disbelief in the fictions of conjuration.

Douglass's account suggests that the culture of chance could be seen as a confidence game. It required ritual play that depended on and reinforced the players' faith in its significance. Yet in a larger sense, virtually every culture is a confidence game: an effort to provide people with a feeling of confidence, with a conviction that they have a meaningful place in the universe and can influence the forces that shape their fate. In fact the modern culture of control made unprecedented claims (far more ambitious than those of the culture of chance) regarding its capacity to promote human mastery, explain the universe, and predict the progress of national greatness. The evangelical-rational consensus exuded a confidence rarely before seen in the world.

Yet throughout the antebellum era, the culture of chance survived. Its traditional forms flourished especially among the people stigmatized by the evangelical-rational consensus as childlike, backward, undisciplined, or simply weird: Native Americans, African Americans, white Southern men, Roman Catholic immigrants, and footloose rogues on the frontier. Most of these groups were also avid gamblers. Respectable Northern Protestants, on the other hand, tended to jettison the cosmological baggage but still displayed a fondness for risk-taking in economic life.

CHANCE, COMMERCE, AND PROGRESS

While old beliefs flourished in eddies and backwaters, the new main-stream culture of chance became heavily commercialized. A nation given over to full-throttle economic expansion moved speculative enterprises to the center of politics, market exchange, and mythic fantasy. Material progress was dependent on the labor discipline and systematic organization that characterized economic rationality. But irrationality was wide-spread as well. In the absence of any government regulation, or even any uniform currency, dreams of fantastic wealth fostered a variety of economic fauna: not only self-made men, diligent achievers on the moralists' model, but also counterfeiters and schemers. These were confidence men—or sharpers, in the idiom of the time. Their success depended less on work than on the manipulation of appearances that often turned out to be misleading. If the self-made man personified the ethic of mastery, the confidence man implied a new spin on the ethic of fortune.

The self-made man and the confidence man depended on each other for their significance; each icon called the other into being. A society thronging with impostors required an official ideal of predictable, plain-spoken selfhood—if only as a counterweight to the centrifugal force of misleading meanings in constant flux. Despite the reverence paid the plodder on ceremonial occasions, though, Americans admired the sharper as well. The country that added bluffing to poker remained fasci-nated by the art of cool deception. And few deceits were commoner than the confidence man's attempt to show that he was really a self-made man. A common tendency to foster mistrust linked the casino and the market.

But that was not all the two realms had in common. In the entrepreneur's imagination, as in the gambler's, dreams of rapid rise or ruin jos-tled for predominance, and despair was redeemed by the promise of starting over. (Americans also changed poker rules to allow for the three-card draw—it offered a fresh start: one was no longer stuck with the hand one was dealt.)[3] All enterprises were enveloped by the atmosphere of risk. In a society where taking chances was a way to win big but also court catastrophe, one could not always distinguish between ventures at *vingt-et-un* and those on the stock exchange.

Gradually, though, moralists began to try. Most republican critics had refused the effort: economic speculation and gambling were twinned, in their minds, as sources of both public and private corruption. But by the

1820s, republicanism had yielded to evangelicalism as the favorite idiom of public scolds. Evangelicals tended to privatize virtue; they were less concerned about the effects of speculation on the public good than about the impact of gambling on the individual. As the language of public morality became preoccupied with personal salvation, mainstream moralists began to seek ways to separate legitimate from illegitimate risk.

One obvious solution was to pose the question: Was the game on the square? This the moralists were often willing to ask of speculative ventures, but almost never of gambling itself. In a calculating bourgeois society, the gambler became just another calculating cheat. In the moralists' collective imagination, the professional gambler—that is, the man who aimed to make a living from the games—was equated with the confidence man.

But honest gamblers (including professionals) rejected that equation. They struggled to distinguish fraud from play. They insisted that the games could be fit on a continuum: three-card monte was outright larceny; faro and other banking games were a toss-up—possibly fair, possibly not; short-cards (poker, brag, blackjack, etc.) were probably the best bet.[4] Among gamblers themselves, there was no blurry middle ground between swindlers and sportsmen. Or so the honest gamblers claimed.

The true sporting man was in some ways a survival of traditional masculinity. He epitomized older notions of risk and redemption amid encroaching market discipline. He disdained the cheat as little more than a timid clerk, obsessed with controlling risk and unwilling to play with uncertainty. He resisted the reduction of gambling to a mere variation on the conniving spirit of commercial life. From his view, the real gambling ethos was the opposite of conniving.

Of course, the true sporting man was an ideal type. Actual gamblers came in many different models; many were as calculating as any clerk. Yet the sporting ideal remained an important alternative ethic. It fostered a readiness to relinquish control over the outcome of the game, to place confidence in the cosmos; it encouraged a willingness to play.

Still, in the developing entrepreneurial society, it was not always easy to distinguish the sportsmen from the sharpers. By the 1840s and 1850s, much of the old culture of chance had been assimilated to the emerging vocabulary of commerce, in which magic became sleight of hand and grace a favor granted by banks or other creditors. (Though not granted freely enough, the New Orleans banks complained in 1848. They wanted three "days of grace" allowed for drafts drawn on New York banks; the New Yorkers would tolerate only one.)[5] Pretenders and poseurs swarmed among the devotees of Fortune, whose connotations were largely reduced to mere wealth and worldly appearances.

Amid such a carnival of misleading surfaces, one could be pardoned some confusion. But if we take seriously the possibility that some games could be fair—that gambling could involve genuine play—we can transcend the too-easy equation of gamblers with sharpers and return to the "sacred significance" of luck, in Huizinga's phrase. Gambling combined a ritual attempt to plumb the mysteries of the cosmos with a willingness to let them remain mysteries—to acknowledge uncertainty, disappointment, and loss as essential parts of life. The gambler, for all his profane ways, may well have been engaged in a form of sacred play.

Since it depended on play, the gamblers' ethos did not demand literal assent so much as a willingness to take certain rituals seriously. Ceremonial performance, not adherence to doctrine, was key. Like Frederick Douglass, many a gambler acquired a sense of confidence from fetishes that his rational self distrusted—these tended to be floating signifiers of luck, unmoored from religious belief or tradition. Silas Greene of Mobile, for example, would always leave the room when his faro bank hit a run of bad luck and pace in the street outside, muttering to himself, fingering his lucky marbles.[6] Yet sometimes the signifiers were more embedded in a coherent worldview: gambling flourished especially among traditionalist subcultures of chance, in which concepts of *mana* persisted overtly.

In the early to midnineteenth century, this tended to mean African Americans and Roman Catholics. The Catholic Church played a critical role as mediator between pagan and Christian beliefs, sanitizing *mana* into grace but still embodying it in material fetishes; in Afro-American Protestantism the conjuring tended to survive on the fringes, rather than at the center. Both traditions contained *mana* in orthodox notions of Providence, but both still fostered the tendency to see a supple universe, suffused with spiritual presences, subject to appeal, negotiation, and propitiation—a world, despite official dualism, where matter and spirit were one.

In contrast, the universe envisioned by evangelical rationalists was very much an all or nothing affair, filled with irreconcilable dualisms and baffling contrarities: matter and spirit, will and Providence, human mastery and natural law. Despite revivalistic countertendencies, it was an increasingly disenchanted world, devoid of miracles, shifting allegiance from an ethic of fortune toward an ethic of mastery. It was a cosmos where grace was etherealized and melded with moral action, where effort was rewarded, and orderly progress guaranteed.

This was the ultimate expression of the culture of control, reaffirmed in its ultimate test, the Civil War. Only Lincoln had the words to give that conflict tragic depth; his contemporaries (at least in the North) retreated to a complacent providentialism, hailing the Union victory as a divine judgment on the secessionist rebels. As the Civil War ended slavery and transformed the United States into a single nation, it also validated the cultural hegemony of evangelical rationality—the vision of a society whose inevitable progress was part of a divine plan.

But this noontide of Providence was a long time coming, and was never untouched by the shadows of chance. The creed of progress had to overcome the inertia of alternative beliefs; official dogma concealed unofficial heresies, which more honestly faced the arbitrariness at the heart of life. The culture of control was not a natural environment; one had to be socialized into acceptance of it. The process was often incomplete, if it occurred at all. The power of chance remained difficult to deny—especially amid the unpredictable lurches of a volatile economy. During the antebellum decades, as market expansion accelerated and confidence games proliferated, the critique of gambling became shriller, but to little or no avail. Fortune and Providence continued to coexist, often in individual minds as well as the society at large.

The career of Robert Bailey epitomized those contradictory cultural tensions. An American man on the make, Bailey was at once gambler, womanizer, and *bourgeois gentilhomme*—not to mention an unsuccessful candidate (twice) for the United States Congress. He was born in 1773 in Staunton, Virginia. His father was killed in the Revolutionary War; his widowed mother taught school and kept a tavern. Early on the boy learned to dance and play cards, two skills he deployed in his lifelong effort to win legitimacy among the gentry. Yet he could never quite pull off the pose. Dismissed by the elite as a mere adventurer, Bailey took pen in hand to defend himself. In his *Life and Adventures* (1822), Bailey used a variety of rhetorical strategies: he distinguished himself, a traditional sportsman, from the swarm of sharpers he claimed were around him; he promoted his own invention, a spring-loaded faro dealing-box, as a mechanical solution to the moral problem of ensuring fair play; and he commended himself, as a contrite sinner, to the care of Providence. Southern honor, modern technology, and evangelical Protestantism mingled to reveal a man struggling for self-vindication in a changing moral landscape.

THE GAMBLER BETWEEN WORLDS

Bailey began with evangelical conventions. "I do freely confess my own iniquities, and trust in the forgiveness of a merciful God," he wrote. "I will guard youth against the course I have travelled through life, and I will make a full and candid statement in these sheets of all things, which, at this time, affects me much, and of which I do sorely repent." His first gambling experience was pitching pennies with an older boy; the first who could produce more heads in three throws would win the other's pocket knife. The older boy won, Bailey recalled, by "retaining two heads under his thumbs"; the sorrowful loser went home to a whipping. Would that he had learned from it! Bailey wrote, taking the hard line: "parents, suffer not your children to play at any game whatever, however innocent it may appear, it is vicious, and all vice is a link of the same common chain."[7]

For years he remained a naïf with respect to gambling. Even as a young man, with a wife and children and a farm near Staunton, he remembered, "I attributed every thing to luck in card playing, had no conception of the tricks and inventions which I myself have since learned." On a horse-trading trip to Philadelphia, he and a friend were sucked into a game of loo and lost close to two thousand dollars; after a sleepless night, Bailey felt "entirely disqualified for business next day" and "determined to hazard another chance"; he dropped another two thousand, and soon learned his cardplaying companions were little more than "banditti."[8]

At first tempted not to pay the sharpers, Bailey resolved on reflection to do so, in order to preserve his reputation. In the society Bailey sought out, even a fraudulent gambling debt was a debt of honor. The prominent planter Robert Wormeley Carter demonstrated this in 1794, when he mortgaged a valuable piece of property to meet the obligations of his son, who had been fleeced by confidence men in a Fredericksburg tavern. Twenty years later, an attorney for Carter's heirs would argue that the planter had acted from a false sense of family honor, and that even honest gambling debts were legally null and void. But among the more traditionalist gentry (and those who yearned for their acceptance), honor (like "character") remained a matter of surface display well into the nineteenth century.[9]

Appearances were crucial to one's social standing among the Virginia aristocracy; but they also could be deceiving, especially when one moved beyond familiar surroundings into an anonymous world of strangers. As Bailey observed in drawing a moral for young men from his encounter with the sharpers: "shield yourselves against the insidious and fawning smiles of men, whose faces beam with conciliation and courtesy, but whose hearts is [sic] a spring of malevolence and artifice." These were the quintessential confidence.men.[10]

In despair at the prospect of financial ruin, Bailey repaired to his hotel room, wrote an affectionate farewell to his wife, and prepared to slit his wrists; just then (according to his account) his "favorite servant"— tipped off by Bailey's oddly timed request for his razor—burst in on him and saved his life. It reminded Bailey, he said with characteristic imprecision, of the Lord's last-minute intervention to stop the sacrifice of Isaac. This was one of many turns of fate that Bailey characterized as "providential."[11]

Yet he continued to gamble. Indeed he became shrewder and better at it. He bought a "Daredevil horse" named Buciphulus, entered him in the many races around central Virginia, and won every purse in sight. At the track, he took to consorting with "gentlemen of the first respectability and wealth. . . ." During a race-meeting at Charlottesville, one of these gentlemen offered Bailey a cut of the winnings if he would allow Buciphulus to lose. Bailey refused, whereupon the same man attempted to corrupt Thomas Glenn, Buciphulus's jockey. Tom told Bailey, who advised him to accept the bribe and win the race anyway, to punish the would-be sharper. The conniving gentleman died soon after, while Bailey persevered in his "course of vanity neglecting my family as before, idolizing pomps and vanities from place to place."[12]

One successful pomp was the faro-bank Bailey opened at Sweet Springs, Virginia. He ordered his dealers "to suffer no person to bet but gentlemen, and to exclude all common persons, youths always to be excluded, and they were never to be suspected of unfairness in conducting the game, for I had much rather lose the whole bank, than any gentleman should be dissatisfied. . . ." He was equally attentive to the ladies' needs. Though he had a reputation as a libertine, his dancing was so fine that they judged him "competent to be a gentleman" and "honored [him] with the management of their balls," Bailey reported.[13]

For his faro-bank, Bailey rented a room in the Court House, which he also allowed to be used for dancing. What this cost him in money he made up in status. But one night he ran into a problem. He had assembled "a large company of gentlemen . . . all flushed with wine and a plenty of money" and ready to spend it at faro, when the ladies sent a messenger saying they wanted the room for a ball. When he refused, the ladies ostracized him, dismissing him as "that gambler Bailey."[14]

The epithet wounded him, as he took great pains to distinguish between gamblers and sportsmen.

> A gambler I shall define to be one, whose only pursuit and study is the business of general gaming, destitute of all honor and honesty, constantly studious in finding subjects of prey, and always inventive in schemes to allure and seduce them to a contest, in which they employ all their art in innumerable ways, regardless of the truth, to purloin from the pockets of those who thus fall a prey to their machinations, the price of infamy. . . . On the other hand a sportsman may be defined to be a highminded liberal gentleman, attached to amusements regardless of loss or gain; his motto is honor, his shield is judgment; no insidious tricks does he practice to vanquish his adversary, fortune is his friend, misfortune is his foe; he is most commonly a man of fortune, or he should be one; but permit me here to remark, that sooner or later, either pursuit terminates in bankruptcy or wrechedness; my friends beware of their bewitching invitations, you may be trapped in defiance of all resistance.[15]

In Bailey's formulation, the gambler was merely a confidence man; the sportsman was a gambler who played fair, who was actually willing to risk loss and bear it with dignity. But both figures, Bailey reminded his readers as he returned to his evangelical mode, were fated to end as losers.

Bailey's experience at Sweet Springs typified his entire adult life. He was constantly seeking an entrée into genteel society, finding himself excluded, and seeking revenge. When the ladies snubbed him at Sweet Springs, Bailey hired the services of their fiddler for the rest of the season so that no more balls could be held except at his own pleasure. When a certain Dr. Thurston wished him removed from a ballroom at Winchester, Bailey confronted the doctor in Brady's tavern, a local watering hole. He pulled Thurston's nose, knocked him down, and threw him out the window; "the new sash is called Bailey's window to this day," he wrote proudly. A better man might have suffered in silence, Bailey admitted, but he was no saint. Like most men he acted "in conformity with the dictates of his nature, which is weak and fallacious."[16]

Despite his evangelical rhetoric, Bailey remained attached to the excesses of the eighteenth-century gentry. His simulation of "Southern honor" included frequent choleric rages and lots of illicit sex. He was always defending his precarious honor, challenging snobs to duels or threatening to horsewhip them. He liked women, and they apparently liked him, too; he records innumerable erotic dalliances—not only with "women of pleasure," but with comely widows and likely housekeepers. His original wife and children receded from the narrative as he recklessly spilled his seed about the Virginia landscape, living with at least two women for extended periods, impregnating others whenever it suited him, leaving a trail of bastards from Winchester to Richmond.[17]

Amid the cumulative evidence of his escapades, Bailey's didactic outbursts began to seem ridiculous. Perhaps he sensed this. Midway through his account he abandoned the evangelical idiom and embraced a worldlier outlook, one more consistent with his own conduct. Rather than condemning gambling *tout court,* he insistently returned to the distinction between sharpers and sportsmen. The question was not whether he played, which he freely acknowledged, but whether he played fairly. To those who accused him of swindling, he demanded to know "whether they had ever seen me guilty of one ungentlemanly transaction." Abandoning the stance of contrite sinner, Bailey slid into the more comfortable role of outraged gentleman.

He insisted he belonged among the best men of the state. "I deny that I am a gambler; I sport and play, but with whom? With members of congress, with members of your state legislature, with attornies [*sic*], judges, doctors, and merchants; such are my respectable competitors, all of whom will say, that I have ever acted in the most honorable and liberal way of playing, indeed too liberal for my own good." If the assembly and other public departments were purged of gamesters, "there would not remain a sufficient number to carry on the government, according to the Constitution." Gaming, he declared, was "a natural passion, which many men cannot restrain, so far as it applies to me, I freely confess, it affords me much pleasure"—and hundreds of other men in "the most honorable offices" would say the same if they spoke honestly. The law should take account of the imperfections of human nature and seek to regulate this "natural propensity" rather than abolish it.[18]

The key task, from Bailey's view, was "to suppress and totally obviate" the "nefarious practices" of confidence men—especially crooked faro dealers. To this end, he claimed, he invented Bailey's dealing-box. It was patented in 1812 and it would, he was certain, ensure fair play if it were widely enough adopted. A modern, mechanical solution would underwrite adherence to traditional standards of honor.[19]

Toward the close of his narrative, Bailey made a feeble effort to pick up the evangelical thread. One night, while he was running a faro-bank near Hagerstown, Maryland, his creditors caught up with him and he was jailed for debt. Alone and in irons in his cell, he could do nothing (he said) but read the Bible and pray; then he "vomited up a lump almost as large as an egg" and felt better, eventually deciding that "it was the Almighty's will to raise me once more." Providence soon intervened: one of his gamester friends prevailed on Bailey's creditors to take the prisoner's promissory notes. Bailey was released but still had to sneak out of town at night to avoid the angry men who had lost to him at faro. Having eluded his pursuers, he learned that a recent girlfriend had borne him two new little bastards, twins he called Esau and Jacob.[20]

Despite his pious stance and penchant for biblical references, Bailey's didactic conclusion remained risibly unconvincing. After a long peroration concerning the universality of the wagering impulse, the need to license gambling rather than trying vainly to suppress it, and the justice of hanging swindlers, Bailey put in a final plug for his dealing-box. "If you are determined to indulge in such follies," he advised, make sure the dealer's box is stamped with the name "Bailey." Accept no substitutes. "But my advice is as before, don't play at all," he concluded lamely, commending his soul to God and forgiving his numerous enemies.[21]

Bailey's memoir was published in 1822. In the five years he had left he managed to squeeze in some further adventures: two unsuccessful runs for Congress, a stint as a newspaper publisher in Kentucky, constant lawsuits and recriminations with creditors and neighbors. Amid another round of litigation in 1827, he foiled his antagonists by dying.

Try as he might to emulate the evangelical or the entrepreneurial spirit, Robert Bailey could not shake his aspirations to a more traditional model of masculinity. His appetite for pleasure made it easier for him to impersonate a gentleman planter than a plain-spoken Protestant Christian or a rational capitalist—though his book contained traces of both styles of thought. On one point he was consistent: fraud and play were not to be confused. The sharper and the sportsman were profoundly at odds.

During the 1820s and after, that opposition became more difficult for most Americans to understand. Feverish speculation in land, shipping, railroads, cotton, and other commodities fed prolonged but uneven economic expansion. The bourgeois merger of economic rationality and evangelical morality contained a powerful utilitarian component, and popular notions of motivation reflected this mix of dominant values. Self-interest was increasingly assumed to be the prime mover in human affairs and increasingly defined in narrowly commercial terms.

The emerging worship of money dissolved older notions of honor, as Marx famously said, "in the icy waters of egotistical calculation." It was hard enough to tell confidence men from self-made men, let alone sharpers from sportsmen, in a society where the most celebrated forms of risk-taking all seemed bent on the same object: financial gain. For many Americans, the culture of chance was about to be reduced to a penumbra of the market.

A VAST LOTTERY

With his usual acuity, Alexis de Tocqueville linked the widespread obsession with economic risk to the intensified awareness of chance in a mobile society. "Those who live in the midst of democratic fluctuations have always before their eyes the image of chance; and they end by liking all undertakings in which chance plays a part." American commerce was "a vast lottery," Tocqueville wrote; individuals undertook business "not only for the sake of the profit it holds out to them, but for the love of the constant excitement occasioned by that pursuit." Amid unpredictable fluidities of fortune, the life of an average American "passed like a game of chance."[22]

Despite evangelical opposition, actual lotteries continued to flourish—along with the metaphorical lottery that constituted the economy as a whole. The imagery used to sell lottery tickets reflected the rising hege-

mony of cash, though vestiges of tradition
survived. In 1831 Fortuna appeared in
a chariot, holding a cornucopia full of
coins, which were spilling out on the
ground; over her horses floated
three banners labeled "$25,000,"
"$50,000," and "$100,000." By
1851 Fortuna was still dropping
coins from her cornucopia, but
she wore a turban and wings, and
seemed to be stepping ashore from
the ocean. The imagery may suggest

A lottery advertisement, Boston, 1831.

the increasing exoticism surrounding the culture of chance, as overt
devotees of Fortune became darker and more marginal; it may also associate the lottery with the uncertainties of the sea, and the possibility of
crossing boundaries from one state of existence to another. Whatever the
nuances of this obscure iconography, one conclusion is clear: while older
meanings of Fortune survived, for a large part of the population—especially the free white males—Fortune's meaning
was being narrowed to monetary gain.[23]

Middle- and upper-class women put a different spin on the embourgeoisement of Fortune. In accordance with the emerging domestic
ideal, marriage was supposed to be the counterweight to the atomizing forces of market-based
individualism. It was supposed to create an indissoluble union between two mutually interdependent people—a relationship that would
resist and ultimately transcend the corrosive insecurities of an entrepreneurial society. But like
other social institutions, marriage was unsettled
by mobility and the spreading emphasis on free
romantic choice. Marriage had always been a
risky business: the perquisites of patriarchy and
the hazards of childbirth made it especially so
for women; men and women alike, moreover,
risked the pain of losing partners or children to

A lottery advertisement,
Boston, 1851.

the cruelties of fate. Yet as American society became more individualistic and American culture more romantic—as Fortune became more bourgeois—the risks of marriage became more present to popular consciousness.

Especially female consciousness. In a mobile market society, women were less dependent on their local communities and families of origin, which could be hundreds or thousands of miles away, and more dependent on the man they chose for a mate. For women in need of economic as well as emotional security, deciding on a partner could be like buying a pig in a poke—one could be signing on for permanent separation from kith and kin as well as allying one's fortunes to a potential failure (not to mention a bounder or a bully). Or one could get lucky.

Dregs in the Cup, William Sydney Mount, 1838.

Given the high stakes of the marriage choice, it should come as no surprise that young women looked to fortune-telling as a form of romantic forecasting. William Sydney Mount's *Dregs in the Cup* (1838), depicts a familiar scene from many a middle- or upper-class parlor: tea leaves made an easily domesticated augury, tidier and more convenient than fingernail parings or urine. In "The Sybil's Leaves" (1835), fortune-telling literally became a commercially marketed parlor game, designed to flesh out hazy fantasies about one's marital prospects. It consisted of cards that could be shuffled and dealt; each described a prospective mate. The game also contained a card with a "Prologue" that explained the game's rationale:

> *The marriage vow may surely be compar'd,*
>   *In all its chances, to a Lottery scheme,*
> *When ev'ry individual is prepar'd*
>   *To realize the fancies of a dream.*
> *In Lotteries, a few small prizes gain'd*

> *Tempt others to the same uncertain wheel,*
> *As though Dame Fortune all her treasures rain'd,*
> *And would to each her countenance reveal. . . .*
> *Alas! two-thirds receive a worthless blank,*
> *Consigning them to wedded wretchedness.*[24]

The domestication of Fortune was by no means a trivialization. Domestic life was increasingly charged with emotional significance; it was the scene of the individual's deepest and most enduring commitments (or so at any rate the dominant norms implied, and so many people felt). Hence the family was also an arena of risk, not merely of comfort and safety—as its celebrants and later its critics charged. Even in a fortunate match, the hazards were genuine; the likelihood of loss was real. The culture of chance could persist even in the apparently well-policed precincts of the bourgeois family.

Risk was pervasive in the antebellum United States, but the ritualized risk of gambling was more flagrant in some regions than in others. Travelers agreed with the British Captain Frederick Marryat, who observed that gamblers "carried on very quietly" in the Northeastern states, but in the South and Southwest their play was "as open as the noon day."[25] The gamblers' ethos was shaped by its geographical settings. In the Southeast, gambling continued to express notions of masculine honor and social hierarchy; in the Southwest and in the major cities it provided occasions to enact more fluid, egalitarian, and individualistic forms of male rivalry. But everywhere the true sportsman sought to distinguish himself from the common sharper.

The distinction was made most insistently and explicitly in the more settled sections of the Southeast, where one could hear endless restatements of Bailey's distinction between the two types. The sharper was a mere greedy conniver; the sportsman, in contrast, was willing to play and lose gracefully; losing, indeed, could be more important to him than winning. Like the Mohegan chief, he affirmed his stature by exhibiting nobility *in extremis*—and by giving things away.[26]

The "big man" among the planter class was enmeshed in a complicated web of indebtedness: the more generously he loaned money, the more people became dependent on his largesse; the more lavishly he borrowed, the more able he was to afford the display that reinforced his authority. Besides, some debts were more urgent than others. As William

Grayson of South Carolina put it in 1852, "A gambling debt is a debt of honor, but a debt due a tradesman is not." The ideal of the gambler as a gentleman amateur led to an odd casuistry among upper-class Southerners. As one told the British visitor Harriet Martineau, a gentleman "may game, but not keep a gaming house." This was where Bailey got into trouble. At every turn, would be professional gamblers met upper-class disdain for mere trade.[27]

The attempt to make gambling into an aristocratic ritual was easiest to sustain among the horse-racing set: entry costs were high; the sport was dominated by such wealthy landowners as John Randolph of Roanoke, who made every race an occasion for competitive (sometimes intersectional) rivalry and lavish conviviality. But even in this area, the link between gambling and elite authority was increasingly compromised by commercialization. The triumph of commerce was signaled by the growing prominence of horse-racing promoters in the 1840s—men like Cadwallader Colden of New York and Yelverton Oliver of Virginia, who served as middlemen between owners and tracks.[28]

Though the aristocratic pose remained appealing, the ubiquity of trade promoted ambivalence, even among prosperous planters. In every planter's soul, alongside the would-be aristocrat there dwelt an agrarian capitalist. Disdaining the cash nexus, he nevertheless derived his livelihood from participation in an international market that often rewarded calculation and usually punished insouciance.

A more immediate obstacle to the appropriation of gambling by any particular class was that its popularity was virtually universal throughout the South. It may be, as Rhys Isaac has argued, that "an intensely shared interest" in a cockfight or horse race, "crossing but not leveling social distinctions, has powerful effects in transmitting style and reinforcing the leadership of the elite that controls the proceedings and excels in the display."[29] But that was truer in 1740 than in 1840, as Isaac's own work demonstrates.

Even in the South, the embourgeoisement of American culture was redefining the social meaning of gambling. By the 1820s, Southern gambling was less a signifier of superior status than of cross-class male resistance to the encroachments of evangelical rationality—in particular the bourgeois reverence for disciplined labor. In the South, more flagrantly than in other regions, gambling was intertwined with a broader attachment to leisure, which even slaves embraced (when they could get away

with it) and which constantly scandalized Northern moralists. One
fumed at the frivolity of the Arkansas plain folk in the 1850s. "Life is to
them but a play-day, and the question of every morning is—how to kill
time?" The answer was often gambling. "No business is so important at
any time as to prevent them from attending the horserace, the cockfight,
or any other kind of sport." A minister en route from Pine Bluff to Little
Rock in 1853 complained bitterly about the consequences of this enthusiasm. He had hired a blacksmith to repair some household items before
he (the minister) left town. But the blacksmith stopped twice to watch
two cockfights; the job was delayed, and the minister missed his train.
Work yielded primacy to play, the well-regulated life to the vagaries of
the moment. This would not be the first time (nor the last) that gambling
embodied resistance to the Protestant ethic of self-mastery.[30]

Resistance was often strongest on the frontier. Despite the drubbing
that Frederick Jackson Turner has received (with good reason) from recent historians of the American West, his inferences about individualism
still make some sense. Unattached men on the fringes of settlement fell to
gambling as a form of competitive play. On rivers and railroads and other
highways of trade as well as in boom towns near gold mines and oil fields,
gambling was an opportunity for masculine self-testing, a highwire act
without a net. But for the less fortunate, it could also be a hopeless compulsion—one that hordes of sharpers swarmed to exploit.

During the antebellum decades, river commerce created a masculine
world that was dirtier and more dangerous than the one later mytholo-
gized by Mark Twain and lesser writers. Along the Ohio, the Mississippi,
and countless smaller tributaries, a floating proletariat of flatboatmen and
keelboatmen mixed casual, hard labor with equally casual bouts of abandon. Men without women (except the occasional prostitute), they crowded
into fetid dens in New Orleans, Cincinnati, and Natchez-Under-the-Hill
(the swampy riverbank neighborhood that respectable folk learned to
avoid); they drank bad whiskey and regularly lost their pay to sharpers
running crooked games of faro and three-card monte.[31]

On the big paddle-wheel steamers themselves, the settings were
sometimes more opulent and the rituals more complex than merely the
bilking of drunks. Riverboat passengers often carried a lot of cash for
business transactions, were away from their friends and family, and were
bored stiff from the want of something to do or even something to look
at. They were also away from women, who were barred from the upper

decks where the gambling took place. Occasionally the riverboat gambling scene resembled Turner's all-male vision of frontier democracy.

Classes—even races—forgot their social differences when they sat down to play cards. As astonished Europeans observed, on the river, army officers and cotton planters, common clerks and rogues, all played together, "laughing together, swearing together, and the names of Bill, Dick, and Harry passing familiarly between them!" So the Marquis de Chevalier described his trip down the Mississippi in 1835. Eastern and Northern businessmen cast off bourgeois restraints to mix it up with vagabonds, "to go it with a perfect looseness," as the English actor Joseph Cowell put it, "there [on the river] *Jack was as good as his master.*" The leveling, liberating fluidity of the river would be given poetic expression by Mark Twain; here we can glimpse its social basis.[32]

The river's liberating effects varied dramatically. To head south on the Mississippi was to pass through a land of black slavery and (increasingly) white paranoia. This was hardly a liberation. But if one stayed the course, the voyage ended at New Orleans, "the jumping-off place"—a place where slavery existed but was less dualistically defined by race, where people came in various shades of black, brown, and white, where quadroon dances and salt-and-pepper crap games were part of a vibrant creole culture.[33]

Or, to take another example of the river's complex influence: consider the experience of the raftsman, and its transfiguration into art. The raftsman's work was demanding and dangerous, we can be sure—transporting cumbrous hogsheads of tobacco or bales of cotton, depending solely on his own strength, fighting the vagaries of the river. Yet there must have been times when the raft floated with the current, and a late-afternoon glow descended, and someone suggested a friendly game. This was the sort of moment captured by George Caleb Bingham in *Raftsmen Playing Cards* (1847); a pastoral haze envelops a static tableau of cardplayers, stout fellows, hardworking men at rest, leaning on their elbows, legs splayed at random. Adrift in mist, they seem exempt from ordinary time—much as Huck and Jim do in *Huckleberry Finn* (1884), Mark Twain's refiguration of his boyhood of the 1840s, when it seemed always to be Saturday or summer.

The river as a realm of male camaraderie, an escape from the schedules and norms of bourgeois civilization (schoolmasters, bosses, mothers, wives)—these themes all link Bingham's painting with Mark Twain's

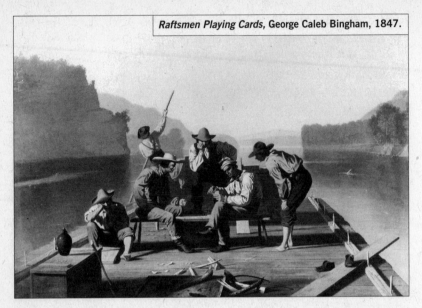

Raftsmen Playing Cards, George Caleb Bingham, 1847.

novel. But there is another thematic connection as well; it may suggest one reason riverboat gambling has preserved an almost mythic stature as an American cultural ritual. That is the tendency, common to Bingham, Mark Twain, and other artists, to imagine the river as a timeless, parallel universe of play. To abandon oneself to its flow was to experience (if one were lucky) the primal plenitude, the stream of endless possibility, courted by tricksters and conjurers. However nostalgic or fantastic this conception of the river as liberator may be, it has at least some historical basis in the fitful freedoms of frontier gambling.

But one did not have to be on the river to experience the sense of democratic emancipation. The historian Hubert Howe Bancroft, recalling the heady days after the discovery of gold in California in 1849, wrote that: "there was an openness in all kinds of wickedness, a dash and abandon quite refreshing. Perhaps they play as heavily at the London gaming houses, and at the German springs, but the charm and freshness of unhackneyed nature is not there. In London, or even at the German springs, one would not often see a Sydney convict, a clergyman not three months from his preaching, a Harvard graduate, a Pennsylvania farmer, and a New York newsboy all betting at the same table at the same time." If the game was on the square (and this was not out of the question, especially during the first three years of the gold rush, when gambling was legal and casinos were operated by leading citizens) the players might catch a glimpse of that utopian realm envisioned by the *alea* players of ancient Rome. The San Francisco games created a world where status, wealth, and power were perpetually fluid, and all men were equal in the eyes of Fortuna—very like the ancient vision, but with "the charm and freshness of unhackneyed nature," at least for men like Bancroft, who by the 1880s (when he published this memoir) was already yearning for vanished frontier vitality.[34]

By 1850, San Francisco was mixing nature with civilization, or at least with aspirations to it. That year saw the completion of the Empire gambling saloon, to the plaudits of the local newspaper: "We do not know of any public room in any portion of the United States of so great an extent, or possessing such elegant decorations and embellishments. Our New Orleans and New York friends would scarcely believe that they could be so far excelled in California." The reference to New Orleans and New York was pointed boosterism: these two cities had set the standard for opulent casinos, beginning with John Davis's place at Orleans and Bourbon Streets in 1827. This would be the pattern for urban gambling, at least the respectable sort: owners of gambling houses would attempt to re-create or simulate aristocratic European excess. Fine Bordeaux would replace rotgut sour mash, gourmet cigars and viands would be provided gratis, and the democratizing ritual of gambling would be surrounded by palatial faux elegance.[35]

The results could be impressive, as Bancroft observed of the San Francisco palaces: "In one the ceiling, rich in fresco and gilt, was supported by glass pillars, pendant from which were great glass chandeliers. Around the walls were fine large paintings of nude female figures, and mirrors extending from floor to ceiling. Entering at night from the unlighted dismal street into an immense room lighted with dazzling brilliance, and loud with the mingled sound of musical instruments, the clink of coin and glasses, and the hum of human voices, was like passing from the dark depths to celestial brightness."[36]

Despite the exalted atmosphere, the democratizing impulse remained. Amid lavish accoutrements, a motley crowd of men met at the tables of the Empire. Professional men rubbed elbows with leather-aproned artisans (free blacks as well as whites) and smoothly operating sharpers. Gamblers' memoirs frequently refer to the regular appearance of gentlemen from the highest circles of public life—attorneys, judges, physicians, politicians, newspaper editors—shoulder to shoulder with mechanics and hod carriers at the roulette table or the faro-bank, even in such respectable towns as Indianapolis, Indiana, or Marietta, Ohio. If gambling was illegal in these localities at the time, then the professional men's presence in the casinos was never openly acknowledged among themselves; they lived tacit double lives. This was a characteristic (male) Victorian resort to a private sphere of pleasure. What moralists might call hypocrisy could be construed by gamblers as creative deployment of multiple identities, a necessary release from a life systematically bound to an ever-tightening morality of self-control. Such conduct challenged conventional categories of virtue and vice.[37]

The challenge became especially sharp in such frontier boom towns as San Francisco—particularly with respect to the ethics of money. "The very qualities most conducive to prosperity in older communities were to some extent out of place here," Bancroft wrote, "men thrived on what else-where would prove their destruction. . . . Generosity, open-handedness, large heartedness, here was the ideal; and if it ran its possessor upon the shoals of bankruptcy, or into a drunkard's grave, it was lamentable, but no such black and accursed evil as parsimoniousness, stinginess, niggardli-ness, or in a word, meanness."[38] The ideal, in short, was something like Robert Bailey's version of the sportsman, as opposed to the mean-spirited cheat. Under the right circumstances, gambling could still epitomize the ethos of a culture of chance, a fine and careless generosity that was in-creasingly at odds with the calculating spirit of the culture of control.

Such a scenario immediately provokes skepticism. Even if class boundaries were fitfully overcome at the gaming tables (itself a large and problematic claim), familiar racial and sexual barriers remained. African Americans, free or slave, remained attached to the culture of chance and often gambled if they had the money. One of the fears that put the citi-zens of Vicksburg in a dither over gambling in 1835 was that slaves were doing it and picking up rebellious ways as well as some cash on the side. But free black people mostly ran their own games and establishments, and in the white man's games, slaves were merely collateral for big-time bets. In San Francisco and other fluid frontier communities, gambling disputes could become an excuse for Anglo assaults on Mexicans and other ethnic minorities. The democracy of gambling was a herrenvolk democracy, for white males only.[39]

Women—apart from the inevitable "sex workers"—fit at best awk-wardly into the gamblers' world of male camaraderie. Women gamblers were few and disreputable in frontier lore. Women dealers were more acceptable, at least in San Francisco, particularly if they exuded the luster of the foreign. The career of the young, attractive, French-born Simone Jules offers a revealing example. She was a popular, honest card dealer and croupier at San Francisco's Bella Union casino during the boom times. She saved enough money to stake herself to her own casino in Nevada City, where she took the name Eleanor Dumont but was eventually dubbed "Madame Mustache" by the miners, due to her luxuriance of facial hair in middle age.[40]

A female gambler was a potentially powerful woman—beyond society's control, concentrating on her own desires and miseries, shamelessly displaying her obsessions, recklessly sorting her chances and worst, perhaps, winning. When she appeared in popular literature, she was often sanitized (and de-sexualized) by sentimentality. Post–Civil War dime novels would make an industry out of this practice. Only gradually did women begin to penetrate the gamblers' preserve.

No one knows what percentage of the riverboat gamblers were frauds; certainly it was an overwhelming majority. In every city, legitimate gambling houses were outnumbered by "skinning houses." The more fashionable ones employed "fastidious ropers"—respectable professional men who brought customers into the establishment and endowed the games with a certain legitimacy, apparently without suspecting that they were rigged.[41]

Like the trickster, the sharper was a consummate actor, even if the pose was simply part of an elaborate social satire. Elijah Skaggs, who organized a vast network of faro and monte dealers throughout the Midwest and South during the antebellum years, was known as "Brother Skaggs, the preaching faro dealer," because of his ministerial costume and abstemious mien.[42] Perhaps the persona was appropriate for someone whose organizational skills were so plainly rooted in the Protestant Ethic, but it also constituted a commentary on the preaching fraternity's well-known horror of gambling—and equally well-known (but furtive) attraction to it.

Gamblers often worked in teams of two to six, posing as Yankee merchants, itinerant preachers, Irish immigrants, naive hayseeds—whatever suited the farce they were about to stage. The riverboat gambler James Ashby regularly passed himself off as a drunken old fiddler traveling with his bumpkin son. While the fiddler, apparently verging on senility, lurched about the cabin playing snatches of tunes, the son belied his dimwitted appearance and picked up pot after pot at poker. Only after Ashby retired a rich man in the 1830s did the truth become widely known: the tunes were coded signals from Ashby to his confederate, describing the players' hands in detail.[43]

Clearly, the professional gambler was also a trickster. Despite his "professionalism," he still liked to play. And despite his determination to accumulate wealth he almost always died broke. Like the men they victimized, professional gamblers could not stay away from the tables. "Play was their bread and butter, and play was in their blood," one historian has observed. "Practically all of them had some game of chance in which they ceased to be the master and became that excited, hopeful thing, the 'sucker.'"[44]

Consider the career of William "Canada Bill" Jones (1820–1877), who was described by his partner as "a slick one. He had a squeaking, boyish voice, and awkward gawky manners, and a way of asking fool questions and putting on a good natured sort of grin, that led everybody to believe that he was the rankest kind of sucker—the greenest sort of country jake." In actuality he was a man of extraordinary mental quickness and manual dexterity, one of the most successful three-card monte cheats who ever set up shop in a room full of rubes. But he squandered all his money at faro. Even if Canada Bill knew the game was rigged, he could not resist. Legend has it that he was stranded in a somnolent Louisiana town, nearly hallucinating with boredom, when he finally found a faro game and began to lose relentlessly. His partner took him aside. "The game's crooked," he warned. "I know it," Canada Bill answered, "but it's the only game in town."[45] The desire to play overcame the certainty of loss—but when play becomes compulsive, is it still play?

The question suggests the limits to the playfulness of gamblers in a commercializing culture of chance. Gambling was not *merely* about money, but it was still—inescapably—about money. Even sportsmen who cultivated indifference to monetary standards of value found it impossible to transcend them altogether—and some succumbed to the same obsessive conduct that characterized the money economy as a whole. For them gambling became a dead end, a self-destructive alternative to viable work. But for others gambling could become at least a fitfully satisfying way of life. Was it a genuine alternative to systematic money-worship? One way to start answering that question is to look at the autobiographies of two antebellum gamblers. The first was a trickster with tendencies to ethical self-justification; the second, a sportsman who insisted there was such a thing as gamblers' honor.

THE CROOKED AND THE STRAIGHT

George Devol was born under modest circumstances in the river town of Marietta, Ohio, in 1829. His lot seemed fated to remain modest when he quit school at thirteen to take a dead-end job, repairing and maintaining commercial rivercraft for other men from sun to sun. But then he discovered he could separate fools from their money at a neighborhood crap game. "I concluded to either quit work or quit gambling," he recalled. "At last one day while we were finishing a boat that we had caulked . . . I gave my tools a push with my foot, and they all went into the river. My brother called out and asked me what I was doing. I looked up, a little sheepish, and said it was the last lick of work I would ever do . . . I told him I intended to live off fools and suckers. I also said, 'I will make money rain'; and I did come near doing as I said."[46]

Within a year Devol was running his first keno game. Having won and lost $2000, he borrowed $300 from the man who had won it from him, Cole Martin, to buy a keno set. Martin, who admired "a young man who tries to help himself," brought his men around from his own faro game to "start this young man's game." They began playing $1 a card at midnight; by 6 A.M. they were playing $10 a card. Devol was taking 10 percent. "They all got stuck," he recalled. "That night my receipts amounted to $1300." Eight months later he was regularly multiplying that sum many times over in a single night. "Then I began to think I was a blooded boy; and soon began to take the girls out riding and to wine suppers, and to play the bank higher than a cat's back, as the old keno game was a great producer." But steady accumulation was not in Devol's line.[47]

Like other men driven to succeed, he was obsessed with making money, but he also wanted to have fun making it with theatrical tricks. The Mississippi riverboats offered that opportunity. Devol became a master of three-card monte, going partners first with a man named Posey Jeffers and later for many years with Canada Bill. Amid a population thronging with counterfeiters, the diddlers sometimes were diddled. He and Jeffers were packing up the three-card monte game one night on the run from Saint Louis to Saint Charles, Missouri, when up stepped a stranger to play. He bet $5000 twice, losing both times, "then walked away as if to lose $10000 was an everyday thing with him," Devol recalled. We then closed up our 'banking house,' well pleased with ourselves." The next day they discovered why the loser had been so calm: the crisp new bills drawn on the State Bank of Missouri were all counterfeit. Bogus bills allowed gamblers to play without fear of loss, even if they could not guarantee a win.[48]

Devol himself usually orchestrated the confidence game. Having ingratiated himself with the slaves at every cotton or sugar plantation between Memphis and New Orleans, Devol was able convincingly to impersonate a prominent planter, which he did when the plantation wharf provided a timely means of escape from outraged victims. Once, after he had won four $500 bags of silver playing three-card monte with some Arkansas chicken farmers heading home from market, he sensed a surge of resentment among the losers and decided it was time to jump ship. "This is my sugar plantation," he said as an impressively pillared mansion hove into view. "You should have seen the chicken men look at me when I landed with my sacks; and all the niggers came to shake hands and say 'Glad youse back, Massa George,' (for I knew all the niggers on the coast)." Devol's account suggests that the black population along the river served as a kind of chorus for his theatrical events; whether this was actually the case is of course an open question, and if it was, there is the further question concerning what (if anything) the slaves got out of participating in the scam. In any case, Devol enjoyed playing a variety of roles. When it suited his need to elude pursuers, he could impersonate a black deckhand or musician as well as a white planter.[49]

To Devol, a square game was boring; it provided too few opportunities for craft and guile. Once in a five-handed poker game on the steamer *Natchez*, Devol found himself among friends. "We were playing on the square, with a straight deck of cards and for a small limit. I could enjoy myself in such a game for a limited time; then the old desire to play my tricks would come over me, and I could not resist the temptation." When it was his turn to deal he slipped in a cold deck with sixteen aces, raised the limit to $20, and dealt four aces to each of the other players. Everybody won but him, and it took a little while for the rest to see the humor while Devol was doubled over with sidesplitting guffaws. Having amused himself (if no one else), he returned to a fairer (and presumably duller) game.[50]

Besides detailing Devol's buffoonish delight in his own tricks, his autobiography also revealed his sporadic efforts at composing an apologia. His motives, he insisted, were more complex than greed; he was not a mere moneygetter. The anti-Semitism that runs through his autobiography was traceable, like other midnineteenth century strains of this malady, to a process of self-purgation through allegorical projection. Devol invariably described the "hook-nosed sons of Abraham" he encountered on the river as archetypes of venality, even greedier and more devious than he was (and hence more likely to fall prey to his wiles). For Devol, as for other gentiles caught up in dubious commercial ventures, the Jew constituted a collective Other on which he could project whatever anxiety he may have felt about his ill-gotten gains.[51]

Preachers played a slightly different role. They appeared repeatedly in Devol's narrative, always in the guise of furtive gamblers who—like Devol's other victims—are convinced that they can see the corner turned down on the card they want to follow, and that they can thus outwit the monte dealer (who has bent that corner precisely to mislead them). Invariably they would lose a sizeable chunk of cash, not to mention gold spectacles and manuscripts of sermons—all of which Devol would magnanimously return, when the ministers came begging to his stateroom. Such episodes were meant to demonstrate that "ever since the days when Joseph's brothers gambled for his coat of many colors when they put him in the pit, the desire to venture in games of chance has been rampant in every human breast, and even 'men of the cloth' have proven no exception to the rule."[52]

The universality of gambling was more than a matter of fun and games, Devol claimed, as he thrashed about for justifications. You cannot teach a dog or a pig to gamble, he wrote, "hence gambling is proof of man's intellectual superiority." Since biblical times, when men cast lots to divide the land of Canaan and decide that Jonah was the cause of the storm, "men have been addicted to . . . settling matters by chance." This assertion is puzzling, as Devol himself was rarely willing to leave matters to chance.[53]

Devol was less a gambler than a sharper, but he proudly claimed allegiance to a gambler's ethical code—which he contrasted favorably with commercial mores. "A gambler's word is as good as his bond, and that is more than I can say of many business men who stand very high in the community," Devol wrote. "The gambler will pay when he has money, which many good church members will not." Speculative commodity investing, in his view, was little more than legalized betting. "The Board of Trade is just as much a gambling house as a faro bank. Do not the members put up their (and sometimes other peoples') money on puts, calls, margins, and futures? Do not some poor people have to wait a long time in the 'future' before they get the money some rascal has put up and lost? Talk about the morality of gamblers. They are not thieves and swindlers . . . ," he concluded a little weakly.[54]

But wasn't Devol's own trade the barest-faced swindle imaginable? Well, yes and no—in many ways the suckers were getting just what they deserved, Devol argued with bold casuistry. "When a sucker sees a corner turned up, or a little spot on a card in three-card monte, he does not know that it was done for the purpose of making him think he has the advantage." He thinks, of course, that the player does not see it, and he is in such a hurry to get out his money that he often cuts or tears his clothes. When suckers lose, "they are mad, because they are beat at their own game"—which is little better than trying to steal money from a blind man. How can they expect sympathy? The monte dealer was simply teaching dishonest people a lesson. So Devol claimed, in all apparent seriousness.[55]

Like other apologists for gambling, Devol placed great stress on knowing how to lose. A true gambler was never a "kicker" or "squealer," never the sort of player who would continue to insist that the the money he had lost was still "his" money; on the contrary: "the gambler considers the money he loses, against any game, as lost: and it belongs to the person who won it, and you never hear any [gamblers] do any kicking."[56]

The gambler's ethic resembled the soldier's: in defeat a stoical calm, in victory a reliable generosity. Devol insisted he was faithful to this ideal. Preachers were not the only beneficiaries of his magnanimity, he declared. He never took any money from a friend and never took more than anyone could afford. He always consulted with the ship's clerk to make sure the losers had sufficient money for their passage home and a cash cushion besides. If they did not, he would provide it. Like Canada Bill, to whom he paid sentimental tribute, Devol was sensitive to the needs of the poor, including those who were poor because they had lost to him. Or so at any rate the Mississippi sharper claimed.

John O'Connor probably would have scoffed at Devol's ethical pretensions. In *Wanderings of a Vagabond* (1873), which he published under the pseudonym John Morris, O'Connor recounted his adventures as an honest gambler among crooks. He drew a hard line between the two categories and insisted that he had never crossed it. His story shows how a traditionalist gambler's outlook—what one might call a persistent ethic of fortune—survived amid the widespread commercialization of chance.

According to Morris's account, he was born in 1833—like Devol—in Marietta, Ohio, which he described as a thriving town with "a fine little wharf." Methodists and Presbyterians were the ruling powers. They had brick churches, while the Catholics' and Baptists' were wooden. None but the godly could hold office; groggeries, billiard tables, and the like were forbidden. The only available liquor was at the Old Hickory Tavern, an overnight hostelry. Morris's father was a partner in the firm of Giles & Morris, tailors. They were Irishmen who believed in the adage that "It's time enough to bid the devil good morning when you meet him"—so they never bothered to prepare for misfortune. And whenever they had a chance, they closed up shop for a variety of leisure pursuits: hunting, fishing, quarter-horse racing, cock- and dogfighting, bull and bear baiting, whatever they could cook up on the spur of the moment.[57]

Both Morris's parents died of cholera when he was a baby; Mr. Giles became his guardian. The boy soon developed a taste for novels and books of travel, much to his foster parents' dismay. They wanted him to take his father's place in the firm; he wanted a vagabond's life. The conflict was typical of many described in antigambling tracts as well as memoirs. The gambler, reformers assumed, was the victim of an overactive imagination, perhaps the result of premature exposure to fiction and other risky stimulants. Avoiding productive labor, the gambler-to-be wasted time and money building "castles in the air"—a phrase that linked him (at least in the reformers' imaginations) with that other fantasist, the masturbator.[58]

Whatever Morris's predelictions for fantasy, he did not have to travel far to begin to gratify them. The back room at Giles & Morris provided a glimpse of a parallel universe, one that was officially condemned by the puritanical town fathers. Here as elsewhere in the gamblers' social universe, Jack was as good as his master; respected professional men sat down with sons of toil. They played poker, brag, euchre, all-fours, whist, vingt-et-un, and faro. The boy watched, learned, and eventually left town,

knocking about the Ohio and Mississippi river towns, finally heading for
bigger game as a faro operator in New York.[59]

Morris's career, as he presented it, was a constant struggle to run an
honest game among hordes of sharpers and the police who protected
them. Perhaps the low point came when was arrested for running a faro
game in New York, fined $50 (which he paid), and kept in prison with-
out explanation for days, fed only hardtack and cold, greasy broth. Finally
the police lieutenant offered to release him if he never came back to town;
his faro equipment would, of course, be confiscated. Not so fast, said the
kid, insisting he should be allowed to keep his means of livelihood. In the
end the police relented, but Morris had to pick his spots more carefully
in the future.[60]

The big problem, as Morris saw it, was that legislators' attempts to
abolish gambling had only created more corruption. As states and localities passed statute after statute to prohibit gambling, the legitimate operators were forced to close while the sharpers proliferated under police
protection. Antigambling legislation provided a host of new opportunities for bribery and graft. Like Bailey, Morris insisted that the trick was to
regulate gambling, not try vainly to abolish it. An honest game, in his
view, was a thing of beauty.[61]

And so was an honest gambler. "None stand higher as a class, in the
scale of probity, than gamblers," Morris wrote. The gambler was simply
"a person willing to back his opinion, whenever he is in possession of any
money with which to do so." He was brave, perhaps given to "excessive
cleanliness" and extravagant display but also to largeness of spirit—liber-
ality and hospitality, courtesy and affability. And he was a genuine democrat. "The gaming-table equalizes all who take their seats before it,"
Morris wrote. "It is a peculiar mart of trade, where cringing and flattery
are not part of the stock, and in no way belong to it." The true gambler,
from this view, transcended the sordid subterfuge of commerce and embodied plain-spoken sincerity.[62]

The sharper, on the other hand, spoiled the real gambler's reputation
by aping his outward appearance. He was merely a confidence man.
"Sharpers are selfish, crafty, and avaricious, and in no case are they ever
moved by the liberal and generous impulses which characterize the true
gambler," Morris wrote. He delighted in exposing the hypocrisies and
crudities of the sharping fraternity—such men as Henry Price McGrath,
"an ignorant, uncouth, and unmannerly loon" who had nonetheless

made a fortune at his New York skinning house. In him, "fraud, avariciousness, insolence, jealousy, and cowardice" were more developed than in any other con artist Morris knew. "His entertaining qualities consist in being a good eater and drinker, singing snatches of blackguard songs, telling stories decidedly bordering on the indecent, and chattering learnedly on the merits of various racehorses—a subject about which he knows as much as the method of squaring the circle, or the secret of perpetual motion." McGrath was a familiar type of blowhard, a titan of knowingness who surrounded himself with sycophants.[63]

Morris declared open war on McGrath and his ilk. No compromise was possible. "So conflicting are the interests of gamblers and sharpers, that if the former possessed the power, the latter would be so completely crushed out, that not a two-card box could be found in America." The solution to the problem of sharpers was within government's reach: make cheating at cards a felony, and the whole deceitful tribe will disappear "like hoar-frost before the morning sun."[64]

Of course, it was not so simple, as Morris realized. In state after state and city after city, the pattern repeated itself. Waves of abolitionist legislation made gambling more dishonest, more sinister, and more corrupt— but no less widespread. Hubert Howe Bancroft noted the disastrous impact of criminalization on gambling in San Francisco: after 1852, when gambling was made illegal, the opulent palaces became mere skinning houses and grew progressively seedier as well as more violent. In every town of any size, judges, police, mayors, and other city officials were bought off right and left. Devol told of winning a watch at monte from the mayor of Indianapolis. The sharper returned it privately; the mayor was relieved and promised his benefactor a future favor. That very night Devol was arrested for gambling illegally and taken before the mayor. His honor let Devol off with a big fine, which he later remitted over drinks after the prosecutor had departed.[65]

Everywhere the pattern was the same: official condemnation, unofficial tolerance. Throughout Virginia in the 1850s, for example, faro was illegal; but the law was enforced only in Wheeling (which apparently had a reputation for rectitude)—and there only sporadically. The trick to getting around it, if you were a faro operator, was to pay the city marshal $100 and offer him a 5 percent cut. This seemed to satisfy him, and faro proceeded in Wheeling.[66]

The difficulty with legislative remedies stemmed, in Morris's view, from reformers' refusal to distinguish between honest gambling and fraud. He was onto something. As Ann Fabian has observed, the prominent antigambling crusader Jonathan Greene simply collapsed all gambling into rational (albeit dishonest) economic calculation: there was no distinction, from Greene's perspective, between gamblers and sharpers; all gamblers were cheats.[67] Greene and other reformers denied that gambling could have any independent cultural existence; to them, it was merely an illicit version of the money mania that pervaded the entire society. There was no doubt that money was a big part of most gamblers' motives, but the reformers' reductionist assumption revealed a characteristic failure of the bourgeois imagination, one that has persisted to our own time: the inability to imagine that gambling could be about anything *but* money.

Morris despised Greene as merely another confidence man in moralist's clothing. "No charlatan ever had a wider field for his operations," Morris wrote, charging that Greene used mirrors and other hidden devices to identify marked cards. Greene falsely claimed expertise while he really just practiced sleight of hand, but his rhetoric seemed to be working. His moral tirades seemed to Morris like water on a stone, wearing away tolerance, promoting the common assumption that gambling was essentially vile.[68]

The result, in Morris's view, was a proliferation of draconian statutes that went unenforced because the enforcers were bribed to look the other way, and a corrosive growth of disrespect for legal authority in general. Cynics and moralists might scoff, but Morris was perceptive: laws against gambling bred lawlessness, not only among sharpers but among politicians, police, and judges. The wagering impulse resisted all attempts to stamp it out.

Yet opponents of gambling did their damndest. During the antebellum decades, antigambling rhetoric escalated dramatically and moralists' hostility toward the practice acquired unprecedented ferocity. Their arguments blended secular and religious inflections into the idioms of evangelical rationality. The republican suspicion of "the speculating spirit" ebbed gradually, resurfacing mainly in times of economic panic (the late 1830s, the late 1850s). Though some reformers still fretted that gambling upset a deferential social order (as Stith had a century earlier), most gradually refocused their perceptions. In their developing discourse, gambling was a contagion that threatened the body politic, but it was also a per-

sonal malady that menaced the individual—his body, his soul, his immediate kin. In the popular culture of evangelical rationality, the gambler
was transformed from a hell of a fellow to a pathetic slave of passion.

THE REDEFINITION OF MANHOOD

Eighteenth-century elites had usually been content to let rich boys and
ruffians hang out at the same horse races and cockfights. Indeed it was in
their interest to do so. These were occasions when men could strut pub-
licly and planters could parade their supposed superiority. But evangelical
rationality introduced a new morality of masculine self-control, reinforced by the fear that gambling upset social hierarchy by promoting
promiscuous social mingling as well as drunkenness and violence. As this
new norm became central to bourgeois visions of civic improvement,
gambling—by any one—began to seem a threat to civilization itself.

So at any rate it appeared to some of the citizens of Vicksburg, Mississippi, during the summer of 1835. The respectable men of the town
had been grumbling for months about the gambling hells along the
river—nests of vice where drunks erupted in violence over disputes at
cards, where hapless boatmen lost their shirts to crooked dealers, and
where (it was rumored) a black slave could sit down and bet, win or lose,
like a white man. Finally the murder of a notorious dealer provoked the
local elite to action. A mob of upright citizens stormed the seedy boat-
house where a number of gamblers were sleeping, dragged them to a
poplar grove just outside of town, and hanged eleven of them. The
Vicksburg lynchings show how high the stakes could get in the battle
over gambling, especially on the frontier, where the very principles of
public order seemed up for grabs.[69]

There was more going on in Vicksburg than simply the survival of
concern about gambling's threat to hierarchy. Evangelical rationality
seeped into the antigambling discourse, giving old suspicions a sharper
edge. New secular theories merged with evangelical moral strictures to
promote a prudential disdain for excessive risk. In 1839, two years into
the long depression touched off by a stock market panic, the *Boston
Weekly Magazine* warned against "The Fluctuations of Fortune." Over-
trading, the frenzied pursuit of fortune, produced a severe and opposite
reaction, widespread misfortune. "All these evils are produced by a gen-

eral striving to obtain more than our average and rightful proportion of the good things of life; and by using unrighteous maneuvers to effect our object." Extreme fluctuations of fortune paralleled chills and fever in the body: only gradually would they subside, just as a pendulum would only gradually resume its normal movement after being pushed too far in one direction.[70]

These physical analogies, crude as they were, expressed a widespread impulse to refigure the ideal man as a steady and disciplined achiever, resistant to the allure of fortune's fancy. In a phrenological chart (also published in 1839), for example, Josiah Graves described a cranial shape that characterized a particular type of gamblers' behavior: "When [hope of success is] perverted, [these] men expect more than is reasonable, are everlastingly scheming, or building castles in the air, trying their luck in lotteries, and c., and c." In reform literature, the tendency toward unbridled fantasy linked the gambler with the masturbator—two especially virulent embodiments of that antitype of success, the idle dreamer.[71]

Ideals of disciplined achievement suited Christian businessmen's needs for new forms of labor discipline. Gamblers, like drunkards, challenged the emerging mythology of self-made manhood. This would never do. Under the aegis of evangelical rationality, the gambler was recast from an epitome of masculine selfhood to a pathetic antiself—a slave to his destructive habit and frequently a suicide. (The hapless Hamburg gamblers, who "perished by chagrin or despair" according to an 1806 survey, were occasionally retrieved to prove the point.) What traditionally had been a form of self-assertion was transformed into self-negation. The gambler's manic-depressive oscillation between joy and sorrow comported ill with the secularized Protestant ethic of unending improvement, civic or personal. So, for that matter, did the speculator's comparable rhythms of life—though they were compared to the gambler's with increasing rarity, usually in times of economic distress. In the depression year of 1859, a *Harper's* contributor rallied the dispirited, presenting them with an alternative to the risk-taking model of manhood: "the practical man."[72]

According to this author, the "truly practical man" never cravenly curries favor with fortune. Indeed he is "the only master of her chances . . . neither madcap nor coward, and proof alike against her smiles and frowns." Unlike the obsessive risk-taker, "the practical man is a match for fortune, and able to meet and master her on her own grounds" How? By hewing to "a scale of substantial values," measured by "a scale of reasonable probabilities." Of course he makes mistakes, "but he has studied chances till he has found the main chance, and in his ruling policy the element of uncertainty is so combined with the element of risk, that the risk serves to quicken and vitalize the whole combination—as the oxygen in the atmosphere, in itself so inebriating and consuming, gives spirit and life when mingled in moderate proportions with the more solid and nutritious nitrogen. To change the figure, he aims to live and work in the temperate zone of sound sense and solid strength, and he is not in danger of running off into tropical fevers and polar icebergs, for he is content to be warmed without being burned, and to be cool without being frozen." Against the manic-depression of the gambler or the speculator—slaves to an ethic of fortune—the practical man posed the virtues of systematic moderation. His ethic of mastery might not bring him great wealth, but it would guarantee steady success.[73]

Yet to counsel moderation was insufficient. One did not live by "reasoned probabilities" alone. Evangelical rationalists needed some stronger force for steady practicality, some more substantial counterweight to the frenzied pursuit or fitful propitiation of fortune. Increasingly moralists found this stabilizing power in the home, which would need some juicing up if it was going to compete with the allure of such disreputable entertainments as gambling. Of course, Americans gamble, the *American Expositor* asserted in 1850, why not? "Our occupations engage us all the time: hands, heart, and head are occupied in money making; and we have comparatively no social enjoyment—no real home joys. Yet we must have some change, a real, go-ahead, American would be crazed if it came not. Hence excitement is sought after—excitements of any kind—of strong drink—of gambling, and c. [*sic*]" For the young boy whose father was always away at his business, gambling was an escape from a dull and gloomy household. The task for parents was to make family life more fun than the cockfight around the corner. This was the impulse behind the domestication of betting games into board games, often with cumbersome didactic agendas—*The Reward of Merit, The New Game of Virtue Rewarded and Vice Punished,* and the like. But it would take more than board games to stem the contagion of gambling.[74]

What the reformers needed to generate was real revulsion, and that came from the emotional intensity of evangelical Protestantism—a movement that spread nationwide, in bursts of revivalist enthusiasm that swept across the countryside and eventually flared up in major cities as well. It was as if Protestant critics knew an alternative religion when they saw one. Gambling, they sensed, was an alternative way of addressing and perhaps even influencing the mysteries of fate. By the 1820s and 1830s, ministers were producing dozens of antigambling tracts which nearly all followed a comparable pattern. *The Lottery Ticket: An American Tale* (1822) may stand for an entire genre. A decent, industrious farmer with a young wife and family is seduced into buying a lottery ticket with the intention of paying off a mortgage bequeathed him by an improvident father. The seducer is the mortgage-holder himself, who knows a little something about acquiring money without effort.

The farmer wins the lottery and is drawn into the world of male camaraderie at the local tavern—"the coarse jests, the buffoonery," the endless demands for "treats" from newfound "friends" congratulating him on his good fortune. All this "tended to produce a dissipation of mind, most unfriendly to industry and virtue," not to mention "a gaiety, which rendered every-day pleasures irksome and insipid, and gave him a craving desire for convivial company, which home could not satisfy." Even then, "the image of a beloved wife" restrains him from actually gambling.[75]

When he does succumb to the amusements of the alehouse, his downward spiral begins. It ends only when he has become hopelessly mired in drunkenness and debt and is jailed for his inability to meet his obligations. On his release, he and his wife pass their old home, now in ruins—the focus of bourgeois hopes, the scene of collaboration between the sexes, the symbol of masculine achievement. What they see is the desolation of a powerful pastoral idyll, caused by the mere purchase of a lottery ticket. The farmer breaks down, embraces his wife and children, reads the parables of the prodigal son and the lost sheep, and recovers the "virtues of self-government and self-denial." *Exeunt Omnes.*[76]

In evangelical reform literature, the wife was increasingly cast in the role of cultural superego and called upon to play a contradictory role as inspiration and doormat. As the *Religious Intelligencer* asserted in 1827: "A woman's love is like a plant that shows its strength the more it is trodden upon." This self-sacrificing sufferer was a far cry from the desirous lady gambler. According to the emerging conventions, home was a moral haven, women its protectors, and men's gambling a major threat to it.[77]

It is easy to scoff at formulaic moralism, but there was no doubt a grim reality behind the many tales of gamblers' downfalls. In a society increasingly dominated by competitive individualism and disciplined labor, failure to embrace "the virtues of self-government and self-denial" could no doubt often lead to catastrophe. Evidence of this pattern pervaded the literature of reform.

Many reformers exhibited physical revulsion in the face of the devastation they believed was wrought by gambling. A pamphleteer named William Snelling produced an exposé of gambling in Boston in 1833; it included detailed descriptions of revolting gambling scenes, such as a cockfight at Craigie's Bridge, where a crowd of a hundred boys and men had gathered, including blackguards, swindlers, and reprobates as well as "sons of the aristocracy of the city" and "honest gentlemen." Whiskey flowed freely: one man was singing obscene songs, another "belching up his bowels with a groan"—appropriately disgusting behavior, Snelling thought, for a blood ritual that depended on systematic cruelty to cocks.[78]

Reformers resorted frequently to the language of illness. Gambling was a "moral contagion," a "sweeping pestilence" that "pollutes the city," wrote Timothy Flint of New York in 1827. The language of social sickness betokened the emergence of bourgeois Christianity, which blended suspicions of avarice with fears of penury. Gambling was castigated for contradictory reasons: it led to unbridled accumulation and inevitable poverty. "We scarcely remember an instance in which a confirmed and persevering gambler did not end his career in poverty," Flint wrote. But the one consistent reason reformers assaulted gambling was that it violated the core value of their version of Christianity: self-mastery.[79]

Religion and psychology melded in antigambling jeremiads; the vice was often characterized in physiological terms. Flint complained that "even females who lead the fashion and give tone to public sentiment, are seen alternately blanching with terror and flashing with rage, around the gambling table." From the reformers' perspective, the pattern was even more disturbing when the gambler was a woman, the supposed source of moral stability in the Christian home. But whatever the gamblers' gender, their wild emotional oscillations were a staple of unrepentant memoirs as well as reformers' diatribes.[80]

The reason the appeal of cards was part of a slippery slope, the Congregational Reverend John Richards told Dartmouth students in 1852, was that "the APPETITE [for gambling] is INSATIABLE." The emphasis on the insatiability of appetites was comparatively new, and was related to the emergence of new, more tightly controlled models of selfhood. By stressing the extraordinary power of sinful appetite, moralists made self-mastery into a form of moral heroism. Those unfortunates who yielded to their yen for gambling would soon find themselves enslaved by the habit.[81] What later generations would call addiction was known to ante-bellum Americans as slavery—a word increasingly burdened with politi-cal as well as emotional freight. It signified the antithesis of personal autonomy. In an era when dependency was increasingly defined (espe-cially for men) as weakness, metaphorical as well as literal slavery pro-voked hostility among the apostles of self-control. Far from expressing his power, in their view, gambling unmanned the gambler.

The same argument could be extended to the culture of chance as a whole. In 1835 *Genessee Farmer* inveighed against the shocking supersti-tions that persisted even among the presumably Protestant people of up-state New York. "We have known farmers who would not on any occasion begin an important operation on 'Friday,' not out of respect to the heathen goddess, after whom that day is called,—but through fear that their progress would be retarded by 'unlucky' events." The problem was not merely impiety but inefficiency: "Such interruptions are heavy clogs on the business of a farm." Fourteen years later, farther west, the *Michigan Farmer* found equally silly superstitions among the farmers of that state. "To trust in signs and the moon, to dreams and visions, to moan over real or fancied woes, and envy others' prosperity, is all idiocy. Be a man in all your resolutions, plans, and conduct, and you will meet suc-cess, yea more you will deserve it." Self-reliant manliness required the re-jection of the culture of chance—above all its main secular ritual, the habit of gambling.[82]

To critics of gambling, the sine qua non of manly success was not sudden wealth but a steady movement toward prosperity. They mingled Christian asceticism and bourgeois prudence, warning against the cor-rupting effects of avarice and accumulation but also insisting, as Weems had in 1810, that "no gambler ever died rich." The secret of the gambler's failure, reformers agreed, was his inability to control his wild imagina-tion. Like the drunkard or the masturbator, the chronic bettor had a ten-dency to build fantastic "castles in the air" that, when they collapsed, left him depleted, exhausted, and despairing. Far saner than this manic-depressive pattern was the path of evangelical rationality.

Or so the reformers claimed. Occasionally, especially during down-

turns in the stock market, they broadened their critique to include speculative investing as well as gambling. But it was hard to sustain this dual
focus. In the emerging moral calculus of success, the gambler was becoming the Other against whom the speculator could define his legitimacy—particularly if his venture turned out to be successful. As the
Jacksonian economist Richard Hildreth wrote in 1840, "When speculation proves successful, however wild it may have appeared in the beginning, it is looked upon as an excellent thing, and commended as *enterprise;*
it is only when unsuccessful that it furnishes occasion for ridicule and
complaint, and is stigmatized as a *bubble* or a *humbug.*"[83] Many opponents
of gambling distrusted the speculator as well. But in a culture intoxicated
with the main chance, reformers faced more difficulty criticizing speculation than demonizing its evil twin, gambling.

A Protestant ethic of mastery gradually merged with secular notions
of progress through will and choice. But that ethic would never have
spread so successfully (the counterevidence was too plentiful) if it had remained merely a set of moral strictures. To compete successfully with
older worldviews, to sustain a successful confidence game, creators of the
evangelical-rational consensus had to offer a compelling and reassuring
account of human beings' place in the cosmos.

This they accomplished by denying chance altogether as they melded
Divine Providence and human will. God had scripted the entire performance—"Nothing Occurs By Chance," moralists insisted—though
the faithful believer could paradoxically choose what role he would play
in this cosmic drama: saved or damned. Private and public salvation were
twinned. Individual and national destinies intertwined as Protestant orators expanded on the idea of America's millennial role. Far from being a
mere accident of fate, the rising glory of America was part of a providential plan. The developing consensus made everything fit a coherent
pattern, from the westward spread of empire to the state of the individual soul.[84]

The mysteries of grace, too, became assimilated to evangelical rationality. The Arminian drift that began in the mideighteenth century intensified through the antebellum era. As Protestants recoiled from the
manic-depressive pattern of revivalistic conversion, more of them redefined the experience of grace as well, moving away from a rhetoric of
fortune and toward an emphasis on the centrality of choice. Rather than
an unpredictable ecstasy beyond human control, the evidence of grace

became an inclination toward predictable moral action—the outcome of a successful joint venture between God and man. But the embourgeoisement of grace occurred primarily among educated white Protestants, the people who most fervently embraced the emergent culture of control. Outside the Protestant mainstream, older meanings of grace survived.

THE SPECTRUM OF SPIRITUAL LUCK

Among African Americans and Roman Catholics, grace remained a form of *mana,* or spiritual luck—its workings in the world were unpredictable and indirect, epitomized in the irregular textile patterns of the Senegambians and their American descendants. In effect these designs were an essential part of sacramental objects, meant to conjure *mana* by emulating its mystery and indirection. Here as elsewhere in the culture of chance, the experience of grace involved an acceptance of indeterminacy, a resistance to the false closure of cosmic certainty.

Of course, it was always possible for mystery to congeal into formula. This was the Protestant critique of Catholic ritual: a covenant of grace between man and God had become a mere covenant of works—an empty, mechanical repetition of essentially meaningless actions. No one who has drowsed amid the droning of a rosary recitation or seen the perfunctory performance of an allegedly sacred sacrament could deny the force of this Protestant assault on inauthenticity.

But the attack on mere form was based on the view from the outside; it came from critics for whom the forms had no meaning. The element of mystery—of irrational faith—had to survive for the ritual or fetish to sustain any spiritual significance. As an early anthropologist of African American folk belief observed, the believer in fetishes "is not foolish enough to worship blindly sticks and stones . . . it is the spirit dwelling within those objects which receives his reverence."[85] The conviction that one might actually conjure *mana*—coupled with the awareness that one might not—was the key to sustaining the mystery and reality of the ritual. Otherwise it was all mumbo-jumbo.

The notion of grace as *mana* depended on "a sense of the nearness of the spiritual world" among the believers. This was the quality that distinguished Catholics from Protestants, according to the Reverend Isaac Hecker. A convert and Catholic apologist, Hecker may have overstated the case. Even a liberal Protestant contributor to the *North American Review,* writing in 1832, admitted that "however we may doubt, we cannot well deny, that separated spirits may, in some mysterious manner, hold communion with our own." These sorts of suspicions kept fortune-tellers, spiritualists, and publishers of dream books in business.[86]

Yet for Catholics, an intimate connection with the spiritual world was not confined to the margins of the faith but was embedded at its core. Patron saints and guardian angels became invisible companions to the Christian believer in late antiquity, and they continued to play that role for centuries. Among the Irish and German Catholics in the ante-bellum United States, the living presence of "the holy ones in heaven among us on earth" was expressed in the doctrine of the communion of saints and enacted in the daily practices of the believer. "Devotions," the historian Ann Taves writes, "presupposed the existence of relationships between faithful Catholics and supernatural beings, and provided a means of interacting with them."[87]

Popular Catholicism mingled matter and spirit, endowing material artifacts with supernatural powers, encouraging prayers for temporal as well as spiritual ends. "Graces and favors"—ranging from the recovery of a sick child to the rediscovery of a lost bracelet—could be obtained in this world as well as the next. The means of grace were material objects, magically charged with *mana:* eucharistic wafers, rosary beads, scapular medals, holy water. One observer of the immigrant Irish in the 1850s noted their reverence for the protective and curative powers of holy water: they would "frequently . . . fill a small phial from the contents of the font and carry it away with them as a precious treasure." Body and soul melded in the enchanted universe of popular Catholicism.[88]

This union was expressed in the metaphor of the church as the body of Christ. The grace received from the communion of saints paralleled the blood circulating in the body: it was, according to Taves, "the sacred substance that kept the body [of Christ] alive." The kinship with magical thinking was undeniable. Despite clerical insistence on the exclusively spiritual meaning of grace, despite priestly disdain for "the delusive piety of wearing scapulars etc. without avoiding sin," to the laity grace remained a form of *mana,* a means of conjuring miracles.[89]

For African American Christians, the situation was a little more complicated. Like many white evangelicals, especially in the backcountry, black believers sustained the notion of grace as an ecstatic, unpredictable experience—a Christian version of spirit possession. Some upper-class white ministers questioned just how Christian it was. The white Presbyterian minister Charles C. Jones, reporting in 1842 on his efforts to bring the gospel to the slaves of Liberty County, Georgia, complained that "they believe in second-sight, apparitions, charms, witchcraft, and in a kind of irresistable satanic influence. The superstitions brought from Africa have not been wholly laid aside." And after a trip through the Southeast in the 1850s, Frederick Law Olmsted lamented that even the avowedly Christian slaves were imprisoned by "a miserable system of superstition, the more painful that it employs some forms and words ordinarily connected with true Christianity." Much the same thing, at much the same time, was being said of Irish immigrants by skeptical Protestant observers.[90]

What white Protestants dismissed as superstition could be a means of maintaining some distance from the dominant culture. Despite the effort of Jones and other ministers to use the Bible as a spiritual sanction for slavery, slaves persisted in seeing it as a conjuring book that melded Hebrew and Christian theological traditions with an Afrocentric cosmos. The hybrid character of Afro-American Christianity encouraged the persistence of bibliomancy and other attempts to conjure *mana*—as Douglass's account of Sandy and the root revealed.[91]

But among the more educated African Americans, this syncretism also fostered a notion of grace uniquely suited to the suffering created by enslavement. The essence of "reconciling grace," for at least some black ministers, was that it cleansed the heart of bitterness, allowing even an oppressed people to accept the inscrutable ways of Providence. From a secular radical perspective, this kind of religion could too easily become an opiate: pie in the sky when you die. But from a believer's view, reconciling grace could offer a flickering but profound insight into the core paradoxes of Christianity—the coexistence of contingency and coherence, doubt and faith. The experience of reconciling grace transcended the cultural oppositions between chance and control; it melded the acknowledgment of arbitrary pain with the affirmation of Providential order.[92]

Reconciling grace fostered an acceptance of conflicts at the heart of existence, above all the conflict between the inescapably cruel accidents of fate and the yearning to embrace some benign principle of Being.

This willingness to live with contradiction, to transcend absurdity through faith, suggests that African American Protestants may have had more in common than they knew with Pascal, Kierkegaard, and William James; they may have been preaching their own vernacular version of Christian existentialism. The notion of reconciling grace animated some of the most profound documents of the age—including Lincoln's Second Inaugural Address, which aimed to cleanse the body politic of bitterness and redeem the random violence of the Civil War by imagining it was part of a Providential purpose, albeit a purpose that human beings could at best dimly perceive.

Reconciling grace encouraged the acceptance of imperfection, in oneself and others; evangelical rationality, in contrast, was implicitly perfectionist. This was what promoted its assimilation to a secular creed of Progress. Through the 1850s, the discourse of grace in mainstream Protestantism reflected a steady embourgeoisement of revivalistic fervor and a gradual abandonment of the rhetoric of fortune. Congregational and Presbyterian ministers (along with some Northern Methodists and Baptists) worked hard to redefine the experience of grace away from the manic-depressive pattern and toward a model more compatible with rational choice. "Evidences of grace," the *Religious Intelligencer* asserted in 1829, could be found "not so much in sudden and powerful convictions, alarming fears and deep despondency, followed by lively hope and rapturous joy (which may sometimes attend conversions from open and flagrant wickedness), as in the gradual understanding and feeling of the truth as it is in Jesus." For ordinary believers, ecstatic oscillations of emotion were no longer on the agenda. "As it is in nature, so it is in grace," the *Intelligencer* concluded—gradual but inexorable growth.[93]

The redefinition of grace required an orderly, progressive cosmos, a universe where God's ways were less mysterious than manifest, where grace conformed to moral convention and the virtuous were rewarded in this world as well as the next, where even the fate of nations reflected divine design. The recession from special providences to general Providence—from a busy, interventionist God to a remote Watchmaker—signaled the disappearance of the miraculous from everyday life. But if God's hand could no longer be discerned in quotidian reality, it could still be seen in world historical events, particularly in the revolution that created these United States and the history of their extraordinary expansion.

Material progress and westward advance could be endowed with a spiritual aura of inevitablity. Gradually this complacent providentialism became the nation's official creed, the sublimest rhetoric of the culture of control. But to become truly national, it had to survive civil war.

THE NOONTIDE OF PROVIDENCE

The developing consensus achieved a paradoxical merger of divine Providence with human striving. Secular and religious moralists united in their disdain for the culture of chance. "Chance, chance is the people's divinity, and wasn't it strange! wasn't it very lucky! . . . is the fashionable vocabulary with which it is apostrophized," the *Atheneum* complained in 1825, insisting that "providential escapes, which have been attributed to accident, or chance . . . should rather be ascribed to higher causes, and holier commands." This appeared to leave open the door to special providences, but most educated Protestants were determined to shut it.[94]

Since special providences were miraculous, unpredictable interventions in the ordinary course of events, they were increasingly at odds with the orderly cosmos of evangelical rationality. "The *order of proceeding* in nature, providence, and grace alike is *gradual*," asserted the *American Biblical Repository* in 1838. God "might have revealed the natural history of the primeval earth to us in his word, but he chose not to reveal what we might better discover for ourselves, and he has left us to gather that history from the organic remains of primitive ages." A belief in inevitable progress—paradoxically achieved through human effort—combined with a common emphasis on harmonies and regularities in nature to link evolutionary science and enlightened Christianity. This was the gradualist consensus at the core of "rational religion."[95]

To be sure, there were tensions beneath the outwardly placid surface of agreement. Accepting ideas of evolutionary development required greater separation from orthodoxy than many Protestant Christians were willing to admit. The "organic remains of primitive ages" could not always be nestled comfortably in framework of divine design; variations over time in the fossil record undermined orthodox ideas of special creation. Uniformitarian visions of steady, predictable geological change over millennia provoked challenges from "catastrophists" among the geologically informed ministry. For men like William Whewell, evidence of discontinuity in geology suggested that the Watchmaker started over on several occasions, remaking the universe (or at least major parts of it) each time.[96]

The catastrophist argument had important religious implications: it seemed to offer empirical evidence for divine disruptions of the natural order (at least in the dim past)—the scientific vindication of miracles. The problem of miracles became central to evangelical rationality. As late as the 1830s, even Unitarians believed that Christian belief required rational assent to miracles as empirically demonstrable facts. This was the view that Emerson denounced as a "corpse-cold" rationalist delusion in his "Divinity School Address" (1838).[97]

But among evangelical rationalists, scientific authority commanded increasing respect: the more readily one embraced a belief in steady progress, the less it seemed to matter whether miracles could be proven or not. Even the catastrophists were willing to consign the age of miracles—and with it, the possibility of special providences—to the distant past. Whatever their opinions on geology, evangelical rationalists were certain that belief in special providences was incompatible with current scientific knowledge.[98]

For the more theologically liberal, science was the teacher, religion the student. Thomas Boucher, writing in the *Herald of Truth* in 1847, looked back fondly on the old belief in special providences as a "vanished dream of the enraptured bard. . . . The world was younger, then: Religion was younger, and science, her instructress, was unborn!" Now we know "that all matter, either in a crude or organised state, is obedient to certain fixed and mathematical laws"; the earth will not "one day bolt from her orbit and, like a hot steed, dash madly across the heavenly arena, to the great annoyance of surrounding worlds!" This emphasis on predictability led to an inescapable conclusion: "*Nothing is done arbitrarily on the part of the Deity.*" An overarching Providence dictated that "Nothing Occurs by Chance." As the *American Agriculturalist* put it in 1848: "'The fool saith in his heart, there is no God'—and so does every one who believes in *chance* or *luck,* whether he acknowledges it even to himself or not."[99]

This repudiation of chance, far from discouraging a sense of human possibility, actually enhanced it. The noontide of providence ushered in the era of self-made manhood. Didactic board games like *The Reward of Merit* and *The Mansion of Happiness* drove home the message that merit and reward were indissolubly linked. Young men's advisers railed against "Fate, Luck, Chance, Happy Stars, Genius, and the rest of those creatures of pagan mythology" which "take no part in the administration of God's providence." Belief in luck led only to indolence.[100]

Emerson caught the conventional wisdom in "Self-reliance" (1841). A classic statement of the newly regnant culture of control, the lecture affirmed a deeply utilitarian ethos as a weapon against the claims of chance. "So *use* all that is called fortune," Emerson advised. "Most men gamble with her, and gain all and lose all, as her wheel rolls. But do thou leave as unlawful these winnings, and deal with Cause and Effect, the chancellors of God. In the Will work and acquire, and thou hast chained the wheel of Chance, and shalt sit here after out of fear from her rotations." For the more daring, the sanctification of will signaled an unambiguous liberation from the oppressive burden of the past. The young Walt Whitman made clear his disdain for the old gods: "henceforth, I ask not good fortune, I myself am good fortune."[101]

Whitman used the language of imperial selfhood, but Emerson, like most Americans, was more circumspect. Though he had abandoned orthodoxy he still sought a way to preserve providentialism by marrying freedom and fate in a secular idiom. In "Fate" (1852), he cited phrenology, the growing preoccupation with racial determinants of character, and "the new science of statistics"—all to show how completely human beings were in the grip of forces beyond their control. Yet fate could be empowering as well as enfeebling, Emerson insisted—neglecting to mention the importance of fortunate birth. Disdaining luck, Emerson turned to the language of racial determinism: "the instinctive and heroic races," he said, were "proud believers in Destiny. They conspire with it; a loving resignation is with the event. But the dogma makes a different impression when it is held by the weak and lazy. 'Tis weak and vicious people who cast the blame on fate."[102]

To avoid weakness and viciousness, Emerson performed a rhetorical sleight of hand. He asserted that "freedom is necessary. If . . . fate is all; then we say, a part of fate is the freedom of man. Forever wells up the impulse of choosing and acting in the soul. Intellect annuls fate. So far as a man thinks, he is free." (One is reminded of the young William James: "my first act of free will shall be to believe in free will.") But Emerson wanted practical as well as philosophical solutions to the problem of freedom and fate. Given his emphasis on the imperial powers of the human mind, he decided that "Fate then is a name for facts not yet passed under the fire of thought; for causes which are unpenetrated."[103] Here we see Providence turning into Progress: unexplained or intractable events were less the result of God's secret plan than of natural forces that would some-day be explained by science. This would be the secular framework that would provide coherence for the culture of control during the second half of the nineteenth century.

The task for the individual, according to Emerson, was to emulate the "heroic races" and cooperate with Destiny. Like Machiavelli, he em-phasized men's ingenuity and adaptability in bending fortune to their will: "every jet of chaos which threatens to exterminate us is convertible by intellect into wholesome force." The mastering of many skills in-volved this process—learning to sail, learning to skate—more broadly, making the best of a bad lot, playing the hand you are dealt. "Cold and sea will train an imperial Saxon race," Emerson said. In a secular universe, the uses of adversity could still be sweet.[104]

Emerson epitomized the consensus that provided moral and ontolog-ical coherence for many Americans' lives throughout much of the nine-teenth century. Providence survived, whether one called it Manifest Destiny or Scientific Progress or Saxon Superiority. Whatever the idiom, History had meaning and purpose and direction; individuals participated in that cosmic drama while they pursued their private affairs offstage.

Yet even as Emerson wed freedom and fate, fissures in the consensus were appearing. The persistent culture of chance evoked the derision of moralists, but certain events were hard to remove from the shadow of the random. The chaotic violence of war has always put schemes of cosmic order to the supreme test, and the Civil War may well have been the most violent, the most destructive armed conflict the world had ever seen.

In many ways, the coming of the war reaffirmed the culture of chance. For elite Southern men still steeped in the gambler's code of honor, the war fed fantasies of redemption through risk. If gambling was a way to demonstrate disinterested virtue through reckless disregard of self-interest, then war was the grandest gamble. As Huizinga observed, since archaic times war has preserved an element of play; it has been the ulti-mate game, the ultimate opportunity for men to match wits against dark fate.[105] So it might have seemed to boys who would be men, flushed with the enthusiasm of raw recruits, on both sides of the Mason-Dixon Line.

The elements of play were no doubt quickly dispersed by the organized violence of battle. As the randomness of fate took on a palpable and menacing form, the experience of the combat soldier made providentialism seem a cruel joke. At one moment a man might be chatting amiably with a companion; at the next he might be cradling a mangled body in his arms. Boys who left home full of faith soon found themselves speaking a different language. An Indiana Union soldier left for the Virginia front in 1862, hoping that "God will bring me safe home." In 1864, amid the carnage and confusion of the Wilderness, he was saved from a lingering death when his belt buckle stopped a bullet. "I have been very *lucky*," he wrote his parents. "I hope I will be as lucky as I have been all along and come out safe."[106]

Those who remained faithful to older traditions could still see special providences at work. A Catholic major general (U.S.A.) was saved from death by a scapular medal which "turned the bullet out of a straight line, to which it returned again, as if to make the power of God more manifest."[107] But whatever their religious persuasion or regional origin, the soldiers festooned themselves with charms, turned to the stars for clues about the future, and took to gambling obsessively. This was characteristic soldiers' behavior in wartime, not unrelated to the absence of atheists in foxholes.

The culture of chance reasserted itself most vigorously among the men in combat—a population sharply aware of the arbitrariness of fate. As Andrew Delbanco writes, "the tumble of the dice and the shuffle of the cards replicated in miniature what seemed the overwhelming randomness of life."[108] Though generals like Stonewall Jackson may have felt they were instruments of God, there was no providentialist consensus at Antietam or Fredericksburg.

On the home front, it was easier to speak of Providence without provoking dismissive laughter. Certainly in the North, Union ideologues routinely referred to the boys in blue as the armies of the Lord; this was the fundamental premise of Julia Ward Howe's "Battle Hymn of the Republic." The most eloquent effort to place the war in a providential framework was Lincoln's Second Inaugural Address; after four years of unspeakable slaughter, it required a profound tragic sense to discern the redemptive possibilities of the conflict—to see the war as a kind of national expiation for the sin of slavery.[109]

Most Northern orators lacked that tragic sense. Like Henry Ward Beecher, who returned to give a speech at the recaptured Fort Sumter in

February 1865, they hailed the Union victory as the punishment of the unrighteous. It was as if the very extent of the carnage demanded cosmic justification. National unity became a sacred cause. Within a few years, even Southerners began to admit that the war's outcome might have been divinely decreed. Providentialist rhetoric transformed the war into a successful confidence game by reinforcing white Americans' confidence in the divinity of their nation's destiny. (African Americans had more concrete reasons to be grateful for the war.)

Ultimately, the Civil War became the centerpiece of secularized providential thought. And providentialism in turn became the official creed of national greatness, at once conservative and progressive. Tested by the chaos of combat, the culture of control emerged triumphant in the stillness at Appomattox. Or so it seemed to the official thought-leaders of the time. Whether the rest of the population agreed remained to be seen.

CHAPTER FOUR

THE WANING OF PROVIDENCE

Not long after Appomattox, First Lieutenant Charles Mabie was discharged from Grant's Army of the Potomac. He returned home to Walton, a hamlet near Oneida, New York. His mother, a devout Christian, died soon after his arrival. For months Mabie brooded about his prospects, confessing his insecurities to his diary. "I somehow feel discontented and restless to day [*sic*]," he wrote on January 30, 1866. "My path is not quite clear to me. I feel a weight on me somehow but what I think to be duty I mean to do. Went to meeting this evening and had a precious time. Oh! I wish I could live as a dying mother wished me to but I am weak but with the grace of God assisting me I mean to try and live an humble Christian life but Oh! temptation I am thy victim . . . ."[1]

The alternating moods of determination and discouragement suggested a familiar Protestant oscillation between manic engagement and depressive withdrawal. The same pattern characterized gamblers, stock speculators, and enthusiastic Christians in the throes of conversion (at least according to their critics). From the evangelical-rational view, the calm acceptance of Providence was the antidote to manic-depressive excitability and the precondition for a life of disciplined achievement. Submission to Providential order and assertion of personal independence paradoxically coalesced.

It is not clear what temptations beset Mabie, but they probably involved his difficulty choosing a means of livelihood. During the early months of 1866, he struggled vainly to leave home and strike out on his own. "I had a talk with Dr. Beard* this morning," Mabie wrote on January 31, "and concluded that as matters are now that it would be best to

*Probably his minister.

remove to some other place but I would rather give 50 dollars than leave old Walton. With all the binding associations I have here it seems hard to break away. One year ago to day I was in the State of Virginia guarding Rebel Officers. But war and Rebellion are now extinct in a measure and things that were then are not."[2]

Judging by his diary, Mabie may have been a typical returning veteran—unable to settle into civilian life after the dislocations of war, yearning to follow the path of duty but finding it difficult to see his way clear. So he stayed around home, sorting through his mother's things, praying for providential intervention. "I am looking for light as to duty but see nothing but darkness before me," he wrote on March 7. And two days later: "When I would do good, evil is present with me. Oh for God's faithful hand to lead me over the troubles of this transitory life and give me a true heart to do his will at *all* times."[3]

The determination to do the Lord's will "at *all* times" revealed the perfectionist strain in the morality of self-mastery—the desire to move beyond weakness and, through rigorous strategies of control, construct an unshakable Christian character. Yet the effort was too much for Mabie, and he alludes frequently (if vaguely) to his difficulties staying on the right path and sustaining faith in Providence. In the end he fell back on scripture. "He hath his purposes and though the Lord slay me yet I will trust in him." Whatever Mabie's trials, they were painful enough to bring the language of Job to mind.[4]

We do not know whether Mabie's faith survived this postwar ordeal. The diary breaks off with Mabie having moved to Oneida to work in his brother's jewelry store, but still hectoring himself in private, still waiting for a providential sign that he has picked the proper path. One thing is clear: despite the confidence of pulpit orators, faith in the nation's providential destiny did not banish the uncertainties and insecurities of everyday life. Young men like Mabie returned from the war, shaken by what they had experienced, unable to find a fresh start in life. Divine guidance was not always available, even to Christians who prayed for it; sometimes they simply had to take a chance.

A lot of people were taking chances after the war. The unsettled economy offered unprecedented rewards for risk, at least to the lucky few. A commercial ethic of fortune flourished amid the glitter of a Gilded Age. Successful gamblers and stock speculators jointly fostered a nouveau riche style. It was on display in the opulent palaces (casinos, hotels, resorts) where paunchy bejeweled sybarites could flash their ill-gotten gains—ill-gotten, at least, from the perspective of the Protestant ethic of mastery. In an economic atmosphere dominated by sharpers and plungers, business and gambling achieved a rapprochement.

The culture of chance survived in less ostentatious ways as well. In the cities, the sporting crowd spread—mixing races and classes, calculation and superstition. African Americans, Roman Catholic immigrants, and other working-class folk continued playing policy (the nineteenth-century "numbers" game), consulting dream books for occult insight into numerology, fondling fetishes for luck. Coexisting with this social world was a more affluent one composed of race track touts, shoeshine boys, barbers, bartenders, and their customers, who were often respectable, professional WASP men.

The sporting crowd's ethic of fortune emphasized the importance of "the breaks" in achieving success. There was something inherently liberating about this notion: it was a portal of escape from the complacent assumption that reward always came from merit. And indeed the post–Civil War culture of chance preserved many democratic features. To be sure, within the sporting crowd there were strong social hierarchies—a vast difference existed, for example, between the clienteles for policy and for high-stakes horse racing. But social diversity persisted as well, as one can see in Horace Bonham's painting *Nearing the Issue at the Cock Pit* (1870).

Nearing the Issue at the Cock Pit, Horace Bonham, 1870.

In a society where a man's rise or ruin could depend on anonymous investors' whims, gambling remained a powerful metaphor for everyday life. The culture of chance continued to draw legitimacy from the indiscipline of the market.

So did the culture of control, as a counterweight to that indiscipline. The centrifugal forces unleashed by economic expansion intensified moralists' fears that society had surrendered to amoral chance. Their ethic of mastery encouraged hostility toward the unreality of speculative wealth and suspicion of the speculator's (or gambler's) "castles in the air." Recoiling from such anxieties, devotees of control clung even more fervently to the worldview I have called evangelical rationality.

During the first decades after the Civil War, the changes in evangelical rationality were minimal. There were new secular and racial inflections, as critics of gambling increasingly associated belief in luck with the more ignorant and backward "races." But the emotional and philosophical foundations of the culture of control remained remarkably consistent throughout the early postwar years. Under evangelical-rational auspices, the battle against gambling was part of several larger campaigns: the worthy against the licentious, the civilized against the barbarous, the enlightened against the superstitious. It was also a struggle to redefine manhood. Wherever evangelical rationality held sway, the moderate Christian gentleman displaced the free-spending "Big Man" as a male ideal. In evangelical rational cosmology, character and destiny were joined. Self-mastery allowed one to cooperate with the providential plan. Against the anarchy of chance, moralists from Beecher to Barnum presented a united (if paradoxical) point of view: an insistence that freedom and fate, science and providence, divine and human will, were merged in indissoluble union.

Yet toward the end of the nineteenth century, this synthesis became harder to sustain. Ideologues of success, stressing the sanctity of work, laid a growing emphasis on human rather than divine will. Conduct-of-life literature tilted increasingly in a secular direction. At the same time, the balancing act between freedom and fate—always a tricky business—became nearly impossible in the face of unprecedented economic and intellectual challenges. The equipoise between free choice and providential order could not survive the appalling conditions created by unregulated industrial capitalism. The sight of sickly children scuffling for garbage in slums was enough, in some minds, to prove that merit did not actually bring reward.

The core of evangelical rationality—the faith in independent self-hood—seemed unrealistic in an interdependent market society, where ordinary people's livelihoods increasingly depended on decisions made in distant cities, on circumstances beyond the individual's control. Darwinian and hereditarian ideas seeped into public discourse, challenging the bases of human choice and threatening to enthrone Fortuna in place of divine design. Little wonder that by the 1890s, to such sensitive observers as William Dean Howells, what had once appeared the work of Providence had come to seem "the world of chance."[5]

The question was what to do about it. Americans acted on their new awareness of accident in a variety of ways. Many sought economic, political, or intellectual strategies for revitalizing the culture of control. Some created new institutions—such as insurance companies—designed to cushion the impact of hazard. Others repeated the old denials of randomness in a secular idiom of evolutionary progress, which satisfied longings for order even as it distorted Darwinian theory. Eventually, still others groped toward new forms of rationality, more flexible and pragmatic than the old moralistic ones.

For many Americans, though, chance remained a central feature of their worldview. For them, the attempt to conjure *mana* could be an everyday event, whether it involved attendance at Mass or a visit to a policy den. This was not simply a matter of working-class play. An ethic of fortune still pervaded enterprise as well as leisure. Gambling was a ritual that seemed to celebrate the promise and peril of American life. The peril was not simply financial ruin; it was a kind of total personal loss, a state of nonbeing that was terrifying but also oddly seductive. The promise was not merely sudden wealth; it involved something subtler and more elusive—the grace of beginning again and ever again. And war's end was a fine time to start over.

THE GOLDEN AGE OF GAMBLING

The news from Appomattox refocused men's attention on the main chance. Impoverished Southerners, black and white, spun off toward the West in search of opportunities they could not find at home. Rural migrants and European immigrants swarmed into cities. Ambitious entrepreneurs quickly saw them as a cheap labor market and did their best to

herd this emergent working class into sweatshops, factories, and tenements. Other venture capitalists deployed more ethereal investment instruments—commodity futures, shares sold on margin, watered stock,
imaginary real estate (castles in the air, indeed). In this frenzied atmosphere, it was more difficult than ever to distinguish self-made men from
confidence men, and legitimate from illegitimate gambling.

During the decades after the Civil War, even long odds at the tables
sometimes looked like a fairer prospect than allegedly more respectable
risks. A sale of mining stock was no better than "the great Oriental Lottery," a bitter Californian observed in 1878; one's chances were as good
in one as in the other. In fact one could argue, a contemporary asserted,
that a straight faro game was superior to many "legitimate investments" on
the San Francisco Stock Board, "in as much as the cards in the stock gamble are dealt in the dark, and the dealers only have the privilege of seeing
them."[6]

Speculation, from this view, was as demoralizing as gambling—and as
direct a threat to manly vitality. "See where the spider weaves its web and,
like a vampire, sucks the life's blood of the [Pacific] coast," says General
Sterne, a character in an antispeculation novel, as he gestures toward the
San Francisco Stock Board. Sterne saves the young protagonist Wily
"from self-destruction[,] and [makes] a man of him" by curing him of
the speculative itch. "Stock gambling is a kind of madness," the chastened
Wily concludes, "nothing is done on merit."[7]

In an laissez-faire economy, riddled by graft and scandal, robber
barons and knights of the green baize were not always easy to tell apart.
The tactics of a Daniel Drew or a Jay Gould differed little from those of
a professional gambler such as Richard Canfield, who owned popular
casinos in Saratoga and Manhattan; the strictness or flexibility of one's
business ethics determined whether one considered these men sharpers
or sports. In retrospect Gilded Age speculators and professional gamblers
look like the same species of fish, swimming about in the same pool.[8]

Their similarity stemmed from the difficulty of preserving social deference in a society that defined status in monetary terms. With so much
new wealth around, the boundaries of polite society became shifting and
problematic, especially when it came to gambling. Wealthy capitalists in
the social register—August Belmont, William Whitney, Leonard Jerome—
might own their own racetracks, but so might John Morrissey, the Irish
street brawler and gambler who helped to transform Saratoga from a

sanatorium to a swank watering hole. Morrissey was a successful prize-
fighter and sometime member of the United States Congress, though he
could never get the etiquette of the capitol down. (Whenever anyone dis-
agreed with him, he demanded the offender step outside.) Morrissey
would not have made any elite guest lists, but he raced his trotters against
Commodore Vanderbilt's in Central Park, and the Commodore was delighted to match up against such a respected judge of horseflesh. Successful gamblers and nouveau riche capitalists inhabited a common realm of
sybaritic excess and theatrical display—the leisure class world that would
later be anatomized and anathematized by Thorstein Veblen.[9]

The carnival of unregulated capitalism celebrated corpulence as a
sign of success. Among legendary stomachs, few were more famous than
Diamond Jim Brady's. Son of a Manhattan saloonkeeper, Brady (1856–
1917) embodied the melding of the business, theatrical, and sporting
crowds. Starting out as a bellboy at the St. James hotel, he didn't drink but
he picked up a couple of other habits: gorging on eels and oysters as he
sauntered up South Street on Sundays; and hanging outside the stage
door of Niblo's Garden, hoping for a chance meeting with Lotta Crabtree, who was in the midst of her starring run as Little Nell in *The Old
Curiosity Shop.* Brady studied bookkeeping and chirography at Paine's
Business College on Canal Street and eventually landed a job as a sales-
man for a railroad supply house. "Between Mr. Brady and the expense account it was a case of love at first sight," his biographer observed.[10]

Brady became the quintessential traveling man, living at company
expense while on the road (which was most of the time), winning his
spending money at faro games, preferring to play for diamonds rather
than cash. Diamonds became his signature, his gimmick, his means of im-
pressing the mighty moguls he had to persuade to buy his goods. A "dead
game sport," Brady gambled constantly but won too easily to derive
much pleasure from it. In the stock market, he became a big plunger; on
the rare occasions when he lost money, he took a what-the-hell attitude.
He built a big country estate on South Branch, Long Island, bought two
champion racehorses, and celebrated his victories at the track with
marathon poker parties at Canfield's midtown casino or champagne and
lobster feasts at Tappan's restaurant on Sheepshead Bay, not far from the
Gravesend racecourse.[11]

Yet for all that, Brady remained under constraints unknown to his in-
dependently wealthy friends. Brady did not want his corporate clients to

know he was rich enough to own a stable of horses—he was afraid of provoking their envy—so he tried to remain anonymous by refusing to use his own name in ownership documents. When the Brooklyn Jockey Club objected to this subterfuge, Brady was forced to resign his membership and retire from the racing business.[12] Gluttonous, convivial, a cooly successful cardplayer, and a prince of a gift-giver, Brady represented the embourgeoisement of the traditional masculine gambler—the convergence of gambling and corporate salesmanship, with the result that even the "Big Man" had to seem smaller than his clients so as not to offend them.

The best illustration of the rapprochement between gambling and business is a poker story (perhaps apocryphal) that originated in Denver in the 1880s. A bank has just opened at 9:00 A.M. when four bleary-eyed young men appear, having stumbled across the street from an all-night poker game. One holds an envelope, the contents of which he furtively reveals to the clerk. The player demands a $5000 loan, with the contents of the envelope as collateral. The astonished clerk is about to stammer a refusal when the bank president walks in from his own all-night poker game. The loan applicant shows his collateral to the president, who quickly opens the safe and begins stacking sacks of $20 bills on the counter while upbraiding the clerk: "In future, do not forget, sir, that four kings and an ace are always good in this institution for our entire assets, sir, our entire assets." One can almost see the president's dewlaps flapping with consternation.[13]

In a society that celebrated risk, the gambler remained an enticing figure—but in some circles more than in others. A few sectors of the economy were more openly beholden to luck, more willing to dispense with diligence, than the mythos of self-made manhood generally allowed. Certainly this was true of the theatrical business. Picking "lucky hits" on Broadway was even trickier than picking them on Wall Street; every venture was a gamble.

No wonder, then, that theater people and gamblers tended to inhabit the same social universe of bars and casinos. The memoirs of the theatrical producer George Tyler recalled this sporting crowd at the turn of the century, and revealed its core belief in luck. Escaping the quiet life in Chillicothe, Ohio, in the 1880s, Tyler rode the rails West to Tucson, Arizona, and eventually Truckee, Nevada, losing lots of spare change to

Mexicans, Chinese, and even a few "American" gamblers. His father, alarmed at the boy's wayward ways, leased the local opera house in Chillicothe so his son could manage it, and stay home for a change.[14]

Young George made such a name for himself as a theatrical manager that he soon decided to head for New York. He took a job as a printer on the *New York World*, "What with backing my own judgment about horses and always living a trifle better than I could afford, . . . I was never more than one jump ahead of the sheriff," Tyler recalled. Eventually his friend Harry Askin, "a first class all around chance taker," persuaded him to embark on a joint venture in Philadelphia, a revue called (what else?) *Miss Philadelphia*. The secret of his success, here and elsewhere, Tyler said, was "my genius at getting cash in exchange for pretty dubious checks." This sort of confidence game was the stock-in-trade of theatrical promotion.[15]

What was refreshing about Tyler's recollections was the complete absence of any of the usual moral lessons and the frank admission that luck played a central role in his career. When his play *The Christian* became a hit, Tyler said he felt like "a grocery clerk who has just won the Calcutta sweep." An enterprise founded on the vagaries of public taste was not likely to foster faith that merit would be rewarded; instead it encouraged an insouciant skepticism about such matters. "Every time we stubbed our toes we said it was bad luck, and every time we landed a success we said it was good judgment," Tyler recalled of the turn of the century days. His irony undercut providentialist assumptions by exposing their ex post facto quality. In theater as in real estate or stocks, success made it easy to match reward and merit—but only in retrospect. There was no use trying to predict theatrical success, Tyler concluded: it "operates like success in roulette. When your number comes up, it comes up, and that's about all."[16]

This sensibility embodied a crucial alternative to dominant values. In a secular, commercial culture of chance, an ethic of fortune survived—a stoic acceptance of fate, combined with a cheerful willingness to relinquish control over outcomes. Though it was rarely articulated, this outlook survived among the sporting crowd who congregated in various venues after the Civil War, from Dodge City, Kansas, to the Lower East Side of New York. The sporting crowd translated the fickle ways of fate into the American vernacular, as "the breaks."

THE NEW SPORTING CROWD

For many Americans, belief in the breaks was a psychic necessity—a release from the moral closure of secular providentialism. Ministers might preach of merit rewarded, but even Horatio Alger acknowledged that luck was as important as pluck in achieving success. Decades ago, Louis Hartz recognized "how frequently Ragged Dick came to riches as a result of falling asleep in the snow and being found by a portly widower or rescuing a child from disaster and winning eternal gratitude." Yet Alger held onto an implicitly providential framework: his heroes earned their good fortune through relentless energy—they were always up and doing, on the lookout for opportunity. No wonder they got all the breaks.[17]

Vernacular common sense questioned even this modified version of secular providentialism. In 1882 the humor magazine *Puck* (an American version of the English original) published an imaginary boardinghouse conversation on "Good Luck and Good Acts." A suspender peddler asserts that "people fare according to their acts," recalling a man who saved the life of an heiress and (in Horatio Alger fashion) was later married to her. An old lady and a skeptical plumber disagree, piling up numerous incidents that show "good luck to be the reward of crime" and bad luck "the penalty of virtue"—a man who loses his legs after saving two ladies from drowning; a murderer, released from prison in improved health, who starts a barroom and makes a tidy fortune; the old lady herself, who, having renounced religion, learns that she has inherited thirty thousand dollars from her uncle and that her husband has been elected to the legislature. "I know the Sunday-school superintendent may fall on a banana and break his neck," she says, "while a gambler may dance on the same leveler [i.e., the banana] as sure-footed as a chamois." Rewards and punishments, at least in this life, were unrelated to moral worth. The suspender peddler falls silent.[18]

The idea of the breaks, like grace, had nothing to do with merit. It succinctly summarized the capricious power of luck, which was a reality (for good or ill) to most Americans. Yet success mythologists from Russell Conwell to Andrew Carnegie continued to assume that a providential arrangement of rewards and punishments operated in this world as well as the next—despite the daily evidence to the contrary. The more they focused on the centrality of human effort, the more likely they were

to make this assumption. Then as now, many among the truly lucky refused to believe in luck.

The vernacular ethic of fortune provided a bracing alternative to the
soporific bromides of success. It promoted a healthy skepticism regarding
the human capacity for mastering fate, recalled the wisdom of Ecclesiastes, and offered relief from the closed system of work and reward.
"There was only one saving concept here [in the United States], the concept of luck or as ultimately translated into the American vernacular, the
'breaks,'" Hartz wrote.[19] However obliquely stated, the notion of the
breaks constituted a form of grace, an undeserved favor from God or
man. Belief in the breaks remained embedded in the ritual practices and
tacit assumptions of ordinary people, especially the sporting crowd.

Their key assumption was that worldly success often had little to do
with human effort and even less with human morality. Against the secular providentialism that sanctioned existing inequalities, this insight was a
potent egalitarian weapon. Despite the sharpening of class divisions after
the Civil War, a rough democracy survived among the sporting crowd—
albeit in some venues more than others. Cockfights still created a collage
of social types; so did off-track betting parlors, known in the late nineteenth century as "pool-rooms."

There were many pool-rooms throughout New York, three in the
neighborhood of Wall Street, and the crowds there epitomized the het-
erogeneity that made moralists squirm. "Gray-haired, respectable-looking
old men, portly brokers, sleek business men, anxious young clerks, dirty,
unshaven specimens of humanity—all jostle together during the hours of
business," one observer noted in 1892. "Caste is disregarded, social barriers are broken down, the man with two dollars and a heap of luck is as
good as anyone else—better than anyone else, in fact, if he is the only
lucky one." Belief in luck sustained, however imperfectly, a democratic
impulse among the gambling fraternity.[20]

Yet there was no single worldview among gamblers. Despite their
common skepticism regarding providential pieties, the sporting crowd revealed a wide range of attitudes toward chance. Preferences for particular
pastimes suggested varying commitments to calculation. Gambling could
be ranged on a continuum from the agonistic games (horse racing, cockfighting, poker, blackjack), which required competition and skill, to the
aleatory games (faro, roulette, lotteries, policy), which simply required the

player to cast lots with blind Fortuna.[21] If the agonistic games encouraged calculation, the aleatory games promoted superstition—a resort to the rituals of conjuring *mana* or manufacturing luck, the time-honored custom of the culture of chance.

But the agonistic games always preserved an element of chance as well. Even the shrewdest handicapper knew that horse races could not be controlled (except by cheating) and even the cleverest poker player realized that the luck of the draw could make or break him. Winning required getting a few breaks as well as taking advantage of them. The inescapable importance of the breaks helped agonistic gambling remain a favored means of affirming traditional ideals of masculinity—which were a live alternative to the self-controlled bourgeois version.

Risk and manhood were still twinned. For men and boys in small Southern towns and Northern urban backstreets, racehorses and fighting cocks were surrogate selves. Samuel Rutherford, a successful businessman from Wilmington, Delaware, recalled his boyhood home of the 1880s and the male world of the stables across the B&O tracks—the "odors of leather and poor whiskey" mingling with those of human sweat and horse manure, the "dusty pictures of celebrated horses and an occasional partly clothed actress," the hostlers and stable boys who would "bet on anything" from the scarred pitbull in the corner (dogfighting was popular, too) to the gamecock strutting and screeching in the street outside.[22]

Rutherford kept his own birds for "friendly battles" but never entered them in the fights staged by the older men—contests that "usually ended in death or serious injury to one of the contestants." In Wilmington as elsewhere, ritualized, vicarious violence validated masculine identity, a process summed up in the title of the cockfighters' leading magazine, *Grit and Steel*.[23] Breeding and training birds were necessary but not sufficient components of success. The most careful preparation could never substitute for the owners' courage to risk death and dismemberment—albeit at second hand, by identifying with animals locked in deadly struggle. To critics of cockfighting, this symbolic descent into animality was one of the most disturbing features of the sport. To cockfighters it may have been one of the most appealing.

Gamecocks acquired a special symbolic significance in the post–Civil War South. (*Grit and Steel* was published in Gaffney, South Carolina.) Southern sporting men characterized "gameness" as "that quality of spirit which sustains a fighting cock no matter how badly he may be pun-

ished." In the aftermath of Appomattox, it was easy to elide this spirit
with memories or fantasies of Confederate martial valor. Fast, aggressive
cocks were compared with Stonewall Jackson, Robert E. Lee, and
Nathan Bedford Forrest: birds and men alike embodied courage, tenacity,
and eagerness to attack even when the odds were against them. The
Southern mythology of manhood acquired a more pronounced regional
inflection.[24]

In the frontier West, poker preserved elements of traditional male rivalry, too; but it was so subject to the wiles of the calculating cheat that
alea often disappeared altogether. The play constantly threatened to degenerate from a contest among equals to a confidence game between
sharpers and shils. The most famous Western "gamblers" were often not
gamblers at all, but clever con artists, tricksters in the tradition of Devol
and other riverboat shysters.[25]

The career of John Henry "Doc" Holliday illustrates the pattern.
Born in 1851 in Fayetteville, Georgia, he was a shy boy with a speech impediment and tubercular tendencies. When he was thirteen a young slave
girl named Sophie Walton came to the Holliday house. She was fright-
ened and lonely and a wizard at cards who managed to win all the young
master's spending money; when the family moved to Atlanta in 1865, she
moved with them. From Sophie, John learned faro and put-and-take; he
also learned how to count cards, compute odds, and deal from the bottom of the deck. Meanwhile, he and his brother were studying to be dentists.[26]

Circumstances conspired to present John with a more intriguing career. Postwar Atlanta could support only a limited number of dentists,
and John was diagnosed with tuberculosis at twenty-one. So it made sense
for him to head for Dallas, where the dry air might do his lungs good and
the prospects for young dentists were more promising. In Dallas, John's
dental practice foundered but his gambling career flourished. Putting Sophie's skills to work, he quickly developed a reputation as a sharp player,
acquiring a superb pair of Will & Finck card-trimming shears along with
a taste for finely tailored clothes and excellent bourbon.[27]

Repeatedly fined for violating the Dallas antigambling ordinance,
Holliday fled to Denver and ultimately to Dodge City. There he struck
up good relations with the law enforcement community, which included
Wyatt Earp and Bat Masterson. (Earp tried unsuccessfully to persuade
Holliday to join him in a mining venture in Prescott, Arizona.) Holliday

spent the rest of his short life drinking hard, dealing cards, and pulling knives or guns on anyone who accused him—correctly or not—of cheating. Once in a while he even practiced dentistry. Holliday died of tuberculosis, complicated by pneumonia, in 1887. He was thirty-six.[28] A colorful figure, he seems to epitomize the "Western gambler"—except that he was less a gambler than a sharper. Like Wild Bill Hickok and other poseurs, he was not really willing to leave things to chance.

Still, in the life Holliday chose, success depended heavily on the breaks. The line between calculation and chance was arbitrary, defined only by the rules of the game—which in turn could be evaded or bent. Risk remained essential to the Western gambler's ethos. So it should come as no surprise that Western gamblers like Holliday and Hickok have followed their Mississippi predecessors into the pantheon of popular culture as icons of masculine coolness.

Women were not allowed to enter most gaming dens, except as prostitutes. Occasionally one heard of female gamblers, but they were the exception that proved the rule. Like Madame Mustache, such women gamblers as Alice Ivers Duffield adopted (or were assigned) masculine traits: "Poker Alice" carried a Colt revolver, which she used expertly, and smoked long black cigars. To play in the boys' club, girls had to check conventionally feminine traits at the door.[29]

Horse racing also offered opportunities for affirming masculinity, through the traditional high-stakes risk-taking but also through a more analytical and methodical (perhaps even statistical) approach, more suited (if successful) to the market model of systematic accumulation. There were still plenty of big-shot plungers hanging around the racing business after the Civil War, men like John "Bet-a-Million" Gates, the barbed-wire magnate from the Great Plains who would bet (it was said) on which of two raindrops would reach a windowsill first, but who preferred the action at the track. As his nickname implied, Gates was notorious for wagering huge sums and losing without blinking an eye.[30]

But post–Civil War racing also gave rise to another sort of gambler, the ancestor of the modern handicapper. The prototype was George "Pittsburgh Phil" Smith (1862–1905), who started out as a cork cutter in a Pittsburgh factory but soon escaped to Chicago, where he hung around pool halls betting on baseball and horse races—most of the time successfully. Eventually he amassed enough cash to head East, where he intended

to develop a scientific method of playing the horses. The theatrical producer George Tyler, like most of Phil's contemporaries, was impressed by
the "absolutely disinterested calculations" the man brought to the sport.
"Everything was figured out to a gnat's head beforehand," Tyler recalled,
"weights, distances, jockeys, records, wind, weather, all doped out and
added up with mathematical exactness, and the chances of crooked work
taken into account along with the rest. And he didn't miss once in a blue
moon." Phil owned a stable, but when he began to bet on his own horses
out of sentiment, said Tyler, "he gave it up and went back to his calcu-
latin' ways."[31]

Phil "had the composure of one of those wooden cigar-Indians that
were everywhere in those days," Tyler wrote, and he was famous for his
coolness at the end of a race—one would never have known it when the
man had just won, say, eighty thousand dollars. This sort of sangfroid had
been essential to the professional gambler's persona for decades; amid the
rapid oscillations of joy and sorrow that were supposed to be inseparable
from the experience of gambling, this capacity to mask one's emotions
became a kind of quiet personal heroism. Another version of the ethic of
fortune, stoical conduct reaffirmed the connection between agonistic
games and manliness. Yet horse players (like poker players) also had particular practical reasons for cultivating coolness. A careful evaluation of
evidence really could mean the difference between defeat and victory;
some horses were faster under certain conditions than others, some jockeys more skillful. (Phil's favorite was Tod Sloan, the brilliant rider who
perfected the forward crouch; Phil paid Sloan four hundred dollars for
every race he won, just to be sure there was one jockey who was actually
trying to win.) The close-your-eyes, stick-a-pin method was for ladies
and amateurs.[32]

Even the smartest horse player or poker player needed a break from
time to time. But the breaks were more completely in charge of faro and
policy. Those aleatory games encouraged a more overt resort to fetishism
and divination, a more palpable sense of luck's presence as an embodied
spirit. They were also more open to women. *Mana* remained the basis of
the culture of chance in a variety of settings, from policy dens and faro
banks to boards of trade and conjurers' huts. Despite official disdain for
superstition, old beliefs survived.

THE ENDURING MARRIAGE
OF MATTER AND SPIRIT

In faro, unlike poker or vingt-et-un, "one simply selected one's card or cards and then waited for judgment to be rendered," passive before the mysteries of fate. Even critical observers agreed that an honest faro game, if one was lucky enough to find it, was a game of "pure chance." This was precisely what made faro so seductive for everyone, from Kansas cowboys to Eastern businessmen, during the postwar decades. As one New York journalist noted in 1873, "day games" were conducted "in Ann, Fulton, and Chambers streets, for the accommodation of business men, many of whom have acquired the bad habit of seeking solace for the vexations of legitimate transactions in the delights of faro." It was, they said, "a fairer game than the cunning and unscupulous gambling of Wall Street."[33]

Fairer, maybe, but not necessarily more lucrative. Indeed the very fairness of John Chamberlain's downtown casino, one reporter noted, "renders it all the more dangerous to society," a place where "heads of heavy concerns" could "fritter away their capital at faro." In the shadow of the New York Stock Exchange, a few honest games of faro undermined the ethos of accumulation and seduced "rational capitalists" into paying homage to Fortuna.[34]

The presence of archaic beliefs could be even more palpably felt in the policy dens. If faro was a way of undermining accumulation by (unwittingly) propitiating Fortuna, policy was an arena for putting *mana* in the service of money. African, Native American, Christian, and Jewish traditions all associated casting lots with the conjuring of occult knowledge. Policy and other street gambling games encouraged the commercialization of ancient divinatory rituals. Given the endless possible meanings that could be attached to numbers, and the gamblers' need for some kind of ontological reassurance, it is small wonder that the policy office was a hotbed of divination, especially numerological dream interpretation. According to the reformer Anthony Comstock, the policy den was "surrounded by all the sense of mystery with which the gambler clothes his schemes." It was "supersition's stronghold," he wrote in 1883. "The negro dreams a dream, the Irishman or woman has a 'presintiment,' and the German a vision, and each rushes to the 'dream-book,' kept in

every policy-den, to see what number the dream or vision calls for."[35]
Policy dens were hothouses for nurturing the culture of chance.

Lotteries and policy games were not simply pastimes of the poor and
ignorant; their clientele included "even men accounted shrewd on Wall
Street," one observer noted. They tended to play the lottery itself (where
it existed) rather than policy, but they exhibited all the same symptoms of
the superstitious mind, according to skeptical observers. What was particularly striking to a New York observer in 1873 was the players' fascination
with the lottery ticket as a kind of magical artifact. "To the thousands
who constantly have one or more such bits of oblong paper in their
pockets there seems to be a strange fascination in the possession." The
lottery ticket was a fetish, an embodiment of luck or *mana,* a potent emblem of pure potentiality. No wonder there were "hundreds of men who
constantly but carefully invest in the delusive bits of paper and give to

> —airy nothings
> A local habitation and a name,

from their reveries based on the mere possession."[36]

Like traditional fetishes, lottery tickets materialized luck. But the lottery ticket was also a disposable fetish, easily discarded when it turned up
a loser. It is tempting to link the disposability of fetishes to the spread of
a commercial society, in which cash became a kind of *mana*: once the
ticket had lost the potential power of attracting money, it no longer possessed a fetishistic charge, and became a piece of trash.

But the process of commercialization was not the whole story. For
many Americans, *mana* remained more than money, and the culture of
chance involved more than a taste for gambling. Homage to Fortuna continued to imply a complex constellation of values—a worldview that acknowledged the power of chance. Gambling was only one ingredient in
a stew of beliefs and rituals concerning luck.

One reason the stew kept its savor is that new immigrant groups kept
adding to it. By the 1880s, Irish and Germans were joined by Italians,
Slavs, and Russian Jews in the East, Chinese and Mexicans in the West.
Many of these groups brought a culture of chance in their baggage. A recent study of the Chinese in Fresno notes that "in the traditional Chinese
view of the universe, fate's hand was the tiller and life was a gamble. For

most nineteenth-century Chinese it was better to be born lucky than clever. The Chinese courted fate through astrologers, soothsayers, geomancers, and gambling. Wherever a large group of Chinese laborers congregated, somewhere, somehow, gambling went on. Any event could be bet on, but the most attractive bets (and games) revolved around randomness rather than skill. Nothing could substitute for luck."[37]

The official mythology of immigration presents "the huddled masses, yearning to breathe free," clamoring for entry at "the golden door." Immigrants, from this view, were (and are) upwardly mobile, progressive individualists, seeking economic opportunity and political freedom. But in recent decades historians have begun to complicate this picture. Many nineteenth-century immigrants, it turns out, were displaced by modernizing forces in their home countries; they left in search of liberty to preserve their traditions. Venturesome traditionalists, they were not so much uprooted as transplanted, sinking old roots in new soil. Gradually they and their progeny grew into something different. But old ways were not forsaken overnight, and old beliefs concerning luck were some of the last to go, if they went at all.[38] The perversities of fortune seemed even more apparent in the new land—especially for the poor and uneducated, who were more vulnerable than the more privileged to infectious diseases, industrial accidents, and the unpredictable lurches of an unregulated market economy. Immigrants needed all the *mana* they could conjure.

Much the same could be said of black freedpeople in the South. Many remained on or near the premises of the plantation, often at the mercy of their former masters and the increasingly virulent racism of the Jim Crow era (not to mention the everyday perils of poverty). Segregation bred cultural autonomy; in the Mississippi Delta and other areas where blacks could remain insulated from white influence (or escape it altogether), pre-Christian practices survived. In 1875 one white Southern observer complained that the freedpeople were merely maintaining the appearance of Christianity while actually "relapsing" into "paganism." Writing in 1903, the former South Carolina slaveholder and eminent biologist Joseph LeConte declared that postbellum white flight from the low country had left the black population isolated from progressive forces, stewing in their own cultural juices, "gradually relapsing into fetishism and African rites and dances."[39]

What "paganism" meant was not always clear. Sometimes it was simply "the universal horseshoe branded on the door of negro cabins as a bar to witches and the devil," as a *Lippincott's* contributor noted in 1870. "There are also the 'conjuring gourd' and the frog-bones and pounded glass carefully hidden away by many an old man or woman, who by the dim light of a tallow candle or a pine torch works imaginary spells on any one against whom he or she may have a grudge." Fetishism was by no means confined to the old folks. Patsy Moses, an ex-slave interviewed for the Federal Writers Project in the 1930s, recalled the pervasiveness of amulets among the young and strong, fifty or more years before: "De big, black nigger in de corn field mos' allus had three charms around he neck, to make him fort'nate in love, and to keep him well, and one for lady luck at dice to be with him. Den if you has indigestion wear a penny round de neck." The courting of "lady luck at dice" was part of a larger courtship system; wearing charms was a way of soliciting a whole range of favors from Fortuna, conjuring *mana* to ward off everything from sexual rejection to indigestion.[40]

Another ex-slave and conjurer, William Adams, confirmed the power of belief in charms: "Some folks won't think for a minute of goin' without lodestone or de salt and pepper mixture in de little sack, tied round de neck. . . . When one have faith in sich an de accidentally lose de charm, dey sho' am miserable."[41] Adams put his finger on the crucial element of faith, which transfigured the commonplace, creating a sacred bundle from a little sack of salt and pepper. Sacred bundles, unlike used lottery tickets, were not disposable. They preserved a religious significance.

The sustaining of a sense of the sacred often involved the synthesis of magic and Christianity. And some rituals, such as "the method of divination by turning the sifter," crossed racial as well as religious barriers, even in the segregated South. A journalist named Sara Handy discovered that this form of divination was "extensively practiced by the negroes and poor whites of the South" when she traveled there in the 1890s. It was, she wrote:

another African survival, the Hoodoo man of the tribe using a shield instead of the sifter. Two chairs are placed back to back in such wise that the sifter rests between, edge on edge, so lightly that a breath will serve to disturb its equilibrium. The diviner, who is no

Hoodoo, but preferably a man of standing in the church, takes his place away from chairs and sifter, and, with lifted hand, chants slowly,—

> "By Saint Peter, by Saint Paul,
> By the Lord who made us all,
> If John Doe did thus and so,
> Turn sifter, turn and fall."

If the person named is innocent, the sifter remains motionless; if he is an accomplice, it shakes without falling; and if he is guilty, it turns and drops with a clang.[42]

Whether the whites picked this ritual up directly from the blacks, or whether their use of it involved some obscure blending of Elizabethan folk memory and African American practice, is anybody's guess. What is clear is that even in the post–Civil War years, the conjuring of *mana* could proceed under Christian auspices, and that even for Protestants, ordinary household objects could acquire occult significance.

Magical thinking thrived in the cities as in the countryside. In 1885 a writer in the *Atlanta Constitution* estimated that "perhaps a hundred old men and women practiced conjuring as a profession in that city, telling fortunes, locating lost and stolen goods, and casting spells upon people and cattle." It is safe to assume that their clientele was large and interracial. Even fifty years later, when the folklorist Harry Middleton Hyatt was compiling his classic *Hoodoo-Conjuration-Witchcraft-Rootwork,* his informants told him that "in the South . . . 90 per cent of Negroes is been trained in that *hoodooism* and 40 per cent of the whites believed in *hoodooism.*" However inexact such statistics may be, they represent resistance to the disenchantment of the world, in the most avowedly Protestant section of the United States.[43]

Catholic Christanity sanctioned syncretism more overtly. New Orleans became the capital of syncretist belief and ritual; Catholic and African traditions blended to sustain a rich mix of voodoo and other hybrid forms of magical practice. As late as the early 1900s, a typical New Orleans good luck charm was a sacred bundle containing "about fifty black pepper seeds, some glistening mineral like polished lead but brittle as coal, flakes of dried herbs, crumbs of moldy bread, a wisp of hair, the half of a white bean, and a tarnished brass medal of St. Benedict." To make it work, you wet it with rum every Friday (except Good Friday), then made the sign of the cross over it. Such practices revealed that syncretism was another word for *bricolage*—the vernacular "science of the concrete" identified by Claude Lévi-Strauss as a key component of *The Savage Mind*.[44]

One can see this science at work in the American Southwest as well. Don Pedro Jaramillo (1829–1907) was a Catholic faith healer in Los Olmos, Texas. He charged nothing for his services. The instruments of his art included a statuette of the Virgin of Guadalupe, a candle, a handkerchief, a bottle containing "oil of seven herbs" with an image of himself on the label, a set of fortune-telling cards, and a horseshoe mounted on a plaque surrounded by a collage of images: the Sacred Heart of Jesus, Joseph and Jesus, a head of garlic and the Buddha, Saint Martin and a beggar. Christianity mingled with naturopathy and a vague evocation of Eastern religion. This sort of syncretism later characterized the popular religious movement called Santeria that would emerge in parts of Latin America in the early twentieth century and claim such respectable adherents as the Mexican president Francisco Madero.[45]

Despite this mélange of images, syncretism was not the same as confusion, except to a clergy bent on rooting out superstition. Most Catholic priests were far less intent on that task than their Protestant counterparts. As a result, vernacular Catholicism was shot through with magical thinking, particularly with the belief that certain objects contained the power to protect their possessor from physical (as well as spiritual) harm—with the conviction that some material things could be endowed with *mana*.

Faith in materialized *mana* pervaded popular Catholicism throughout the late nineteenth century (and, one could argue, most of the twentieth as well). In Irish, Italian, and other immigrant households, holy water continued to serve as a balm for flesh as well as spirit. Images and icons played a similar dual role. "PAID WITH HIS LIFE FOR LOSING A CHARM," the *New York World* reported in 1901. "Longshore Friends of John Kennedy, Who Was Murdered, Say His Luck Deserted Him," the article continued. "Friends along the wharves who knew and liked big John Kennedy, the longshoreman, attribute his murder to the loss of a charm—the image of a saint—which he wore about his neck. Yesterday, without a word of warning or a threat, Rinert Christensen, runner for a sailors' boarding house, entered a saloon at No. 400 West Street and shot Kennedy dead."[46]

Kennedy could have bought a scapular medal, a tiny statue, or a "holy card" with a saint's picture on it at one of the little shops that sold sacred goods, often alongside parish churches. Or it might have been a gift from a family member or a parish priest. Whatever the artifact's source, Kennedy added to its orthodox significance (which may have been minimal) by transforming it into a "charm."

African American Protestants had to be a little more careful when they went in search of *mana*. Protestant Christianity was less openly tolerant of syncretism, especially in congregations whose ministers were committed to uplifing the race from rural ignorance and pagan superstition. Yet even educated blacks in Philadelphia and other Northern cities consulted conjurers for "hands" to keep witches and other bad luck away. Gradually, as the Smithsonian scholar Carolyn Long has observed, urban conditions promoted commercialization of magic: "the 'Voodoo drugstore' began to replace the conjurer, the root doctor, and the Voodoo queen as a source of charms and potions."[47]

But commercialized magic was still magic. These beliefs and practices were not mere isolated "survivals" but part of a larger worldview. As the historian David Brown writes, "Conjurers traditionally obtained the force or power they employed in their work from the spirit world of the dead and from nature, and understood the power they manipulated as either morally neutral or ambivalent." Or as an old black man from Tin City, Georgia, put it: "I know deah is luck and unluck and some people kin wuk it." Luck was a spiritual force that pervaded everyday life and that sometimes could be successfully manipulated. This belief was at the core of a coherent world picture, an alternative to the dualism of both the orthodox Protestant and mainstream scientific perspectives—the image of a universe where matter and spirit were married.[48]

Yet, however numerous its devotees, this outlook continued to lose legitimacy during the decades after the Civil War. The golden age of gambling was also the triumphant epoch of evangelical rationality—the moment when that worldview became the consensus of educated opinion. Its philosophical basis, the partnership of divine and human will, had been articulated before the war by Northern intellectuals. After the Union victory, belief in that partnership became the core of a national creed. From this view, Americans were willing freely what was happening providentially, anyway: the westward advance of moral and material progress. Freedom and fate converged in a harmonious universe, governed by divinely ordained natural law. Gambling had no place in such an orderly cosmos. Nor did any other form of homage to Fortuna. Under Protestant Christian eyes, the culture of chance retained a demonic aura. Conjuring *mana* seemed little different from consorting with Satan.

THE APEX OF EVANGELICAL RATIONALITY

Images of the devil tell us a lot about ourselves. They embody what we most want to distance, yet still find attractive. Nineteenth-century American Protestants imagined the devil in a variety of forms, but all bore a family resemblance to one another. The devil was a gambler, a developer (or speculator), and sometimes, especially toward the end of the century, merely a doofus. In whatever guise, he was (according to Andrew Delbanco) "universally familiar, with nothing alien or even grotesque about him."[49] Long before Hannah Arendt coined the controversial phrase, the banality of evil was becoming a social fact—epitomized in the changing imagery of Satan. Sometimes he was appealing in his resourcefulness and bland persuasiveness (two useful qualities in a society based on self-salesmanship), and sometimes he was simply silly.

The comic devil-as-gambler emerged by 1890, in P. T. Barnum's *Dollars and Sense; or, How to Get On*: a ridiculous cartoon figure surrounded by cards and dice, with the caption "Luck."[50] To Protestant moralists, gambling represented the broader foolishness of belief in luck, which they implicitly sensed was a rival to their own doctrines. The image of the devil as a gambler captured the moral stakes in the war on gambling (at least from the warrior's point of view). This was not simply an attempt to reform individual conduct, as the war on alcohol claimed to be; this was an attempt to abolish an alternative culture.

Despite its broad implications, the critique of gambling preserved its evangelical emphasis on saving the individual soul. But gradually,

"Luck," 1890.

the language of moral corruption acquired medical qualities as well. The rhetoric of Anthony Comstock revealed a greater emphasis on psychological than on spiritual matters. Though he denounced lottery organizers in traditional terms as "too lazy to work, too cowardly to be openly vicious," he also resorted to more viscerally charged idioms. He was plainly horrified, for example, by the psychic atmosphere that youthful smokers created: "the blue smoke curls above their heads as it puffs out of their mouths in fantastic forms," he reported breathlessly. "Parents," he warned of billiard parlors, "such an atmosphere is dangerous to your son. The contagion of sinful influences fills the air, and the poison will corrupt the better nature of your boy."[51] The rhetoric of moral (or immoral) influence dissolved Protestant Christianity into the pre-Pasteur language of public health. Gambling and other vices created another form of miasma, the invisible noxious gas that was thought to cause epidemics in cities.

For Comstock, gambling ultimately unmanned the gambler. Like earlier reformers, he reversed the conventional criteria of masculine prowess. The result was a reconfigured notion of manhood, more suited to the countinghouse than to the cockfight. Addressing "business men" directly, Comstock clarified the cash value of antigambling reform. Of horse-pool betting parlors, he warned that "a clerk who frequents these places, and is brought under their seductive influences, is not to be trusted in office or store. The wild excitement that fires his brain will unman him. The things he would not do he will do." The loss of self-control, in short, was a threat to the essence of the gambler's manhood, his free will—as well as a threat to his employer's investment.[52]

Other antigambling reformers, depending on their social or geographical location, resorted to other idioms. Southern ministers joined their Northern counterparts in stressing the dangers of risk, uncertainty, and excitability versus the calm and control of the domesticated household, but the source of those threats, for the Southerners, was less the heartless world of commerce than the sinful one of traditional male amusements. From Alabama to Virginia, evangelical reformers sought to sever the connection between cockfighting and Confederate valor. Assaulting the traditional linkage between gambling and masculinity, they joined the boosters of the New South in promoting a new notion of the Southern man—domesticated, moderate, self-controlled, and ready to get down to business.[53]

Secular critics of gambling sometimes took a more idiosyncratic approach. During the 1890s, German socialists in Saint Louis attacked the existence of slot machines in working-men's saloons for a variety of reasons: the machines preyed on the poor; they discouraged education, self-development, and upward mobility among the working class; and they offered reformers an excuse to shut down all recreational watering-holes. As a pamphlet concluded in 1894: "We must have STRICTLY DECENT DRAMSHOPS" to keep the bluenoses at bay.[54]

But this was a minority view. Most critics of gambling conceived it of a piece with drinking, masturbation, and other sins against self-mastery—and they linked those apparently private issues with larger public ones. From the evangelical-rationalist view, a self-controlled citizenry created a harmonious polity. That was the assumption that lay behind the United States Supreme Court decision (1879) to uphold the Mississippi ban on lotteries: by generating widespread mania, the court held, lotteries "upset the checks and balances of a well-ordered community."[55] Private and public disorder were fused.

The key to maintaining that balance, reformers agreed, was the family. From antebellum times to the end of the century, reform literature presented domestic ideals as the chief casualty of the gambler's vice and the chief agency of his redemption. Bret Harte dramatized but also distanced himself from this view. In his short story "The Luck of Roaring Camp," (1868) California miners adopt a baby boy, the offspring of Cherokee Sal, a local prostitute who dies in childbirth. Having disposed of the nonwhite, unmarried mother (an unthinkable presence in nineteenth-century fiction), Harte sanctifies her mixed-race son—a "mighty small specimen" who "has n't mor'n got the color," the miners say. That is, the baby's skin has only a faint tinge of "color," the miner's word for gold. He is almost white, but not quite.[56]

The baby's presence, and the responsibility for his care, transforms the camp from a collection of hovels to a respectable hamlet and redeems a few rough-hewn souls in the bargain. Eventually the miners take to calling the baby "The Luck," for the regeneration he has brought to Roaring Camp. Real luck, Harte suggested, is not the gambler's kind, but the shot at self-transcendence offered by the acceptance of familial responsibilities. Personal morality and bourgeois respectability cohere in the domestic household—epitomized by the spotless, whitewashed cabin the miners fix up for The Luck. With only a few dissenters, the miners even agree "to build a hotel in the following spring, and to invite one or two families to reside there for the sake of The Luck, who might perhaps profit by female companionship."[57]

But Harte quickly resists this move to full domestication. He cannot allow "decent" (i.e., married, white) women to enter this male utopia. So he intervenes in the miner's plans, unleashing a late-winter flood that sweeps through Roaring Camp. The next morning the whitewashed cabin is gone, and "the pride, the hope, the joy, The Luck, of Roaring Camp had disappeared." A relief boat soon returns from down river with a miner named Kentuck, who is holding the dead baby in his arms. When the other men tell The Luck's protector that he is dying, too, "a smile lit the eyes of the expiring Kentuck. 'Dying!' he repeated; he's a takin' me with him. Tell the boys I've got The Luck with me now;' and the strong man, clinging to the frail babe as a drowning man is said to cling to a straw, drifted away into the the shadowy river that flows forever to the unknown sea."[58]

Harte refigured luck, enveloping its older meanings in sentimental Christianity. The Luck is a redemptive infant Christ child, but not one who could be allowed to grow to adulthood in a respectable Victorian setting. He is, after all, a little mixed-race bastard, the product of a union between a "sinful" Indian prostitute and one of her "white" clients (who remains anonymous). It was as if The Luck could never entirely outgrow his disreputable origins, any more than he could shed the color in his cheeks.

While Harte's story suggested the limits of regeneration through domestication, the idea remained a guiding principle of antigambling reform. Domestic ideals could focus strategies directed at women as well as men. In 1891 a minister from Chicago told how he had begun to wean several female gamblers from waywardness: "at a gathering of these young women several were compelled to leave the room when 'Home, Sweet Home' was played on the piano."[59] Reminders of home renewed commitments to abstinence. The domestic ideal extolled a realm of wholeness, an intimate providential order, where risk and uncertainty were kept at bay by love; in this sense it recalled the original etymological connection between nostalgia and homesickness. Yet the utopian home looked forward as well as backward: it was not merely a refuge for childlike innocence; it was on the front lines of the cultural war against chance—an agency of progress, a means for preparing productive, rational citizens.

Gamblers, it was assumed, were unproductive and irrational. Indeed, gambling was often merely the outward and visible sign of an inner and spiritual lack—a perverse attachment to superstitious and backward ways. The high levels of intemperance and illiteracy in Louisiana, the *Nation* asserted in 1884, could be directly traced to the persistence of the lottery in that state. Personal conduct had broader social and economic consequences. Edmund Crapsey, in his 1873 survey of gambling in New York, complained that one of the chief problems created by the lottery was the amount of capital it withdrew from "productive industry."[60] This is a strikingly modern formulation, the sort of complaint one would expect a "rational capitalist" to make about the man-hours lost to alcohol and drug use. In the discourse of evangelical rationality, concern for "productive industry" linked moral and economic perspectives.

The gambler's fundamental flaw was his disregard of the sanctity of work. In this he was not alone. "The multitude shirk labor," the former Unitarian minister O. B. Frothingham observed in 1883: gambling was only one example of a national obsession with getting something for nothing. "Witness the rage for speculation, the crowd at the exchange, the throng of adventurers on the street, the disgraceful phenomenon of stock gambling, the great company of people who live by their wits, wait for something to turn up to their advantage, haunt the patent-office, dog the steps of inventors, borrow money, live on their friends, hang to the skirts of successful schemers." Trolling for shirkers, Frothingham cast a wide net. Anyone who wanted to muddle through life without systematic labor— maybe getting lucky, maybe not—could be charged with social parasitism and childish dependence. Only those who were committed to their work became, in Frothingham's scheme of things, independent citizens, beholden to no one.[61]

Yet gambling and other forms of idle risk were more than mere escapes from honest labor. They also stimulated and satisfied "the passion for nervous excitement" that pervaded American society—and that betrayed "the immaturity of our social development," according to Frothingham. The frenzy of high-stakes betting was "one of those perilous devices by which men try to infuse romance into their otherwise dull existence, to add zest to their experience, to drag some portion of heaven down to their clay." Food, wine, prostitutes, dancing, even "lascivious music" could fill this need momentarily by providing a few spasms of excitement. But of all such vices, gambling was "the most fascinating because the most intense, the most lasting, and the most social. It brings the greatest number of stimulants together, and exerts their power on the most sensitive nerves." At first elevated by his "wild infatuation," the gambler was eventually ruined by it.[62]

Frothingham's critique, like Comstock's, epitomized the growing influence of a psychological idiom in antigambling literature. But conservative clerics like Comstock placed the language of bodily danger alongside traditional Protestant moralism, while rationalists like Frothingham discarded much of Christian tradition altogether—notably the long-standing suspicion of lucre. The gambler's error, from Frothingham's secular and progressive view, was not avarice but indifference to money. "Not only is he destitute, as he must needs be, of any perception of the divine import of money as a sign of man's supremacy over the lower spheres of nature, he equally lacks comprehension of its higher social advantages. He is animal and passionate through and through." Gambling was an enemy of progress, a form of regression to childhood dependence and animal passion. As society became more refined, more widely persuaded of "the divine import of money," gambling—like intemperance and other vices—would gradually disappear. So Frothingham and some of his contemporaries surmised.[63]

The deification of money was usually not as flagrant as Frothingham's, but it was by no means confined to the few. During the 1880s and 1890s, as the sanctity or at least the morality of property became an article of faith among business apologists, gambling could be portrayed by its critics as a kind of blasphemy, a desecration of society's most sacred substance. Property embodied morality, chance amorality: to submit the former to the latter was at best a category mistake, at worst an inversion of moral hierarchy. Gambling, on this view, laid an axe to the foundation of cosmic order.

During the Gilded Age as in the antebellum era, the critique of gambling involved more than cards and dice: it was an assault on a whole way of thinking and being, an attack on a culture of chance. Reform literature insistently linked gambling with ignorance and superstition. "Fortune is still a goddess, and to her shrine throng the devotees of pleasure," Frothingham observed. "The number of people who hang about the confines of the hidden world, and play with the dice-boxes of destiny, is amazing. There is a morbid curiosity to peer into the secrets of Fate and to get the start of Providence." This was what accounted for the licensed lotteries of Europe; despite the long odds, popular belief persisted that one might capture the power of luck.[64]

Even in Protestant America, Frothingham reported, "the border land of Providence is occupied by superstition." In that strange country of the mind, "the laws of reason being suspended, miracles are looked for as events of course." Before the Civil War, liberal Protestants and secular rationalists had begun tacitly to agree that the age of miracles was over. But the borderland of Providence was a part of the world that had not yet been disenchanted. The same could be said of the gambling room, which was (according to Frothingham) "a nest of superstitions." Consider the sporting character who took a spider in a box to Monte Carlo: the bottom of the box was painted half red and half black, and whichever side the spider stayed on, the gambler judged the fortunate one. (Spiders continue to play a similar central role in African divination.) "No Roman augur was ever more diligent in searching for signs and omens" than the typical gambler, wrote Frothingham; "no sailor at sea, no savage in the wilderness, no necromancer or alchemist or seeker after the philosopher's stone, was ever more credulous." And gamblers' superstitious tendencies were enhanced by the mysteries of their trade—the arcane language, the odd artifacts with glyphlike markings. Fetish objects ranged from the rabbit's foot in the gambler's pocket to the slot machine (invented in 1887), an ornate and stylized device for dispensing money—the modern *mana*—in accordance with mysterious, hidden principles. (See pages 7 and 8.) No wonder the gambling room was pervaded by "a species of glamour," in the original etymological sense of magical spell.[65]

By the late nineteenth century, to criticize gambling was to criticize a broad and general worldview as well as a particular vice. Belief in luck attracted vitriolic scorn from captains of commerce and their ideological allies. "There is no such thing in the world as luck," P. T. Barnum asserted in 1890, echoing generations of denial among ideologues of success. Luck was merely the alibi of the lazy man. "I never knew an early rising, hardworking prudent man, careful of earnings and strictly honest, who complained of bad luck," Henry Ward Beecher announced in 1886. Luck had no existence apart from the wistful projections of the unsuccessful.[66]

Fortune received equally rough treatment. Purveyors of middle-class pieties reduced its meaning to wealth alone, and then transformed it from a blessing to a burden. As Gail Hamilton told the readers of *Young Folks* in 1866, "poverty seems to be favorable to the best mental and moral

training of a vast majority of persons."[67] The alleged advantages of inherited wealth were in fact mere temptations to indolence; poverty, by
comparison, provided ennobling incentives to rise in the world. This sort
of nonsense has survived and even flourished down to the present. Its
staying power stems from its capacity to legitimate status quo economic
inequalities.

The suspicion of good fortune was rooted not only in lame apologetics for the rich but also in classical and Puritan tradition. "He has not
acquired a fortune, the fortune has acquired him," said Bion of Athens in
the third century B.C.E. Nineteenth-century American writers reformu-
lated the notion in Protestant terms. In *Ben-Hur* (1880), one of Lew Wallace's many sententious characters declared that "a man is never so on trial
as in the moment of excessive good fortune." The notion that good fortune puts us on trial recalled Puritan ideas concerning the corrupting effect of riches. The reduction of fortune to moral temptation was a small
but significant campaign in the cultural war on chance.[68]

The larger aims of that war remained the same in the 1890s as they
had been fifty years earlier. Not simply gambling, but also the superstitious worldview behind it, had to be eradicated. Enlightened liberal
Protestants joined scientists and other secular sorts in a sustained assault
on popular superstitions. "Though they may seem trifling and harmless,
they need careful watching," an *Outlook* author warned parents in 1895,
advising them to nip "superstition in the bud," however appealing their
children's fancies might seem.[69] From the evangelical-rationalist view, superstition disregarded religious and secular ideas of order—both of which
depended on the assumption of a universe governed by natural law.

While these assumptions had been in place since the antebellum era,
toward the end of the century they acquired a more distinctly secular
tinge. Many devotees of control developed an outlook that can loosely be
labeled "positivism." By this I mean neither the social positivism of Auguste Comte nor the logical positivism of twentieth-century analytical
philosophy. The positivism in question was less a systematic philosophy
than a habit of mind affecting the educated classes: journalists, academics,
novelists, and more than a few ministers. Gradually it reshaped evangelical rationality.

Positivism depended on a belief that the entire universe—including
all human life—was ruled by deterministic laws discoverable through scientific inquiry. Science was an Easter-egg hunt; once the eggs were gath-

ered the game would be over: the laws governing the universe would be fully known. Some laws were as yet undiscovered, but it was only a matter of time. At some not-too-distant date, all the apparent mysteries of the cosmos would be explained once and for all. To accomplish this end, positivists embarked on innumerable projects of categorization and classification, seeking to assemble the parts of the universe and discern the mechanisms that governed their actions. This search for order paralleled the preoccupations of industrial capitalists and altered the rhythms of everyday life, through the spread of factory discipline and the creation of standard time zones (which first appeared, at the railroads' urging, in 1883). A mechanistic worldview reinforced the rationalization of time and space.

From the positivist view, what were called random events were simply those for which we had not yet discovered a law. "Either law or chance—these are the only alternatives," John Fiske announced in the *Popular Science Monthly* in 1873. Fiske was an avowed positivist and a disciple of Herbert Spencer's deterministic scheme of progress; he regarded the invocation of chance as a confession of intellectual failure. "Chance and luck are merely aliases for ignorance," Thomas Henry Huxley wrote in an *Introductory Science Primer,* published in the 1870s and distributed in schools on both sides of the Atlantic. Positivistic scientists were united in their disdain for any acknowledgment of randomness.[70]

So were Protestant moralists. Chance is "only a negation—the denial of intelligence or design," the Presbyterian magazine *Hours at Home* declared in 1870. "Every advance from ignorance to intelligence in all the departments of science, disproves, by the most positive evidence, the doctrine of chance and asserts an overruling providence." Fourteen years later the *Unitarian Review* assailed "gambling for the sake of Christ." Apparently harmless fund-raising had ominous side effects—raffles and bingo were more sinister than they appeared. "The worst feature of all these customs is that they encourage the appeal to chance, and they make that thought stronger: whereas we want to do everything we can to weaken that [thought], and fix our minds upon the idea of order and providence in the least as well as the greatest." Even gambling for charitable ends, from this view, promoted a dangerous alternative worldview.[71]

In many ways, the Gilded Age marked the apex of evangelical rationality—the coming together of Protestantism, liberal individualism, and positivistic science in a philosophical consensus that papered over intellectual divisions and somehow made cultural contradictions cohere (at least for a significant minority of the population). The journalist John Bigelow summarized the evangelical-rationalist perspective in 1895. A superstitious belief in chance kept gamblers at the tables, he wrote, but they failed to realize that "there is no such thing as chance. What we commonly term chance or luck is simply a mode of expressing our ignorance of the cause or series of causes of which any given event is the inevitable sequence." Under the sway of his passion, the gambler slid steadily away from rational awareness of causal sequences; eventually he was "reduced to the level of a beast of prey." The desire to do unto others the opposite of what he would have them do unto him, when frustrated, turned inward and led to suicide. Belief in Chance and Luck put the gambler on the slippery slope to self-destruction; belief in Providence and Progress put the rational citizen on the firm path of self-mastery.[72]

But by the time Bigelow was writing, this kind of optimism required a studied indifference to a ferment of destabilizing change. The most obvious instability was the increasingly violent class conflict bred by industrial capitalism. Less apparent but equally serious were the spread of Darwinism and other intellectual movements that reasserted the power of chance against familiar ideas of cosmic order. At the fin de siècle, even acolytes of Providence were haunted by an increasing awareness of accident.

THE SPECTER OF RANDOM FORCE

The growing concentration of power in a nouveau riche plutocracy, responsible to no one, made paeans to Providence ring increasingly hollow. Rich men still paid tribute to the partnership of Providence and will, as Junius Morgan (J.P.'s father) did at a testimonial dinner in 1877: "A kind providence has been very bountiful to us, and under this guidance, the future is in our own hands." But such self-congratulation was hard to swallow under certain circumstances. Consider the election of 1888: Grover Cleveland won the popular vote and Benjamin Harrison the electoral college—thanks to Matthew Quay, the Republican boss of the Pennsylvania legislature. When Harrison announced "Providence has given us the victory," Quay snapped: "He ought to know that Providence hadn't a damn thing to do with it." What really mattered was the huge number of Republicans Quay had "compelled to approach the gates of the state penitentiary to get [Harrison] elected."[73] Like other rhetorical strategies too readily deployed, the invocation of Providence could come to seem stale and insincere. Too many inappropriate examples could exhaust the metaphor's carrying capacity.

The most palpable challenge to Providence came from the everyday unpredictability of life, which was inescapable under any economic system but accentuated under laissez-faire capitalism. "The propensity to treat the events of human life as accidental or the sport of chance was never more nearly universal than it is to-day," Bigelow said in the 1890s. The "heathen goddess" Fortuna presided over "the Boards of Trade and the Stock Exchanges"—and over the publishing industry as well. In *The World of Chance,* published in the panic year of 1893, William Dean Howells recounted the fortunes of an aspiring young writer, S. N. Ray, to underscore the centrality of caprice in the courtship of literary success. Ray's publisher Brandreth tells him that "there are no laws of business. There is nothing but chances, and no amount of wisdom can forecast them or control them." Howells realized that luck was threaded throughout the fabric of entrepreneurial society, making it more interesting but less just than a carefully managed utopia.[74]

Yet neither Howells nor his Christian socialist colleagues could rest content with randomness. They were troubled by the cruel contingencies of capitalist fate and by the resemblance of the market economy to a destructive game of chance. The Social Gospel minister Washington Gladden argued that "speculating on margins—that is, betting on the future value of stocks or produce"—was "simply gambling, nothing more nor less."[75] It was a zero-sum game, in which one man's success required another one's failure, and therefore, in Gladden's view, it was the opposite of legitimate trade,

> To say that gambling in margins is as bad as faro or roulette is a very weak statement; it is immeasurably worse. It is far more dishonest. The gambler in margins does his best to load the dice on which he bets his money. It is, moreover, far more injurious. By this practice values are unsettled; business is often paralyzed; the price of the necessaries of life is forced upward. The poor man's loaf grows small as the gambler's gains increase.[76]

Gladden was groping toward a social critique of chance in the economic realm—a critique more humane and capacious than the moralistic diatribes against speculation that had characterized republican tradition. Rather than accept the volatility of the business cycle as an expression of *Natural Law in the Business World* (the title of a textbook of the time), Gladden recognized that contemporary economic arrangements were products of human choice and could be changed. That dawning awareness prefigured a broad, creative response to laissez-faire capitalism. The emergence of social democratic thought and its public policy expression, the welfare state, involved more than merely repairing the cracks in the evangelical-rational consensus. It required a new, more flexible frame of mind—more sensitive to the abrasions of accident in individual lives, less insistent on the power of will to master fate.

Yet some difficulties were subtler and deeper than the ones posed by the casino economy. Among the subtlest and deepest was the challenge presented by Darwin to natural theology—the synthesis of Providence and scientific law, which had been the basis of enlightened cosmology for decades. As George Levine writes, "there could be no role for the random in natural theology. [The British theologian William] Paley saw chance as only an 'appearance' resulting from the ignorance of the observer, or as an occasional consequence of multiple laws intersecting, and where he found it he immediately justified or compensated for it." And for most of the nineteenth century, Paley's was the authoritative voice behind the evangelical-rational synthesis.[77]

Darwin was as uncomfortable with chance as any other Victorian Protestant or scientist. Nevertheless, he found it indispensable: minute chance variations, he concluded, were the origin of new species. He could not account for those variations, but he knew that they lacked "any Lamarckian connection to particular environmental conditions, to parent stock, to need, or to any recognizable goal." By default, Darwin was moving toward an emphasis on randomness as the basis for novelty in nature; yet the apparently random variations eventually cohered to create an adaptive synthesis. "Nearly all steps leading to evolutionary change seem to be controlled entirely or largely by accident," writes the biologist Ernst Mayr, "yet the final product of evolution is perfection in adaptation." This was a kind of order, but it was not a providential one.[78]

Still, Spencer, Fiske, and other prophets of progress did their best to deny the waning of Providence. They merged Darwinian and Lamarckian views in a synthesis that preserved cosmic purpose. The persistent faith in progress was the key to what may have been the most remarkable feat of late-nineteenth-century intellectual history—the transformation of Darwinian evolution into a language of linear advance. Rather than reasserting the significance of the random (which a careful reading of Darwin might have prompted one to do), popular Darwinism merely reassured human beings of their centrality and superiority to the rest of creation—not to mention their own ancestors. There was no warrant for this in Darwin's writings, but there was a powerful need in his interpreters to contain the subversive and perhaps even nihilistic implications of his work.

Perhaps the only American intellectual who resisted that need was Chauncey Wright, the "Cambridge Socrates." As Louis Menand has observed, Wright was a stellar example of a Victorian type—the freelance thinker who published meagerly but conversed brilliantly. His main distinction lies in the people who listened, among them Oliver Wendell Holmes, Jr.; Charles Sanders Peirce; and William James. Wright considered himself a true positivist and the Spencerians frauds, because they muddled fact and value. Unlike them, Wright refused to meld the scientific evidence of evolution with metaphysical faith in progress. Almost alone among his contemporaries, he was willing to face the centrality of the random in Darwinian theory.[79]

Wright had been preoccupied with chance in nature even before *The Origin of Species.* In 1858, he published "The Winds and the Weather" in the *Atlantic Monthly,* which argued that the capriciousness of weather thwarted human efforts to predict it: "Unlike planetary perturbations, the weather makes the most reckless excursions from its averages, and obscures them by a most inconsequent and incalculable fickleness." But it was this very fickleness, according to Wright, that activated organic change in plants and animals, killing some organisms prematurely through drought, flood, heat, and cold, allowing the more fortunate organisms to survive. The similarity of this argument to Darwin's is striking, and Wright was thrilled by the publication of *Origin.* "Darwin became his hero," as Menand says, and the two men corresponded.[80]

The Metaphysical Club met for nine months in 1872. One can imagine the younger men's fascination with this talented conversationalist, who spoke enchantingly of "cosmical weather," despised conventional wisdom, and boasted the acquaintance of Darwin himself. In an intellectual climate dominated by evasive banality, Wright's intellectual honesty must have been bracing to young men in search of straight talk. But his emphasis on the omnipresence of uncertainty led him to the brink of nihilism, if not beyond. His rigorously consistent positivism justified his motto: "where we cannot be certain, we can affirm nothing." In a universe pervaded by uncertainty, he thought, moral action was impossible. Of Wright's three famous interlocutors, only Holmes was even half-content with this conclusion. Peirce and James, as they matured, sought ways to make more sense of randomness. (James in particular recoiled from Wright's "Nulliverse.") But from Wright they retained a distaste for Spencerian pomposities, and a clearer understanding of Darwin than that of most of their contemporaries.[81]

Much "evolutionary" thought misread Darwinian theory to preserve providential progress. For many liberal Protestants, this containment project involved yoking Darwinian evolution to a Paleyite argument from design. The Harvard geologist Nathaniel Shaler, writing in the *Andover Review* in 1889, typified the tentative theism of this view when he made design the more sensible alternative to chance: "either intelligence in the high form in which we find it in man is the result of a fortuitous concatenation of unadjusted impulses dependent on one chance in a practically infinite number of possibilities, or . . . the life of man is the product of control. In the end it is left to the student to judge which of the two views is most [*sic*] satisfactory to his spirit." There was no doubt which alternative Shaler would choose.[82]

Fiske and other Spencerians were equally confident that a Darwinian universe could be made to cohere morally. The ascent of man, Fiske believed, involved the evolution of intelligence through natural selection, and "the order of mammals with greatest prehensile capacities, the primates with their incipient hands, were the most favourable subjects in which to carry on this process." In his evolutionary scheme, the growth of brain size required the lengthening of infancy, and sustained maternal nurturance allowed human intelligence—and eventually human society—to flower.

At this point, without encountering any breach in the cosmic [evolutionary] process, we crossed the threshold of the ethical world, and entered a region where civilization, or the gradual perfecting of the spiritual qualities, is henceforth Nature's paramount aim. To penetrate further into ths region would be to follow the progress of civilization, while the primitive canoe develops into the Cunard steamship, the hieroglyphic battle-sketch into epics and dramas, sun-catcher myths into the Newtonian astronomy, wandering tribes into mighty nations, the ethics of the clan into the moral law for all men. The story shows us Man becoming more and more clearly the image of God, exercising creative attributes, transforming his physical environment, incarnating his thoughts in visible and tangible shapes all over the world, and extorting from the abysses of space the secrets of vanished ages.[83]

Here as elsewhere in late-nineteenth-century evolutionary thought, Darwin disappeared amid the mists of cosmic optimism. Fiske's synthesis merged biological, social, and even spiritual evolution in a two-stage framework of progress. The first stage was the evolution of primate and eventually human intelligence through natual selection. The second stage was the evolution of human civilization: it still depended on the survival of the fittest, but the process acquired a vague religious aura. For Fiske, human evolution could be sharply distinguished from that of all other creatures: the emergence of Man brought God back into the picture. Nature began selecting for "spiritual qualities." It would be hard to find a more ambitious effort to preserve a providential order on scientifically defensible grounds.

This cosmic optimism remained the stuff of banquet oratory for a good quarter century after the Civil War, but by the 1890s Fiske's progressive platitudes were showing signs of strain. The problem went beyond the sheer banality of his formulations, or the difficulty of discerning the spiritual qualities in a luxury ocean liner. The fundamental flaw in Fiske's or any other effort to claim Darwin for cosmic optimism was that natural selection in fact had nothing to do with progress. As Stephen Jay Gould and many other scientists have observed, "The basic theory of natural selection offers no statement about general progress, and supplies no mechanism whereby overall advance might be expected."[84] Darwinian "laws," even if they could be described precisely, operated apart from any intention or meaning. There was no teleology, except in an exclusively naturalistic sense. Thus from the providentialist point of view, Darwin's "law" of natural selection represented a surrender to chance. And, since the human intellect could not be exempt from the rules governing nature, evolution was no more subject to human than to divine direction. Despite the efforts of Fiske and other popularizers to evade the implications of Darwin's work, many thoughtful observers began to sense that it directly undermined the foundation of evangelical rationality, the linkage of Providence and will.

In principle, release from evangelical rationality could be a liberation from a narrowly anthropocentric belief in evolutionary progress—a liberation that has still not been fully accomplished today. Gould writes that "Darwin's revolution will be completed when we smash the pedestal of arrogance and own the plain implications of evolution for life's nonpredictable nondirectionality." Or as Darwin himself put it, more succinctly, in the margin of Robert Chambers' *Vestiges of the Natural History of Creation*: "Never say higher or lower."[85]

Darwin's late research on earthworms brought this point home, as Adam Phillips has perceptively shown. Darwin discovered that worms continually created vegetable mold as a digestive byproduct; in effect, they did "the inexhaustible work that makes the earth fertile." Far from being the emissaries of death (with which they were traditionally associated), worms were—however inadvertently—on the side of life. According to Phillips, Darwin knew that these lowly creatures told us "something about resilience and beneficial accidents: that it may be more marvellous when the world happens to work for us, than to believe that it was designed to do so."[86] Darwinian chance, in short, could underwrite a sense of wonder.

But during Darwin's own time, neither theists nor secularists were prepared to make this argument. Whether one believed in Providence or Progress (or both), the big issue raised by Darwin was the need to reconcile randomness and design. For a while, Fiske and other popularizers contained the Darwinian threat in a dynamic, dualistic framework of progress. But only for a while.

By the 1890s, Darwinian theory was one among several intellectual challenges to the synthesis of Providence and Will. The rise of hereditarian psychology and the stress on social interdependence in the emerging "science" of sociology both tended, in different ways, to undermine the familiar faith in autonomous choice, even as Darwinian natural selection threatened to shatter the providentialist argument from design. For those inclined to doubt, religion offered fewer comforts in times of trial.

Mark Twain was one such doubter. There was a time, during the 1880s, when he had joined in the national chorus of praise for "our great century," accepting the complacent equation of technological and moral progress. But everything in his experience as a pilot on the Mississippi, as a reporter in the boom towns of Nevada, as a beneficiary and victim of a volatile economy, conspired to undercut this secular faith in an orderly cosmos.

Mark Twain believed in luck. He was convinced that he had been a lucky man until the mid-1880s, when his propensity for risky investments led him to sink tens of thousands of dollars in the disastrous Paige typesetter. Neck deep in debt, he was forced to move his family out of their Hartford home and resume the life of an itinerant funny man (which he hated) simply to meet current obligations. His dream of a tranquil life as a man of letters was over. He may have destroyed it himself, more than half deliberately. He would have been bored to death in Hartford, perhaps visited daily by the doddering Harriet Beecher Stowe—the very emblem of the faded New England tradition he both despised and revered.

In any case, Mark Twain never had a chance to be bored by Hartford gentility. Circumstances ensured that his faith in Providence would be superficial and short-lived. By the time he was in his fifties he was committed to a darkening vision of a universe ruled by accident, without meaning or purpose. This was a peculiarly modern version of the culture of chance, shorn of any connection to larger cosmic meaning.

The critical event in Mark Twain's disillusionment was the sudden death of his daughter Susy from meningitis, at twenty-four, when he was in England on tour. He was standing in the dining room of a rented house in Guildford, thinking of nothing in particular, when a messenger handed him the cable telling him Susy had died. "It is one of the mysteries of our nature," he recalled nearly ten years later, "that a man, all unprepared can receive a thunder-stroke like that and live."[87]

Susy's death sealed the pessimism of this middle-aged writer. For Mark Twain, chance had become less a portal of possibility than an agent of disaster. Railing years later against the perverse tricks of fate, he wrote bitterly to Howells, whose own daughter Winnie had just succumbed to an undiagnosed illness: "It is my quarrel that traps like that are set. Suzy and Winnie given us in miserable sport, & then taken away."[88]

The meanings of "sport," at the time Mark Twain chose the word, were various and revealing. They included spontaneous mutation in plants or animals and the staking of money on risky or speculative propositions. And for Mark Twain himself, descending into a world without purpose, the darker connotations of "sport" resurfaced as well—the implications articulated by Gloucester in *King Lear.* Sport was prodigal, unpredictable, amoral, absurd: everything that Providence was not. Sport was the cruel joke of a demented deity.[89]

The death of a child, for all its frequency in the nineteenth century, nevertheless put faith in Providence to the test. Parents who were able to affirm belief could transform the arbitrary verdict of nature into "God's will." Mark Twain refused this ritual affirmation and ended in despair. His experience was neither typical nor untypical; it was a thing unto itself. Many Americans may have had stronger faith, or fewer trials, and lived out their lives in serenity. Who knows? The inner lives of most people remain a closed book to historians.

But by the 1890s, few educated Americans could deny that a host of social and intellectual developments (not to mention the ever-present pull of personal experience) had begun to reassert the claims of randomness. Against the reassurances of Fiske that the universe still made sense, Theodore Dreiser, Frank Norris, and other naturalistic novelists portrayed human beings buffeted by what Dreiser called "the forces that sweep and play through the universe." In Dreiser's *Sister Carrie* (1900), the motif of fortune's dice underscores the centrality of chance in shaping human fate, and the decline of Carrie's lover Hurstwood begins when he steals from a safe that has accidentally been left open. In Norris's *McTeague* (1899), a lottery activates the central movement of the plot, and the characters inhabit a purposeless Nature that reduces them to "the sport of chance."[90]

Such views were unusual but not unique. Many a skeptical imagination was haunted by the specter of random force—the power of amoral chance, as resistant to ritual conjuring as it was to the doctrines of Providence. New idioms of control would be needed to exorcise it.

{CHAPTER FIVE}

THE INCOMPLETE TAMING OF CHANCE

ew of Mark Twain's contemporaries echoed his accusations of the cosmos. Most educated Americans continued to profess belief in a providentialist consensus, though they gradually recast it in a form more flexible than evangelical rationality. Figures as different as John D. Rockefeller, Sr., and Thorstein Veblen collaborated unwittingly in creating a new managerial outlook that became the main foundation of the twentieth-century culture of control. Whatever their differences, managerialists shared a common faith in organizational technique—rather than personal morality—as the best means of containing the chaotic impact of unregulated markets (and, indeed, of disorder in general). Management subsumed moralism, without supplanting it. Rockefeller was almost a parody of the disciplined Protestant achiever, and Veblen (despite his ironic pose) was as horrified by waste as any bourgeois moralist. A morally charged commitment to efficiency linked capitalists and their critics.

To make life function more smoothly, managerial thinkers developed a new interpretation of random events in human experience. Instead of denying chance, they tamed it, to a variety of ends.[1] Rockefeller and other corporate chieftains formed monopolies that aimed to minimize economic risk; Social Gospel ministers pursued antigambling reforms that aimed to provide alternative outlets for the wagering impulse; social scientists embraced probabilistic thinking that acknowledged the existence of chance but robbed it of its power by reducing it to a handful of "outliers."

Yet the resort to statistics could have unintended consequences. The cult of numbers seemed to satisfy the positivist demand for precise measurement, but the numbers themselves represented likelihoods rather than certainties. As scientists and philosophers turned to probabilistic thought, they found themselves on the threshold of a new intellectual universe—one where positivist demands for certainty could no longer be adequately met. The postpositivist worldview resonated with avant-garde art and literature as well as with the vernacular culture of chance. More sophisticated thinkers, led by Charles Peirce and William James, willingly abandoned the quest for certainty. For them as for many of their successors, chance became less a portent of chaos than a portal of possibility. To their relief, the effort to tame chance would remain forever incomplete.

But among most educated professionals in the United States, that sort of philosophical openness remained unusual. From the 1890s through World War I, academics, journalists, ministers—the major contributors to public discourse—remained committed to some alliance between Providence and Progress. Those who sought to further that alliance through civic reform began to call themselves Progressives, and historians have done so ever since—despite the diversity of characters covered by that label.*

Progressive aims ranged from the alleviation of human suffering to the reorganization of government on a businesslike basis. What most Progressives had in common was a desire to channel the chaotic energies of the marketplace to more humane and productive ends. Many were still inspired by millennial dreams, but they sought the Kingdom of God on earth through social efficiency. They recast Victorian certainties in secular, managerial forms.[2] The process was halting, uneven, and unfinished. Nevertheless, by the 1910s the American social landscape did, indeed, look more manageable—at least to the business and professional elites who were concerned about such matters—than it had forty years before.

CAPITALISTS AND PROGRESSIVES

In the effort to manage the explosive entrepreneurial economy, capitalists themselves led the way. The creation of monopolistic corporations was

---

*Throughout this book, I use "progressive" to refer to a general belief in progress and "Progressive" to mean those early-twentieth-century reformers who used the word as a self-description.

the single most successful effort to minimize risk and ensure predictable profitability. And Rockefeller was the single most successful monopolist.

John D.'s father, William "Doc" Rockefeller, was a smooth-talking purveyor of trinkets, dreams, and magic elixirs, the sort of shape-shifting confidence man who flourished on the margins of the midnineteenth-century marketplace. His son, in contrast, epitomized the self-made man whose plain living and plain speaking—according to the dominant mythology—would counteract the deceit and debauchery of the confidence man.

John D. Rockefeller, Sr., embodied success through system, the stabilization of market sorcery through economic rationality. This was an increasingly common pattern in late-nineteenth-century entrepreneurship. From childhood to senescence, he was obsessed with control—of himself, of his environment. Even his admirers, such as the journalist William Inglis, admitted there was "something bordering on the super-human, perhaps the inhuman" in Rockefeller's "unbroken, mechanical perfection of schedule."[3] There was more at work in Rockefeller than the Protestant ethic. Rockefeller's obsession with control was rooted in reaction against his father's infidelities and unreliabilities.

The preoccupation of Doc Rockefeller's son with eliminating chance, whatever its personal sources, had important public consequences. The dream of predictable profits animated his drive to rationalize the oil industry, which he did by means of monopoly power. The Standard Oil empire, even after its formal dismemberment in 1911, set the pattern for the twentieth-century economy of oligopolistic, multinational corporations.

Rockefeller combined Christian moralism with a reverential attitude toward money. As a young clerk in Cleveland, starting out in the 1850s, he recalled that he would "gaze longingly" at a four thousand dollar banknote in the company safe. The implicit admission that the bill carried an "almost . . . erotic charge," his biographer Ron Chernow writes, was particularly remarkable in this eerily disciplined man, who insisted "I never had a craving for anything."[4]

Soon he had saved enough to start his own shipping business, and made a tidy fortune supplying produce, flour, ham, and other commodities to the Union troops in the Civil War. Yet the war was a piddling opportunity compared to the oil spurting from the streambeds of northwestern Pennsylvania. The trick was refining it into kerosene—"the poor man's light," in Rockefeller's words—and getting it to market. With one of his Cleveland partners, an Englishman named Maurice Clark, Rockefeller plunged into the oil business.[5]

To the fastidious Rockefeller, the oil fields presented a satanic vision, a hell in need of harrowing. Like miners in the California gold fields, wildcatting drillers swarmed over the slippery landscape, in search of the single lucky strike that would set them up for life. Decent enough fellows, Rockefeller thought, but they had no system. They were little more than gamblers, and their risk-taking tendencies did little for the moral tone of the region. Such boom towns as Oil City, Pennsylvania, were literally infused with gambling: card sharps and prostitutes proliferated, and the air was filled, as one visitor recalled, with "the slap of cards on the whiskey-stained tables of groggeries." Rockefeller picked his way through this fallen world, grimacing in distaste but following his own aphorism: "Success comes from keeping the ears open and the mouth closed."[6]

From the outset, his circumspect attention to detail paid off. He removed the risk from a risky business. To suspicious bankers who equated refining with gambling, Rockefeller presented himself as an ascending success whom bankers would one day covet as a customer. He borrowed huge sums, but distanced himself from speculative plungers. He dumped one of his partners, Maurice Clark's younger brother James, because (said Rockefeller) "he gambles in oil. I don't want this business to be associated with a gambler." He never had a losing year. Though money carried a magical frisson for this worldly ascetic, the key to his success was his capacity to manage his secret passion.[7]

While obsessive attention to detail was the centerpiece of Rockefeller's managerial strategy, belief in Providence played a major role as well. More than most rich men in the Gilded Age, Rockefeller conceived himself to be an instrument of divine purpose. When he missed a train that later wrecked, he wrote to his wife: "I do . . . regard the thing as the *Providence of God*." When he said "God gave me money," he really meant it—but not in quite the self-sanctifying way his critics assumed.[8] He meant that God had entrusted him with the money, and that it was his responsibility to use it in godly ways. The basis of Rockefeller's philanthropy, this doctrine of stewardship sustained his sense of the sanctity of money, while containing its fetishistic and erotic charge in a providential order—a kind of spiritual money laundering.

Rockefeller's disdain for gambling reflected his lifelong commitment to controlling wayward impulses in himself and his surroundings. Other leading monopolists shared his views, if not their Christian basis. The freethinker Andrew Carnegie, who created Standard Oil's counterpart in the steel industry, was outraged when his right-hand man, Charles Schwab, was seen gambling at Monte Carlo. "I feel . . . as if a son had disgraced the family," he cabled Schwab. Men at war against chance in business had little tolerance for chance in pleasure.[9]

The corporate taming of chance did much to enrich a handful of lucky people (nearly all of whom denied the existence of luck) but did little to reduce randomness in the lives of the less fortunate. Indeed, for anyone who was not the direct beneficiary of unchecked monopoly power, the new managerial strategies created less security, not more. To their critics, men like Rockefeller were merely confidence men—disguising collusion by creating dummy corporations; bribing legislatures wholesale, on the sly. "Mr. Rockefeller has systematically played with loaded dice," the muckraking journalist Ida Tarbell said in 1906, "and it is doubtful if there has been a time since 1872 when he has run a race with a competitor and started fair."[10]

By the turn of the century, more and more Americans were being struck by the fundamental unfairness of monopoly power—not only unfairness to the monopoly's competitors but to its customers and workers as well. Muckrakers like Tarbell played a crucial role in spreading the word. Exposing Rockefeller's ruthlessness, his resort to bribery and perjury as well as his clever concealment of his own responsibility for illegal acts, Tarbell made his invocations of Providence seem like the pratings of a pious old hypocrite—which in many ways they were.

Monopolies may have made profits more predictable for their shareholders, but they accelerated the transformation of the American economy into an arena of amoral struggle. As risk-taking rogues prospered, the words of the French poet Charles Peguy came to seem appropriate to the United States: "no one could suspect that times were coming," Péguy wrote, (remembering France in the 1880s), "when the man who did not gamble would lose all the time, even more surely than he who gambled."[11] Contented diligence in one's calling was no longer sufficient for success. The flagrant display of unmerited rewards called secular providentialism into question. Why did the virtuous suffer, and the wicked prosper?

Social upheaval and class warfare gave the question a sharper point.

From the late 1870s through the 1890s, striking railroad, steel, and mine workers fought frequent skirmishes and even a few pitched battles with National Guardsmen, Pinkerton detectives, and other gunmen hired by threatened executives. Mass unemployment swelled the ranks of the "tramps," trudging across vast territories in search of work and food. From Pittsburgh and Chicago to Saint Louis and Coeur d'Alene, Idaho, even comfortable Americans sensed their society was coming apart at the seams. No wonder they found it harder to see the world as Tennyson had in 1850:

> One God, one law, one element,
> And one far-off divine event,
> To which the whole creation moves.[12]

For decades, Americans had quoted those lines as the poetic expression of providential progress. By the 1890s, such notions of universal harmony were difficult to sustain.

Still, it was equally difficult to reject cosmic coherence altogether, as the reception of Darwinism demonstrated. A few interpreters of Darwin saw his work as a sanction for struggle: strife was the law of life, they claimed, among businessmen as well as beetles; the fittest survived and the weak were their rightful prey. But in a culture still suffused with Protestant Christianity, such crude biological analogies served as little more than literary conceits. A handful of novelists and social scientists resorted to them (Frank Norris, Theodore Dreiser, William Graham Sumner), but only Sumner followed such ideas to their bleak conclusion. Meanwhile, most Americans—and certainly most businessmen—recoiled from any notion of a world cut off from moral order.[13] The question was how to resurrect a more flexible sense of order, one more able to contain the inescapable facts of contingency.

What was needed was a democratic and pluralistic culture of control, one with a less brittle intellectual basis than the partnership of Providence and Will—and a less oppressive social basis than the monopolistic corporation or the company town. The people who called themselves Progressives began to create this culture around the turn of the century. Some seemed more preoccupied with efficiency than with justice, but at their most humane they laid the foundation for the twentieth-century welfare state. Whatever the ultimate consequences of their reform efforts, the

Progressives developed new political and intellectual strategies for containing the corrosive power of chance.

Chance, to be sure, had always been corrosive; vulnerability to disaster had been a constant component of human consciousness. But the rise of industrial capitalism sharpened the sense of unpredictability in the human imagination of disaster. In preindustrial times, it was possible to persuade oneself that calamities were natural and even somewhat predictable events—seasonal famines and epidemics, for example, seemed an inescapable part of an unchanging cosmos. But under industrial capitalism, new kinds of calamities occurred, unconnected to natural cycles but clearly related to policy decisions made by particular people. When fate had a human face, it was harder to accept hardship as a decree of destiny.

The Progressive movement, for all its ideological and cultural contradictions, was at bottom animated by a humane desire to mitigate the destructiveness at the heart of capitalist development. The sacrificing of workers' economic security on the altar of profitability was too much for Progressives to take; they wanted to counteract the random forces of the market with a reassertion of the public good. Progressive ideology was a more flexible and secular version of evangelical rationality; it still contained the evangelical emphasis on enforcing the ethos of self-control (as in the prohibition crusade and the first "war on drugs," both conducted under Progressive auspices). But it also depended on the new managerial language of social efficiency and pragmatic compromise (which even such Protestant moralists as Theodore Roosevelt and Woodrow Wilson could learn to speak).

What brought many Progressives together was the ideal of a revitalized civic culture, especially in the city. Within the few decades since the Civil War, immigrants and native rural folk alike had crowded into urban areas in search of sweat shop or factory jobs. Slumlords promoted a riot of unregulated real estate development. Jerry-built tenements proliferated within the city; industrial wastelands sprawled on its fringes. The typical metropolis resembled nothing more than a mere "accident, a railway, water, or industrial accident," according to one reform journalist—who like many Progressives was repelled by the appalling conditions of the modern slum. Municipal reform meant a variety of enterprises: cleansing the city government of corruption and the city streets of filth, replacing political cronyism with planning expertise as the chief criterion for public office; raising government revenues to create and maintain public spaces;

developing social insurance and other schemes designed to salve the abrasions of accident in ordinary people's lives. What Progesssives described somewhat vaguely as "the social idea" was an attempt to create a humane civic order from "the hideous anarchy and accident" of the American city—to use the journalist's Brand Whitlock's phrase.[14]

Perhaps the most anarchic force at work in the late-nineteenth-century city was capitalism itself. Despite capitalists' perverse tendency to label themselves "conservatives" (then and now), they usually sought to conserve nothing except their own and their shareholders' profits. It was still possible, of course, to claim that monetary rewards were the result of meritorious work; but as largely unregulated financial and real estate markets made men rich overnight, the link between hard work and wealth became looser in many minds. Indeed as Washington Gladden and numerous other critics argued, what happened at the Boards of Trade and Stock Exchanges was often "simply gambling, nothing more nor less."[15]

By the 1890s, the effort to distinguish gambling and legitimate business involved ever more difficult rhetorical contortions. The rhetoric of success and failure reflected the influence of an ethos of chance taking—even of play. The words "winner" and "loser" became stand-ins for one's station in life.[16] This subtle shift from Providence back toward Fortuna betokened the survival of a secular culture of chance in the belly of the capitalist beast. Similar nomenclature—the use of such terms as "banking games," for example, to categorize faro and roulette—suggested attempts to legitimize gambling by associating it with business.

Wondering "What is Gambling?" in 1895, John Bigelow raised some discomfiting comparisons—discomfiting, that is, to anyone concerned about contrasting business virtue with gambling vice. What, he wondered, was "the ethical distinction between between putting one's money on a wheel of fortune" and "underwriting a policy of insurance" or "buying shares in a corporation"? In a providentialist culture of control, determined to distinguish between virtuous businessmen and vicious gamesters, these were subversive questions. What if the captain of industry were really no better than a common gambler?[17]

Few Progressives were willing to risk this question. Most maintained a sharp distinction between legitimate business and gambling; they aimed to regulate the former, extirpate the latter. Many Social Gospel ministers believed that it was possible to remove the gambling element from business by prohibiting speculative practices, such as buying and selling on margin. As the Methodist Reverend H. C. Vrooman wrote in 1891: "The Christianization of business on a mutualistic basis is the immediate hope for the final elimination of that monster of 'chance,' which has ruled the world for so long."[18] Apart from moral exhortation, it was not clear how Vrooman intended to accomplish that goal.

But the basic principle, at least, was clear. For most Progressives, mutual gain was the key to differentiating Christianized business from gambling: in a fair commercial transaction, both parties get what they want; in gambling the winner takes directly from the loser. "There is no mutual exchange. The desire of the one is that the other shall lose," the Yale philosopher Frank Freeman wrote in 1907. "Gambling, then, in the nature of the case causes a loosening of social ties. It sets each man's hand against his brother and this is of the very essence of immoral action."[19]

For decades, observers of American culture had wondered whether this sort of critique could be made more broadly. Tocqueville was the most prescient, when he identified "individualism" as the fragmented underside of egalitarianism. "Not only does democracy make every man forget his ancestors," he wrote, "but it hides his descendants and separates his contemporaries from him; it throws him back forever upon himself alone and threatens in the end to confine him within the solitude of his own heart."[20] Freeman, like other Progressives, overlooked the possibility that the "loosening of social ties" he linked to gambling might be traced as well to a more diffuse social tendency: the competitive individualism at the core of market society.

But individualism was a widespread cultural ethos with deep reserves of moral legitimacy. Gambling had none. Policy, faro and other betting games had numerous unsavory associations with an urban underworld: they promoted police corruption (and vice versa); they tempted the unwary to lose self-control. Progressives saw "gambling hells" as appropriate targets for extinction, alongside whorehouses and (sometimes) saloons as well. Maintaining Comstock's fervor, they gradually embraced a more capacious outlook. In the end they were extraordinarily successful.

By 1910 legal or illegal gambling had hit a low ebb, rarely matched before in our history. Horse racing survived in Kentucky, Maryland, and a few other select locations—though even New York banned the sport from 1910 to 1913. On the frontier, antigambling campaigns achieved unprecedented gains. At least for a while, the forces of systematic self-control sustained the compliance of the majority. The effects were remarkable. "Well, things ain't just the same," said a storekeeper in northern Arizona, "six months after the gambling curse had been lifted" in 1908: "I don't sell as many silk shirts and giddy neckties as I used to; but I figure out I sell a whaling sight more pork and beans—and get paid for them." Staples of life displaced the fripperies of fashion: this was the sort of comment that resonated with Progressive moralism.[21]

Like the Prohibition movement, the Progressive crusade against gambling tapped into middle-class longings for stability and social cleansing. Casinos and saloons suffered from their association with an urban underworld of prostitution and political chicanery. Respectable folk were tired of compromises with corruption, ready to reconceive their secularized Protestant ethos as a unifying national creed. This would require a little less Protestantism, a little more pragmatism—the beginnings of the shift toward a managerial culture of control.

One can see that transition clearly in the changing approach to gambling reform. In *If Christ Came to Chicago* (1894), the Reverend William T. Stead quoted a gaming house proprietor's interpretation of the failure of reform: "Simply that the fever has broken out all over the body corporate. There are small games all over the city and invariably will be as long as the legal outlet for the disease is closed." To Stead this was merely the counsel of fatalism, yet later Progressives would find it at least partly persuasive. The public health idiom of fever encouraged a more flexible approach—one that recognized gambling as a symptom of some deeper disturbance that might have to be addressed if the sickness were to run its course.[22]

Biological language also underwrote a more pragmatic approach to gambling reform. The sociologist W. I. Thomas identified what he called "the Gaming Instinct" in 1900; it was rooted, as commentators before him had disapprovingly noted, in the desire for risk and excitement. But Thomas dropped the tone of disapproval. His adoption of the neutral term "instinct" represented a move away from the bullying moralism that characterized Comstock's thrusts at corruption. Thomas's greater psychological subtlety surfaced in such remarks as: "our problem is not to explain the gambler, but to explain the business man"—that is, the prudently calculating bourgeois. Rather than mere moral weakness, the gambler's obsession with risk represented a hunger for excitement that must be assuaged. The question was how.[23]

Complications arose when the Progressives moved from diagnosis to remedy. The more secular and pragmatic reformers (Walter Lippmann, Jane Addams) began to wonder how thrill seekers might be satisfied by more acceptable entertainments—how the gambler, for example, might give up his titillation at the tables and still live "a life that shall be truly interesting" (in Lippman's revealing words).[24]

Lippmann's patronizing phrase suggests how the managerial ethos could justify manipulative social policy. The early decades of the twentieth century were the golden age of "democratic social engineering"—an oxymoron that captured the Progressive faith in the experts' capacity to manipulate the masses toward "wholesome" ends. The Progressives' taming of chance was rooted in the humane desire to mitigate the cruelties of laissez-faire, but also in a less attractive longing to make the entire society function more efficiently—a longing that was often shaped by racist assumptions. In fact, the emergence of racial hierarchies supposedly based in science provided a new, secular set of categories for sustaining cosmic order. For many Progressives, eugenics became a centerpiece of reform, and "perfecting the race" became as important as promoting "the social idea."[25]

Scientific racism was only one symptom of a much broader social tendency—an eagerness to contain randomness in biological categories and make chance behave in accordance with "natural law." Faith in the natural harmony of Providence and Progress had been a cornerstone of evangelical rationality for decades. The doctrine had faced and largely evaded an unprecedented challenge in the spread of Darwinian thought after the Civil War. John Dewey summarized that challenge retrospectively in 1910: "In laying hands upon the sacred ark of absolute permanency, in treating the forms that had been regarded as types of fixity and perfection as originating and passing away, the *Origin of Species* introduced a mode of thinking that in the end was bound to transform the logic of knowledge, and hence the treatment of morals, politics, and religion." Darwin's emphasis on chance, change, and novelty in nature allowed all sorts of thinkers to question whether this or that allegedly timeless ideal was adapting successfully to evolving social conditions.[26]

Yet Dewey and his Progressive contemporaries, like earlier evolutionary thinkers, avoided the full implicatons of Darwinism by applying it inconsistently. Certain ideas—democracy, science, progress—remained exempt from the gimlet gaze of skeptical inquiry. Recalling the rhetorical strategies of Fiske and Spencer, Progressives like Dewey and Lippmann sanctified Darwinian progress as a secular version of Providence. But they redefined mastery as management rather than will—the organization of collective expertise rather than the celebration of individual effort.

The managerial version of Darwinian progress invoked a variety of deterministic idioms to create a vision of global mastery. The reach of this rhetoric depended on the intertwining of beliefs in the superiority of Anglo-Saxon civilization and the inevitablity of its advance. Senator Albert Beveridge, a leading Progressive, showed how a Darwinian rhetoric of empire could tame chance in his argument for the annexation of the Philippines:

> It is destiny that the world shall be rescued from its natural wilderness and from savage men. Civilization is no less an evolution than the changing forms of animal and vagetable life. Surely and steadily the reign of law, which is the very spirit of liberty, takes the place of arbitrary caprice. Surely and steadily the methods of social order are bringing the whole earth under their subjection. And to deny that this is right, is to deny that civilization should increase. In this great work the American people must have their own part. They are fitted for the work as no people has ever been fitted; and their work lies before them.[27]

The ideology of imperialism came the closest to providing a secular substitute for the old synthesis of Providence and Will, as orators like Beveridge summoned Anglo-Saxons to a destiny at once biologically and divinely decreed.

Yet perhaps the major idiom of Darwinian progress—and certainly the longest-lived—was technological determinism, which often worked in tandem with doctrines of white supremacy to sanction the spread of empire. From the technological determinist's perspective, material advance was the engine of social evolution; human values and beliefs were always lagging behind institutional change. Factories and railroads, for example, created new economic institutions, then people spent decades formulating new cultural values that reflected the new institutional reality. This was the pattern the sociologist W. F. Ogburn would describe as "cultural lag." Nowhere was it more apparent, evolutionary progressives believed, than in the persistence of the culture of chance amid the triumph of industrial capitalism. Ordinary folk stubbornly refused to adjust their thinking to conform to principles of linear cause and effect—or what the economist Thorstein Veblen called "the discipline of the machine."[28]

In *The Theory of the Leisure Class* (1899), Veblen excoriated the belief in luck, which he found among "leisure class" sportsmen and other native-born groups as well as immigrant peasants and preindustrial folk generally. It was, he thought, a mere relic of primitive animism. As Veblen put it, making his own utilitarian standards explicit: "apart from all question of the beauty, worth, or beneficence of any animistic belief, there is a place for a discussion of their [*sic*] economic bearing on the serviceability of the individual as an economic factor, and especially as an industrial agent." Belief in luck was sand in the gears of the industrial machine and therefore an impediment to progress. The mainspring of efficiency, in contrast, was a work force with heads uncluttered by superstition and filled instead with matter-of-fact understanding of cause and effect. Non-gamblers, all.[29]

Sounding like nothing so much as a twenty-first century social scientist discussing "obstacles to modernization in the Third World," Veblen wrote: "This lowering of efficiency through a penchant for animistic methods of apprehending facts is especially apparent when taken in the mass—when a given population with an animistic turn is viewed as a whole." Veblen did not specify which populations in the United States might be so afflicted, but he gave a hint of how widespread he thought the problem was when he noted that "the gambling spirit which pervades the sporting element shades off by insensible gradations into that frame of mind which finds gratification in devout observances." The dead game sport and the superstitious charwoman had more in common than they knew.[30]

The culture of chance, for Veblen and other evolutionary Progressives, included the religious as well as the secular devotees of *mana*—anyone who sought to conjure grace through ritual. Some critics of gambling sympathized with the religious aspirations that hovered around it: John Bigelow admitted that "the gaming table may become as effective a means of grace as the communion table," insofar as both might promote an awareness of our dependence on an inscrutable Providence.[31] But Veblen wanted no part of dependency; his ideal of the rational technician was a reprise of republican manliness.

Yet Veblen's apotheosis of mastery, like Emerson's, continued to be celebrated in a deterministic framework. The mechanisms of industrial-

ization worked inexorably; values would automatically evolve to meet the
new industrial conditions. The discipline of the machine would gradually
stamp its imprint on the laboring population; rationality would spread.
Meanwhile, we would have to live with the confusions created by cultural lag.

The vision of a huge plan of progress, unfolding under the direction
of Science rather than God, was the managerial substitute for evangelical
faith in Providence. Both the religious and secular idioms allowed room
for a paradoxical coexistence of free will and determinism, and both denied the very existence of the random. Despite his radical pose, Veblen
had more than he let on in common with respectable church ladies. Under Providence or Progress, the philosophical consensus remained fundamentally the same.

Yet on the boundaries of the consensus, a new intellectual universe
was beginning to take shape. The emergence of probabilistic, statistical
thinking suggested a new way of taming chance—not by pretending it
didn't exist, but by reducing it to an outlier or a standard deviation. This
was the thinking behind many Progressive reform proposals, especially
those insurance plans aimed at creating collective responsibility for individual loss.

Statistics underwrote infant schemes of social insurance—giving mu-
tuality some institutional foundation and material reward. As early as
1891, disciples of the utopian Edward Bellamy had grasped that unemployment compensation suggested "how to counteract chance" in the
economic realm. European social democrats put similar insights into public policy. British social insurance derived from "slate clubs" that had been
organized as mutual insurance and betting operations by the working
class, and which were eventually superseded by the British National Insurance Act of 1911—the purpose of which was "to build 'a new foundation of averages' in place of 'the old foundation of chance.'" Actuarial
tables and group liability would contain the impact of accident under industrial capitalism—at least in Great Britain. In the United States,
Theodore Roosevelt's efforts to implement social insurance met con-
gressional opposition, and the creation of a successful program awaited
the New Deal.[32]

Nevertheless, probabilistic thought was seeping steadily into American culture by the turn of the century. The growth of life insurance firms
was only the most obvious example of the spreading institutional base for

statistical thinking. Marketing research was another; some observers thought it might even lead to the quantification of good taste. The literary critic Hamilton Wright Mabie wrote in 1894 that "the mind revolts against chance as a determining factor in any field, but the persistency of its revolt in this particular field [publishing] is evidenced by the constantly repeated effort to secure trustworthy data regarding the relative popularity of books. These efforts assume that there are principles of taste or conditions of culture determining the choice of books, which may be discovered if the data can be collected."[33] Here as elsewhere, statistical information presented itself—at least to one enthusiast—as the crucial instrument for plumbing the mysteries of the public mind and decoding the dark secrets of public taste. It was, in other words, another instrument for extending a managerial culture of control.

Even when it was socially humane, this culture could still be philosophically vacant. Statistics might acknowledge the existence of chance but rob it of any real significance. Yet the mere acknowledgment of chance opened hitherto undreamt-of possibilities to more venturesome thinkers. Probabilistic thought promoted uncritical faith in statistics but also led to the abandonment of the positivist quest for certainty. The postpositivist intellectual universe was more ecumenical, less hostile toward the culture of chance. Indeed, even as rationalists like Veblen derided superstition, many other educated Amercans were becoming more fascinated with it, even sympathetic toward it. A seismic shift in sensibility was under way.

THE RESURGENCE OF THE PRIMITIVE

The "fondness for old follies," as one commentator called it, swelled steadily during the waning two decades of the nineteenth century. By the 1890s, mass-circulation magazines were full of reporting on folk beliefs. Popular historians dredged the past for superstitions from Elizabethan to Victorian times. Intrepid reporters ventured from the swamps of south Georgia to the wild west coast of Ireland, collecting odd rituals and charming fancies for cultivated audiences. The American Folk-Lore Society, founded in 1888, created a scholarly discipline to complement the surge in public fascination. Folklorists quickly began compiling lists of omens, portents, charms, and other bits of arcana peculiar to particular localities or ethnic traditions. About all this activity there was sometimes a sense of urgency, a feeling that these strange beliefs had to be recorded before they vanished from an increasingly disenchanted world.[34]

The growing fascination with folklore revealed an implicit recognition that progress had a price. Collectors of "old follies" were animated by a notion that in the passage to modernity, something of value and beauty might have been lost. The sense of loss was reinforced, ironically, by the widespread faith in social evolution—and especially by the tendency to express it in pseudo-Darwinian metaphors. If the human race was an organism, evolving toward an ever more complex existence, then there might be a point at which the adulthood of civilization began to signify decline. To think of the Anglo-Saxon as the most advanced "race" was also to think of it as the one most likely to begin losing its vitality. Projection of childlike qualities onto subject peoples provided paternalistic justification for imperialism but also suggested that the imperialists would be superseded as they faded into senescence and the subalterns grew to vigorous maturity. If civilizations resembled individual organisms, then progress could be come a self-canceling scheme. Social as well as personal decay—and ultimately death—was always on the agenda.

The common analogy between individual and social development made nostalgia the companion of belief in linear progress. In the popular imagination, romantic reverence for childhood combined with pseudo-Darwinian theories to create a powerful primitivist impulse. Primitivism fed an attraction for "the childhood of the race"—whether it was located in premodern Europe or among the childlike folk of the present. The catchphrase "ontogeny recapitulates phylogeny" captured the alleged biological parallels between children and savages. To Americans who felt increasingly "overcivilized"—vulnerable to "race suicide" (as Theodore Roosevelt warned) and afloat in a spiritual void—both children and savages embodied freshness, vitality, and spontaneity. And both groups clung to amulets, charms, and faith in luck—a way of looking at the world that could only be called superstitious.[35]

Longings to reconnect with childhood fostered the fascination with folklore, spreading it beyond a small circle of scholars. "Many who do not care for folklore as a subject of research are pleased to have recalled to them the fancies, beliefs, and customs of childhood," wrote the folklorist Fanny D. Bergen in a preface to her edition of *Current Superstitions* (1896). Yet Bergen's colleague William Wells Newell, in an introduction to the same volume, reasserted progressive assumptions as a counter-weight to sympathy for childish beliefs. He defined superstition as "a belief respecting causal sequence, depending on reasoning proper to an outgrown culture." The less technologically advanced a culture, the less control its people could exercise over their environment, and the more "chance events" it was a necessary to explain by superstition. Accident pervaded "all human conduct," but "uncertainty appears to be the greater, the reaction against the natural conditions less definite, the more primitive is the life." Newell, anticipating the anthropologist Bronislaw Malinowski's famous argument that magic is premature technology, showed how professional scholars could dismiss superstition as childish reasoning—even as some of their colleagues began openly appreciating its charm.[36]

This was not simply a case of the boys against the girls. It may be that men were more socialized to disdain superstition, women to appreciate its charm, but many thoughtful Americans embodied contradictory attitudes within themselves. Mark Twain's fiction, for example, revealed one man's profound ambivalence toward conventional ideas of human advance. Long before his financial disasters and his daughter's death, when he was still half-attached to belief in progress, Twain bemusedly satirized the supersitious child-world in *The Adventures of Tom Sawyer* (1876). Tom Sawyer and Huckleberry Finn are both veteran conjurers, though they adopt different methods for, say, removing warts. (For Huck, the mojo is a buried, bloody bean; for Tom, a dead cat.) But Tom is a little more credulous, wrapped in his own self-confirming cocoon of beliefs, festooned with amulets and charms. He refuses to swim with Injun Joe and Huck "because he found that in kicking off his trousers he had kicked off his string of rattlesnake rattles off his ankle, and he wondered how he escaped cramp so long without the protection of the mysterious charm. He did not venture outside until he found it." Tom experiences a spiritual crisis when a marble, which he buries with all the proper incantations, fails on being exhumed to have produced "all the marbles you ever lost" in a hole dug to contain them. "Tom's whole structure of faith was shaken to its foundations," Mark Twain wrote, noting that Tom forgot all the times this had happened before.[37]

Mark Twain's attitude toward Hannibal was more complex than mere nostalgia. Despite the sometimes elephantine whimsy that enveloped his evocations of it, Hannibal was the mother lode of memories Twain mined for his greatest work; it was also the playground of his imagination. Twain's creative remembering helped make Hannibal an emblem of free play as well as foolish superstition. Indeed, as Huck Finn realized, there was an element of play in the use of amulets and charms, not to mention the deployment of other superstitious rituals; a boy did not have to be as credulous as Tom to participate in paying homage to Fortuna.

Thinking back, Mark Twain recreated a child's experience (or fantasy) of almost pure potentiality, a truly enchanted universe. "Saturday morning was come, and all the summer world was bright and fresh, and brimming with life," Twain wrote in the talismanic beginning to *Tom Sawyer*. "Cardiff Hill, beyond the village and above it, was green with vegetation, and it lay just far enough away to seem a Delectable Land, dreamy, reposeful, and inviting." The child world of Hannibal met and mingled with the worlds of memory, desire, and imagination; play was the lingua franca of this "Delectable Land."[38]

And by the time Twain was writing his novels, play was increasingly confined to the sphere of childhood; for most adults, especially respectable Protestants, serious play was often little more than a memory—or an observation of the playful, childlike Other. As Victorian adulthood began to seem oppressive to the WASP bourgeoisie, the alleged childishness of African Americans and other ethnic minorities began to seem less a cause for contempt than a reason for sentimental bemusement or even covert admiration.

The commercial culture of chance reflected that growing complexity. The imagery in cartoons and sheet music was full of ridiculously ignorant Irish and black gamblers, cool but irresponsible frontier gamblers, and exotic but ominous gypsy fortune-tellers.[39] In short there were stereotypes aplenty, including straightforward exercises in the assignment of racial traits. The "coon songs" of the Gilded Age played endless variations on common racial caricatures. Gambling appeared in almost all of them. Will Heehan's song "Every Race Has a Flag but the Coon" (1901) was typical.

> *Just take a flannel shirt and paint it red,*
> *Then draw a chicken on it, with two poker-dice for eyes,*
> *An' have it wavin' razors round its head;*
> *To make it quaint, you've got to paint*
> *A possum with a pork chop in its teeth;*

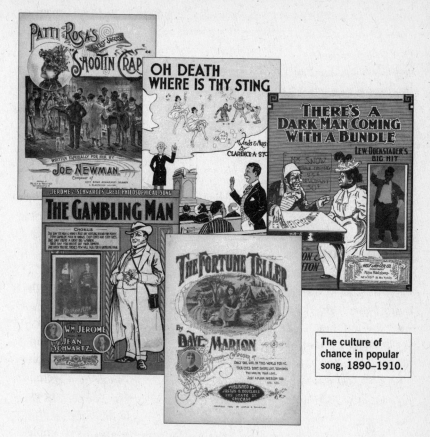

The culture of chance in popular song, 1890–1910.

> To give it tone, a big ham-bone
> You sketch upon a banjo underneath,
> And be sure not to skip just a policy slip,
> Have it marked four-eleven-forty-four.[40]

(In policy lore, that number combination possessed mystical associations with the promise of a big win.)

Heehan's coon song was contemptuous; others were burlesque. But most were patronizing evocations of black people's supposed preference for spending and play over thrift and work. Gambling was a necessary component of the carefree Sambo stereotype, gone to the big city. No longer just a rural buffoon, the citified Sambo knew how to enjoy women and liquor as well as "rollin' de bones." He was ignorant, ungrammatical, and prodigal, but he had fun. Indeed his prodigality constituted the core of his appeal.

I've got money now to throw to the birds,
I buy my chickens by the herds—

says a successful gambler in a coon song of 1899. Behind the racist sneer, coon songs contained a foretaste of what would become the main attraction (to whites) of African American cultural style in the late twentieth century: its apparent ease and freedom from unnecessary self-constraints.[41]

African Americans who stayed in the rural South acquired a different but related symbolic significance. In the Northern white imagination, Southern blacks became embodiments of local color, exotic remnants of a regional social fabric that was already fraying under the standardizing impact of industrialization. Yet some local colorists were more than mere purveyors of nostalgia. Charles Waddell Chesnutt was a highly educated light-skinned black North Carolinian whose stories of plantation life after the war were eventually published as *The Conjure Woman* (1899).[42]

Chesnutt created two narrators for these folktales. One is an Ohio businessman named John, who buys a ruined North Carolina plantation with the hope of resurrecting its vineyards and raising grapes commercially. He is a representative of rationality, an imperial modernizer with plans to develop this backward, colonial economy. John's wife, Annie, who accompanies him on this venture, is subject to bouts of neurasthenia—the late-Victorian term for protracted depression. The second narrator is the oldest ex-slave on the place, Uncle Julius, who entertains John and Annie on the front porch of the big house with tales of the recent past.

Through Uncle Julius, Chesnutt evoked the enchanted universe of the African American folk, during and after slavery. Chesnutt's own view of Julius's stories was complex and elusive. He was as skeptical and bemused as John or any other educated person; he was careful to provide evidence for naturalistic explanations of most of the magic in the tales—enough to make Julius look like little more than a clever confidence man.[43] Yet Chesnutt also took these stories seriously. He recognized that the beliefs they described, however absurd from the rationalist point of view, were a legitimate effort to sustain spiritual meaning and social connection in lives full of arbitrary violence.

The story "Sis' Becky's Pickaninny" suggests the largest significance of Chesnutt's vernacular culture of chance. John begins by reporting that Annie, having temporarily rallied when they first moved to North Carolina, has relapsed into "a settled melancholy, with vague forebodings of impending misfortune." John tries reading novels to her and arranges for the "hands" to serenade her with "plantation songs"; friends drop by; frequent letters arrive "from the North"—"nothing seemed to arouse her from the depression into which she had fallen." Then one day John notices Julius fingering a small object as they sit together on the porch. He asks what it is, and Julius tells him it is a rabbit's foot: "'I kyars it wid me fer luck, sah.'"[44]

John slips into a lecture. "'Julius,' I observed, half to him and half to my wife, 'your people will never rise in the world until they throw off these childish superstitions and live by the light of reason and common sense.' . . . 'It is ridiculous,' assented my wife, with faint interest." Julius insists the rabbit's foot has brought him good luck for forty years: "'I had a good marster befo' de wah, en I wa'n'y sol' erway, en I woz sot free; en dat 'uz all good luck.'" John, ever the rationalist, rises to the bait. "'But that doesn't prove anything,' I rejoined, 'Many other people have gone through a similar experience, and probably more than one of them had no rabbit's foot.'" It is the classic rationalist response to superstition.[45]

Julius says he will demonstrate the power of a rabbit's foot by telling the story of Sis' Becky, who is separated from her infant son Mose when her master, the feckless Colonel Pendleton, sells her to buy a prize racehorse named Lightnin' Bug. Aunt Nancy is left in charge of Mose, who cries and cries for his mother, refuses to eat, and starts to look so "peaked" that Aunt Nancy takes him to Aunt Peggy, the conjure woman down on the Wilmington Road. In exchange for "a mess er green peas," Aunt Peggy takes Mose for the evening, and works a root on him that turns him into a hummingbird, who flies away to visit his mother. A few days later she turns Mose into a "mawkin' bird," with similar results: Sis' Becky feels happier and closer to Mose, and Mose feels "mo' pearter en better 'n he had be'n fer a long time." Finally, in return for Aunt Nancy's "best Sunday handkercher," Aunt Peggy arranges with a "hawnet" to sting Lightnin' Bug repeatedly on the knees. Seeing its swollen joints, Pendleton insists the horse was defective from the start and tries to cancel the deal, but the horse-trader refuses to return Sis' Becky. Aunt Peggy mixes up a voodoo bag, buries it in Sis' Becky's yard, and conjures her into a grave and mysterious illness. Deciding that "a lame hoss wuz better n' a dead nigger," the horse-trader relents, and Sis Becky is reunited with Mose, who from then on could whistle like a mockingbird.[46]

John dismisses Julius's story as an "'ingenious fairy tale,'" but Annie declares that "'the story bears the stamp of truth, if ever a story did.'" When John tells Julius that the story "doesn't establish what you set out to prove,—that a rabbit's foot brings good luck," Julius says of course it does—just ask the "young missis" here. "'I rather suspect,' replied my wife promptly, 'that Sis' Becky had no rabbit's foot.' 'You is hit de bull's eye de fus' fire, ma'm,' assented Julius. 'Ef Sis' Becky had had a rabbit's foot, she nebber would 'a' went th'oo all dis trouble.'" John leaves the two talking, and when he returns Julius is gone. But from that day forward, Annie's health improves dramatically. Within a few weeks, after she has recovered completely, John discovers she has been carrying Julius's rabbit foot in her handkerchief.[47]

"Sis Becky's Pickaninny" captures the complexity of the African American culture of chance. As in his other stories, Chesnutt described a cosmos characterized by fluid boundaries between animals and humans, nature and the supernatural. People conjured *mana* to sustain communal and familial ties against the destructive power of slavery. But the frame-story of the rabbit foot suggests that *mana* could still cross the racial divide. Annie is lifted from her languor by her belief in Julius's story, her perception of his logic, and (most important) her acceptance of his rabbit foot. The boundaries between mind and body turn out to be fluid, too. Chesnutt's fiction recreated a world where cosmic truths are multiple, shifting, and elusive—but also potentially omnipresent.

In this pluralistic universe, conjuring preserved a therapeutic value. Its results were not scientifically verifiable in any positivistic sense, but they were results nonetheless. Its truth lay in ritual performance rather than empirical demonstration. But its "illocutionary force" could heal the body as well as the soul. This power was something a rational capitalist like John could never acknowledge.

Recognizing the limitations of John's worldview, Chesnutt granted the conjure woman her dignity and wished her clients well in their search for *mana*. Perhaps more important, he also recognized the centrality of play in the culture of chance—not merely play-acting (though that was part of it) but the creation of a parallel universe. In a sense, conjurers and their clients enacted the imaginative freedom of the artist. Their willingness to play (with ideas, rituals, artifacts) constituted the source of their creativity. In turning them into the subject matter of his own art, Chesnutt acknowledged his kinship with them and his dependence on them.

Both Chesnutt and Mark Twain celebrated the culture of chance as a source of artistic inspiration, a mix of memory and desire, and a realm of childlike freedom. This combination appealed profoundly to to a broad swath of the literate public—not only the middle-class folk who flocked to Mark Twain's lectures, but the more educated elite who subscribed to the *Atlantic,* where Chesnutt's stories appeared. The attractions of a playful and childlike culture arose in part from its inaccessibility—at least to the sober and responsible adult. For the Protestant middle and upper classes, amulets were becoming mere amusements. In Chesnutt's 1899 story, John notes in passing that the rabbit's foot had acquired a "jocular popularity among white people . . . " Other charms took the form of vacation souvenirs. Like the "lucky spoons" sold at the 1893 Chicago World's Fair, at the Liberty Bell Exhibit in Philadelphia in the 1890s, or at any of many other tourist attractions, souvenir charms embodied memories of respite from routine.[48] Adult responsibilities (at least in the dominant culture of control) left little space for the free play of the imagination; that was for children (at least in the idealized bourgeois vision of domesticity) and childlike races.

With supersition and childhood linked to a realm of freedom that was largely unavailable to adults, small wonder that "old follies" began to be taken more seriously—not merely as charming reminders of childish things but also as a legitimate way of apprehending the universe. The experience of seeing one person's religion turn into another's superstition led many educated people on both sides of the Atlantic toward a more ecumenical appreciation of previously scorned rituals and a more relativistic understanding of religious truth. A series of articles and letters in the *Athenaeum* on "Other People's Superstitions" concluded that "it is quite usual for persons professing one creed to condemn in the main the tenets of an alien creed, and at the same time to adopt the superstitious beliefs and practices connected with that creed." Other observers agreed that the reflexive, implicitly rationalist dismissal of superstition had begun to ring hollow.[49]

After decades of anticipating a millennium, in which the shadows of occult lore would yield entirely to the noontide of Protestantism and science, evangelical rationalists were forced to acknowledge the stubborn persistence of superstition, even among the educated. Under these circumstances the old derision began to seem hypocritical at best. In 1895 the British *Spectator* predicted that "we ought to expect and to prepare ourselves for a reaction setting in before very long in favor of 'superstition.'"[50]

By then the reaction was already well launched. Even sentimental commentators on superstition, who emphasized its childishness, began to take it more seriously as a form of perception and even knowledge. The folklorist William Wells Newell, who associated superstition with "an outgrown culture," admitted that the survival of such beliefs was owing to "more than the unintelligent and unconscious persistence of habit." Superstition made sense; it made things explicable in ways that continued to resonate, even with a skeptical modern intelligence. It expressed the feeling that even the most matter-of-fact empiricist might experience, the sense that one is in the presence of something uncanny, something unexplained. As *Scientific American* mused in 1891, "Nobody can fully explain the states of his own inner consciousness, or tell the reasons why, when [one is] in apparent good health, the atmosphere is luminous with transcendental glory, and anon is shadowed by dimly comprehended specters."[51]

This was a key move: from observation of the peculiar beliefs of primitive folk to meditation on the mysteries of our own "inner consciousness." Gradually the study of folklore shortened the distance between "us" and "them," revealing that civilized people and savages shared similar fears and longings. "The fairy-tales and ghost-stories of the countryside reveal a facet of universal human nature in a naive and ingenuous manner not to be discovered in any other development," Dr. Daniel Brinton wrote in 1898. "Deep down in the heart of man bides the firm conviction that he dwells in the midst of an unseen world, peopled with beings of strange powers, who move incessantly athwart the plans of his own life." Omens and portents, amulets and charms and conjuring rituals were all ways of acknowledging those powers and attempting to propitiate them.[52]

"For some strange reason," Brinton wrote, "there has been a wonderful revival within the past decade of nearly every medieval superstition, under various guises, in the most enlightened centers of the world. The practitioners of this modern sorcery, instead of concealing, advertise their claims, and urge them on the community under pseudo-scientific names and jargons. Palmistry, astrology, sympathetic magic, the doctrine of signatures, hiero-therapeutics, and all the farrago of fifteenth-century thaumaturgy, flourish to-day in Boston and New York, in Paris and

Chicago, to a degree surpassing anything known three centuries ago." By the end of the nineteenth century, Europeans and Americans alike viewed beliefs they had once dismissed as irrational with renewed fascination and respect. It was becoming harder to claim that superstition was confined to the ignorant and backward peoples of the earth.[53]

The reasons for this ferment may not have been as strange as Brinton supposed. By the time he was writing, the evangelical-rationalist consensus had begun to crumble. The problem was not simply that chance was inevitable in economic life, but also that the synthesis of Protestantism and science was no longer secure. The cosmology for the comfortable, created by Spencer and his popularizers, was now under siege from scientists and philosophers. By the turn of the century, neither the cosmos nor the individual seemed as unified or predictable as earlier generations had thought. European and American thinkers alike were challenging determinism on scientific grounds. Charles Peirce, the sometime mentor of William James, was one of several philosophers of science who began to develop a probabilistic notion of causality and a statistical idea of law. Such mathematicians as Henri Poincaré were increasingly willing to question claims to precision within their own and related disciplines, emphasizing the limitations of human senses and instruments. Chance was becoming more than an alias for ignorance: it was becoming a palpable force, with consequences both calculable and incalculable.

The consequences were fitfully apparent in discussions of evolutionary theory: biologists and later geneticists could openly confront the randomness in Darwinian theory instead of concealing it behind schemes of linear progress. Philosophers could, too, though only a few did so. Peirce was among the most perceptive. One of his earliest mentors had been Chauncey Wright, with whom he shared the intellectual intimacy of the Metaphysical Club. Recalling Wright's emphasis on the uncertainties of "cosmical weather," as well as his understanding of Darwinism, Peirce argued that to see natural laws or uniformities in nature as the result of evolution was to see them "not to be absolute, not to be obeyed precisely. It makes an element of indeterminacy, spontaneity, or absolute chance in nature," he wrote in 1891. We had to expect "a certain swerving of the facts from any formula."[54]

For anyone who demanded certainty, this could be disturbing news. It suggested, as the philosopher Ian Hacking has written, that "there are no constants in nature, over and above those numbers upon which we increasingly settle." "Natural law" was a statistical construction of regular-ity amid the chaotic unpredictability of the universe. "Chance pours in at every avenue of sense," Peirce wrote. "It is of all things the most ob-trusive." Statistical concepts of regularity allowed scientists to continue formulating orderly explanations while they acknowledged the obtru-siveness of contingency. Chance was becoming a legitimate category of scientific thought; certainty was becoming problematic. Among physicists (including even amateurs like Henry Adams), the discovery of X rays sig-naled the existence of cosmic forces that could not be mechanically measured; the conundrums of quantum mechanics were only a few years away. At the highest theoretical levels, positivist assumptions were crum-bling.[55]

Yet as Hacking makes clear, the theoretical acknowledgment of in-determinism allowed scientific practice to proceed as if certainty were still a viable goal. Statistical thinking tamed chance, at least provisionally. The probabilistic revolution reduced random occurrences to predictable unpredictability. In the "normal science" of the laboratory, chance re-mained little more than the standard deviation, the exception that proved the rule. Scientists might well grant its importance in theory while they remained positivists in everyday practice. In this way, the culture of con-trol could absorb and defuse the challenges posed by chance.

But outside the laboratory, the taming of chance remained less com-plete. The most direct challenge to established certainties—and the one best known to the general population—came in human psychology. Rather than a static collection of faculties creating a unified self, the psy-che began to seem fluid, filled with contradictory and often irrational im-pulses. Freudian psychoanalysis was only the most systematic formulation of this more dynamic understanding of human consciousness; novelists from Dostoevsky to Conrad were also engaged in recovering what D. H. Lawrence called the "primal, dark veracity" of unconscious instinctual life. American writers embarked on their own version of this quest. Theodore Dreiser probed the self-defeating obsessions bred by sexual de-sire; Stephen Crane explored "the delirium that encounters despair and death" in war; and Frank Norris returned repeatedly to the theme of de-generation, as his protagonists yield their humanity to the overwhelming power of "the brute" within them.[56]

For a broad range of artists and intellectuals as well as psychoanalytic thinkers, the unconscious mind evoked ambivalent fascination. As the home of archaic, unresolved yearnings, the unconscious possessed a double significance—it was the shelter for the superstitious beliefs that survived anachronistically in the modern mind, yet also the refuge of an emotional truth that had somehow become more elusive in a disenchanted world. The modernizer's pride in how far we have come coexisted with the primitivist's longings for lost vitality. Relief at throwing off "old follies" accompanied regret at their passing.

From the psychoanalytic perspective, it was not clear whether savage traits could be so easily surmounted. Freud and his followers, in effect, presented a secular doctrine of original sin. The apparent moral and intellectual advances of modern civilization, from the Freudian view, had created a mere crust on a caldron of eros and aggression. The discovery of the unconscious coincided with anthropologists' discovery of "the mind of primitive man"; psychoanalysis and other forms of depth psychology claimed to reveal the persistence of primitive thought patterns beneath the veneer of civilized morality. Superstition, it seemed to many, was less a remote remnant of superseded thought than a universal tendency of human consciousness. The most apparently civilized people were unable to repress it entirely.

Why were even educated people still attached to such silly customs as carrying lucky charms or refusing to travel on Fridays? Part of the answer, as always, was that life (and death) remained largely unpredictable and inexplicable, even among the more fortunate. The unspoken feeling that one was being toyed with by the gods was not confined to the socially marginal, as Mark Twain and Howells both understood. It was understandable that even literate folk might want to keep capricious malevolence at bay by any means necessary—including archaic rituals, half-ironically evoked.

Yet the new prestige of superstition stemmed from a more specific source as well: the conviction that beliefs thought to be magically efficacious might tell us something about the murky relation between the mind and the rest of the physical world. As the psychiatrist H. Addington Bruce observed in 1911, it was not surprising that superstitious rituals sometimes actually worked. Consider the great variety of rituals that have apparently charmed away warts—everything from rubbing a bean on the afflicted area, then throwing it in a well, to burying a bag filled with as many stones as there are warts to be removed. "In the light of modern discovery regarding the influence of the mind on bodily states," Bruce wrote, "it should surely be obvious that when cures are effected by such dissimilar charms it is not the particular charm but the faith it inspires that brings about the cure."[57] This conclusion was consistent with traditional beliefs regarding fetishes. Without faith, the fetish was nothing but trash; with it, the mojo might really make its owner stronger and braver; the conjuration of *mana* might heal physical ills—especially if their origin was obscurely emotional. Certainly Uncle Julius's rabbit foot worked for the dispirited Annie.

The annals of voodoo as well the lives of the Roman Catholic saints were full of such mysterious recoveries; during the late nineteenth century, the study of folklore began making them known to an educated public. The audience was receptive: Protestants had long had their own subterranean tradition of "soul-cure"; during the early 1900s it spread and fragmented into a variety of therapeutic agendas: Christian Science, New Thought, psychoanalysis, and other varieties of "mind cure," as psychotherapy in general became known. The new therapies "made what in our Protestant countries is an unprecedented use of the subconscious life," William James observed; they promised *Power Through Repose* (as did Annie Payson Call's best seller of 1906)—regeneration through reconnection with nature's "great powerhouse of being." The notion of the universe as a source of endless energy pervaded the mind-cure movement, preserving an abstract, modernized version of *mana*. There were no mediators between the self and the force at the heart of universe; all of the magic had to be concentrated in the self alone and its allegedly limitless powers of renewal. The disenchantment of the world might require the reenchantment of the self.[58]

Psychotherapists renounced magical mediation through material objects, but still merged matter and spirit with respect to the human individual, by stressing the centrality of mental attitudes to bodily health. The ferment of mind-cure arose from a broad dissatisfaction with mainstream religion and medicine—pastors and doctors who couldn't help when faced with neurasthenia or other mysterious forms of nervous illness. Psychosomatic pain had intellectual consequences. By encouraging a more fluid understanding of the relationship between mind and body, mind-cure promoted a distrust of Cartesian dualism, the philosophical basis of evangelical rationality; it also encouraged a more capacious un-

derstanding of what had previously been dismissed as meaningless superstition. By the 1910s, perceptive observers (including psychotherapists)
realized that superstition survived because it worked psychologically—at
least some of the time. Maybe the rabbit's foot really could conjure
enough confidence for a man to succeed in courtship or a woman to cure
herself of the blues. Belief in one's ability to capture *mana,* as Chesnutt
implied, could be a form of therapy.

The renewed interest in the therapeutic value of superstition involved a search for alternatives to modern modes of consciousness and
conduct. Educated Americans began to recognize that behavior they had
thought backward and futile was more complex and rewarding than it
had seemed. They also started to suspect that chance might pay a far
greater role in the universe than evangelical rationality had acknowledged.

The intellectual recovery of Fortuna was taking place at about the
same time that her temples were being shut down all across the land.
While the actual practice of gambling was less tolerated than ever before,
"the gambling spirit" acquired unprecedented luster. The revitalization of
chance took various forms, ranging from a masculine cult of risk that
could easily meld with Theodore Roosevelt's "strenuous life" to the
more serious philosophical explorations of William James.

THE GAMBLING SPIRIT

The new respect for the gambling spirit was part of a continuing conversation about manhood. Comstock and other evangelical moralists defined
manliness as self-mastery and submission to chance as emasculation. Yet
the examples Comstock chose suggested a haunting possibility: was the
creed of calculating diligence merely a morality for clerks? Nietzsche
posed the question most pointedly, but even High Victorians wondered if
the issues were more complex than Comstock and his ilk imagined. "The
gambling element in life," the Reverend John Ware told an audience at
the Boston Music Hall in 1871, was a near-universal tendency to take
chances for the excitement of it—for the hell of it, Ware might have said,
as he traced the impulse toward risk taking to primordial, volcanic energy.
Its effects on the compulsive gambler were truly appalling to behold.

"When the breath comes fast and hard; when the heart pulses painfully, as the tug for victory comes; when the eyes strain, the hands are clenched, the teeth are set, and the whole body is rigid, and the quick words leap, and the odds grow more fearful, and are dared to the brink of ruin, then you see the awful end to which with rapid stride this 'harmless thing' [gambling] hurries. It fastens like a vampire upon those who yield to it." The stakes in risk taking were spiritual as well as physiological. The ultimate risk was to resist Christianity by submitting to blind fate; to live a Christian life, in contrast, was to live in accordance with the divine law of Providence.[59]

All this was conventional enough, but Ware veered in a new direction when he asserted toward the end of his sermon that "this gambling element in itself is no unmitigated evil." Because God made it universal, there must be some use for it; indeed it might well be "the secret instinct and impulse which suggest and carry on great enterprises, which give tenacity in presence of difficulties, and prevent defeats from growing into despairs. It is this spirit which spurs us when flagging, and supplies new hope when old hopes fail." It brought Columbus to the New World, cheered Washington at Valley Forge, subdued a wild continent, and built a great American nation. The gambling spirit, for Ware, was an essential force that had to be harnessed but should never be suppressed.[60]

This stream of vitalism remained subterranean for years, but gradually surfaced toward the end of the nineteenth century. A growing preoccupation with masculine vitality returned the gambling spirit—though not gambling itself—to respectability. "Gambling is reprehensible, but the spirit that underlies it is noble," wrote a *Forum* contributor in 1891. "A genuine gambler is a great man gone wrong, and gambling is a misdirection of courage and energy and enterprise—of all those attributes that make man most manly."[61]

Social scientists, such as W. I. Thomas, used a Darwinian framework to link "the gaming instinct" with a fundamental life force. Even the most familiar "pleasures and pains," he argued, "go back for the most part to instincts developed in the struggle for food and rivalry for mates." Gambling was no exception. It was "a means of keeping up the conflict interest and securing all the pleasure-pain sensations of conflict activity with little effort and no drudgery." It acquired a special resonance as our daily lives became more shackled to industrial routine: unlike most occupations under industrial discipline, "in gambling the risk is imminent, the attentions strained, the emotions strong. . . . " Whatever pathological forms it might take, "the gaming instinct is born in all normal persons. It is one expression of a powerful reflex fixed far back in animal experience." Christian moralists had urged their audiences to transcend their animal impulses, but the revaluation of the primitive undercut this morality. If animality was vitality, then maybe even Christians could use a dose. And maybe taking chances was a way to keep the red blood coursing through our veins. The idea of a "gaming instinct" redefined risk as a fundamental life force.[62]

There was something peculiarly modern about this metaphorical revitalization of gambling. It did not, for example, involve a rehabilitation of planter-class prodigality; fin de siècle devotees of the gambling spirit celebrated *agon* over *alea*. The rhetorical rehabilitation of gambling drew on romantic and liberal tradition to celebrate the striving male self.

The founding document in that tradition was Goethe's *Faust* (1808, 1832), a romantic reinterpretation of the traditional tale in which a wandering conjurer/doctor, weary of life and longing for lost vitality, makes a pact with Mephistopheles: his soul in exchange for mastery of the world. In Goethe's version the focus is on Faust's restless pursuit of intense experience. Faust agrees that if he should ever say to the passing moment "Abide, you are so fair," Mephistopheles can have his soul. The conjurer/doctor is the ultimate gambler, betting his immortal soul on his ability to sustain a life of endless striving. In the end Faust is saved because God (or Goethe) approves that sort of life. "Who ever strives with all his power, / We are allowed to save," the angels say.[63]

The celebration of action without an object was an important covert strain in Victorian notions of heroism. It was best to have a clear and noble goal, but if one was not immediately in sight, action alone was preferable to inaction. "How dull it is to pause, to make an end, to rust unburnish'd, not to shine in use!" says Tennyson's Ulysses (1842). By 1900 such sentiments had been detached from Protestant moorings and pressed into the service of a revitalized masculinity, more activist but also more aimless than Victorian manliness had been. Theodore Roosevelt quoted Tennyson's words as the epigraph to *The Strenuous Life* (1900), which repeatedly celebrated risk-taking as a path to regenerated manhood.[64]

But by the end of the century, masculine risk-taking no longer lacked an object. Roosevelt urged his audience of middle- and upper-class men to look at the regenerative possibilities of empire. Business executives and salaried employees who feared the softness of sedentary life could find revitalizing force (at least vicariously) by supporting imperial adventures in the Caribbean and the Pacific. The value of empire was not just economic; it was psychological, social, and moral. Imperial struggle demanded a resurrection of martial virtue, which could serve as a powerful antidote to the corrupting effects of commerce while at the same time securing new sources of national wealth. Empire would dissolve the tension between prosperity and virtue. Or so Roosevelt, Beveridge, and other imperialists claimed.

And their message resonated with a large portion of the (white, male, middle- and upper-class) public—men who may well have felt hemmed in by domestic or organizational routine. Despite their continued exposure to the random movements of the market, their opportunities for risk-taking were limited. These were the sort of people who developed a new appreciation for the gambling spirit and its military manifestations, who recognized that some agonistic games of chance required the same sort of coolness under fire that we prized in our fighting men. Poker was the best example: "What a school of control it is!" announced the author of a poker manual in 1900. "Officers in the army and navy are always capital players because they are taught to restrain their tempers and emotions in the line of duty until it becomes second nature to them. Look at Admiral Dewey's face and see a crack poker player." Real men took risks with a poker face.[65]

The recovery of the gambling spirit could either undermine or reinforce a broader ethic of fortune. The typical approach to risk was more disciplined than spontaneous. As the example of Admiral Dewey suggests, the celebration of self-controlled risk-taking could lose sight of luck altogether and affirm a conventional male ideal of success through will and personal moral responsibility—a ideal that still pervaded advice to young men. In "A Divergence of Views Concerning Luck," the *Century* offered straight talk from an uncle to his nephew, who had complained of a run of "hard luck"—running his motor car into a cow, failing at his lessons, losing his credit at the shops. What bosh, says the uncle, pull your socks up, boy. "We have outgrown the use of charms and amulets. The civilized world has ceased to believe in the evil eye or 'controls.' It is time that we also outgrew the belief in luck."[66] One did not have to be a social scientist to mix moralism and manliness with metaphors of evolutionary progress. Admiral Dewey would no doubt have nodded his assent.

Yet the effort to reimagine the gambling spirit sometimes promoted an updated version of the ethic of fortune. Such novelists as Norris and Dreiser appeared to be creating a new type of risk-taking business hero, the Faustian gambler who dared to sport with Chance (which, like Fate or Force, was often capitalized in naturalistic novels). "Chance!" cries Magnus Derrick of Norris's *The Octopus* (1901). "To know it when it came, to recognize it as it passed fleet as a wind-flurry, grip at it, catch at it, blind, reckless, staking all upon the hazard of the issue, that was genius." And in *The Pit* (1903), when Norris's protagonist Curtis Jadwin is first drawn into trading in commodity futures, the author can barely contain himself: "In the air about him he seemed to feel an influence, a sudden new element, the presence of a new force. It was Luck, the great power, the great goddess, and all at once it had stooped from out the invisible, and just over his head passed swiftly in a rush of glittering wings." This was as close as an aspiring young American novelist could come to capturing the mysterious power of *mana*.[67]

But despite this fascination with the white-hot experience of hazard, naturalistic novelists tended to punish their protagonists, whose hubris nearly always led to their doom. Sporting with Chance was a dangerous business. Cooler heads tended to prevail. Hence the popularity of Admiral Dewey or fictional heroes like Owen Wister's *The Virginian* (1903), for whom risks were an opportunity to exercise formulaic manliness. Still, even wild-west adventure tales could sometimes rise above formula. A. H. Lewis's Wolfville stories presented a woman gambler, Cherokee Hall, as a voice of stoical wisdom regarding the acceptance of mysterious fate:

Life is like stud-poker; an' destiny's got an ace buried every time. It either out-lucks you or out-plays you when it's so inclined; an' it seems allers so inclined, destiny does, just as you're flatterin' yourself you got a shore thing. A gent's bound to play fa'r with Destiny; he can put a bet down on that. You can't hold six kyards; you can't deal double; you can't play no cold hands; you can't bluff destiny. All you-all can do is humbly and meekly pick up the five kyards that belongs to you, an' in a sperit of thankfulness and praise, an' frankly admittin' that that you're lucky to be allowed to play at all, do your lowly best tharwith.[68]

Or as the epitaph for another Wolfville resident stated:

JaCK KInG
LIfE AiN'T
iN
HOLDING A GOOD HAND
BUT
In PLAYing a PORE HAND
WeLL[69]

Such sentiments constituted a counterforce, however provisional, against the blustering, moralistic denials of luck that continued to blow across the American cultural landscape.

Yet the rediscovery of the gambling spirit could also lead in more philosophically profound directions. The vitalist longing to recover some sense of spontaneity in the universe was not reducible to mere reassertions of manliness. Consider the case of William James (1842–1910). He recoiled from the progressive vision of a perfectly managed world—"fie upon such a cattleyard of planet!" he wrote, as he sought to imagine a moral equivalent of war, an opportunity for revivifying risk, but in the service of peaceful purposes.[70] This in itself was a far more humane and capacious agenda than Roosevelt's strenuous life, but James's longings for revitalization led him further afield, on a search for supernatural meaning in what he feared was a meaningless universe. This modern quest was motivated by moral concerns: James wanted to vindicate ethical action in the world without resorting to providentialist conventions (secular or religious).

James became our greatest philosopher of chance. By the time he died in 1910, he had developed a point of view that in effect retranslated the insights of older, polytheistic cultures of chance into a modern philosophical idiom—down to and including his sympathy for mind-cure and other therapeutic departures from dualism. His radical empiricism was an extraordinarily imaginative effort to descibe and imagine a pluralistic universe, forever resistant to unified or dualistic explanation—"a world of pure experience," as James called it, "a big blooming buzzing confusion, as free from contradiction in its 'much-at-onceness' as it is all alive and evidently there."[71]

For James, "pure experience" became a kind of *mana,* a primal plenitude melding spirit and matter, thoughts and things. The experiential stream was unpredictable, unmanageable, and liberating. It overflowed conceptual categories and inundated theoretical systems, creating fresh opportunities for human risk—without which, James believed, neither belief nor moral choice was possible. In a culture that disdained the very idea of chance, James resurrected it and made it the center of his developing worldview. From the outset, his entire philosophical and moral project pivoted on the possibility of randomness in the universe, as an escape hatch from the prison house of Victorian certainty.[72]

In the 1870s, James had conversed with Chauncey Wright at the Metaphysical Club, and like Peirce had come away persuaded by Wright's insistence on the omnipresence of chance in nature. But unlike the nihilistic Wright, for whom chance was the assassin of cosmic order, James viewed chance as an opportunity for making meaning from cosmic disorder. Unlike most of his contemporaries, James refused to ignore the contradiction at the heart of the progressive consensus: between human freedom and deterministic natural law.

That conflict loomed especially large for James—a young man with strong spiritual yearnings, training to be physician in the relentlessly positivist atmosphere of post–Civil War medicine. For the scientist or skeptic, the question was clear: How could one reconcile familiar ideas of personal moral efficacy (not to mention religious belief) with the various mechanistic systems that were displacing traditional ideas of Providence?

Peirce addressed this question in the language of science and logic; James's idiom was more frankly personal and psychological. He articulated his struggle with particular clarity in two classic essays: "The Dilemma of Determinism" (1884) and "The Will to Believe" (1896). The first presented chance as an escape from a deterministic universe; the second resuscitated Pascal's wager, adducing a new, pragmatic set of reasons for gambling on God.

In "Dilemma," James made his ethical concerns central from the outset. He told the Harvard Divinity students that he would "disclaim openly on the threshold all pretension to prove to you that the freedom of the will is true. The most I hope is to induce some of you to follow my own example in assuming it true, and acting as if it were true." His first move was to observe that ideas of order in the world were rooted in the need for subjective satisfaction—what James would call, in another context, "the sentiment of rationality." He took aim at the most hallowed principle created by that sentiment, in either its evangelical or positivist forms: "the principle of causality, for example, what is it but a postulate, an empty name covering simply a demand that the sequence of events shall some day manifest a deeper kind of belonging of one thing with another than the mere arbitrary juxtaposition which now phenomenally appears? It is as much an altar to an unknown god as the one St. Paul found at Athens."[73]

James wanted to dissolve the chains of determinism by resurrecting the claims of chance. This was a daring move, one that he was sure would run afoul of responsible thinkers—who held that "chance is something the notion of which no sane mind can for an instant tolerate in the world. What is it, they ask, but barefaced crazy unreason, the negation of intelligibility and law?" Here James caught the dogmatic tone that had characterized both religious and secular assaults on chance for centuries: one is reminded of the stark choice posed by John Fiske between chance and law. But in fact, James said, there was nothing "intrinsically irrational or preposterous" about the notion of chance; we had merely become used to seeing it censoriously.[74]

Chance in itself was neither good nor bad. (No more than the forces of fate, or *mana*.) Indeed, chance events might sometimes satisfy the sentiment of rationality, James observed: chance "may be lucidity, transparency, fitness incarnate, matching the whole system of other things, when it once has befallen, in an unimaginably perfect way." All that you mean by calling it chance is that this is not guaranteed, that it may fall out otherwise. James was astonished that "so empty and gratuitous a hubbub should have found so great an echo in the hearts of men."[75]

Yet James may have glimpsed an explanation for the horror of chance, when he observed that "the idea of chance is, at bottom, exactly the same thing as the idea of gift,—the one being simply a disparaging, and the other a eulogistic, name for anything on which we have no effective *claim*."[76] James had hit on an extraordinary insight here. The uncertain, unclaimable quality of chance was what made it so offensive to the rationalist mentality in either its evangelical or managerial forms—a mentality that despite (or perhaps because of) its providentialism and determinism had fostered more faith in human mastery over fate than any previous body of Western thought. The culture of control (secular or religious) made claims on everything and everyone, bringing faith in system to the inner as well the outer environment. Chance was a stench in the nostrils of both the moralist and the manager. But for James, it was a portal of possibility—a gift from the cosmos.

James's revaluation of chance, however challenging to conventional morality, was done for moral reasons. He wanted to salvage some intellectually sound basis for ethical action. He found it in the idea of a pluralistic universe, a universe of "indeterminate future volitions" where we could still act as if moral choices mattered. Chance, from this view, was "the vital air which lets the world live, the salt which keeps it sweet." Without it we inhabited a flat, dead cosmos.[77]

For James, the idea of a pluralistic universe was more satisfying than the evasions of the "soft determinists" who claimed to find free will in conformity with universal law. In its openness to accident, the pluralistic universe posed a fundamental challenge to traditional ideas of Providence. If Providence survived in James's cosmos, he admitted it would have to be a little less than omniscient, a little more like a chess master facing an amateur opponent: the master knows how the game will turn out (he will win), but he does not know all the moves.[78]

In a culture still deeply committed to divine omnipotence, James's choice of metaphors was daring and significant. His deity might ultimately be in control, but in the meantime was at least willing to play. He was more like a trickster-god from a polytheistic culture of chance than like the Calvinist Jehovah of James's ancestors. The element of play was for James irreducibly connected with his own sense of the uncertainty at the heart of the universe—his feeling that, however predictable an outcome may seem, events "may fall out otherwise." Denying the basic premise of traditional faith in Providence, he argued that chance vindicated a morally meaningful universe.

In "The Will to Believe," James gave that argument a more explicitly theistic turn. The essay was a Protestant resuscitation of Pascal's wager, which in its original Catholic form struck James and his audience alike as laughably unpersuasive. Belief that masses and holy water brought salvation was not a live option for liberal Protestants; it lacked "the inner soul of faith's reality." But pose the possibility that faith might satisfy our deepest passions, unleash ethical energies, revitalize our very being—then the odds shifted dramatically. James was willing to accept Pascal's wager if the benefit to be gained was a renewed sense of moral engagement with the world. Otherworldly salvation was secondary. To the observation of

Ivan Karamazov that without God, everything is permitted, James in effect replied yes, but we can still act *as if* some things are required of us, and we will live more intensely if we do.[79]

James's yearning for intense experience led him to revalue risk and elaborate his vision of a pluralistic universe. In the introduction to the *The Will to Believe and Other Essays* (1897), he assaulted the positivist ideal of the completely explained cosmos. "Ever not quite" was the reasonable philosopher's response to claims of unified explanation.

> After all that reason can do has been done, there still remains the opacity of the finite facts as merely given, with most of their peculiarities mutually unmediated and unexplained. . . . The negative, the alogical, is never wholly banished. Something—'call it fate chance, freedom, spontaneity, the devil, what you will'—is still wrong and other and outside and unincluded, from *your* point of view, even though you be the greatest of philosophers.

Quoting "a gifted writer," James continued:

> "Not unfortunately, the universe is wild—game-flavored as a hawk's wing. Nature is miracle all; the same returns not save to bring the different. The slow round of the engraver's lathe gains but the breadth of a hair, but the difference is distributed back over the whole curve, never an instant true,—ever not quite."[80]

The writer was Benjamin Paul Blood, a freelance religous thinker with whom James corresponded toward the end of his life. James was put off by the monistic assumptions of traditional mysticism, the desire to blend with the oneness of the deity or the cosmos, but Blood's refusal of closure appealed to him. The last piece James wrote was a tribute to Blood called "A Pluralistic Mystic."[81]

Pluralism gave James a way to reject dualism as well as monism. He aimed not only to refute false unity (idealist or materialist) but also to bridge the false division between subject and object. Consciousness, he insisted, was not an entity but a function—the process of conjuring concepts from "immediate sensible life," the world of pure experience. That notion was as close as James came to articulating an ontology, to answering the question that philosophers from Hume to Wittgenstein have thought was the most important, maybe the only question in philosophy: Why is there something rather than nothing? "Who knows?" James wrote. "The question of Being is the darkest in all Philosophy. All of us are beggars here."[82] Pure experience postulated a manyness-in-oneness, blurring all the old boundaries between thoughts and things, subjects and objects.

Mental life, for James, was inextricably engaged with material and emotional life; his impatience with conventional epistemological boundaries led him frequently to resort to fluid metaphors—perhaps most notably "The Stream of Thought" in *Principles of Psychology* (1890). Unlike traditional atomistic empiricism, radical empiricism aimed to comprehend "the relations that connect experiences" rather than separating the experiences into discrete data. It also took seriously the many forms of "fringe consciousness," from dreams and hallucinations to religious visions, that traditional empiricism refused to acknowledge were "real." James's pluralistic universe was full of unexplained phenomena and unpredictable contingencies, an unfinished cosmos that invited us to participate in its continuing creation.[83]

The crucial aspect of a pluralistic, chance-filled universe remained, for James, its capacity to inspire and engage significant moral action. He was the the most profound example of a broad upsurge in popular vitalism that continued after his death. By the 1910s, yearnings for psychic and physical regeneration coursed through the dominant culture, seeking scientific and philosophical legitimacy. Philosophers like James and the French vitalist Henri Bergson addressed enthusiastic audiences. In 1912 Bergson was nearly mobbed by fans when he spoke at Columbia University. He was the creator and celebrator of the *élan vital*—the mysterious demiurge at the core of his conception of "creative evolution." Much of this ferment depended on the renewed respectability of chance in public discourse.[84]

The naturalist John Burroughs defended a vitalist conception of evolution in 1915; the central evidence in his argument was the pervasiveness of chance in organic life: "the books are never balanced; there is purpose, flexibility, indeterminateness, a shaping of means to an end, and ever-changing finity, movement which perpetually defeats the tendency in matter to a dead equilibrium." Burroughs was no scientist; he believed the life force to be more accurately characterized by "the creative impulse of Bergson" than by "the mechanical and fortuitous selection of Darwin." The desire to find purpose in the universe still provoked a recoil from blind chance.[85]

Burroughs's musings, however muddled, suggest what a wide range of thinkers was groping toward James's notion of an open universe. Even the anthropologist A. G. Keller, a disciple of the dour positivist William Graham Sumner, admitted that the range of the inexplicable was infinite: subtract scientific knowledge and you still get infinity. As a result, belief in luck was likely to survive indefinitely—though perhaps not as widely as in the days of primitive animism.[86]

Well into the early twentieth century, vitalist yearnings continued to animate a fitfully resurgent culture of chance. Sometimes even the work ethic seemed to be growing more supple, as youth workers such as Luther Gulick and G. Stanley Hall groped toward a new appreciation of the ways that play could foster a coherent cosmos and a satisfying sense of self. These were the sort of insights that would be fully developed by Johan Huizinga in his classic *Homo Ludens* (1938).[87]

The tendency to question accepted hierarchies of work and play, adulthood and childhood, bestowed new intellectual legitimacy on luck. Childlike spontaneity could be linked with the acceptance of inscrutable fortune. An *Atlantic* editorial of 1917, "Io Fortuna!" revealed some of the connections. Dismissing all the bluster about mastery of fate and captaincy of soul, the author recommended the wisdom of the child, who lived in the immediate present, in accordance with the whims of Fortuna: "And his deepest secret is this, that he looks on all fortune as adventure. For it is not for nothing that upon one stem have grown the two words, *Happen* and *Happiness*."[88] It would be hard to find a clearer rejection of the belief that satisfaction could be seized through conscious effort—the basis of the core American mythos, the pursuit of happiness.

But such subversive gestures remained idiosyncratic. The probabilistic revolution was placed in the service of managerial purpose. In the actuarial tables of insurance companies, the risk assessment studies of government planners, or the market research of major corporations, a new conception of the cosmos emerged—one that was all the more orderly because it acknowledged and aimed to contain the occasional eruption of disorder. The taming of chance underwrote the rise of sorting and categorizing institutions in both the private and public sectors of advanced industrial society.

Even play fit into the managerial picture, as a healthy sign of instinctual vitality. Animal instincts were normal (and normality itself was a statistical construct), but they needed appropriate outlets. Play was no exception, and the language of "recreation" provided a new idiom for orchestrating the recapture of lost spontaneity. Recreation referred to something satisfying but fundamentally unserious, a sport or hobby that would re-create the player's capacity to perform in the workplace where it counted. Gambling did not fall into this category; throughout the first two-thirds of the twentieth century it remained more restricted than ever before (or since) in American history. It is possible to see the epoch from the 1910s to the 1970s as a period characterized by the formation and consolidation of a managerial culture of control.

Under these circumstances, James's resurrection of chance became a modernist gesture of liberation. In a society committed to fine-tuning the organization of everyday life, where the actual practice of gambling was driven to the margins of society and placed under unprecedented surveillance, randomness and risk acquired a fetishistic charge—especially to the artistic and literary avant-garde. As in archaic cultures, chance became a path to esoteric knowledge, or perhaps simply an entry into the Jamesian world of "pure experience," that realm of spontaneity that seemed so threatened by managerial strategies of containment. At least in some minds, gambling as metaphor succeeded gambling as fact. The triumph of management intensified the allure of accident.

{CHAPTER SIX}

THE UNCERTAIN TRIUMPH OF MANAGEMENT

The dream of reason bred monsters. A century of total war posed unprecedented challenges to managerial faith in human mastery. Totalitarian systems in Germany, the Soviet Union, and China revealed what could happen when cultures of control were backed by state power. Yet in wartime, even democracies eventually yielded to the technocratic imperative, accepting the slaughter of innocents in the name of national policy. The more systematic the effort to manage military outcomes, the more unpredictably destructive were the human consequences.

Total war intensified the palpable presence of chance and—as always—people in and out of uniform turned to fetishes to ward off misfortune. In the streets of Paris, during the summer of 1918, the citizens of that citadel of rationality took to wearing amulets for protection against air raids and the heavy artillery fire of the German gun Big Bertha. A favorite was a tricolor badge depicting a boy called Rintintin and a girl named Nénette, child heroes of popular fiction. Parisians with such a charm could venture forth without fear—or so many of them hoped.

The resurgence of luck fetishes in wartime prompted a British observer to consider their larger significance. To the *New Statesman,* "even after generations of science, rationalism, materialism, and doubt, the human passion for some visible protection against invisible evil shows itself in the revived popularity of amulets and mascots at the present time." The editorial concluded:

We have not yet discovered truth, nor do we make great efforts to do so. What we long for is an easy and magical means of salvation.

Our faith is weak, but our credulity is strong, and we are at least second cousins once removed to the savage who believes that a pair of
kingfisher's eyes will secure him against sleeplessness, Have not
Nénette and Rintintin conquered Paris? And is not Paris the capital
of this Europe of ours?[1]

In the United States, the appeal of amulets was less urgent. No Big
Berthas were booming in the streets of Manhattan or Chicago. The civilian population was more endangered by homegrown superpatriots than
by enemy fire. Facing a distant foe, some American Progressives viewed
wartime production needs as an opportunity to institute a regulatory
state. Their hopes were disappointed, but the end of the war did see a
move at least toward welfare capitalism, if not social democracy.

The legitimation of managerial thought represented a shift in the
dominant idiom in the culture of control, from morality to efficiency.
Business and academic elites employed a new language of expertise to re-
balance tensions that had characterized American society since the early
nineteenth century—between the market's potentially anarchic promise
of perpetual novelty and the broader social need (even among capitalists
themselves) for stability, regularity, and predictability. Through the nineteenth century, evangelical rationalists had posed this conflict in its classic
forms: sybaritic consumption against virtuous production, aristocratic
luxury versus republican morality. But by the early 1900s, managerial
thinkers had a new formula.

In *The New Basis of Civilization* (1907), the economist Simon Nelson
Patten departed decisively from previous moral commentary on political
economy. He argued that expanding consumption would not undermine
labor discipline but would reinforce it. Workers would embrace productive habits in order to buy more things and make a better way of life.
Good consumers would make good producers as society moved from
agrarian scarcity to mass-produced abundance. Experts like Patten would
bring their managerial skills to overseeing the dynamic, upward-spiraling
equilibrium between production and consumption. American society
would become a busily humming, ever-expanding "social system," as a
later generation of social scientists would call it.[2]

Frederick Winslow Taylor, the father of scientific management, and
Henry Ford, the pioneer of the five-dollar day, were having similar thoughts
at about the same time. By timing work segments and recombining them

more efficiently, Taylor wanted to bind workers to a regime of relentless productivity, which they would embrace (he thought) in exchange for higher pay. Ford thought similar motives would keep workers on his assembly lines, though he could not resist spying on them to make sure they spent their money prudently. Leisure was acceptable only if it harmonized with work. Taylor's and Ford's policies implemented Patten's ideas.

Several decades, two world wars, and a Great Depression later, Patten's dream was finally realized—more or less—in the post–World War II United States. It was the Fordist moment, the fulfillment of the managerial agenda of orderly economic development, under the oversight of a partnership between big business and big government. Popular support for such policies stemmed from widespread yearnings for safety and stability, longings for refuge from Depression and War. The Keynesian "mixed economy" of the midcentury decades was probably the most flexible and humane version of the culture of control American policymakers had yet tried to implement with any success.

But it was one thing for Americans to support an efficiently managed economy and quite another to embrace the ideal of "personal efficiency" in their everyday lives. Workers resisted Taylor's scientific management of their work and Ford's surveillance of their leisure. Ordinary Americans continued to enjoy themselves in idiosyncratic ways, including gambling—the antithesis of efficient productivity, the apotheosis of economic waste. While managerial ideals dominated mainstream public discourse, a vernacular culture of chance flourished where people actually lived. Around kitchen tables, on street corners, in neighborhood bars and churches, there were countless opportunities for sustaining an alternative moral economy—a worldview that elevated generosity over productivity and redefined apparently wasteful activity as a potential means of grace.

The triumph of management was limited and uncertain. Even managerial thinkers themselves felt some discomfort with the consequences of their ideology. By midcentury, to some observers, a labor force locked in an endless cycle of earning and spending evoked the specter of a regimented society. American conformity was hardly totalitarian, but it seemed close to fulfilling Tocqueville's fear that democracy might feed the body and starve the soul. Or so said a growing chorus of cultural critics.

Meanwhile, a more palpable threat hovered constantly in popular consciousness, as postwar foreign policymakers committed the United States to a Cold War with the Soviet Union. This decison led to the creation of a national security state—a labyrinth of secrecy and surveillance that institutionalized the managerial drive for control more systematically than ever before and that sponsored the reductio ad absurdum of managerial thought: the nuclear arms race. Nuclear strategists used game theory and other forms of probabilistic thought to "think the unthinkable"—plotting mass destruction with spurious precision. The quest for national security created an atmosphere of permanent insecurity. Even in the prosperous postwar United States, the dream of reason could still breed monsters.

ADJUSTMENT AND ANXIETY

The tension in managerial thought was due to the mixed marriage that produced it. One partner was pragmatism, which prized uncertainty; the other was positivism, which demanded a sure thing—and assumed that science could deliver it. To the extent that pragmatism remained true to its Jamesian origins, managerial thought sustained an experimental and self-critical cast of mind; to the extent that pragmatism yielded to positivism, management thinkers succumbed to fantasies of technical mastery. The strategies of managerial rationality were balanced between chance and control.

John Dewey's thought epitomized this equipoise. Philosophical pragmatists, he argued, confronted "the precarious and perilous" in human life, without concealing uncertainty behind a metaphysical facade of false unity. "Our magical safeguard against the uncertain character of the world is to deny the existence of chance, to mumble universal and necessary law, the ubiquity of cause and effect, the uniformity of nature, universal progress, and the inherent rationality of the universe." We have used scientific technique to make the world more predictable and controllable, Dewey wrote, "but when all is said and done, the fundamentally hazardous character of the world is not seriously modified, much less eliminated."[3]

For Dewey, the hazardous character of the world was a prod to philosophy and science. "The striving to make stability of meaning prevail over the instability of events is the main task of intelligent human effort."

While secular providentialism merely asserted the sanctity of the existing social order, pragmatic philosophy could involve "us in the necessity of choice and active struggle." And by coming to terms with "genuine hazard, contingency, irregularity and indeterminateness in nature," scientists could better realize their own agenda of technical mastery. The scientific method, Dewey asserted, "adds greater control to life itself . . . mitigates accident, turns contingency to account, and releases thought and other forms of endeavor."[4]

In one sense, Dewey's argument embodied the can-do, "peculiarly American" spirit that has so often been associated with pragmatism—the experimental way of life that says anything goes, everything is up for grabs. But everything was not up for grabs in the application of pragmatism to policy. Dewey tended to exempt "scientific method" from scrutiny, even when its practitioners' claims to science were dubious. Unlike James, who distrusted "the Ph.D. octopus," Dewey welcomed the professionalization of knowledge, especially in the new "social sciences." As early as World War I, those emergent academic disciplines became organized in quasi-public entities—the National Research Council, the Social Science Research Council—that epitomized the managerial ideal of organized expertise.[5] Aspirations for professional legitimacy encouraged social scientists to exaggerate positivist claims of objectivity and value-neutrality.

The social sciences depended increasingly on statistical survey research. In theory, probability should have loosened the hold of positivistic assumptions; in practice it reaffirmed them. Belief in numerical precision undermined the acknowledgment of uncertainty and reinforced key positivist distinctions: between fact and value, the observer and the object of his study.

As managerial thinking grew dependent on positivist assumptions and methods, it became more embedded in corporations, universities, and government agencies—and more susceptible to their institutional purposes. Pragmatism often became merely "what works." The blooming buzzing confusion of James's pure experience was sometimes lost in the denatured language of technical expertise. But this was not the whole story. Some thinkers in the Progressive tradition took a more chastened approach, more sensitive to the limitations of positivistic science, truer to the Jamesian pragmatic tradition of openness to the unexpected.

Managerial thought took on the coloration of its historical moment. In the business culture of the 1920s, it appeared as welfare capitalism—

no longer as concerned with "the social idea" as Progressive reform had been, but still a legitimate effort to soften the impact of accident on workers' lives, and a major departure from older dismissals of luck (good and bad). Corporate executives like Gerard Swope and Owen D. Young pioneered employee insurance plans designed to protect workers against misfortune; some of these policies became models for the New Deal programs of the 1930s, including Social Security.[6]

The attempt to balance safety and risk linked managerial liberals with labor unionists. From the outset, union organizers had to urge reluctant workers to risk taking a stand now in order to gain security later. A. Philip Randolph, who headed the Brotherhood of Sleeping Car Porters, demonstrated this strategy in a fictitious dialogue between a New Negro union man and a suspicious old-timer. "'You've got to take a chance just as white workers have done. Nothing ventured, nothing gained,' says the organizer, who quickly contradicts himself: 'Of course today you're not taking any chances. Success is a sure thing with organization. You can't fail.'"[7] A little scary at first, joining a union ultimately meant betting on a sure thing, escaping from the constant threat of layoffs to a utopian realm of steady work. So workers, weary of want, must have hoped.

With the collapse of capitalism in the early 1930s, longings for security intensified and spread. The Great Depression created a huge constituency for the taming of economic chance. The dominant response to the catastrophe, as Franklin Roosevelt brilliantly realized, was fear. But along with fear there was a sense of shame. "I would go stand on that relief line," an unemployed businessman told Studs Terkel. "I would look this way and that and see if there's nobody around that knows me. I would bend my head so nobody would recognize me. The only scar that is left on me is my pride, my pride." Embarrassment and humiliation accompanied feelings of failure.[8]

In such an anxious atmosphere, security became an emotional as well as an economic goal. Yearnings for reassurance underwrote the authority of experts—not only credentialed psychotherapists but freelance counselors like Dale Carnegie, who identified "the feeling of importance" as a universal goal and who listed a string of obscure academic degrees after his name on the title page of *How to Win Friends and Influence People* (1936). Even quantitative social scientists could help to satisfy the longing to belong to a comforting whole. By the 1930s, opinion pollsters believed that they had discovered a cohesive mass audience—"the American public"—and a modal personality type—"the average American." Since many Americans shared the pollsters' naive faith in numbers, they accepted social scientists' statistical constructions as accurate descriptions of themselves. The desire to fit in reinforced the normative power of statistical aggregates. As one of George Gallup's interviewers observed at the end of the decade, "eight out of ten [respondents], after answering a question, will either ask directly what most people said about it or will remark indirectly 'I suppose nobody else said that.' They are delighted if told that everybody said it. It makes them feel that they were right."[9]

Polling provided an apparently scientific basis for belief in a homogenous American Way of Life—a transcendant collective identity for a society in search of security, a vision of classless cultural nationalism that informed everything from Popular Front rhetoric to Frank Capra films. Social science and corporate-sponsored entertainment developed symbiotically, as moviemakers and radio programmers used standardized formulas to reach audiences defined by market research. Gallup and Capra were partners in the creation of a mythic American identity.[10]

The drive for economic security required technical expertise as well. Roosevelt created a "Brains Trust" of experts, among whom were Raymond Moley (one of his chief political advisers), Rexford Tugwell (a leading advocate of government planning and head of the Resettlement Administration), David Lilienthal (a director of the Tennessee Valley Authority and later head of the Atomic Energy Commission). The "Brains Trust" signaled the reorientation of managerial technique from private to public purposes. The Depression had given sudden urgency to the task of reducing economic chance without pretending to eliminate it. This was the characteristic New Deal policy. Whether subsidizing farmers for not growing cotton, devising social insurance for elderly and disabled workers, or providing direct grants to the dependent poor, New Deal liberals revived the Progressive "social idea," seeking to create a core of economic stability amid the random movements of the market.

Toward the end of the New Deal, some of Roosevelt's experts began to attend to Keynesian theory. In Keynes's work, the effort to balance chance and control was made explicit. Keynes himself recognized that gambling metaphors captured motives at the core of capitalism. In *The General Theory of Employment, Interest, and Money* (1936), he observed: "the game of professional investment is intolerably boring and overexacting to anyone who is entirely exempt from the gambling instinct; whilst he who has it must pay to this propensity the appropriate toll." Chance was an inescapable element of economic life under capitalism, and the stock exchange could aptly be compared to a casino. But governments had a responsibility to promote capital development in ways that benefitted the entire society, not just a handful of lucky investors. "When the capital development of a country becomes a by-product of the activities of a casino," Keynes wrote, "the job is likely to be ill-done." Seldom has the argument for regulating capital markets been more succinctly stated.[11]

By using fiscal and monetary policy to encourage aggregate demand, Keynes argued, governments could lower the stakes of the game without driving investors and entrepreneurs away from it altogether. Without effective consumer demand for his products, the individual entrepreneur operates "with the dice loaded against him. The game of hazard that he plays is furnished with many zeros, so that the players *as a whole* will lose if they have the energy and hope to deal all the cards," the economist wrote, with a flurry of mixed gambling metaphors. But "if effective demand is adequate, average skill and average good fortune will be enough." The key to prosperity was taming chance sufficiently to reduce inequalities and sustain a high level of demand (either through direct public investment or indirect encouragement of private investment), without dampening the "animal spirits" of entrepreneurs or investors. Keynesian economics was a balancing act between chance and control.[12]

Keynes was wise enough to realize that gambling metaphors were finally insufficient to capture cosmic uncertainty. Risk was calculable, at least up to a point; uncertainty was not.

> By "uncertain" knowledge, . . . I do not mean to distinguish what is known for certain from what is only probable. The game of roulette is not subject, in this sense, to uncertainty. . . . The sense in which I am using this term is that in which the prospect of a European war is uncertain, or the price of copper and the rate of interest twenty years hence, or the obsolescence of a new invention. . . . About these matters, there is no scientific basis on which to form any calculable probability whatever. We simply do not know![13]

Keynes's frank admission of uncertainty paralleled William James's. It was a declaration of independence from the rule of rigid natural laws and spurious metaphors.

By the late 1930s, just as Keynes's work was beginning to find an audience among New Deal policymakers, business leaders revived their own managerial vocabulary. Whole industries, such as advertising, owed their existence to their skill in helping clients sustain profits amid the fluctuations of the business cycle. The collapse of the early 1930s had called their claims into question, but during the later part of the decade the advertising industry began to reassert them on the basis of statistical market research. Advertising apologists tamed chance rhetorically, with reference to expertise rather than simply work. An agency pamphlet from 1939 captured this departure from familiar business rhetoric by juxtaposing "Brains" versus "Luck," a chess piece versus a pair of dice.[14]

The preoccupation with "Brains" could be harnessed to business as well as government ends. The economic mobilization for World War II provided the opportunity for corporate leaders to reclaim expert authority and reshape representations of the American Way of Life. Visions of corporate-sponsored abundance filled the magazines of the war years. The war and its aftermath brought a business version of Keynesianism to the center of public policy. This approach to managing the business cycle depended more on monetary than on fiscal policy and more on private than on public investment—though military spending remained a crucial component of postwar prosperity. The postwar reconfiguration of managerial ideology involved a shift from social democratic to corporate idioms as the dominant language of public discourse.[15]

Within that discourse, the idea of America's redemptive role was reinforced by the emergence of the Cold War, which like World War II could be construed as a struggle for the soul of humankind. The Soviet threat, actual and imagined, gave new life and urgency to the old millennial dream that the United States would be the savior of the world. In 1947 the Truman Doctrine gave the dream official backing: the United States, said Harry Truman, would "support free peoples who are resisting attempted subjugation by armed minorities or by outside pressures"—whenever and wherever such conflicts arose.[16] Without using religious language, this extraordinary, open-ended commitment nevertheless cast God's New Israel in a providential role of unprecedented scope.

By the early 1950s, everyone from suburban pastors to congressmen in search of subversives routinely contrasted the "religious principles of democracy" with "godless communism." In his inaugural address in 1953, President Eisenhower reaffirmed the Manichean pattern set in place by Truman. "Freedom is pitted against slavery; lightness against the dark," he said, urging free people everywhere to come together against the communist menace. "To produce this unity, to meet the challenge of our time, destiny has laid upon our country the responsibility of the free world's leadership."[17] Successful nations, like successful individuals, were carrying out a providential plan—in which even nuclear weapons might play a necessary part.

While secular providentialism provided the moral superstructure for managerial thought, postwar prosperity provided the economic base. American victory had vindicated Fordist methods of mass production and Taylorite preoccupations with maximum productivity. The development of a secure, unionized, and comparatively affluent labor force underwrote the fulfillment of Patten's dream: an economy in dynamic equilibrium between production and consumption. Well-paid workers were the engine of economic growth; as Patten had predicted, good consumers made good producers. The sociologist Talcott Parsons gave this vision of equilibrium academic legitimacy in his summa of functionalist sociology, *The Social System* (1951).

Everything fit into the functionalist framework. Even the apparently unproductive suburban family had a role to play: it was an institution, Parsons decided, that was made for "intimacy maintenance." From this perspective, play became *recreation*—re-creating the individual's capacity to perform where it counted, in the workplace. An older idiom of morality gave way to a newer one of normality—itself a statistical construction. An eclectic psychology of adjustment, using shreds and patches of theory from behaviorism to psychoanalysis, expressed the hegemony of the normal.[18]

But one does not have to look very hard to find strains in managerial thought. Almost as soon as white-collar workers achieved a measure of security, some Americans began to suspect it had come at a fearful price. The very idea of society as a self-regulating system evoked the blank, impersonal face of modern authority—which everyone knew could be turned to sinister ends. By the 1950s, college sophomores had learned to call their epoch "Kafkaesque." C. Wright Mills, David Riesman, and William Whyte all played variations on the theme of managers' entrapment in the huge organizations that now dominated the economy. For the epigraph to his *White Collar* (1951), Mills chose Péguy's prediction that "the man who did not gamble would lose all the time, even more surely than he who gambled." To Péguy, the man who did not gamble had been the good family man, the citizen content with his lot; to Mills he was the bureaucrat trapped in "the enormous file." Other sociologists were more sanguine, but neither Riesman's "other-directed man" nor Whyte's "organization man" could escape being identified as emblems of conformity.[19]

Complaints about conformity became, in effect, the official critique of managerial thought. Social scientists, literary intellectuals, and a host of other critics worried about children who were too tractable and managers who had lost the capacity for independent thought. Historians increasingly turned to Tocqueville to describe what they deemed to be the greatest threat to American democracy—a "virtuous materialism . . . which would not corrupt, but enervate, the soul and noiselessly unbend its springs of action."[20]

At its most menacing, the idea of a perfectly managed society evoked the specter of totalitarianism. Victor Klemperer's diaries and other recollections of life under dictatorship reveal that victims of totalitarian rule at first viewed random events as a threat (the Jewish Klemperer worried whether or when he would draw "the black lot" and be singled out for extermination despite his Protestant religion and Gentile wife) but gradually came to see chance as an ally in their efforts to elude the Nazi state.[21]

In an age when social control seemed all too efficient, journalists associated unpredictable behavior with individual freedom. When pollsters underestimated Eisenhower's margin of victory in 1952, the radio commentator Edward R. Murrow rejoiced in the people's victory over managerial expertise. "They demonstrated, as they did in 1948 [when the pollsters mistakenly predicted Dewey's victory], that they are mysterious and their motives are not to be measured by mechanical means," he said. The embarrassment of the pollsters, Murrow mused, "restored to the individual some sense of his own sovereignty. Those who believe that we are predictable . . . have been undone again," and we have once again been released from their "petty tyranny," Murrow concluded.[22]

As a managerial culture of control acquired unprecedented power and influence, "the individual" became a threatened hero. He acquired many forms (almost always male)—the doomed, unadjusted protagonists of George Orwell and Aldous Huxley's dystopian fiction; the isolated existential heroes of Camus and Sartre; the tough, stoical gunslingers of Westerns and film noir. Like Dashiell Hammett's detective Sam Spade, these risk-takers realized that "the good citizen-husband-father . . . could be wiped out between office and restaurant by the accident of a falling beam," that "men died at haphazard . . . and lived only while blind chance spared them."[23] Heroism required constant awareness of contingency.

For some critics, conformity was more than a matter of taste: it signified a surrender to an empty managerial cult of efficiency, an abandonment of one's authentic self. Consider a scene from J. D. Salinger's *The Catcher in the Rye* (1951). Holden Caulfield, prince of maladjustment, holds forth against "phonies" as he recalls banging around Manhattan. To kill time he went to the movies at Radio City Music Hall, that glittering monument to Fordist gigantism. "I came in when the goddam stage show was on," he says. "The Rockettes were kicking their heads off, the way they do when they're all in line with their arms around each other's waist. The audience applauded like mad, and some guy behind me kept saying to his wife, 'You know what that is? That's precision.' He killed me."[24] The Rockettes' merger of mass entertainment and managerial norms evoked reverence from the conformist and scorn from the maladjusted man.

In the academy, humanists rallied to the defense of individual freedom and contingent possibility. Historians (if not social scientists) recoiled from determinism. In *Chance or Destiny* (1955), Oscar Handlin used providentialist and positivist traditions as foils. Handlin told the story of eight turning points in American history, all of which pivoted on chance events—such as the sudden storm on the James River that prevented Cornwallis's escape from Yorktown in 1781. An earlier age might have called this providential, but Handlin aimed to discredit exclusive reliance on "impersonal forces"—religious or secular—as explanations for major historical events. Manifest destiny was not an analytic option. Broad technological, economic, or demographic changes could shape available choices, Handlin admitted, but not determine them. For Handlin as for William James, the inescapability of chance validated free will and choice against the claims of causal law.[25]

Even at the height of the Cold War, a few mainstream critics saw the managerial ideal of efficiency as a common fault of capitalists and communists, especially as it shaped their shared obsession with mastering nature. "The 'control of nature' is a phrase conceived in arrogance, born of the Neanderthal age of biology and philosophy, when it was supposed that nature exists for the convenience of man," wrote Rachel Carson in 1951.[26] Her critique of technocratic hubris would become central to the emerging ecology movement. Carson put her finger on a fundamental weakness in managerial idioms of control—not simply the ethical vacuity and aesthetic boredom they induced, but the spuriousness of their claims to mastery.

Statistical strategies for taming chance were far more problematic than their proponents acknowledged. Economists and other social scientists made probability theory the standard of practical rationality, whether or not it had anything to do with how people actually made decisions. In fact, statistics had serious limits as a mode of managing choice, even within the insurance industry (the supposed citadel of probabilistic thought). Actuaries exercised enormous power over policy, but not all branches of the business could make use of their methods. Even a mortality table could not be constructed from data without a good eye and hand—the ability literally to draw a curve freehand through a cloud of points. Fire and maritime insurance remained innocent of probabilistic thought, dependent as ever on underwriters' judgments. Shipwrecks resisted statistics.[27]

The importance of personal judgment persistently undermined positivist claims to impersonal truth. As early as 1927, Werner Heisenberg had articulated the Uncertainty Principle in physics, which emphasized the impossibility of making precise measurements without taking the position of the observer into account. The problem was far more glaring in the social sciences, as the pollster Elmo Roper admitted in 1949. Statistical sampling, he told his staff, was based on "the assumption that human beings (interviewers) will cease to behave like human beings when ordered to do so by a statistician in an ivory tower." Probabilistic methods could not depersonalize the encounter between the pollster and the public.[28]

The tension between the drive for statistical control and the ever-present power of contingency was most apparent in the use of game theory to manage the nuclear arms race. Game theory got its start in John von Neumann and Oskar Morgenstern's *Theory of Games and Economic Behavior* (1944, 1953), as an effort to bring mathematical rigor to financial decision making when one faced incomplete information. But during the Cold War, it acquired a special resonance as a means of planning moves and countermoves against the Soviet Union.

Game theory offered apt models for the rivalry between the superpowers, which was characterized by nothing if not incomplete information on both sides. John McDonald's *Strategy in Poker, Business, and War* (1953) brought gambling and the arms race together by articulating the "minimax" principle. Said McDonald: "Good strategy requires the use of the principle of 'minimax,' that is, a policy in which a range of high and low gains is adopted on the assumption that one might be found out. But to avoid being found out one obscures the specific pattern of play by randomizing the strategy with chance plays." Though the stakes were millions of lives, the game could go on, filled with feints and counterfeints, dummy missiles and real ones, double agents and deliberate deceptions.[29]

This was the ultimate expression of the muddle at the core of managerial thought—apparently rational means in the service of wildly irrational ends. For most Americans, the promise of national security could not dispel their persistent fear that they were helpless before the ever-present possibility of nuclear war. The ideal of adjustment could not dispel the actuality of anxiety. The confusions of the moment were aptly summarized in the self-canceling advice of Roy Rogers, the television cowboy, to his youthful audience: "Be brave, but don't take chances."

Attitudes toward gambling reflected similar contradictions. During the first two-thirds of the twentieth century (and especially the postwar decades), legal restrictions on gambling were more stringent than at any time before or since in American history.[30] And the cultural sanctions against gambling became more capacious than ever, combining moral and medical idioms of disapproval. Yet actual as well as metaphorical gambling remained attractive, even among the managers themselves.

Part of the reason for this was that gambling, like other institutions in the managerial era, gradually became rationalized. The key to rationalization was the emergence of pari-mutuel betting in the 1910s and 1920s. Odds were set automatically, by combining all bets in a common pool and playing off the amounts bet on each horse against the the amounts bet on the others; the horse with the most bettors had the shortest odds. Pari-mutuel betting deprived bookmakers of the power to set odds unilaterally and—perhaps more important—made racing receipts subject to taxation. Private wagering could be a respectable source of public revenue, though only a few states took advantage of the possibility until the 1960s and 1970s.[31]

The emergence of organized crime syndicates also signaled the rationalization of gambling. In the illicit as well as the licit economy, the big guys drove the little guys out of business, and government aimed to make sure it got a piece of the action or else shut down "the rackets" altogether. Abolition was still the main policy goal, but some states began gradually to emphasize regulation as well. The prospect that gambling could be a source of public revenue appealed to the managerial mentality, and opened the door to more tolerant state policies in the last third of the twentieth century.

MANAGING THE GAMBLER

During the comparatively flush times of the 1920s, the "gambling spirit" remained an honored part of a mythic national identity. "I think that Americans, of all the nationalities, most profoundly believe in luck," wrote the literary critic William Rose Benét in 1928. "We began as a nation by gambling on the future of a continent. Most of our great industrial pioneers have been inspired gamblers. We are the three-card monte men of the world. We regard life as a faro layout. We have roulette wheels spinning in our brains, and anything is likely to turn up. That is why we cling tenaciously to our individual enterprise and open competition." It was also why we often took risks without regard for the consequences, since "the best gamblers worship their intuition and proceed as it dictates, without pondering the thread-hung sword that waits to fall. . . . We plunge on a guess, on the great American 'hunch,' at a flicker in the brain we become mad mystics."[32]

After the market crash of 1929, celebrants of gambling faced a tougher task. Cash-strapped state governments remained reluctant to consider legalization as a means of revenue. (Nevada was the exception that proved the rule: casino gambling was legalized there in 1931, and Las Vegas eventually became a top attraction for high-rollers, an efficient money machine for fugitive crime bosses, and—by the 1960s a focus for uninformed speculation by journalists about the meaning of America.) Even legitimate risk-taking was in low repute in the wake of the crash. To those who defined adjustment as a measure of mental health, the unadjusted gambler was plainly a figure in need of clinical management. To those who feared society had become all too well managed, the gambler held a certain faded glamor. But in public discourse generally, gambling was more thoroughly pathologized than ever before, as its critics skillfully blended moral and therapeutic themes.

True Story magazine captured the mix in "Gambler's Hell," a story supposedly told by Warden Lawes of Sing Sing Prison. When Jim Harrison, one of his prisoners, tries to hang himself in his cell, Lawes says, "It was part of my duty to help him escape whatever complex had driven him to this desperate act." It was 1938, and already prison wardens (at least in women's magazines) had begun to talk like psychiatrists. The warden persuades Jim to tell his story, which resembles that of every other ruined gambler in the reform literature. Tormented by guilt over his failure to support his family, Jim seeks self-destruction as escape from self-accusation. He is saved by the combination of talk therapy and old-time religion; the very day he attempts suicide—which happens to be Christmas Day—he receives a present from his daughter, a Bible. The word of God, combined with the words of the warden, pulls him back from the brink.[33]

Despite its psychological basis, the contrast between the gambler and the well-adjusted citizen continued to draw strength from religious sources. Protestant opposition to gambling persisted according to precedent, through World War II and beyond. Denominational statements of principle struck familiar notes. For the Baptists, gambling was "an act of greed" and "a potentially compulsive habit." For the Lutherans, it promoted the hope of gain without production, the desire for escape from "the realities of life," and an unwholesome competitive spirit. For the Methodists it was "nonproductive, creating no new wealth and providing no useful service." Catholics, in contrast, continued to argue that gambling in itself was not a sin; only gambling to excess was.[34]

The fissures between Catholics and Protestants surfaced in a continuing debate over bingo during the 1950s. The game was technically illegal in most states, but police generally looked the other way when it was played for charitable purposes. In 1957 New York State held a referendum on the legalization of bingo. The Federal Council of Churches inaugurated a "BIG NO" campaign; such Protestant magazines as the *Christian Century* inveighed against the proposal as the first step down a slippery slope. The Jesuit journal *America* begged to differ. It was certainly true, the editors admitted, that "gamblers can get themselves abysmally deep into the mire of evil." Betting beyond your means is an unalloyed ill; but church bingo? Come on! Votes should be cast without prejudice or preconception. "The BIG NO campaign of the Council of Churches seems to us to be propagating more than their fair share of both."[35]

The measure passed, but Protestants kept their guard up. In 1963, when James Cardinal Cushing of Boston said he would no more condemn a fling at cards than he would a glass of whiskey, the Methodist Lycurgus Starkey took to the pages of the *Christian Century* to articulate his outrage.

> Gambling offers artificial risks in the hope of excessive gain. . . . results depend not on effort or ingenuity but on the turn of a wheel, the throw of the dice, the odds on a race or the drawing of a number.
> The Christian knows that ultimately life is not a gamble, a risk, a game of chance. Rather, life is lived in the Providential care and keeping of the Lord of history, whose self-giving love has been disclosed in Jesus Christ. Understanding the universe as a purposeful, consistent creation, the Christian will take the odds of life and transform them into the will of God.[36]

This was the orthodox Protestant ideal of a well-adjusted life, unchanged since the nineteenth century. But from the 1930s through the 1950s, the managerial version of adjustment fostered newer, secular orthodoxies based on technical expertise rather than divine decree. Despite their apparent novelty, these modes of thought often reinforced a familiar morality of self-control, and a traditional Protestant disdain for gambling. Among the most influential new orthodoxies was psychoanalysis.

Freud's work contained the seeds of secular providentialism. In *The Psychopathology of Everyday Life* (1904) and other essays, he pioneered the idea that slips of the tongue and other apparently random events were clues to our unconscious life. Used with care, this was a fruitful insight, but it could easily degenerate into a dogmatic denial of chance. Freud's followers became so preoccupied with uncovering false accidents that they overlooked the power of real ones. As psychoanalysis became an orthodoxy it began to resemble Calvinism: every occurrence, no matter how apparently fortuitous, could be fit into an overarching scheme of interpretation. Ambiguities fell away and provisional insights hardened into a self-contained system of thought.[37]

This process was apparent in the psychoanalytic critique of gambling. Its locus classicus was Freud's essay "Dostoevsky and Parricide" (1928), which asserted that the novelist's gambling mania was a substitute gratification for masturbation.[38] The psychoanalytic critique maintained the perspective of evangelical rationality, joining the gambler and the masturbator as slaves to an overmastering passion. Psychoanalysis became a secular justification for the ethos of self-control.

Edward Bergler's *The Psychology of Gambling,* which went through several editions from 1936 to 1958, typified the transformation of psychoanalysis into an adjustment psychology. The impulse to gamble, he claimed, could be traced to the desire described by Dostoevsky's fictional gambler: "*to challenge Fate.*" Bergler reduced this wish to its allegedly familial origins: "We have only to substitute, for fate, the child's typical picture of its parents, and we have in a nutshell the gambler's psychic situation." The psychodynamics of gambling, from this view, were all too simple: "the main cog in the mechanism of gambling," according to Bergler, was "the unconscious wish to lose as a penalty for masochistically tinged aggression against parental authority." The gambler was not a romantic risk-taker, but a neurotic loser.[39]

This was the case, Bergler insisted, even among gamblers with pretensions to skill. Gambling with calculation, as in poker or horse racing, "may seem rational, and it is certainly more intellectualized than the 'pure' types [roulette, lottery, and other games dependent wholly on luck], but psychoanalytically even these gamblers are still, in effect, sacrificing to the pagan god of omnipotence." There was nothing rational about that.[40]

Though psychoanalysis was not the only psychiatric orthodoxy in the midcentury decades, it was the most useful in providing new legitimacy for old suspicions of gambling. This was especially apparent when the gambler was female. Resolutely patriarchal, midcentury psychoanalysis reaffirmed male distrust of women taking risks in public. A 1949 film, *The Lady Gambles,* revealed how conventional therapeutic wisdom could surface in mass entertainment. A young couple, played by Barbara Stanwyck and Robert Preston, is honeymooning in Las Vegas; she gambles compulsively. Divorce looms until the truth is unearthed by the husband, with help of a wise psychoanalyst. The truth is that the young wife blames herself for her mother's death in (the wife's own) childbirth. Losing at gambling is a way to expiate her guilt—a fantasy her unmarried and suspiciously mannish sister encourages. Discovering the truth allows the wife to break the cycle of self-punishment and reaffirm her domestic role.[41]

Mass entertainment pathologized the male gambler less insistently.

The Mississippi or Western gambler, ensconced in a mythic frontier past, remained an icon of masculinity for an era anxious about conformity. In *Mississippi Gambler* (1953), Tyrone Power persuades Piper Laurie to join him on his wanderings, after a long courtship. Concern about an overly adjusted society sanctioned male fantasies of escape from domestication.

"Maturity" was the touchstone of psychological health in the mid-century decades. The concept cut two ways. It meant acceptance of labor discipline, domestic responsibilities, conventional definitions of adult behavior—everything the gambler notoriously disregarded. Gamblers just wanted to play, and play was for kids. But if maturity was a euphemism for conformity, the prescription became more problematic. Gamblers' playfulness might be a refreshing alternative to an overly managed life. More commonly, though, the orthodox analysis remained in place: along with his other neuroses, the gambler was a case of arrested development.

The sharpest statement of this view was Franklin Frazier's *Black Bourgeoisie* (1957), a scathing portrait of middle-class African Americans. For Frazier, the sporting crowd's ethic of fortune was the scourge of disciplined achievement. "The spirit of play or make-believe has tended to distort or vitiate the ends of their most serious activities," he wrote. Since black people were often excluded from white professional associations, they set up "reading societies" to offset that exclusion, but those turned into social clubs for drinking and playing poker. "Playing, then, has become the one activity which the Negro may take seriously."[42]

The consequences, in Frazier's view, were appalling. Black professionals took recreation more seriously than work: a physician told Frazier he would rather lose a patient than see his favorite team lose a game. Since even educated black people rarely read books, Frazier charged, "their conversation is trivial and exhibits a childish view of the world." The burden of his argument was simple: black folks were going to have to grow up if they expected to be integrated into mainstream white society. They were going to have to stop "playing seriously" and start working seriously.[43]

Frazier's assault on the black bourgeoisie was a variation on persistent themes in the postwar critique of gambling: it was wasteful, it was irresponsible, it kept the poor man down. There was something to all these arguments, especially when they were used to characterize legalized gambling as a regressive tax on the poor. Yet most critics neglected this social impact and focused instead on familiar moral concerns. We need to encourage advancement through "effort and merit, rather than the passive anticipation of chance," said Joseph Carlino, the speaker of the New York State Assembly, arguing in 1963 against the legalization of off-track betting. The work ethic survived in secular form.[44]

The stakes in the legalization debate, many commentators agreed, concerned the nation as well as the individual. Attorney General Robert Kennedy warned in 1962 that "corruption and racketeering, financed largely by gambling, are weakening the vitality and strength of this nation." Gamblers, Kennedy concluded, "are taking a chance which the nation and its economy cannot afford." Like Victorian moralists before him, Kennedy worried about the public consequences of private acts. He implicitly invoked the hydraulic depletion model of decline in the body politic, a model deployed by moralists since the eighteenth century. Nations, like individuals, could lose their "vitality and strength" if they indulged in nasty habits. Poorly adjusted persons, Kennedy implied, could create a poorly adjusted economy.[45]

But few law enforcement officials were as militant as Kennedy on the subject of gambling. Judges and prosecutors argued openly that the suppression of gambling was a quixotic goal. Only legalization made sense. The history of horse racing since World War II seemed to bear out their arguments. It gradually reacquired some legitimacy, first as an instrument of managing government fiscal policy and later as a form of family entertainment. During the Second World War, the federal government sanctioned the sport as a means of siphoning off excess cash chasing goods unavailable due to wartime shortages. After the war, promoters built bigger race courses and attracted a broader middle-class audience to tracks in a handful of states.[46]

The spread of pari-mutuel betting reinforced the idea that gambling could be a source of public revenue. In larger cities like New York, the war on gambling became part of a broader effort to flush out municipal corruption and ensure complete collection of taxes on the metered pari-mutuel take. After the Second World War, the federal government began to monitor bookmakers more closely, demanding they buy a fifty dollar stamp and fork over 10 percent of their receipts. The sporting crowd was under managerial scrutiny as never before. But unlike the moral reform of previous eras, the midcentury managerial war on gambling stressed regulation as well as abolition. It was a struggle, at the top, between the rivalrous claims of organized crime and organized government.[47]

Gamblers themselves remained shadowy figures in managerial thought, though social scientists tried to plumb their motives. Some revived the Progressive notion that gambling was a safety valve for the frustrations of a working class life. As they milled around the bars and pool halls of urban ethnic neighborhoods, sociologists discovered that horse players were motivated by the hope of "beating the system" and temporarily mastering fate. Will your ship ever come in? asked a sociologist of a gambler. "No," was the reply, "but what else have I got besides this?" When he hit a long shot, a winner crowed: "What do you think I am, a nobody?" Gambling offered the chance to be a somebody, however fleetingly—a fitfully rewarding experience that eased adjustment to everyday life.[48]

The task, for postwar managerial thinkers as for their Progressive predecessors, was to come up with wholesome substitute gratifications. As late as the mid-1960s, diagnoses of gambling were still posing the familiar questions of the social engineer: "What other cultural devices are available to middle class and lower class men that can be as effective in bolstering a sense of of independence and self-determination and that so compellingly exercise skill and mental powers? What else might be done to brighten the lives of working-class women?"[49]

These were serious questions, posed by decent people with honorable intentions. But they did not really catch the cultural complexity of gambling—its ritual invocation of an alternative logic of life. To understand the persistence of gambling in the managerial era, we need to return to its larger context in the vernacular culture of chance. From the 1920s through the 1960s, beyond the boundaries of responsible opinion, a magical worldview flourished.

There were good reasons for this—not merely the influx of immigrants who still believed in conjuring *mana,* but the relation of supposed superstitions to serious and legitimate religious longings. As the British writer G. K. Chesterton observed in 1933, "the depths of a superstition . . . are still depths." Unlike "evolutionary educators," who glibly assumed that all fundamental questions were (or were about to be) solved, superstitious people acknowledged the ineradicable mystery at the heart of existence. "They do not shout with vulgar conceit at finding nothing but shallows. There is something in the grossest idolatry or the craziest mythology that has a quality of groping and adumbration. There is more in life than we understand," Chesterton said.[50] That admission was the core of the culture of chance, and the key to its survival.

THE BORDERLANDS OF SUPERSTITION

By the 1920s, a number of thoughtful observers agreed that superstition was more than a sign of ignorance. Writing in the aftermath of World War I, the English essayist Robert Lynd observed that many dunderheads were free from superstition, and many wise heads were full of it; echoing William James on "the sentiment of rationality," he argued that belief or disbelief in luck was dependent on temperament rather than reason. "During the war the men who carried mascots were not noticeably inferior to the men who did not," Lynd wrote, noting the curious irony that the nation that introduced the worship of reason, France, was the one that was fondest of mascots. There may be, he concluded, a more interdependent relationship between rationality and superstition than we had previously imagined.[51]

Certainly the two modes of thought coexisted in twentieth-century America, where it became possible to clothe the rankest superstition in the language of science. As the anthropologist Elsie Clews Parsons told her colleagues in 1942, "soothsaying is illegal in Massachusetts and so the other day when a fortune teller arrived in my village she gave out that she was a Problem Lady." Whether telling fortunes or solving problems, a variety of experts ministered to the public's insatiable need to know what happens next. As Parsons wrote:

> From the stars you cast a horoscope or you foretell an eclipse. Dream of fire and you fear your house is going to burn down, or if you are being analyzed, that you are bent on something, say suicide. To learn whether you are to live or to die, you roll a pebble under your foot or you open your mouth to a thermometer. You choose a proper mate—a Water person if you are an Earth person—and a propitious wedding day or, as the Committee on Social Adjustment of the Social Science Research Council suggests, you look up in a matrimonial expectancy table your matrimonial risk.[52]

Parsons was not equating superstition and science. Like Lynd (and William James), she was making a subtler point. There were certainly times when it would be foolish to ignore scientific evidence of probable future events—the evidence of the thermometer, say, rather than that of the pebble. But there were also times (especially if the science in question was social science) when the choice of predictions was really a toss-up.

Whether one chose a mate on the basis of astrological lore or the matrimonial expectancy tables was largely a matter of temperament.

And one's temperament was shaped by one's immediate circumstances (as well as one's genetic inheritance). As always, those whose lives were most precarious were the strongest believers in luck. Consider the superstitions of the American airmen in World War II. The poet and bomber pilot John Ciardi put their situation succinctly in his diary: "we live by accidents," he wrote. He and his comrades had figured the odds at 2 to 1 that they would complete a full tour of duty (thirty-five missions). Given these bleak prospects, airmen covered their planes with good luck symbols: great poker hands, four-leafed clovers, winning dice rolls. They embraced rituals and fetishes: one never went on a mission without his Bible and a scarf made from the parachute of a dead friend; another, a professional dancer, carried a small jade goddess given him by Martha Graham. Others renamed their thirteenth mission as "12-B" and wore the same shirt, unwashed, every time they went up. And when they completed their tour, the fortunate fliers were issued certificates of membership in the "Lucky Bastard Club."[53]

The airmen embodied the survival of superstition in the heart of managerial rationality. The flying of B-29s could not have been all cold logic. There was something truly marvelous about the human capacity to construct a huge fortress, then lift it off the ground and move it through the air. This was true as well of other technological "miracles" of the twentieth century. Some of these, such as the B-29, were the product of systematic calculation; others, such as the discovery that mold on cheese kills bacteria, were quite accidental—though Alexander Fleming's penicillin breakthrough clearly illustrated the adage that "fortune favors the prepared mind." The technological triumphs of managerial rationality did not extinguish the capacity for wonder. But they also did not extinguish the need to propitiate fortune. Managerial rationality could mass-produce B-29s, but it could not tame the chances of death in combat.

Superstitious beliefs predominated in extreme situations, such as the combat airmen's, or in subcultures that mixed pleasure, danger, and strangeness into sublimity. Few subcultures were more sublime than the gypsies—known more formally as the Rom or Romany. During the early decades of the twentieth century, gypsy encampments became familiar sights in the American countryside, at once fascinating and sinister. To the *gajo* (a nongypsy of any ethnicity), gypsy culture offered a seductive blend of magic, sensuality, and nomadic freedom. But it also carried an aura of menace.[54]

Gypsies were notorious for thievery, and there is ample evidence that the reputation was deserved—at least from the *gajo* point of view. Without sentimentalizing them or ignoring the frauds they sometimes worked on innocent people, one can also see that their indictment for theft needs to be qualified. Their morality was particularist, not universal; it did not apply to dealings outside their own community. And they often provided genuine services to their *gajo* customers.

The relationship between gypsy and *gajo* was more complicated than that of the con artist and dupe. The gypsy fortune-teller frequently provided her clients with pragmatic advice or at least peace of mind. She was not merely a cynical trickster; often she believed in premonitions and portents, in dream books and evil eye charms. Like the crooked gambler, the gypsy fortune-teller was both a calculating operator and a credulous representative of the vernacular culture of chance. The gypsies' outlook constituted an alternative worldview, embedded less in words than in a way of life—one that was increasingly difficult to fit into industrial capitalist society. The modernization of gypsy life involved the transformation of itinerant rural rogues into sedentary urban tricksters.

Most of the Rom came to the United States between the Civil War and World War I from Romania, Russia, and Serbia. By the late 1930s, there were anywhere from seven thousand to twelve thousand living in New York City, and comparable colonies in Philadelphia, Baltimore, Saint Louis, and other cities. Before the coming of the automobile, they led a mostly untroubled rural existence, at least according to one of their New York "kings," Johnny Nikanov. "When I was a little knee-high boy the U.S. was gypsy heaven," Nikanov told the *New Yorker* writer Joseph Mitchell in 1942. (Nikanov, by his own account, was anywhere from forty-five to seventy-five at the time.) In those days, Nikanov recalled, "there wasn't no motorcycle cops, and you could camp just about anywhere. . . . And there was a violin in every family—or at least a guitar—and you didn't have to get drunk to feel like dancing."[55]

But by the early 1930s, the gypsies' situation was changing. Cars complicated the picture. Gasoline was expensive and work was increasingly scarce. Skilled *gajo* metalworkers were eager for any job they could find, even tinkering with small repairs. Gypsy men, squeezed out of the trade, could not make enough to pay for gasoline. Economically pinched *gajos* were more sensitive than ever to being "gypped," and gypsies found it harder to make a fast getaway after a successful confidence game. As John-nie recalled, "along about this time [1932–1933], I don't know why, but the whole country turned against gypsies. Them motorcycle cops would chase us across one state line and then some more cops would chase us across another state line. Pretty soon we didn't know where the hell we was at. Whole sections of the country had to be dodged or they'd put us on a chain gang, or try to. Even the carnivals turned against us."

Under economic and cultural pressure, the Rom reluctantly drifted away from their nomadic traditions into urban tenement neighborhoods.

Gypsy fortune-teller, Mineola, New York, 1932.

This move demoralized the men but not the women, who became more ambitious and successful in their efforts to separate credulous customers from their life savings. Gypsy "kings" like Johnnie, meanwhile, grew adept at manipulating the welfare system and managed to get most of their people on the relief rolls. This was a tricky business, as gypsies could not provide the kind of data routinely requested by government agencies. No longer as mobile as they had been in the earlier part of the century, they nevertheless continued to elude census takers, truant officers, police detectives, and other agents of managerial rationality.

Like other participants in the vernacular culture of chance, gypsies constructed a syncretist world view, a spiritual bricolage. On the feast of Saint John the Baptist, they brought patent medicine bottles, whiskey bottles, any empty bottles they could find to the local Eastern Orthodox church to be filled with holy water—which, like many Roman Catholics, they believed had medicinal properties. But only occasionally—usually for funerals—did they avail themselves of other institutional church services.[56]

Gypsies believed as fervently as their fortune-telling clientele in the predictive power of dreams. An old queen of con artistry from California, one of the richest gypsies in the country, retired to Brooklyn. She had a dream that money would soon be worthless, so she converted all her cash to diamonds, which she sewed into the linings of her coats and petticoats. As Detective Daniel Campion (NYPD) said, "One reason they understand superstitious people, they're about as superstitious as they can be themselves. They see signs everywhere, signs and warnings, especially the women. . . . Sometimes one of them has a premonition, and the family suddenly packs up and moves. And one thing you're always sure to find when you search a gypsy is a good-luck charm of some kind."[57]

Children needed more than one charm. A small gypsy child might wear a protective vest like the one from Kansas in the 1920s, now housed at the Smithsonian Institution. It is festooned with fetishlike objects—glass beads, tiny plastic toys, and bits of shiny metal—all of which (at least in combination) were assumed to keep bad luck at bay. Clearly gypsies believed in the possibility of conjuring *mana,* even as they manipulated that belief among the *gajo* population. The closest gypsy equivalent to *mana* was *baxt,* which meant "luck," "fate," or "destiny." *"Baxt,"* a contemporary gypsy told the writer Isabel Fonseca, "is the occupying idea among the Roma on this earth." *Baxt* was the key to moral character; as another gypsy said: "Every person is part Judas, part Christ. Only luck decides him."[58]

African American conjurers also sustained the belief in luck. They continued to attract a wide audience among whites—in Norfolk, Virginia, in the 1930s, one practitioner estimated that 40 percent of the whites and 90 percent of the blacks believed in conjure. Such numbers were largely but not entirely subjective—they reappeared often in other observers' estimates from other Southern and Midatlantic cities. By the 1920s and 1930s, African American folk beliefs were probably the most vital element of the vernacular culture of chance, especially in the East and South. (Hispanic and Asian influences were more significant in the West.) Black conjurers or root doctors

Gypsy child's protective vest, Kansas, 1920s.

catered to a huge biracial clientele in a variety of settings, from plantation to ghetto. The Great Depression, two world wars, and a cold war whipped up a persistent atmosphere of general anxiety to go with the everyday sorts of worries conjurers traditionally addressed. In Harlem and the French Quarter, on Beale Street in Memphis and on Peachtree in Atlanta, whites and blacks alike demonstrated their faith in adapting archaic rituals and beliefs to modern circumstances. African and European traditions, such as the magical (and diabolical) significance of the crossroads, survived in the lyrics of Delta bluesmen like Robert Johnson. As late as the early 1960s, an old black man in Piedmont, North Carolina, put a pumpkin on his head and did a dance in order to read minds. And in the same period, the black popular press was still full of advertisements for Easy Life Mixture, Black Cat's Oil, Heifer Dust, Lovin' Powder (25 cents), and Extra Fast Lovin' Powder (35 cents). Magic remained popular and profitable.[59]

It also remained practical, or so its practitioners claimed. Conjuring and root work often embodied a pragmatic "science of the concrete." The performance of certain rituals could exert a curative power, through the curious interaction of mind and body. If you wanted your job back, whether you were in Philadelphia or Little Rock, you wrote your boss's name on a piece of paper and put it in your shoe while you went about your business, chewing a John the Conquerer root. (John the Conquerer was a folk hero of the black oral tradition, an icon of potency who could be traced to slavery times.) In the 1920s and 1930s, you could find lucky beans in New Orleans and lucky buttons in Mobile, lucky glass in Saint Petersburg, Florida, and a lucky heart plant in Fayetteville, North Carolina. African American folk beliefs mingled and merged with Elizabethan traditions in North Carolina, with Caribbean lore in New York, and with Irish and Italian Catholicism in New Orleans.[60]

The vernacular culture of chance was not a neat ethnocultural patchwork but a syncretist stew, served up on secular as well as religious occasions. Many conjures involved Christian prayers, such as the Memphis practice of shaking lucky pinto beans in one's hands while reciting the Lord's Prayer, then saying "in the name of the Father, the Son, and the Holy Ghost." The promise of magical efficacy in everyday life still lingered around the rituals of the Roman Catholic Church, and this made them attractive to nominal Protestants, especially African Americans. Well into the post–World War II era, even educated black Protestants per-

formed Catholic rituals and carried Catholic charms. Belief in an enchanted universe also survived among evangelical revivalists, who held
that the truly converted would see a shooting star on the way home from
camp meeting. ("Lord, if I'm truly saved, shoot me a star," was a popular
prayer of the homeward bound.) Protestant and Catholic Christianity still
blended with older animistic beliefs.[61]

One striking example of the syncretist mix was Old Divinity, a
ninety-six-year-old black man from Mississippi interviewed by a white
woman journalist named Ruth Bass in the early 1930s. Old Divinity was
a "tree talker," which meant he spent a lot of time cultivating a relationship with a certain tree, learning its language, studying it, and listening to
it under all sorts of conditions. "Best to stay in one place and take what
de good Lawd sends, lak a tree," Old Divinity said to Bass, whose sentimental rendering of his speech veered toward parody. Old Divinity was a
faithful Baptist who was buried with various good luck charms, the most
important of which was his Saint Anthony medal.[62]

In New Orleans and Harlem, among other places, Saint Anthony
was the patron of gamblers—as well as the patron of lost objects. In a
sense, the popularity of his images suggested the links between gambling
and awareness of inevitable loss, between playing apparently pointless
games with abandon and cultivating a certain kind of subversive Christianity. High and low mingled in an animated universe. Hoodoo and
Christianity came together in the effort to conjure *mana.* When one of
Harry Middleton Hyatt's informants from Fayetteville, North Carolina,
told him how to make *goopher* dust, syncretist ritual unfolded into a vindication of imagination. After you get some graveyard dirt, he said, "*yo'*
carry it through de watah and de watah puts what chew call a Christian spirit on
it. . . . *Think about yore dust* [i.e., the eventual fate of your body] *den luck*
will come. . . . 'Tie it up [in a sacred bundle]' . . . *Yo' give it a spirit of imag-*
ination wonder." This was the core of the performative conception of
truth: the seeker sought not to verify empirical reality through experiment, but to constitute emotional reality through ritual. The conjuring of
mana, or spiritual power, involved the creation of "a spirit of imagination
wonder."[63]

There was nothing ethereal about that spirit. It was embedded in the
detritus of everyday life. Seemingly trivial details carried cosmic meanings. And nowhere were those connections clearer than in the luck beliefs
associated with gambling. The world of fortune-telling, dream books,

and conjuring overlapped with the world of hot tips, sure things, and gambler's hunches. Dream books, numerology, and other forms of divination flourished among crap shooters and policy players. The voodoo drugstore could also serve as a numbers drop. The sporting crowd's ethic of fortune sustained a symbiosis between the wagering impulse and a wider realm of omens and portents. For everyone from pious washerwomen to racetrack touts, this vernacular culture of chance may have sometimes offered a titillating mix of pleasure and danger—much as experiences of "the sublime" were said to do by Romantic aesthetes—but it also offered participation in an alternative way of life.

BETTING AND BELIEVING

Even during the first half of the twentieth century, the most racially segregated epoch in American history, the sporting crowd continued to encourage the coming together of classes and races. Bookie joints, floating crap games, and similar settings provided some of the few venues where blacks and whites might fraternize, however occasionally and fleetingly. Part of that openness stemmed from the prominence of outsiders in the white sporting crowd: Jews, Italians, Southern boys in flight from evangelical stolidity.

The gamblers' alternative economy provided opportunities for ambitious men outside the white Protestant mainstream. In Chicago during the early twentieth century, one of the flashiest and most successful professional gamblers was an African American. John "Mushmouth" Johnson entered a lucrative interracial partnership with an Irish American gambler named Tom McGinnis, as co-owners of the Phoenix Policy and Bung-Loo Company. The policy bank prospered, and by the time Johnson died in 1907, he had become a major philanthropist in the black community. Through the 1930s, while blacks never broke into bookmaking, they did own their own casinos, which served an integrated clientele and paid protection money to the same cops and judges the white-owned establishments had to pay off.[64]

White people and black people bet on the same horse races, prizefights, and lotteries—and often deployed the same rituals of divination. As late as the beginning of World War II, many black conjurers in Southern and border cities reported that nearly half their clientele was white.

The conjurer served many purposes, but one was helping people puzzle out what number to play. In New Orleans in the 1930s and 1940s, a WPA guide reported, many people of all races thought of nothing but numbers and lottery. "Hundreds of white people make it an inseparable part of their daily lives. They seem to find in the game an escape, an almost glamorous rainbow trail with hope and a pot of gold always ahead. And sometimes they win. Many families seem to supplement their incomes constantly by scrupulous attention to every detail in the art of playing lottery."[65] For blacks and whites alike, the vernacular culture of chance allowed apparently irrational means to serve rational ends—a reversal of the nuclear strategists' procedure.

Still it would be a mistake to suggest that the culture of chance was a roistering free-for-all of racial diversity. There were severe limits to racial mixing in this era of *apartheid:* as in San Francisco during the gold rush, the sporting crowd brought footloose men of various ethnicities into sweaty proximity, creating animosity as well as camaraderie. But in surveying the evidence that documents the vernacular culture of chance, one is struck less by diversity than by the centrality of African American influence. In New York, New Orleans, and other places where the sporting crowd liked to congregate, black people played a crucial role in sustaining the symbiosis of betting and believing.[66]

Most African American gamblers wanted to contact the Lord, but not through regular channels. Rather than consult a minister, who might or might not be sympathetic, they turned for advice to spiritualist "mothers" whose storefront churches could be found in many urban black neighborhoods by the 1930s. For these women, as for others before them in Christian tradition, heterodox spirituality was a path to female power. Some, like Ida Carter of Hogansville, Alabama, or Aunt Caroline Dye of Newport News, Virginia, were modern Marie Leveauxs—hoodoo women with occult powers.[67] Other "mothers" were more explicitly Christian, albeit syncretic and idiosyncratic. The Reverend Maude Shannon was head of her own independent church, the Daniel Helping Hand Mission, in New Orleans. Like other African Americans in that city, she had borrowed the Italian Catholic custom of celebrating Saint Joseph's day. In 1931 she built a special altar in the saint's honor and invited everyone in the neighborhood for a big feed, which included "lucky beans." In subsequent years, word got out among the sporting crowd; local gamblers would "come to get the lucky beans and leave money behind," Reverend

Shannon reported. How devoted they were to Saint Joseph is open to question, but the gamblers' mere presence at Shannon's church underscored the interdependence between their apparently trivial pursuits and a syncretist cosmology.[68]

Similar symbioses surfaced in other cities. In Memphis during the 1920s and 1930s, professional gamblers used conjuring techniques to attract good spirits (customers) and repel bad ones (police). One way was to burn an old shoe with a mixture of sugar, onion hulls, sulfur, and Hearts Cologne in the heel; another was to make a cross with two old shoes (the crossroads as well as the Christian symbol), put a teaspoon of sugar in each heel, and burn that cross.[69] Black migrants from the South carried their conjuring beliefs in their battered valises. By the 1920s, in Harlem, Pittsburgh, Chicago, and Detroit, a mix of hoodoo, Christianity, and numerology created cosmic coherence for gamblers—most of whom were recently arrived migrants from the North American South or the Caribbean. Belief in that cosmos encouraged betting and vice versa.

The most popular betting game in Harlem was the numbers game, which resembled older forms of policy or lottery.[70] The numbers had an extraordinary impact on everyday life in Harlem. "The avid playing of numbers enormously multiplied the appetites of the credulous in the science of numerology," the writer Claude McKay recalled. "Harlem was set upon a perpetual hunt for lucky numbers." Any conceivable object or event could acquire numerological significance, either by yielding information directly (house numbers, laundry tickets) or by connecting with the interpretive scheme of a dream book or a hoodoo doctor. Stepping in dog excrement was good luck, crossing a funeral procession was bad; but both actions had lucky number combinations associated with them.[71]

In Harlem as elsewhere, hoodoo fetishes and rituals blended with Christian practices. Psalms 4, 57, and 114 were considered the gamblers' psalms and were sold on parchment. They were meant to be read while burning Prosperity Oil and Lady Luck incense, before a lithograph or statue of Saint Anthony. Conjurers readily incorporated Christian icons into their business, but also kept up a brisk trade in traditional and modern hoodoo charms—lodestones (sometimes nourished with iron filings), miniature bone hands (increasingly plastic—a trend deplored by the conjurers), snake vertebrae, rabbit's feet, Lucky Dog perfume, and John the Conquerer root.[72]

The persistence of root work in Harlem revealed the continuing connection between urban blacks and their rural past. It also epitomized the linkage of matter and spirit in the culture of chance. A magic root—what could more aptly signify the earthly dimensions of *mana*? Like other fetishistic rituals, root work sustained (and claimed to satisfy) erotic longings for grace—for the sense of oneness with the cosmos that the lucky gambler or lover might feel. As in other traditions, love was the riskiest gamble of all, exposing one to incalculable gain or loss, mixing transcendent longings with insistent physical needs. A root doctor on Lenox Avenue made the link between gambling and eros explicit, at least from the male point of view: "Y'know the women and the numbers, they's both jus' alike. Ain't neither of 'em can hold out long when yuh got Big Johnny [Big John the Conqueror root] workin' fo' yuh." The courtship of Fortuna was paired with the courtship of flesh-and-blood women—who in turn often deployed love charms to catch or keep a man. *Mana* carried an erotic charge, melding sex and spirit.[73]

Body and soul came together in the African American language of luck. Though she sought guidance from an invisible spiritual world, Martha White of New Orleans described her gambling strategy in earthbound terms: "You gotta stick to your numbers. They bound to come out sometimes. It's just like feedin' up a little ole shoat. You gotta fatten that pig up first. Then you kills him. And you gotta play your hunches. You gotta play what comes to you. Dreams is a good way. Everybody plays their dreams. Sure I got me a dream book." Dreams were the path between visible and invisible worlds, and for some African Americans (as for Iroquois and Yoruba) the very basis for an alternative, gambler's worldview.[74]

There was nothing inherently irrational about this perspective. Regular numbers players viewed their bets as a sensible investment. Given the kinds of jobs available to them, this attitude made some sense. "If I had to choose between work and the Lottery, I would sure take Lottery, 'cause I feels I can make money and still have my time to myself," said White. It was no sin, but rather a way to avoid stealing (at worst) or frivolous spending (at best). Numbers players reasoned that if they tried to save small change, they would probably spend it, while if they bet it on a number, they couldn't get it back, and they might get something more for it. Many players cultivated a methodical betting style and a long-range perspective, which the academically sanctioned numerology of econometrics has declared to be economically rational. According to the academic conjure-doctors, if a numbers gambler bet a dollar thirteen hundred times over ten years, he or she could confidently expect to hit a $550 pay-off at least once, not to mention smaller wins that would offset the initial investment. Black people in Harlem, like poor people throughout the United States in the interwar period, were suspicious of banks and ill-served by them. Money bet on numbers was not being withdrawn from bank deposits. As an alternative form of banking for the bankless, numbers gambling could constitute a rational investment.[75]

Along with monetary payoffs, numbers, policy, and lottery offered a variety of tangible and intangible rewards. Numbers runners saved bettors time and trouble. Lottery offices were suffused with sociability: in Philadelphia, some elderly black women recalled, they would get together with their girlfriends every morning to pick their numbers; if somebody hit, there was bound to be a party, and money would circulate some more. In every city, the numbers apparatus provided job opportunities for dozens if not hundreds of unemployed or underemployed African Americans. It also created culture-heroes: living lives of glittering excess, black numbers bankers evoked admiration from lesser folk, who were often beneficiaries of the big shots' largesse. Numbers banks even extended loans, pooling gambling debts into a capital fund for local residents who lacked collateral or credit. The "numbers racket" constituted a legitimate part of the informal economy in black communities throughout the country.[76]

The connections between formal and informal economies were indirect but revealing. During the 1920s, when the winning number was the total sale on the New York Stock Exchange for the day, one black numbers banker rented an office on Wall Street so he could more easily pick up inside dope. In Harlem he won respect as "the Negro on Wall Street." During the bull market of the late 1920s, even symbolic association with the formal economy was a source of legitimacy, but the crash of 1929 revealed that there was not that much difference between playing the numbers and speculating in stocks. "My savings of a lifetime of hard work are all tied up in the stock market at an appalling loss," an African American from Pittsburgh wrote to the manager of the New York Stock Exchange in 1931, "yet I am not a hard loser, but have resorted to the 'Number' game to try and retrieve at least a part of my losses."[77]

Respect for chance remained woven into the fabric of black people's everyday life. This outlook reflected the centrality of *play* in African American cultural traditions. Conjuring was a ritual performance that depended on the playful assemblage of apparent junk. The conjurer's worldview was a syncretist agglomeration of hoodoo, Christianity, and numerology—another version of spiritual bricolage. Gambling reinforced this playful "science of the concrete," and vice versa; the result was a symbiosis between betting and believing. Other pastimes also encouraged respect for risk and chance. The game of escalating insult called "the Dozens" ("Yo' mamma . . . ") was a form of improvised verbal play that placed a premium on maintaining poker-faced composure while taking outrageous social risks.[78]

Sometimes African American play was a way of constantly shuffling and recasting outcomes (as with cards or dice). Improvised solutions came from play, which tapped subrational logics and associations. It often involved performance, but in the deepest sense the performer was oblivious of the need to win. In music, sport, or ritual conjuring, this deepest form of play was pure, unself-conscious prodigality.

Perhaps the richest expression of African American play was in the area of music. Blues and jazz were rooted in the same subsoil of experience as African American superstitions: anxiety concerning the uncertainty of fate. "Can't tell my future, I can't tell my past, Lord it seems like every minute sure gonna be my last," sang Willie Brown of Mississippi. Like other tragic cultural forms, the blues translated fundamental philosophical issues into concrete experience—the nearness of nonexistence, the pain of feeling estranged from the dominant idioms of order, the longing to be at home in the cosmos. In "Crossroads Blues" (1936), the Delta bluesman Robert Johnson brilliantly used an ancient emblem of chance to explore his own sense of alienation.

> *I went down to the crossroads, fell down on my knees.*
> *I went down to the crossroads, fell down on my knees.*
> *Ask the lord above for mercy, say boy, if you please.*
> *Mmmmm—standing at the crossroads, I tried to flag a ride.*
> *Mmmmm—standing at the crossroads, I tried to flag a ride.*
> *Ain't nobody seem to know me, everybody pass me by.*[79]

Universal feelings of abandonment and isolation acquired an especially sharp significance for black people living under the American version of apartheid. Playing the blues was a way of exorcising the specter of random force, turning cosmic uncertainty into a song—or, in the case of jazz, into an opportunity for improvisation. Jazz musicians sought escape from the controlled linearity of classical Western modes into a realm of pure play, beyond time—the same sort of unified experience courted by a gambler on a hot streak or an athlete "in the zone." The aim was not a rejection but a loosening of cosmic order, the creation of a place of grace.

The African American sporting crowd situated exalted experiences in apparently sordid places (sordid, at least, from the viewpoint of respectable morality). The white sporting crowd provided a similar mix of high and low, rationality and irrationality; it was dominated by Italians, Jews, and other ethnic and regional outsiders who had less access to public legitimacy than black gamblers did within their own communities— who in fact were often associated with organized crime. As the phrase suggests, even lawless behavior was being brought under managerial control. Gambling, like other forms of vice, could repay a steady return on investment. Despite such gestures toward economic rationality, sporting men of various ethnic backgrounds sustained the connection between betting and believing—the location of the wagering impulse within a wider culture of chance.

In part, the ethic of fortune was sustained by nostalgia for frontier freedoms (actual or imagined). Almost as soon as the frontier officially closed, mythographers began enveloping it in an elegiac haze. The frontier gambler became an icon of twentieth-century masculinity. Part of his appeal was his prodigality. Consider Riley Grannan, an adventurer, gambler, and plunger from Kentucky who died in the silver town of Rawhide, Nevada, in 1908. The eulogy delivered at his funeral by W. H. Knickerbocker, a defrocked Low-Church Episcopalian from Louisiana, was reprinted twenty years later. It caught the largest significance of the sporting crowd's ethic of fortune.

Knickerbocker described Grannan as a "dead game sport," renowned among local lowlifes for his generosity and good cheer. The world said he wasted his money by trying to brighten the lives of prostitutes and drunks, but (Knickerbocker asked), "Did it ever occur to you that the men and women who inhabit the night-world are still men and women?" The man who brought them happiness was still a benefactor to humanity. "Riley Grannan may have 'wasted' some of his money this way." But if he did, he was emulating God himself, who was hardly an example of economic efficiency.

> Did you ever stop and think how God does not put all His sunbeams into corn, potatoes, and flour? Did you ever notice the prodigality with which He scatters these sunbeams over the universe? . . . Wasted sunbeams, these? I say to you that the man who by the use of his money or power is able to smooth one wrinkle from the brow of care, is able to change one moan or sob into a song, is able to wipe away one tear and in its place put a jewel of joy—this man is a public benefactor.[80]

Characters like Grannan lived in memory and mythology, though the world they inhabited grew more marginal as the managerial ethos spread. Still, on street corners and in barbershops and bars you could play a number, pick a horse, bet on a baseball game. With the triumph of Progressive antigambling reform, the sporting crowd retreated further into the shadows of respectable society, where they gambled as enthusiastically as ever. Casino owners went to imaginative lengths to stay in business, including anchoring "gambling ships" just offshore from Los Angeles and beyond the reach of its laws. But most professional gamblers followed time-honored tradition and paid off the police. As in the nineteenth century, laws against gambling were often left unenforced, for a fee.[81]

There were also turf struggles between the gamblers themselves, which tended to result in the survival of the more efficiently organized syndicates. As a tool for economic survival, rationalization occasionally worked. In Harlem during the early 1930s, Dutch Schulz's syndicate attempted with some success to take control of the numbers game. Local numbers bankers resisted quietly, but the éclat of the earlier years began to ebb. Schulz based the winning numbers on the betting statistics at various mob-controlled racetracks, and depended on his lieutenant Abba Dabba Berman to manipulate the reported amount of the pari-mutuel take so that only lightly played combinations won. Berman, referred to enviously by Vito Genovese as "the Yid adding machine," ensured Schulz a predictable profit—for a little while. Schulz and Berman were assassinated by rival white mobsters in 1935, but even before then they had lost control of the numbers in Harlem. Their attempt to rationalize the numbers was limited and short-lived.[82]

In smaller cities, undercover gambling was a less complicated proposition. Warren Nelson, who became a successful professional gambler in Las Vegas in the post–World War II era, remembered starting out as a keno dealer at the Mint Cigar Store in Great Falls, Montana, in the early 1930s. The keno game was in the backroom; women were not allowed there, but could play through a window in the foyer of the ladies' room. The game was shut down occasionally by the sheriff, but only when a local citizen complained. With the end of Prohibition in 1933, gambling stayed undercover in Great Falls but went wide open in the mining town of Butte. Nelson moved there and discovered the best gamblers were the migrant Mexican beet pickers, who would play poker, smoke marijuana, and laugh all day long as their piles of chips ascended. Nearly every restaurant, bar, and roadhouse in the Rocky Mountain West had at least one slot machine on the premises, put there by syndicates, which split the profits with the proprietors.[83]

Farther east, slot machine operators were more circumspect. On warm summer afternoons during the early years of the Second World War, the phone would ring in Davidson's Tavern, at the intersection of Front Street and West Broadway in East Saint Louis, Illinois, about a hundred yards from the Mississippi River and directly under the east end of the Eads Bridge. Ernie, the manager, would answer it and say, "Yes. Yes. Yes. Okay." Then he would hang up, get a hand truck out of the backroom, take the slot machines methodically, one by one, to the basement, then sweep up the area where their pedestals had been. When the state police arrived, he would serve them roast beef sandwiches with horseradish. As soon as the cops left, Ernie would return the machines to their places.[84]

Scenes like this were repeated throughout the Mississippi Valley, and in the Northeast and Middle Atlantic states, from the 1920s through World War II. Often the person on the other end of the phone line was a local politician; in East Saint Louis in the 1940s it was probably Dan McGlynn, the lawyer and fixer who oversaw relations between the police and the gambling community. Like other forms of "vice" in this officially abstemious era, gambling could be tolerated if it was decently hidden.

Public gambling survived in select locations, some exuding glamor. At the Algonquin Hotel in New York City during the 1920s, the Thanatopsis and Literary Inside Straight Club endowed ferociously competitive

poker with an aura of celebrity. In Hollywood during the 1930s the ownership of racehorses brought vicarious self-enhancement to Hal Roach,
Bing Crosby, and other newly rich men.[85] But the vast majority of the
white sporting crowd was seedier, flashier, and less respectable than
Crosby and Roach. The life of Titanic Thompson provides an idiosyncratic example of a common social type.

Thompson was born Alvin Clarence Thomas in a log cabin near
Rogers, Arkansas, in 1892. His father was a sporting man who left town
when the baby was five months old. His mother remarried a hardworking honest man, and almost as soon as young Alvin was old enough to
imagine getting away from a life of earnest toil, he was beginning to
plot his escape. He began accumulating a stash by pitching pennies with
schoolmates and winning bets with strangers on rigged propositions. He
once bet his dog Carlo against a tourist's fancy fishing rod that Carlo
could fetch a rock from the bottom of a creek. The tourist agreed, but
said they better mark the rock so they knew the dog brought back the
same rock thrown in. Alvin agreed and drew an X on the rock—having
spent the previous day covering the creek bottom with similarly marked
stones. Alvin won the rod.[86]

This would become his favorite form of gambling—the proposition
("I'll bet you I can . . . "), particularly one weighted in his favor. When he
was sixteen he left home, betting he could make a better living by trick-
ery than by hard work. He was right, but it took a little while. Alvin got
a job selling maps in southern Missouri, but picked up more cash from
playing dice, pool, and poker (his apparent sincerity made him a good
bluffer). After a stint with a medicine show operator who called himself
Colonel Bogardus, Alvin headed for Memphis and full-time gambling.
He'd learned how to palm dice and won consistently at craps.[87] He spent
a few more years working the gambling circuit in the mid-South, including the golf clubs, where he proved an adept at the game. By the end of
the First World War, he was ready to head for New York City—but not
before he had renamed himself Titanic Thompson.[88]

Thompson arrived in New York during the early 1920s, at about the
same time as Nick Dandolos, better known as Nick the Greek. Dandolos
was a rich kid from Crete, the son of a prosperous rug merchant, the
grandson of a shipowner. He was a good card player but a reckless bettor
who quickly became known as a big loser (and an occasional cheat, out

of desperation). When he came to New York, he had won nearly a million dollars in California and carried a suitcase full of cash—nearly all of which he lost to a crack team of Jewish gamblers. Dandolos became the butt of stand-up comics, who called him Saint Nick: "Only recently has it been learned," they would say, "that Santa Claus is really a native of Greece, not the North Pole, and he's showered his gifts on a group of people who don't even bother to put up a Christmas tree."[89]

Thompson was more consistently successful than Dandolos. A trickster who liked to win through subterfuge, Thompson pretended ineptitude on the golf course, often losing the match but more than making up for it in side bets on propositions concerning indvidual shots. ("A G-note says I sink this putt.") He once bet a local mark he could throw a pumpkin over a two-story hotel in Reno; he found a baseball-size pumpkin, flung it over the building, and collected the bet. Throughout his gambling career, Thompson was a shrewd operator. He learned how to calculate odds from a former math professor named Pat McAlley, and he always did his damndest to minimize the role of luck.[90]

But neither Thompson nor any other professional gambler could eliminate luck altogether. (Attempts to reduce gambling to system were the butt of satirical humor—as in the Marx Brothers' movie *A Day at the Races* [1937], in which Chico sells Groucho a collection of betting books, which Groucho never bothers to use.) Nor would the sporting crowd have wanted to eliminate luck. No matter how systematic their efforts to control outcomes they still felt a powerful attraction to uncertainty and risk, to feinting and bluffing—in short, to play. Gamblers, even men like Thompson who might more precisely be designated sharpers, were contributing to an alternative moral economy.

The gamblers' moral economy existed beyond the managerial quest for systematic control. If the dominant capitalist economy sanctioned self-discipline and steady accumulation of money, the gambler's economy valued prodigality and periodic circulation of money. To be sure, not all gamblers adhered to this ethos: as Nick the Greek complained after one of his big losses, "The real tragedy is that those sharp sonsabitches won't ever put none of that money back into circulation. It's just like you dropped it down the john and flushed it away."[91] But Nick's bitter disappointment suggested that most gamblers expected big winners to put some if not most of their winnings "back into circulation." The sporting crowd still sustained an ethic of fortune—an alternative to managerial rationality. Less fully but in the end no less decisively than the African American version, this ethic pointed toward an alternative cosmology, a symbiosis of betting and believing.

The clearest presentation of the sporting crowd's worldview was in Damon Runyon's work. Runyon created the most enduring image of the twentieth-century gambler as a social type. Despite their wise-guy mannerisms, Runyon's gamblers displayed many traditional sporting traits. For starters, they never ratted on a friend. Like Arnold Rothstein, who survived in the hospital for two days after he was shot at the Park Central Hotel but refused to name his assassin, they "died game"—as Runyon praised Rothstein for doing.[92]

They also rarely died rich, though they may have lived well. This was usually due to their insouciant disregard for saving money. They never refused help to a tapped-out friend or passed up a bet at long odds. One of Runyon's characters, a horse player named Regret, was modeled on Abba Dabba Berman. Runyon was less interested in Berman's ability to rig the numbers than in his propensity to lose at the track despite occasional big wins. (Regret was the name of the Kentucky Derby winner in 1915.) Although Dutch Schulz paid him $10,000 a week for his service to the numbers racket, Berman died in possession of $87.12. Surrounded by gamblers like Berman, and given himself to losing big at the track, Runyon concluded that "All Horseplayers Die Broke."[93]

In its emphasis on circulation rather than accumulation, and on the creation of authority through giving, the gamblers' moral economy resembled the preindustrial gift economies described by anthropologists and cultural historians. The acceptance of chance as a source of potential beneficence, a gift from the gods, involved an implicit rejection of the linear march toward perfection enshrined by the culture of control. In a sense, Runyon's gamblers inhabited an eternal present, epitomized by his use of the historical present tense—"So I says to this guy, I says . . ."—a usage inspired by the gamblers' own, which Runyon faithfully transcribed. Runyonland was a world elsewhere, where gambling was a way of killing time.

For Runyon, the sporting crowd's ethic of fortune was more than a moral economy. It was also a cosmology that connected gambling, loss, and redemption—implying there was no redemption without loss. Those implications surfaced in Runyon's most famous story, "The Idyll of Miss Sarah Brown" (1932). Its hero, Sky Masterson, was modeled on Titanic Thompson. "The Sky" is a big guy from Saint Louis who is constantly on the move, looking for action wherever he can find it. From the Gideon Bibles he reads in hotel rooms he learns not to welsh on his bets, but he is not above tricking his opponents—as when he tricks Big Nig at the Polo Grounds by claiming he could toss a peanut from the pitcher's mound to the box seats behind home plate, winning the bet by weighting the peanut with a little piece of lead.

The Sky's great preoccupation, though, is not with winning but with playing, preferably for the highest possible stakes. "In fact," Runyon writes, "the reason he is called The Sky is because he goes so high when it comes to betting on any proposition whatever. He will bet all he has, and no one can bet any more than this." Money means nothing to him: "as far as The Sky is concerned, money is nothing but just something for him to play with and the dollars may as well be doughnuts as far as value goes with him. The only time The Sky ever thinks of money as money is when he is broke, and the only way he can tell he is broke is when he reaches into his pocket and finds nothing there but his fingers." The Sky is a quintessentially traditional gambler in his willingness to risk total loss.[94]

That outlook comes across clearly in his courtship of Miss Sarah Brown, the doll with "hundred per cent eyes," who plays cornet for the Salvation Army mission. When The Sky asks her how the soul-saving business is going, she says: "I worry greatly about how few souls we seem to save. Sometimes I wonder if we are lacking in grace."[95] The Sky determines to find a way to save some souls for her, though she spurns him after she discovers he is a professional gambler. He finds Nathan Detroit's crap game floating in a room over a Fifty-second Street garage and proceeds to lose his entire bankroll in a futile attempt to win the soul of Brandy Bottle Bates, or anyone else who cares to bet. The proposition is that if they lose they have to attend a prayer meeting at the mission, but no one loses because Brandy Bottle's dice are loaded. The Sky figures this out eventually and is about to pull a revolver from his pocket when Miss Sarah Brown bursts in, full of outrage.

"If you wish to gamble for souls, Mister Sky," she says, "gamble for your own soul." She bets him two dollars against his soul, rolls Brandy Bottle's dice, and wins. They leave together and once they are out in the

street, Miss Brown tells him: "'You are a fool.' 'Why,' The Sky says, 'Paul
says "If any man among you seemeth to be wise in this world, let him become a fool, that he may be wise." I love you Miss Sarah Brown,' The Sky
says." Miss Brown refers him to the second verse of the Song of Solomon, and the story concludes with The Sky happily beating a drum in
the Salvation Army band, and Mrs. Sky blissfully unaware that she won
her husband's soul with a pair of loaded dice.[96]

Of course, it is all a joke, made even more ludicrous in its later incar-
nation as a Broadway musical. It would be foolish to impose too solemn
a meaning on Runyon's story. But it does suggest some provocative connections between a certain kind of gambling and a certain kind of grace.
The Sky embodies the subversive paradoxes of Christianity: he risks all to
gain all; he behaves foolishly to become wise. Eventually he demonstrates
the meaning of grace to a woman who fears she is deficient in it, despite
her appearance of piety.

The gambler's attraction to loss, even to self-destruction, was part of
the aura of danger that made gambling sublime. But there was more than
a titillating frisson at work in gambling's appeal: the figure of "the loser"
became an oddly powerful specter in a society that deified winning and
denied defeat. Incurably prodigal, the gambler refused to hoard money;
instead he kept "throwing it away," seeking a kind of grace through what
the theologian Paul Tillich called "holy waste." As Tillich said, "Without
the abundance of the heart nothing great can happen"—without "accepting the waste of an uncalculated surrender" or "wasting ourselves beyond the limits of law and rationality."[97]

The sporting crowd's ethic of fortune melded with a strain of Christianity that celebrated reckless generosity as a means of grace—a strain
very different from the one that sanctified the United States as the savior
of the free world. Few theologians expressed that subversive version of
Christianity more eloquently than an author who called himself Harlem
Pete, in a dream book published in Philadelphia in 1949. "If you want to
be rich, Give! If you want to be poor, Grasp! If you want abundance,
Scatter! If you want to be needy, Hoard!" he wrote.[98] This was a world
view profoundly at odds with managerial rationality, and indeed with the
whole tradition of secular providentialism. It also sounded suspiciously
like the teachings of Jesus.

Baffling as it may have been to Frederick Winslow Taylor, holy waste
remained central to the twentieth-century culture of chance: not only to

its vernacular versions but also to a shadow discourse of risk and redemption that included painters, musicians and poets, novelists, theologians, and philosophers. The triumph of management remained uncertain, and the allure of accident attracted some of the profoundest artists and writers of the age.

{CHAPTER SEVEN}

THE PERSISTENT ALLURE OF ACCIDENT

he new fascination with chance arose from a transatlantic conceptual revolution—the variety of revolts against certainty that historians call "modernism." Virginia Woolf's famous hyperbole remains strikingly acute. "On or about December 1910," she wrote, "human character changed." Even before the guns of August 1914, Woolf heard all about her "the sound of breaking and falling, crashing and destruction." The sounds were metaphorical but nonetheless real. Modernist literary experiments violated grammar, smashed syntax, and outraged propriety; the culmination of those gestures was James Joyce's *Ulysses* (1914–1922)—"the conscious and calculated indecency of a man who feels that in order to breathe he must break the windows," Woolf called it.[1] But the modernist excitement involved more than a bunch of naughty boys thumbing their noses at schoolmarms. It was an extraordinarily complex challenge to accepted categories of understanding, mounted by a diverse assortment of artists and writers, scientists and philosophers—a cracking of the metaphysical foundations of Western thought.

While Taylor and other managerial thinkers continued their effort to systematize everyday life, the ferment of modernism generated compelling new reasons for respecting the power of randomness. From Nietzsche to Freud, modernist thinkers jettisoned ideas of Providence (religious or secular) as metaphysical delusions. Freud concluded in his essay on Leonardo da Vinci: "We are all too ready to forget that in fact everything to do with our life is chance, from our origin out of the meeting of spermatozoon and ovum onwards. . . ."[2]

Yet despite their new sense of the causal role of chance, most modernist thinkers refused an all-embracing relativism and continued to cling to some larger framework of cosmic order. Sometimes this meant succumbing to a secular metaphysics: Nietzsche came to celebrate the *Über-mensch* as a quasi-divinity; Freud allowed psychoanalysis to congeal into a positivist system, as insistent on its timeless truth as any Victorian moral-ity had been; Dewey's openmindedness closed in defense of "scientific method." Still, many other thinkers recognized that science itself was changing, acknowledging indeterminacy even in those fields that had once been bastions of positivist certainty: physics and mathematics. That acknowledgment allowed a more open stance, in the spirit of William James.

For those modernists who remained at ease with ambiguity, chance became an avenue of escape from mechanistic determinism. Rejecting positivism, they refused nihilism as well and sought to sustain a precari-ous balance between the awareness of contingency and the longing for larger meaning. Among the most remarkable were such Christian exis-tentialists as Karl Jaspers and Miguel de Unamuno, whose appreciation for the arbitrariness of life and death led them to a deeper form of reli-gious belief—one that embraced rather than evaded the absurdity at the heart of existence.

It was in literature and the arts, though, that the allure of accident was strongest. Chance had long been a source of inspiration for artists. Leonardo himself had advised aspiring painters in fifteenth-century Flo-rence to attend to the random configurations of everyday life—but only as the raw material for "complete and well-drawn forms."[3] In the early twentieth century, chance began to play some dramatically new roles for painters and poets, novelists, musicians, and choreographers—for a siz-able portion of the artists who by the turn of the nineteenth century were known as the avant-garde. The significance of chance varied in ac-cordance with the artist's purpose and sensibility. For some, such as James Joyce or Marcel Proust, random recollections of past events became a source of inspiration for extraordinarily crafted works. For others, such as Marcel Duchamp or Tristan Tzara, leaving things to chance itself became a method of composition. New forms proliferated—automatic writing, action painting, collage, assemblage. All, in various ways, required artists to allow freer play to forces beyond their conscious control.

Relinquishing intentionality, letting events happen, occasionally be-came more than a method. For some artists at least, it became a path to insight—though it was an open question whether the insight came from the depths of the artist's unconscious or from somewhere else altogether.

Ultimately, the aesthetic of accident aimed to blur such distinctions, along with all the other familiar dualities in the Western tradition: mind and body, performer and audience, art and life. Most accidentalists were tricksters, whose identities ranged from ironist to shaman. The purpose of their projects was often merely to shock the perennially shockable bourgeoisie. But sometimes the accidentalist gesture acquired greater significance. Sometimes it became a way of conjuring *mana* through play, of tapping into the stream of creative energy, the flow of primal plenitude sought by diviners and gamblers when they paid homage to Fortuna. At its most profound (as in Joyce or Proust), the allure of accident could lead to a fleeting experience of grace.

Many American modernists shared in the accidentalist impulse, though it took them several decades to feel its full inspiration. Beginning in the 1930s, the artist Joseph Cornell joined accident and craft, collecting the detritus of commercial life and using it to embody Proustian "*moments bienheureux*" in the glass-fronted boxes that became his signature work. During and after the Second World War, artists and writers created what the historian Daniel Belgrad has called a "culture of spontaneity"— extending the claims of chance against the midcentury managerial consensus.[4] In Charles Olson's "projective verse" and Jack Kerouac's "spontaneous bop prosody," in Jackson Pollock's gesture paintings and Robert Rauschenberg's assemblages, as well as in the more crafted spontaneity of Louise Nevelson's found-object sculptures and Robert Motherwell's collages, an accidentalist aesthetic flourished.

Perhaps its purest expression was the work of the composer John Cage, which incorporated chance by rolling dice or consulting the I Ching, and eventually aimed to open all art to the unmediated randomness of everyday experience. Cage was a central figure (along with the choreographer Merce Cunningham and the artist Allan Kaprow) in the development of the unscripted theatrical events the composer called "Happenings." As Cage and his friends took chance to extremes, they often lost its larger significance. The trickster-artist often became little more than an entertainer, inventing new dance steps in the endless pas de deux between bohemian and bourgeois.

Still, this was not the whole story. American artists who combined chance and craft—Cornell, Nevelson, and Motherwell, among others— created enduring and significant work. So did those modernist thinkers who continued to pose ultimate questions to a contingent universe. Even

Cage sought silence as an opening to divinity, and the theologian Paul Tillich, like Jaspers and Unamuno (and James before them), redefined faith for an uncertain age. And in *Invisible Man,* the novelist Ralph Ellison embedded chance in a rich vernacular context, reaffirming the connections between gambling and grace. They challenged the excesses of managerial control in midtwentieth-century American life, but the origins of their insights lay in the transatlantic modernism of the early twentieth century. To understand American accidentalists, we need to retrace the conceptual revolution that preceded them.

THE MODERNIST TRANSFORMATION OF TIME AND SPACE

The modernist challenge to Western metaphysics was most apparent in the emerging critique of those supposedly a priori categories, time and space. The pioneering critic was William James. In *Principles of Psychology* (1890), James articulated the key insights that would shape modernist thought and eventually inform the aesthetic of accident. Before Gestalt psychologists and Cubist painters, he recognized the unity of the perceptual field: the complementarity of figure and ground, sound and silence. As he wrote: "What we hear when the thunder crashes is not thunder pure, but thunder-breaking-upon-silence-and-contrasting-with-it." His habitual use of hyphens underscored the continuity of perceptual experience: negative space was as important as positive space. What was formerly regarded as a void now possessed a constitutive function, as James acknowledged (in the philosopher Horace Kallen's words) "the democratic consubstantiality of every entity in experience with every other." With the recognition of positive negative space, James opened the door to new ways of appreciating the interconnections between the meaningful and the meaningless, the ordered and the random—as inseparable components of the perceptual flux he would come to call "pure experience."[5]

James's revaluation of experiences and modes of perception previously deemed beneath notice was a characteristic modernist gesture, one he performed to extraordinary effect with respect to the understanding of time. The impact of James's thought on the modernist discourse of time stemmed from his redefinition of consciousness in the brilliant chapter he

called "The Stream of Thought." "Consciousness does not appear to itself chopped up in bits," he wrote. "It is nothing jointed; it flows. A
'river' or a 'stream' are the metaphors by which it is most naturally described. *In talking of it hereafter, let us call it the stream of thought, of consciousness.*" With this insight, James freed human self-understanding from the
atomistic, mechanistic frameworks that viewed human thoughts as discrete, separable entities. "We ought to say a feeling of *and,* a feeling of *if,*
a feeling of *but,* and a feeling of *by,* quite as readily as we say a feeling of
blue or a feeling of *cold.*"[6] As in his comments on spatial perception, James
recognized the meaningfulness of experiences previously thought meaningless. Though a handful of Romantics and mystics had gestured toward
this wholistic understanding of thought, James was the first to name it
precisely and give it philosophical legitimacy.

James's emphasis on the continuous flow of consciousness led directly
to a new understanding of how people experienced time. Bergson called
it "duration" and contrasted it with the mechanically measurable bits of
time displayed on clocks and in railway schedules. (A shift toward standard
time zones began in the 1880s, and World Standard Time was implemented in 1913.)[7] As public time became more standardized and more
pervasive as a means of organizing everyday life, modernist thinkers grew
more skeptical of attempts to quantify the duration of experience. Indeed, they began to question any official effort to impose a single, linear
meaning on time—above all the widespread, complacent belief in inevitable progress that united the governing clases on both sides of the Atlantic.

This secular providentialism was the stuff of metropolitan gentlemen's clubs and overheated drawing rooms—the sort of places whose
windows Joyce wanted to smash. Joyce, Proust, and other modernist authors increasingly turned away from predictable public versions of time
altogether, prompted by the unpredictable stirrings of memory to explore the heterogenous time of private experience. Recognizing the survival of the past in the present, they blurred the boundaries set by clock
time and rejected the determinism of Progress or Providence.

And the key to their recollection was chance. As Proust observed, the
past forever eluded conscious efforts to recall it. "It is a labor in vain to try
to recapture it: all the efforts of our intellect are useless. The past is hidden somewhere outside its own domain in some material object which

we never suspected. And it depends on chance whether or not we come upon it before we die."[8] The taste of a madeleine dipped in tea, the feel of an uneven paving stone underfoot—these unpredictable occurrences trigger the involuntary memories that become, in their sensuous fullness, what Proust called *moments bienheureux:* earthly experiences of grace.

Joyce's views were more ambivalent but ultimately similar. In *Ulysses,* Stephen Dedalus says that memories may be "hidden away by man in the dark places of the heart but they abide there and wait" until "a chance word will call them forth suddenly and they will rise up to confront him in the most various circumstances, a vision or a dream. . . . A scene disengages itself in the observer's memory, evoked, it would seem, by a word of so natural a homeliness as if those days were really present there (as some thought) with their immediate pleasures. A shaven space of lawn one soft May evening, the well-remembered grove of lilacs at Roundtown. . . . " For Dedalus the past is a source of remorse—"agenbite of inwit"—over his failure to attend his mother's funeral; for Leopold Bloom the past is a focus of longing. As he saunters about Dublin, random perceptions repeatedly turn the flow of his mind back to the period twenty years earlier, when he and Molly were happy together, when their son Rudy was still alive. "So it returns," says Bloom of a scene from the past. "Think you're escaping and run into yourself. Longest way round is the shortest way home."[9]

For Joyce, linear schemes of progess were based on an illusion. The past was inescapable: it rose unbidden amid our stream of consciousness, through the unpredictable fluctuations of memory. Such meldings of past and present could become what Joyce called "epiphanies"—sudden surges of spiritual insight that occurred in "the most delicate and evanescent of moments."[10] Like Proust's *moments bienheureux,* Joyce's epiphanies constituted secular experiences of grace—no more controllable by conscious will than any other gifts of Fortuna. Joyce, Proust, and other modernist writers revalued heterogenous, private time against the claims of homogenous, public time. They repudiated the inexorable forward march of progressive and providentialist determinisms in favor of a more fluid understanding of time, more subject to the play of the artist's imagination.

The impact of such experiments on a broader audience is difficult to gauge. Certainly the readers of Proust and Joyce were mostly intellectuals like themselves. But the playful possibilities that literary modernists introduced were popularized and extended through film technology.

"Moving pictures" put space as well as time at the disposal of the artist. As the American filmmaker Edwin S. Porter demonstrated in his pioneering editing techniques, cinema time was reversible and stoppable; cinema space was significantly alterable as well. In working-class neighborhoods from Paris to Chicago, nickelodeon audiences delighted in the visual tricks performed by the early "cinema of attractions." One did not have to be an intellectual to experience the fluid possibilities of time and space—as James and others observed, that sort of openness was characteristic of human minds in general, so long as they were not too cluttered with rationalist categories.[11]

From the 1890s on, the notion that temporal and spatial experience could be broken up and recombined led to a host of transformations in art and thought. The perceptual shift helped to create new strategies of managerial control, as in Taylor's scientific management of the labor process, but also gave rise to venturesome strategies in vernacular as well as elite art forms—the unpredictable, irregular phrasings of jazz improvisation; the fragmented, multiple perspectives in the paintings of Cézanne, Picasso, and Braque. A parallel multiplication of perspectives took place in philosophy and physics. A revolt against old certainties, idealist or positivist, opened the door to pragmatism and relativism and to various cults of the irrational spawned by the primitivist challenge to Victorian values. What these movements had in common was a spirit of resistance to the tyranny of a single point of view. Philosophers as different as Nietzsche and Ortega agreed on the social relativity of time and space and the need for a perspectivist approach to reality rather than any form of absolutism, religious or rationalist.[12]

Absolute time and space, meanwhile, were taking their lumps from physicists. Even as Darwinian evolution was transformed into a synonym for progress, physicists were dismantling the Newtonian foundations of faith in an orderly, progressive universe. In 1883 Ernst Mach dismissed Newton's notion of absolute space, motion, and time as "an idle metaphysical conception." A series of hypotheses and experiments by various physicists showed that time measurement depended on the relative motion of the clock and the observer. The trend culminated in Einstein's theories of relativity. To oversimplify (grossly) their significance: the special theory (1905) replaced the Newtonian notion that space was a static realm of empty matter with the idea that it was dynamic and full of energy fields; the general theory (1915) concluded that "every reference body has its own particular time." While classical physics needed only one clock, Einstein wrote, the new physics required "as many clocks as you like," each set to a different correct time.[13]

The smashing of old forms heard by Virginia Woolf occurred in the laboratory as well as the study and the studio. Einstein's theories called the stability of matter into question: spatial forms were constantly changing shape as their movements were accelerated by countless particles within and around them. Space was not as empty nor matter as solid as older conceptions of the universe had assumed. The discovery of X rays brought the new permeability of matter down to earth. Human flesh could be made transparent through the penetrating power of radioactive isotopes. The boundary between the body and the world was not as firmly drawn as it had seemed.

The crackup of the older cosmology was mostly a theoretical affair. Its impact on the practice of science could still be contained by statistical methods and probabilistic thought. Positivism still reigned in the laboratory and social sciences, despite researchers' occasional bows to the uncertain, provisional knowledge produced by the experimental process. But in literature and the arts, the breakdown of established categories was an invitation to cross old dualistic divisions: artist and audience, self and world, art and life. The rejection of old dualisms reaffirmed the Jamesian notion of consciousness as a stream of "pure experience." Fluid metaphors for thought combined with pluralistic conceptions of the universe, allowing artists to conceive the creative process as openness to the flux of chance events. From this view, art was less a product of conscious control than of receptivity to that flow of primal plenitude, that feeling of pure potentiality, which was known in other contexts as *mana*. The avant-garde and vernacular cultures of chance were linked at the ontological level. Artists and intellectuals, like conjurers, took inspiration from accident.

The modernist revaluation of the random contrasted sharply with older traditions of cosmic doubt. Mark Twain, Melville, and Howells had all viewed a world of chance as a bleak moral void. In *Moby-Dick* (1851), when Pip falls overboard by accident and is rescued quite by chance as well, he wanders about the *Pequod*'s deck, staring vacantly and repeating miscellaneous refrains: "I look, you look, he looks; we look, ye look, they look. . . . Caw! caw! caw! caw! caw! caw! Ain't I a crow?"[14] His nonsense

embodies the specter of meaninglessness in a purely random universe—
or worse, as Mark Twain would have it, the capricious cruelty of the gods
who kill us (or drive us mad) for their sport.

But by the end of the nineteenth century, some writers and artists
feared hazard less than the absence of it—in the iron determinisms, religious or secular, behind the culture of control. James led the effort to
promote more favorable views of chance, less as a metaphysical principle
(metaphysical questions were always bracketed, for James) than as an escape hatch from the stifling predictability of a positivist universe. Chance
offered the gift of possibility. Accidentalist artists and writers took a similar view, declaring chance to be a source of creative insight.

This was more than a matter of triggering involuntary memories—
though that was surely crucial for Proust and Joyce. The creative potential of accident extended to the artist's own mistakes. Indeed, as Joyce's
Stephen Dedalus said, in the midst of an argument with pedants over
Shakespeare: "A man of genius makes no mistakes. His errors are volitional and are the portals of discovery."[15] Starting from different premises,
Freud arrived at a parallel conclusion. In *The Psychopathology of Everyday
Life* (1904), he argued that slips of the tongue and other apparently accidental gestures were actually involuntary clues to the buried life of the
unconscious—which for Tristan Tzara and other surrealists became a
spring of vital inspiration. Whether or not they believed their errors were
volitional, avant-garde artists and writers began to imagine them as portals of discovery.

The redefinition of mistakes (sometimes out of existence) was a key
modernist theme. Surfacing with particular clarity in the improvisational
cadences, chord changes, and harmonic structures of jazz, it resonated
with the emphasis on the spontaneous gesture in automatic writing, collage, and action painting; it blurred the boundaries between the correct
and the incorrect. The new tolerance for error was rooted in a reverence
for spontaneity, in a revaluation of childhood and play, in a romantic critique of civilization that intensified toward the end of the nineteenth
century. Along with many educated persons on both sides of the Atlantic,
modernists were fascinated by "primitive" ideas and rituals, including the
casting of runes and other chance operations involved in divination. Like
chance itself, previously scorned forms of thought (or nonthought) could
be redefined as sources of spiritual insight and authentic experience.[16]

The avant-garde trickster could be a modern diviner or shaman, with the power to penetrate and transform the random dailiness of existence.

But the aesthetic of accident could encourage a different sensibility as well. The erasure of boundaries between art and life could lead to ironic acceptance of twentieth-century mass culture in all its chaotic banality. Then the trickster became an impresario of disorder. Absence of any sense of possible cosmic order led to the celebration of chance, play, and uncertainty as ends in themselves. This allegedly postmodern tendency was actually embedded in the modernist project right from the start. The bohemian aspiration to success by scandal came tricked out in revolutionary manifestos, but was often animated merely by the bad boys' desire to tweak the nose of the bourgeoisie.

The trickster sometimes used chance to elude his audience as well as to subvert the Apollonian forces of order. In Jorge Luis Borges's story, "The Lottery in Babylon" (1944), the narrator spins a fable designed to conceal meaning, rather than unfold it. "I have known what the Greeks did not: uncertainty," he says. "I come from a vertiginous country where the lottery forms a principal part of reality." Early lotteries failed in Babylon because "their moral virtue was nil. They did not apeal to all the faculties of men: only to their hope." But gradually "the Company" redesigned the lottery to have adverse as well as happy consequences: job loss or even murder as well as marital happiness or professional prominence. The lottery was made secret, free, and general, and was run entirely by the Company. Every stage of every life event was made subject to its random operations. "Under the beneficent influence of the Company," the narrator concludes, "our customs have become thoroughly impregnated with chance. The buyer of a dozen amphoras of Damascus wine will not be surprised if one of them contains a talisman or a viper. The scribe who draws up a contract scarcely ever fails to introduce some erroneous datum; I myself, in making this hasty declaration, have falsified or invented some grandeur, some atrocity; perhaps, too a certain monotony. . . ." Nothing, even monotony, was safe from epistemological suspicion; everything was shrouded in doubt. As Borges toyed with his reader, he constantly called his own assumptions into question, implying that radical uncertainty was the precondition for modern existence.[17]

Borges's trickster narrator inhabited a world of fragmented identity, persistent ambiguity, constant novelty. It was the same metaphorical locale occupied by Walker Percy's protagonist in *The Last Gentleman* (1966)—

"the locus of pure possibility" where "what a man can be the next minute bears no relation to what he is or what he was the minute before." Borges celebrated this condition (at least implicitly); Percy yearned for a stable alternative to it. But like many other writers, both assumed that this discontinuous sense of self was an inescapable corollary of modern (and postmodern) life.[18]

The discontinuous self bore an uncanny resemblance to the metaphorical gambler, entranced by the dream of endlessly starting over with every new deal or turn of the wheel. If the dream was a delusion, if gambling was a self-destructive passion, that only increased its aura of authenticity in avant-garde eyes. "The modern element in modern literature," according to Lionel Trilling, was "the idea of losing oneself up to the point of destruction, of surrendering oneself to experience without regard for self-interest or conventional bonds, of escaping wholly from social bonds."[19] This was the dark side of the "gambling spirit" embodied by romantic figures like Poe and Dostoevsky and sentimentalized by American naturalists like Norris and Dreiser; it was self-surrender for its own sake, not as a path to salvation but as a form of intense experience unavailable to the devotees of honest toil. This was serious play with a vengeance.

Two godfathers of the twentieth-century avant-garde, Baudelaire and Dostoevsky, created the image of the gambler as a modernist hero, an acolyte of authentic experience. In *"Le Jeu"* (1857) the poet admires the sublime impatience for intensity that could be found, he thought, in even the most pathetic loser.

> *And my heart took fright—to envy some poor man*
> *Who ran in frenzy to the sheer abyss,*
> *Who, drunk with the pulsing of his blood, preferred*
> *Grief to death, and hell to nothingness* [20]

In *The Gambler* (1866), Dostoevsky's narrator was nothing if not self-destructive, drawn to the tables, he says, by "a strange sort of feeling . . . a kind of desire to challenge fate, a longing to give it a fillip on the nose or stick out my tongue at it."[21] In the end he is punished for his passion, but losing does not seem to matter. All that matters is the endlessly repeated frisson of play. *The Gambler* was an astute exploration of the erotics of gambling—the complex interplay between the narrator's homage to For-

tuna and his equally self-destructive worship of the elusive Polina. In both
courtships, the lover is more preoccupied with the process of pursuit than
its fulfillment.

The twentieth-century heir to Baudelaire and Dostoevsky, the main
modernist connoisseur of the psychology of gambling, was Walter Benjamin. In his *Arcades Project* (1935–1940), Benjamin assembled quotations
from a variety of authors together with his own asides and aphorisms to
create a verbal collage, illuminating the varied significance of the wagering impulse. Like the stock market, he observed, the casino offered
opportunities for paying tribute to the "the inexplicable" in bourgeois
society—the mysterious force that lay behind unintelligible success and
failure. But for Benjamin, gambling was more than a parallel universe for
market exchange. Like Dostoevsky, he recognized its erotic significance.
"The peculiar feeling of happiness in the one who wins is marked by the
fact money and riches . . . come to him from the fates like a joyous embrace returned to the full. They can be compared to words of love from
a woman altogether satisfied by her man," Benjamin wrote.[22]

But the tables embodied more than erotic significance. To Benjamin,
gambling remained a form of divination (albeit, perhaps, a debased one).
"Are fortunetelling cards more ancient than playing cards?" he wondered.
"Does the card game represent a pejoration of divinatory technique?"
Certainly roulette did: its rapid aleatory procedures compressed past,
present, and future into an intense experience of simultaneity, the sort of
experience prized by modernists in flight from bourgeois conventions of
time and space. There was an infinite fullness of being and potentiality in
a single silver ball, bouncing about the roulette wheel—"a hand-to-hand
encounter with Fate" which could bring an overwhelming rush of satisfaction but could also be "cruel and terrible. At its caprice [gambling]
gives poverty and wretchedness and shame—that is why its votaries adore
it. The fascination with danger is at the bottom of all great passions."
Such reflections recalled the self-destructive romantic tradition of Poe
and Baudelaire, burning themselves out with lightning speed. Indeed, a
rapid pace was essential to roulette's divinatory ritual. The speed of the
game made it purely reflexive; there was no time to interpret the workings of chance, only to pay court to its sublime power.[23]

This emphasis on the reflexive gesture was a central feature in the
aesthetic of accident. For surrealists, dadaists, and their successors (including Benjamin), spontaneity was the key to releasing messages from

the unconscious mind, which the avant-garde transformed from a source of neurosis to a seat of wisdom. As the French surrealist Marcel Raymond said, "Only the unconscious does not lie; it alone is worth bringing to light. All deliberate and conscious efforts, composition, logic, are futile. The celebrated French lucidity is nothing but a cheap lantern."[24]

Real lucidity required the recognition that "the marvelous comes to light within *reality*," according to André Breton's *Surrealist Manifesto* (1924); it does not descend from a remote, transcendent realm. "It comes to light in dreams, obsessions, preoccupations, in sleep, fear, love, chance; in hallucinations, pretended disorders, follies, ghostly apparitions, escape mechanisms and evasions; in fancies, idle wanderings, poetry, the supernatural and the unusual; in empiricism, in *super-reality*." Surrealism aimed to demystify the notion that art occupied an exalted sphere, apart from everyday life. "Art is not the most precious manifestation of life," the poet Tzara wrote. "Art has not the celestial and universal value that people like to attribute to it. Life is far more interesting."[25]

The preference for raw authenticity over cooked artifice combined with reverence for the unconscious to place chance at the center of surrealism and dada. Tzara composed poems by drawing words from a hat. Hans Arp made collages by picking up random scraps of paper, shuffling them, then dropping them and gluing them in the configurations they formed when they fell. Marcel Duchamp performed a similar operation with threads on a canvas. Max Ernst created "the decalcomania of chance" by spilling ink between two pieces of paper, then spreading them apart.

These experiments were part of a broader growth of interest in collage among the European avant-garde. In forms as diverse as the Cubist *papiers collés* of Georges Braque and Pablo Picasso and the assemblages of Kurt Schwitters, collage embodied the link between chance and play in art. "Before it is anything else, collage is play," Robert Hughes writes. "The rules of the game are subsumed in what is available—the mailing paper, matchboxes, cigarette packs, chocolate wrappers, stickers, and other stuff in the unstable flux of messages and signs that pass through the flux of a painter's studio. Pushing them around on the paper is pure improvisation, a game with educated guesses played out until the design clicks into some final shape."[26] But the dadaists wanted to give the play a further turn, to reject any pretense of design and make the "final shape" dependent on arbitrary chance rather than the artist's choice (however apparently spontaneous).

In this insistent playfulness, there was an element of bohemian tricksterism, high-jinks *pour epater le bourgeoisie*. But dada also had more challenging aims. It was an attempt to use play to meld categories previously assumed to be opposites—the correct and the incorrect, the ridiculous and the profound. Hans Arp summarized the importance of chance imagery for him. "Chance opened up perceptions to me, immediate spiritual insights. Intuition led me to revere the law of chance as the highest and deepest of laws, the

Merz 410: "Irgendsowas," Kurt Schwitters, 1922.

law that rises from the fundament. An insignificant word might become a deadly thunderbolt. One little sound might destroy the earth. One little sound might create a new universe." Despite their anarchic pose, even devotees of dada were seeking new forms of knowledge through the vagaries of accident. Their playfulness had a purpose.[27]

All the key elements of the aesthetic of accident were present in the ferment of dada and surrealism—the rejection of procedural correctness and controlled intentionality in favor of playful experimentation; the desire to cultivate unconscious sources of creativity; the determination to erase all the old boundaries separating art and life; even the fascination with Eastern philosophy and religion. Arp used the I Ching to pattern chance operations; others would follow. But their interest was substantive as well as procedural. The Zen sect of Buddhism devised meditative practices meant to "bring us in contact with Being or Life which animates all things, and personally feel its pulsation, as when the eye comes in touch with light it recognizes as light," according to the Zen scholar Daisetz Suzuki. This openness to what Suzuki called "immediate knowledge"— and the willingness to forego controlling it—paralleled James's openness to "pure experience" and made Zen tradition appealing to the accidentalist avant-garde. The aesthetic of accident sanctioned irony rather than morality, play rather than work, acceptance of the phenomenal world rather than the commitment to transform it. Still it constituted an imaginative, life-affirming dissent from the technocratic excesses of the managerial culture of control, embodied in the deadening repetitions of the modern factory, as well as in the piles of corpses at Passchendaele and the Somme.[28]

The dadaists and surrealists continued their experiments with chance imagery after World War I, through the 1920s, and into the early 1930s. During that same period, unbeknownst to most people outside the discipline of physics, quantum physicists were completing a quiet revolution that would provide another layer of legitimacy for the aesthetic of accident. In 1927 Werner Heisenberg summarized and elaborated the significance of several decades of experiments in quantum physics. His Uncertainty Principle demonstrated mathematically that it was impossible to measure the position of an electron without disturbing its momentum and vice versa; the very attempt to capture the characteristics of the tiniest particles disturbed those characteristics and altered the results the researcher obtained. At the most microcosmic levels of observation, the observer was always intervening in the thing observed.[29]

Within the discipline of physics, as in other professional scientific communities, uncertainty could be contained by statistical methods. The working definition of truth was embodied in a set of parameters; beyond them were the statistically insignificant "outliers." Like geneticists and evolutionary biologists, quantum physicists found themselves forced to turn from strict causality toward probabilistic prediction (just as in biology, positivist definitions of evolutionary causation yielded to statistical description of natural selection). Most physicists, especially in the United States, bracketed the big philosophical questions, assuming their task was to describe rather than explain the universe.[30]

But outside the laboratory, artists and intellectuals saw Heisenberg's ideas as further justification for the rejection of positivist causality. In light of the Uncertainty Principle, the causal descriptions of classical physics and philosophy could be seen as little more than simplified models of reality. To anyone eager to incorporate chance into one's worldview and work, the shift from causality to probability offered appealing possibilities for scientific legitimacy.[31]

These developments took several decades to reach most nonscientists. Meanwhile, more disturbing events were occurring in Europe. Fascist cultures of control appeared in Italy and Germany, committed to the reg-

imentation of entire societies. Chance, accident, and play acquired a
sharper political edge. As storm troopers strutted through Berlin, Vienna,
and Rome, the Dutch historian Johan Huizinga penned his brilliant
paean to play, *Homo Ludens*. Europe in the 1930s was no place for surrealists or dadaists. Maybe it never had been. For years the leading dadaists
had looked longingly to America, imagining it to be the sort of place
where their experiments would be welcomed. They were not completely
mistaken.

THE AMERICANIZATION OF ACCIDENT:
SPONTANEITY, IRONY, GRACE

Much of the dadaists' fascination with the United States was based on the
mythic equation of America with possibility. When Duchamp and the
painter Francis Picabia arrived in New York in 1925, they immediately
announced that "America is the country of the art of the future." Unfortunately few Americans realized that "the art of Europe is finished—
dead," while the Americans' own was being born. "In Paris, for instance,
everything is perfectly blended and in perfect harmony . . . But here—
from the very instant one lands one realizes that here is a people yearning, searching, trying to find something."[32]

Such pronouncements were a mix of sense and nonsense. They ig-
nored the obvious evidence of corporate-sponsored standardization and
class domination; they confused noise and haste with spontaneity and
freedom. In this they resembled the gaseous fulminations of young American intellectuals. Kenneth Burke was one. In 1925 he declared that "America is Dada in its actual mode of life . . . American intellectuals go to Paris
where they learn to be patriots, returning to America with the religion of
Joe Cook [a vaudeville juggler] and Krazy Kat . . . Dada in Europe is a
prodigal son. In America it is Topsy, and just growed." Like dada, America yoked dissimilar objects together and extended its middle finger to authority—or so Burke believed.[33]

Behind the self-congratulatory nationalism of such statements, though,
there was a complex relation between American culture and dada. More
than a few American thinkers had heeded the example of William James
by making chance an integral component of their worldview. Perhaps

the most remarkable was Randolph Bourne, whose effort to fashion an "experimental life" was cut short by his untimely death in the influenza epidemic of 1918. American modernists had also begun to pay more respectful attention to their own vernacular culture of chance, and particularly to jazz. With its inventions and variations in tempo and harmony, its fragments of melody, its unpredictable squawks and squeals, jazz epitomized the new musical possibilities created by the breakup of old forms.

In the visual arts, despite Duchamp's prediction, those possibilities took longer to assert themselves. Like other modernist traditions in the United States, the aesthetic of accident developed slowly and uncertainly. One of its most original practitioners was Joseph Cornell. Beginning in the 1930s, Cornell's assemblages and constructions embodied the playfulness of the collage tradition, as he translated European surrealism into his own American idioms. Cornell's work depended on lucky finds— shiny marbles, old lithographs, and other scraps of the past he stumbled upon in the second-hand shops of lower Manhattan. He integrated these found objects into carefully crafted designs, the glass-fronted boxes or vitrines that became his signature creations. They were artifactual equivalents of Proust's madeleine—material embodiments of memory that might evoke the same sort of *moments bienheureux*.

In his diary, Cornell called these moments "GC 44." This was a reference to the few months he worked in a garden center and apparently experienced a feeling that everything around him possessed an ineffable significance, if he could only divine it. It was a feeling that later came on unbidden, unpredictably, in a variety of chance situations. For example:

Hotel Eden, Joseph Cornell, 1945.

while he was sitting in an Automat at Forty-second Street and Third Avenue, watching the "typical motley stream of N.Y. humanity" hurry by, he felt "the minutiae of commonplace spectacle" lead him to "an 'on-the-edgeness' of something apocalyptic [i.e., revelatory], something really satisfying." "How marvelously does the decalc sign on the little delivery truck become alive and germinal on such occasions," he wrote in 1954. "GC 44" experiences enchanted everyday life; they constituted a kind of grace.[34]

They also animated his work and reinforced its associations with memories of his childhood. As he recorded in his diary, "On Thursday in cellar dismantling a Parmigliano box a something came as in a far away distant childhood happening trees in summertime a street scene somewhere gone in a flash and leaving nothing but surprise at its unexpectedness—for a moment I must have gone back to a precious childhood moment not recalled since—remarkable, if elusive moment." It was triggered by dismantling a Parmigliano box, which like most of Cornell's boxes, melded images of nineteenth-century bourgeois culture with his own recollections of that culture in its afterglow. Chance perceptions triggered creative withdrawal into memory, which led to assemblages that evoked other imaginative returns to the past. Cornell feared nostalgia, but wisely decided, in the end, that "the attempt to hold as much of the passing beauty as one is able to needs no apology."[35]

Cornell's achievement was extraordinary but idiosyncratic. The main currents of artistic chance flowed elsewhere, away from Cornell's concern with "the passing beauty" and toward more overtly serious uses of accident—"serious," that is, by the emerging modernist standard. The obsessively masculine modernists discounted beauty as a merely feminine (and therefore supposedly trivial) excrescence of Victorian taste. By the early 1940s, catastrophic world events made the making of beautiful things seem a comparatively trivial task, especially for young men of draft age who were not in uniform. Wartime expectations intensified male artists' determination to demonstrate their masculine seriousness.

Certainly there was plenty to furrow one's brow about. The rise of fascism and the resurgence of world war seemed an eruption of palpable evil, inexplicable in its intensity and unassimilable to liberal ideas of rationality and progress. The reigning aesthetic formulas, even modernist ones, seemed inadequate to capture the the enormity of the catastrophe. Dadaist high-jinks became repetitive and trivial; surrealist manifestos slid into affirmation of rationalist orthodoxies, whether Freudian or Marxist; abstraction etherealized into cold formality. None of the existing modernist movements in the visual arts gave form to the fundamental, inescapable fact of the historical moment—the vulnerability of ordinary, innocent people to acts of mass destruction, previously unimaginable in their scale and intensity. The managerial quest for total control had led to total war. The consequences of hubris revealed the tragedy at the heart of the human condition.

Some of the more thoughtful American painters tried to grapple directly with this historical predicament. By the early 1940s, Adolph Gottlieb, Jackson Pollock, Arshile Gorky, Barnett Newman, and Robert Motherwell (among others) had become impatient with the idea of painting as formal experiment. As Gottlieb said in 1943, "This emphasis on the mechanics of picture-making has been carried far enough." The problem was not how to paint, but what to paint. They were convinced they confronted a "crisis in subject matter" and groped for innovative ways to respond to it. Ultimately they created the most celebrated (and reviled) style of the midcentury decades, abstract expressionism.[36]

Abstract expressionists embraced spontaneity as a path to dark truth. As early as 1942, the painter Edward Renouf observed a striking tendency among modern American artists: "the more spontaneously, the more quasi-automatically they worked the more their work expressed the emotional disintegration and desperation that lurked concealed and inhibited behind the compulsive optimism of industrial civilization."[37] Nowhere was this impulse stronger than among early abstract expressionists. Mixing heady draughts of Freud and Jung, they believed that by allowing their unconscious impulses free rein they could re-create the mythic forms—the embodiments of mystery and magical self-transformation—buried beneath the blandness of a managerial society.[38]

This was the rationale behind the pictographs Adolph Gottlieb

painted in the early 1940s. Gottlieb acknowledged that "there was an element of accident to what association, what image would pop into my mind and I would put it down, try to put it down without revision or without thinking it over too much, so that there would be no self-consciousness and there

The Prisoners, Adolph Gottlieb, 1947.

would be a free play." The emphasis on free play combined with the idea that one was expressing an inner world to devalue academic craft traditions. "I don't work from drawings," Pollock said in 1950. "I don't make sketches and drawings and color sketches into a final painting. Painting, I think, today—the more immediate, the more direct—the greater the possibilities. . . . "[39]

By midcentury, artistic possibilities were popping up in unpredictable ways. Pollock started out as a mythmaker, along with Gottlieb and Gorky. But in 1949 he spun out the spontaneous gesture to its logical conclusion. He began the flailing dance of drip painting. That same year, the young Robert Rauschenberg left his Lower Manhattan apartment, took a walk around the block, and returned with an armload of junk, whatever forlorn and fascinating object that happened to catch his eye—the first load of trash he would use to make his "Combines." Through the 1950s and early 1960s, he produced what one critic called "a plastic language of the non sequitur" by combining stuffed goats, shattered umbrellas, razor blades, broken glass, a motley of pasted and graphic elements.[40]

Full Fathom Five, Jackson Pollock, 1947.

Impulses toward spontaneity informed literary experiment as well. The poet Charles Olson, fresh from a prolonged encounter with the writings of Jung, launched a series of influential experiments in automatic writing at Black Mountain College in North Carolina. He called his poetry "projective verse" and emphasized the importance of the syllable as a spontaneous expression of sound. Comparable desires to escape the constraints of conscious control animated the rebellious authors who called themselves "Beats," in San Francisco, New York, and points in between. Diane DiPrima and LeRoi

Jones (later Amiri Baraka) caught the improvisational spirit of Beat poetry when they called their mimeographed literary magazine *Floating Bear,* after Winnie-the-Pooh's makeshift boat. As DiPrima said of the magazine, quoting Pooh: "Sometimes it's a Boat, and sometimes it's more of an Accident."[41]

Jack Kerouac, Allen Ginsberg, and other Beat writers were inspired by improvisational bebop jazz to produce what Kerouac called "spontaneous bop prosody." Through the late 1940s and 1950s, as Charlie Parker and other bebop musicians reemphasized polyrhythmic phrasing and unpredictable chord changes against the highly orchestrated big band sound of swing, Beat poets played with words and sounds, hoping to hear them separate from the organized apparatus of conceptual thought. In a perceptive essay of

Collection, Robert Rauschenberg, 1953–1954.

1961, Jones noted how Kerouac used a primer word, phrase, or question to release the images that flowed toward a "jewel center." Jones cited "a very simple and effective primer" from *On the Road*.

> He asks himself a question, "What is the Mississippi River?" The answer rushes forth: "—a washed clod in the rainy night, a soft plopping from drooping Missouri banks, a dissolving, a riding of the tide down the eternal waterbed, a contribution to brown foams, voyaging past endless vales and trees and levees, down along, down along" (primers) "by Memphis, Greenville, Eudora, Vicksburg, Natchez, Port Allen, and Port Orleans, and Port of the Deltas, by Potash, Venice, and the Night's Great Gulf, and out."[42]

The poetry in that passage, Jones said, arose from the combination of spontaneity and preparation. Like Billy the Kid in Howard Hughes's film *The Outlaw,* the successful spontaneous writer aims before he pulls out his gun. "That is, the spontaneous writer has to possess a particularly facile and amazingly impressionable mind, one that is able to collect and store not just snatches or episodic bits of events, but whole and elaborate associations," Jones wrote.[43] Neither spontaneous bop prosody nor bop itself was simply a matter of winging it. Successful improvisation, in music or literature, depended on deep immersion in existing idioms of composition. The same combination of preparation and play characterized developments in the performing arts during this period: the incorporation of spontaneous gestures in "method" acting, the emergence of improvisational comedy from the Marx Brothers' vaudeville to the inspired riffs of Jonathan Winters.

Despite the need for preparation, improvisation remained a playful performative art—taking chances, inducing exhilaration, refusing closure, remaining open to accident and mistake. Jazz musicians could "engage with their infelicitous phrases," as Robert Walser writes, resituating and reinterpreting them in subsequent statements. In the 1950s and 1960s, Miles Davis and Thelonious Monk demonstrated that the artist's errors, if not volitional, could still be portals of discovery. Davis simply accepted them as consequences of the way he played, incorporating them into his trademark trumpet solos. Monk found mistakes fascinating, returning to them repeatedly, "using musical accidents as material for development and elaboration."[44]

Improvisation was the opposite of Taylor's scientific management, which sought to impose systematic control on a craft and its object. In contrast, improvisers played with their tradition or their material. "You can't force [the clay] completely," a Japanese potter at Black Mountain said. "So you're in tune. You play. It's interrelation, interplay with the clay. But the clay has much to say on its own. You can't really control that. . . . And when you finish a piece . . . the piece is alive."[45] Serious play reenchanted the world.

This potter's refusal of any attempt to master nature, her willingness to let the clay have its say, betokened a broader shift in consciousness, beyond the academy and the artist's studio—the growth of skepticism toward the Western tradition of "subduing the earth" and the ideologies of linear progress that accompanied it. Rachel Carson's critique of the technological misuse of nature resonated with an ecological aesthetic of accident. Writers like Joseph Wood Krutch were drawn to "the mystery, the independence, the unpredictability of the living as opposed to the mechanical." The most perceptive observers had sensed some philosophical significance in the prodigality of nature, the flow of primal plenitude at its core. They had suspected that this blooming buzzing confusion was too chaotic and chance-ridden to be contained in puny human schemes of progress. That insight was what made Thoreau's vision continue to resonate with the postwar culture of spontaneity.[46]

The critique of progress led artists and writers to ask larger philosophical questions. In particular they challenged the various dualistic premises at the basis of Western thought: between subject and object, body and mind, cause and effect. From abstract expressionists to Black Mountain poets, many turned to the writings of Carl Gustav Jung as a passport to new philosophical territory. Interest in Jung focused on his vindication of primitive symbols and rituals as part of a "collective unconscious" and on his concept of "synchronicity"—an "acausal principle" (which he claimed was borne out by paranormal psychic research) that constituted a complement to Western notions of linear causality. But one did not have to wander through the mists of Jungian metaphysics to locate alternatives to dualism. Quantum physicists were deploying the concept of complementarity to describe the puzzling relationship between waves and particles; as discussion of complementarity spread outside scientific circles, it allowed thinkers to move beyond dualistic "either-or" to more inclusive notions of "both-and."[47]

Distrust of dualism fed fascination with the links between primitive and modern mentalities. The similarities reinforced the idea of the artist as shaman, creating and interpreting an augury. This was the posture of the mythmakers among the abstract expressionists, and also of the writer William Burroughs, whose composition technique included cutting up and folding together fragments of printed prose. "I would say," Burroughs wrote, "that when you make cut-ups you do not get simply random juxtapositions of words, that they do mean something, and often that these meanings refer to some future event."[48] Chance art was an act of divination. Reading significance from apparently fortuitous events, Burroughs collapsed the dualistic oppositions at the base of Western thought: sense and nonsense, matter and spirit, chance and necessity.

An even stronger indicator of disquiet with dualism, both Christian and technological, was the spreading preoccupation with Zen Buddhism in the post–World War II United States. Probably the most influential Zen enthusiast was Alan Watts, who wrote frequently on the subject in the 1950s and 1960s. Recoiling from the dualist ethic of mastery over nature, Alan Watts articulated a suspicion that "our attempt to master the world from outside is a vicious circle in which we shall be condemned to the perpetual insomnia of controlling controls and supervising supervision *ad infinitum*." Watts was an intelligent popularizer; he realized that "the *satori* experience of awakening to our 'original inseparability' with the universe" has always been elusive. Still, "one has even met people to whom it has happened, and they are no longer mysterious occultists in the Himalayas nor skinny yogis in cloistered ashrams. They are just like us, and yet much more at home in the world, floating much more easily upon the ocean of transience and insecurity."[49] The very notion that we were (or could be) at home in the world undermined the impulse to master nature.

Watts's teacher, and the crucial intermediary between Buddhism and American culture, was Daisetz Suzuki. He emphasized the philosophical ideal of Zen: "directly to take hold of reality without being bothered by any interrupting agency, intellectual, moral, ritualistic, or what not. This direct holding of reality is the awakening of *Prajna,* which may be rendered as 'transcendental wisdom.'" But Suzuki also rendered *Prajna* as "pure experience beyond differentiation," which allowed "no room for intellection, no time for deliberation. So the Buddhist master urges us to 'speak quick, quick!' Immediacy, no interpretation, no explanatory apology—this is what constitutes *Prajna* intuition."[50] In a nondual tradition, there was no contradiction or even tension between wisdom and action. Suzuki's apotheosis of "pure experience" suggested the common ground between this version of Zen and the spirit of William James.

Most devotees of chance were eclectic in their intellectual tastes. Whatever challenged the objectivist epistemology behind the managerial worldview was congenial to the aesthetic of accident. By the 1940s, many such challenges were in the air—quantum physics, Alfred North Whitehead's process philosophy, Zen Buddhism, French existentialism—promoting the idea that the artistic process was more important than the artistic product. To ignore process was to separate means and ends in accordance with outmoded physics (and metaphysics); it was also to overlook an essential part of Pollock's achievement in his drip paintings, or Burroughs's in his cut-ups.

But as the culture of spontaneity became popularized, the artist's risk-taking persona constantly threatened to degenerate into a pose, one with special masculine resonance in this era when manliness was often defined in regimented ways. Indeed, it is hard not to see the Beats' fascination with recklessness as a boyish rebellion against midcentury notions of male maturity—especially conformity to corporate discipline and acceptance of domestic responsibilities. The distrust of women and their demands (actual or imagined) lay behind many accidentalist gestures, limiting their larger significance. An implicit misogyny fed the bohemian fear of marriage and children as a bourgeois trap, whatever the sexual preferences of the bohemian in question.

The revolt against bourgeois convention coalesced in the figure of the hipster, celebrated without apparent irony by Norman Mailer in "The White Negro" (1957). The hipster, Mailer believed, was a gambler: he must live "the life where a man must go until he is beat, where he must gamble with all his energies, through all those small or large crises which beset his day, where he must be with it or doomed not to swing."[51] This was a problem with the Beat culture of spontaneity—its proponents' constant slide into self-absorption and self-parody.

Kerouac's spontaneous prose could exhibit those tendencies too, as when he wrote: "Great words in rhythmic order all in one archangel book go roaring through my brain, so I lie in the dark also hearing the jargon of the future worlds—damajehe eleout ekeke dhdhkdk dldoud . . . mdoduldltkdip—baseeaatra—poor examples, because of mechanical needs of typing, of the flow of river sounds, words, dark, leading to the future."[52] There were times when Kerouac's prose justified Truman Capote's famous sneer: "That's not writing, that's typing."

Yet despite its descents into vapidity (and misogyny), the Beat culture of spontaneity preserved a potential for protest. Perhaps the most eloquent was lodged in Allen Ginsberg's work. Arriving in San Francisco in 1954 after years of emotional struggle with his mother's madness and his own homosexuality, he followed the poet Kenneth Rexroth's advice and began to experiment with poetic techniques that resembled Kerouac's spontaneous prose. "I thought I wouldn't write a poem but just write what I wanted to without fear, let my imagination go, open secrecy, and scribble magic lines from my real mind—sum up my life—something I wouldn't be able to show anybody, writ for my own soul's ear and a few other golden ears." Extending each line the length of his own breath, he thought of himself as a jazz musician.[53]

He was also a trickster, dwelling on the thresholds of sexual and po-

litical respectability, combining the roles of ironist and shaman. Unlike
Kerouac, he leavened his labor with wit, as in "America" (1956):

*America I still haven't told you what you did to Uncle Max when he came over from
   Russia.*
I'm addressing you.
Are you going to let your emotional life be run by Time *magazine?*[54]

But Ginsberg also longed openly for a realm where body and soul melded
and "everything is holy"—a place of grace.

> *The final wish*
> *Is love*
> *—cannot be bitter,*
> *cannot deny,*
> *cannot withold*
> *If denied:*
>
> *The weight is too heavy*
>
> *—must give*
> *For no return*
> *as thought*
> *is given*
> *In solitude*
> *In all the excellence*
> *of its excess.*[55]

Hymning the excellence of excess, Ginsberg crossed the boundaries that
were so central to maintenance of the managerial culture of control: normality and abnormality, reason and madness, the self and the world. For
all his self-destructive urges, he had more staying power than the bad boys
Pollock and Kerouac.

By the late 1950s the Beats had inspired a spirit of restlessness among
a broad swath of young people. In *The Dharma Bums,* Kerouac presented
Japhy Ryder (Gary Snyder) holding forth on the impending "rucksack
revolution" against "them"—the allegedly complacent majority—"all of
them imprisoned in a system of work, produce, consume, work, produce, consume." The rucksackers would be, in contrast, "all of 'em Zen
lunatics who go about writing poems that happen to appear in their heads

for no reason."[56] There was something prescient about this idea of a popular revolt against the hamster-cage model of happiness, as the counterculture of the 1960s and 1970s would demonstrate in all its inanity and insight. For all their occasional silliness, pop existentialism and Zen lunacy sustained the beginnings of a serious search for alternatives to managerial rationality—a search that would be intensified by the managers' war in Vietnam.

The quest was initially energized by an eclectic mix of influences. Existentialism emphasized the individual's need to make his own meanings in a radically contingent universe; Jungian psychoanalysis heeded messages from the collective unconscious; quantum physics sanctioned ideas of indeterminacy and complementarity; Zen made openness to the universe a precondition of spiritual insight. All these traditions legitimated chance as a source of creativity, but within the culture of spontaneity they created there was a deep division about the nature of the meanings chance disclosed. Did they come from the inner self or the outer world? The first view led to automatic writing, drip painting, and other spontaneous gestures that sought to release the truths of the unconscious. The second perspective encouraged the conjuring of chance by rolling dice or using such traditional methods of divination as the I Ching—not burrowing within the self, but opening outward to the randomness of the cosmos. Both approaches raised problematic issues concerning the actual creation of artistic work by claiming to negate the need for aesthetic reflection and considered choice.

Without reflection, what seemed to be a declaration of independence from managerial culture could turn out to be a form of submission to it. When *prajna* was construed as immediacy, the Zen concept had a way of meshing with American speed—anything to avoid calculation, craft, or thought. Peter Voulkos, an abstract expressionist potter, put it this way: "You try to keep the spontaneity. You can't sit there and think about it for long. You don't have that kind of time with clay." The material itself provided a rationale for Voulkos, but the emphasis on speed subsumed all the arts, even writing. Suzuki quoted the Zen master Tenno Dogo, who stopped a disciple from pondering his advice by saying: "No reflecting whatever. When you want to see, see immediately. As soon as you tarry [that is, as soon as an intellectual interpretation or mediation takes place], the whole thing goes awry."[57]

The danger that even a moment's hesitation might throw the whole process out of kilter suggested a link between *prajna* and the mentality it was meant to supplant, managerial rationality. As early as 1912, Wassily Kandinsky had noted that "a strategy of voluminous production [was] made possible by the embrace of a spontaneous or improvisational style." Craftsmanship took time; spontaneity demanded speed—and so did the assembly line. By identifying *Prajna* with immediacy, Americans made it more compatible with the rhythms of an industrial society. Paradoxically, then, Zen could provide a justification for either sustaining reflection or abandoning it altogether. The Japanese American sculptor Isamu Noguchi would ponder a rock for years before he would decide how (or even whether) to use it, but Olson translated Zen into the idiom of Frederick Taylor: "ONE PERCEPTION MUST IMMEDIATELY AND DIRECTLY LEAD TO A FURTHER PERCEPTION," he asserted in 1950, "at *all* points (even, I should say, of our management of daily reality as of the daily work) get on with it, keep moving, keep in speed, the nerves, their speed, the perceptions, theirs, the acts, the split second acts, the whole business, keep it moving as fast as you can, citizen."[58]

Olson would no doubt have bristled at the comparison, but the disdain for reflection, the obsession with movement, energy, and dynamism as ends in themselves, all placed him alongside ideologues whose social views he abhorred. These qualities also separated him from the actual practice of Zen. As Suzuki wrote: "Zen has nothing to do with rapidity or immediacy in the sense of being quick. A flash of lightning [as a metaphor for intuitive insight] refers to the non-mediating nature of Zen-experience."[59]

For inwardly oriented chance artists, another problem arose from the psychoanalytic understanding of accident as an expression of unconscious drives. In automatic writing or gesture painting, from the psychoanalytic perspective, apparent spontaneity was actually obedience to the immutable dictates of the id. Advocates of automatism assumed that random doodles appeared in accordance with mysterious but inescapable psychic laws—Freudian fate, or Jungian, in Pollock's case. Pollock, who was in Jungian analysis for years, insisted in 1950 with respect to his drip paintings that "I don't use the accident—'cause I deny the accident." The problem with painting images from the unconscious was one of abdicating aesthetic responsibility. As Pollock's contemporary Robert Motherwell observed, the unconscious offered "none of the choices which, when taken, constitute an expression's form. To give oneself over completely to the unconscious is to become a slave."[60]

But when artists acknowledged (even implicitly) that intention and choice were inescapable, they reaffirmed their power to transform the ordinary into something rich and strange—through cooperation with chance rather than submission to it. That outlook allowed the accidentalist tradition to prosper in the later work of Robert Motherwell. As he grew older, Motherwell increasingly preferred pen and paper to paint and canvas; often, he told an interviewer toward the end of his life, "the paper absorbs and dries almost instantly. . . . and I think that unconsciously makes [me] create less considered works; they're more a throw of the dice, you just do it and that's that."[61] In his later career, he also turned to collage, using cigarette packs, candy bar wrappers, and torn paper fragments—"manual chance," in Robert Hughes's apt phrase. They embodied an extraordinary range, from *The Tearingness of Collaging* (1957), which he called "the equivalent of a shudder, symbolically," to the multiple puns in *The French Line* (1960). But all implicitly repudiated the obsession with precision and predictability at the heart of managerial culture. "It's the fore-ordained end that bothers me. . . . There's always got to be an opening for life to creep in," he said in 1991. Spontaneity and chance were the preconditions for life in art.[62]

The French Line, Robert Motherwell, 1959.

Motherwell's use of trash was not simply an attempt to erase the boundaries between art and the rest of experience, as many accidentalists claimed they wanted to do. Like his abstract expressionist colleagues, he preserved a persistent sense that he was making something apart from random dailiness, a vestigial notion of the artist as seer with the power to penetrate and transfigure the banalities of everyday existence. For decades, abstract expressionists had nurtured this exalted conception of the artist's role. But few used the spontaneous gesture as playfully—or as thoughtfully—as Motherwell. The materials of his later work embodied the "both-and' of Zen buddhism, rather than the "either-or" of dualism—yes, the cigarette pack is trash, no, it's not merely trash. Rejecting self-destructive poses, Motherwell revived an unfashionable concern with beauty and pleasure in art.

So did other artists who collaborated with chance by using spontaneous gestures and lucky finds. If Pollock dripped, Helen Frankenthaler poured. If Rauschenberg picked up trash, Louise Nevelson collected discarded wood from furniture factories and vacant lots. "I wanted a medium that was immediate," Nevelson said. "Wood was the thing that I could communicate with almost spontaneously and get what I was looking for. . . . when I'm working with wood, it's very alive. It has a life of its own." Like the Japanese potter or the jazz improviser, Nevelson allowed her material its own autonomy, as she brought her own craft into cooperation with it.[63]

Yet the use of chance imagery could lead away from this emphasis on collaboration with luck and toward a more passive acceptance of it. This was especially likely when the artist cultivated openness to the outer world rather than the inner self. And no one advocated this strategy more consistently than John Cage. His aesthetic of accident influenced a wide range of art, from Rauschenberg's combines and Noguchi's sculptures to Kaprow's "action collages" and Happenings. As devotees of chance imagery gradually turned for inspiration from the canvases of Pollock to the compositions of Cage, they revealed a broader movement in the aesthetics of accident—from psychic automatism to mechanically induced chance, from modernist depths to postmodern surfaces, and from an attitude of bitter alienation toward one of ironic detachment.[64]

The emergence of irony linked accidentalist art with a subtle but enduring shift toward postmodern cultural fashion: a weariness with seriousness, a willingness to play with the materials of mass culture

Moon Spikes IV, Louise Nevelson, 1955.

rather than simply revile them. Amid the postmodern ferment, Cage himself remained enigmatic—issuing orphic pronouncements, staging cerebral antics, and gathering sycophants. Yet in the end even Cage wanted chance to be more than a cosmic joke. The consummate trickster revealed a yearning for grace.

Unlike Pollock, Cage lived a long time, long enough to become a central figure in the aesthetic of accident. Cage was everywhere in the midcentury decades. In Seattle in 1938, he composed music for the Cornish School of Dance, where Merce Cunningham was a student. Cunningham became a dice-throwing choreographer, one of Cage's most frequent collaborators, and eventually his life companion. In New York in 1944, Cage and Cunningham mounted their first performance together, and the young Rauschenberg designed the set for it (as he would many more). At Black Mountain in 1952, Cage staged the first "Happening" with Rauschenberg, Cunningham, Olson, and the composer David Tudor. At the New School in New York in 1958, he taught a course in avant-garde music composition, using the I Ching, to a class that included Kaprow and other young artists interested in chance operations. Cage crossed boundaries between art forms as well as between art and life.[65]

He also defined the cutting edge of accident in art. However far his predecessors had pushed toward spontaneity, he pushed further. His "Landscape 4 Radio" (1951) involved tuning twelve radios to different stations and playing them simultaneously. His "4'33"" (1952) required a pianist to sit at a piano for four and half minutes of silence, punctuated only by the sound of the pianist opening and closing the piano three times (to signify the "movements" of the piece) and the random coughs, murmurs, and rustlings of the concert hall. Cage rejected any distinction between art and the messiness of everyday experience. "I was with [the painter Willem] de Kooning once in a restaurant," Cage recalled, "and he said, 'if I put a frame around these breadcrumbs, that isn't art.' And what I'm saying is that it is. He was saying it wasn't because he connects art with his activity—he connects it with himself as an artist whereas I would want art to slip out of us into the world in which we live."[66]

This vaguely populist enthusiasm for "the world in which we live," combined with frequent complaints against cultural hierarchy, won Cage a reputation as a pragmatic and "characteristically American" thinker—even while his music was often dismissed by professional musicians.[67] To his followers, a Cagean stance of ironic acceptance was a way of jettisoning the ponderous alienation of the abstract expressionists, of playfully embracing the existing social universe—including the overstuffed commodity civilization of the midcentury United States. To those who felt engulfed by the Sargasso Sea of American stuff, the ironist advised: let it wash over you, while remaining bemused and detached. According to Cage, Jasper Johns's replication of beer cans and other mass culture artifacts embodied an appropriate artistic stance toward the larger society: "The situation must be yes and no, not either or. *Avoid a polar situation.*"[68]

The avoidance of polar situations recalled the Zen rejection of dualism and suggested an understandable desire to escape the self-destructive isolation embodied by Pollock's death. It could lead to a constructive engagement with the existing culture, a fruitful alternative to mere negation. But it could also lead to a refusal to comment at all, a mindless replication of mass-produced objects. The determination to erase boundaries between art and life preserved significance only as long as those boundaries remained in place. Eventually, the emergence of boundaryless postmodern culture would transform art into a variety show.[69]

Cage's ideas and example contributed to this trivialization, but his work led in more profound directions, as well. Occasionally the trickster revealed a more serious side. What at first seemed to Cage an epistemological venture, an attempt to formulate a nondualistic way of knowing from the flux of "pure experience," gradually and almost imperceptibly acquired a spiritual dimension. In the end, Cage, too, was animated by longings for grace—for a sense of self-forgetfulness, of oneness with the cosmos, that could best be cultivated through openness to a chance-ridden universe. This variety of religious experience began as an intellectual experiment.

Cage's way of knowing arose from the Zen and modernist emphasis on experience as a flow that could not be cut up into discrete categories and entities. A crucial modernist text was Ernest Fenollossa's "The Chinese Character as a Medium for Poetry" (1920), which made a Jamesian argument concerning the capacity for compression and simultaneity in the Chinese character: "A true noun, an isolated thing, does not exist in nature," Fenollossa wrote. "Things are only . . . the meeting points of actions, cross-sections cut through actions, snap shots. Neither can a pure verb, an abstract motion, be possible in nature. The eye sees noun and verb as one: things in motion, motion in things, and so the Chinese conception tends to represent them." The Chinese character represented the stream of thought in ways that Western languages found difficult. One is reminded of James's litany—"We ought to have a feeling of *and* . . ." etc.—as well as of Joyce's decision to conclude *Finnegans Wake* with the word "the." Similar motives energized Olson's "projective verse"—the term he coined to characterize his poetry's emphasis on the syllable. He wanted "to engage speech where it is least careless—and least logical."[70] Literary experiments served philosophical aims: the desire to make language more fluid so it would more fully embody the flow of consciousness.

Cage was involved in a similar project. He could not escape the force of his own intentions, as he himself implicitly admitted when he used such oxymorons as "chance operations" and "purposeful purposelessness."[71] Ultimately his philosophical purposes led him toward a fluid epistemology that rejected all dualisms, implicitly melding James and Zen.

"The world, the real, is not an object," he said. "It is a process." Drawing on the Asianist William McNaughton's distinction between full (referential) words and empty words (which referrred only to other words), he became fascinated with conjunctions, prepositions, and pronouns. Such words epitomized the representation of time in his compositions as well as our experience of it in everyday life. The attempt to impose discrete boundaries on time truncated our experience. In life, there were many situations where it was impossible to tell when "something is finished and the next begins. . . . " Why not in music as well? he wondered. Abandoning any indicated time measures, he sought to bring a Bergsonian notion of time as duration into the concert hall. (Sometimes the duration was interminable, according to his critics.)[72]

The question inevitably arises: what was the point of such exercises? Merely to play with existing categories and demonstrate their artificiality? Sometimes it seemed so: the dangers of abstraction and solipsism were always present. But in the end Cage's aims were more serious than mere intellectual gamesmanship. They came across most clearly in his veneration of silence. This was partly based on the Jamesian recognition that sounds and silence, like something and nothing, were coexistent. Here as elsewhere, Cage displaced bipolarity with complementarity. But Cage wanted to do more than use silence in music; he wanted to silence the self. From an Indian musician who was studying with him, Cage learned (he said) "the traditional reason for making music in India: 'to quiet the mind thus making it susceptible to divine influences.'" He later said he found a similar formulation in a sixteenth century English text; such meditative world-openness expressed a universal, nondual view of reality. Even for Cage, the aesthetic of accident was not merely an excuse to revel in chaos; chance offered a glimpse of divinity.[73]

For Cage, the grandson of a Methodist minister, the Eastern idiom was more appealing than the Christian, perhaps because Buddhism rejected otherworldliness. "We learned from Oriental thought that those divine influences are, in fact, the environment in which we are. A sober and quiet mind is one in which the ego does not obstruct the fluency of the things which come in through our senses and up through our dreams."[74] Despite his disdain for subjectivist notions of an inner self, Cage here at least acknowledged the importance of unconscious life.

Cage's consistent purpose, as Christopher Shultis has cogently argued, was "diminishing the role of the self in the creative act"—for spiritual as well as artistic reasons. One of his guidebooks was Aldous Huxley's *The Perennial Philosophy* (1940), which contains the following suggestive passage:

> The divine Ground of all existence is a spiritual Absolute, ineffable in terms of discursive thought, but (in certain circumstances) susceptible of being directly experienced and realized by the human being. This Absolute is the God-without-form of Hindu and Christian mystical phraseology. The last end of man, the ultimate reason for human existence, is unitive knowledge of the divine Ground—the knowledge can come only to those who are prepared to 'die to self' and so make room, as it were, for God.[75]

It may be that Cage's lifelong obsession with chance eventually became a spiritual quest, a striving to not strive. ("Teach us to care and not to care / Teach us to sit still," T. S. Eliot prayed in "Ash Wednesday.") Openness to the endless flow of random experience made room for "the God-without-form of Hindu and Christian mystical phraseology." But the initiation of that process involved losing the self of Western dualism and acknowledging the self-without-form of conjure—the nondual view of the universe embedded in cultures of chance. The desire to be emptied of all one's contradictory yearnings and filled with the ineffable sweetness of abundant life—this would be a fair gloss on Cage's notion of susceptibility to divine influences. It would also be a fair, short summary of common Christian ideas about grace.

Some of the most original, heterodox Christian thinkers of the twentieth century—Aldous Huxley, Simone Weil, and Paul Tillich, among others—returned repeatedly to the mystery of grace. They emphasized its incompatibility with the individualist emphasis on self-help, its apparent arbitrariness and caprice, its status as a kind of spiritual luck, inexplicable with reference to human moral or philosophical schemes. Grace was indeed gratuitous, and mysterious. But one thing about it was certain: like Cage's notion of creativity, it required the opening of the self to the cosmos and the cessation of human control—a willingness to lose all in order to gain all.[76]

Tillich was the most prominent American articulator of this insight. A German Lutheran and socialist who fled Hitler in 1933, Tillich accepted a position as a professor of theology at Union Theological Seminary in New York and eventually became a leading articulator of Christian Existentialism. Both Cage and Tillich were successful public performers, though their audiences were different. While Cage captured the imagination of artists and their camp followers, Tillich reached a broader public. His books—especially *The Courage to Be* (1952)—became best-sellers and cult artifacts, the sort of book that serious adolescents would carry around after they had graduated from the *The Catcher in the Rye.* He lectured to overflow crowds on campuses and in cities throughout the country; his face graced the cover of *Time* magazine. This popularity did not arise from an optimistic message. On the contrary: in contrast to Cage's vision of chance, which was fundamentally sunny, Tillich's was dark and troubling. Awareness of contingency, for him, was nothing less than awareness of the uncertainty at the heart of our own existence—the unpredictable but always potential event of our own death. Yet (as with James), for Tillich the encounter with nothingness could be a form of therapeutic revitalization. A sense of imminent nonbeing enriched the intensity of being, indeed gave us "the courage to be."

As Eugene McCarraher has perceptively demonstrated, Tillich's lifelong obsession with "acceptance"—his hunger for a sense of wholeness and reconciliation—stemmed from his own tormented psychic history. His father was a Lutheran pastor and a demanding patriarch; his mother was a far more nurturant figure and the object of his desperate love. She died when he was seventeen, and young Paul was desolate. "Oh abyss without ground, dark depth of madness! / Would that I had never gazed upon you and were / sleeping like a child!" he wrote soon after her death.

The recoil from nothingness and the longing for surrender to oblivion would paradoxically coexist in his work, and would animate his theological concerns throughout his career.[77] Tillich came of age intellectually in the heady atmosphere of Weimar modernism, an atmosphere that sanctioned sexual as well as artistic experimentation. Railing against the "hypocrisy of bourgeois conventionality," he embarked on a career of compulsive promiscuity. From the 1920s through the 1950s, on both sides of the Atlantic, he left behind a trail of seduced, abandoned, and often humiliated women—including, sometimes, his wife Hannah. Their avowedly "open" marriage was marked by countless affairs on both sides, but Hannah was more invested in the relationship, and Paul was the more prodigious adulterer—indeed his erotic obsessions dominated much of his life. When he was not writing or lecturing, he was fondling female students in his office or surveying his collection of sadomasochistic pornography. He merged compulsive promiscuity with a masculine will to power—not an attractive combination, in a theologian or anyone else.[78]

Yet even Tillich, the bon vivant who preached openness to all forms of sensual experience, could not suppress his own longings to be forgiven his trespasses. In his sermon "You Are Accepted" (as in many others), one can hear the voice of anguished yearning for redemption from sin—which for Tillich was not evil action but estrangement from oneself and others including (ultimately) God. Reconciliation with God brought a sense of oneness that recalled the pre-Oedipal bond of mother and child, a sense of "the unity of life, which is grace." Sin was a denial of dependence, an insistence on one's capacity to master fate. God asked for nothing but the acceptance of divine acceptance. "Do not seek for anything; do not perform anything; do not intend anything. Simply accept the fact that you are accepted!" Tillich advised.[79]

This all sounds a little too easy—and desperate—but Tillich's reformulation of grace was not reducible to the sum of his symptoms. Indeed, Tillich's existentialism recalled the promise of pragmatism before it became assimilated to technocratic purposes. Tillich himself was in certain ways the legitimate heir of William James. Jamesian pragmatism, Tillich thought, was a creative expression of the courage to be. The pragmatist and the existentialist shared a common willingness to confront the contingency of fate.

Between Tillich and James the similarities were personal as well as intellectual. Both confronted the specter of nothingness early on in their careers. For James it took palpable form in his recollection of a severely epileptic patient he had encountered as a medical student, while on a tour of a Boston asylum—"a black-haired youth with greenish skin, entirely idiotic"—an image of nonbeing. "*That shape am I,* I felt, potentially," James recalled.[80] But for James's generation the encounter with nonbeing was comparatively idiosyncratic; for Tillich's it was virtually epidemic. He published his major work in the post–World War II era, which he and many of his contemporaries dubbed "the age of anxiety."

The phrase became a cliché, conjuring up images of harried commuters hooked on tranquillizers and gin. But for Tillich and other existentialist thinkers, anxiety had more precise meanings. As he wrote in *The Courage to Be,* "anxiety is the existential awareness of nonbeing," the feeling we have in our bones that we will die. There was nothing abstract or second-hand about this feeling: "it is not the realization of universal transitoriness, not even the experience of the death of others, but the impression of these events on the always latent awareness of our own having to die that produces anxiety. Anxiety is finitude, experienced as one's own finitude."[81]

No wonder death was on Tillich's mind. It was 1952. Auschwitz and Hiroshima, Dresden and Bergen-Belsen, loomed large in Americans' recent memory. The Cold War and the nuclear arms race made mass extinction a palpable possibility. Despite the gradual emergence of postwar prosperity, an atmosphere of doubt pervaded much postwar literature and thought. Abstract expressionist painters were not the only ones brooding about the enormity of evil. The rhetoric of original sin made a comeback among intellectuals, under the aegis of neo-orthodox theology or Freudian psychoanalysis. And for good historical reasons, many thinkers recovered a sense of the tragic conflict in the human condition—between the passionate longing for eternal life and the stubborn fact of death.

The gloomy postwar atmosphere contrasted sharply with the intellectual climate of James's time, when support for the idea of inevitable progress converged from religous and scientific sources. The problem, for the young James, was the determinism behind progressive schemes—the tendency to undermine belief in free will. Rejecting the determinism of either Providence or Progress, James embraced chance as an escape from the iron cage of (evangelical or managerial) rationality. For James, chance was the portal to a pluralistic universe.

For Tillich's intellectual generation, in contrast, the problem had become not an excess of cosmic order, but an absence of it. Despite the pervasiveness of managerial control in social thought, the specter that haunted moral philosophy was not determinism but meaninglessness. Thus chance played a darker role in Tillich's thought than in James's; it was another word for contingency, the whirl of unpredictable events without meaning or purpose that made life seem absurd. What was frightening, said Tillich, was not causal necessity but "the lack of ultimate necessity, the irrationality, and the inevitable darkness, of fate." Under the modern "rule of contingency," the pervasiveness of chance was a source of anxiety.[82]

The question was what to do about it. Positivist faith in secular progress was unthinkable after the war, and religious faith in Providence had become a banal belief in the beneficence of the existing order. Tillich wanted to restore the risk and challenge to the idea of Providence. Faith in Providence was no faith at all if it failed to confront the disorder, uncertainty, and potential meaninglessness of everyday life. "*Faith in Providence is faith altogether,*" Tillich wrote. "It is the courage to say yes to one's own life and life in general, in spite of the driving forces of fate, in spite of the insecurities of daily existence, in spite of the catastrophes of existence and the breakdown of meaning."[83]

Despite his darker view of chance, Tillich joined James in seeing the awareness of contingency as the key to overcoming anxiety and revitalizing one's existence. For both men, risking faith in a secular age was the first step in the lifelong project of making meaning in a contingent universe and cultivating the courage to be. This was not to be accomplished through force of will. As Tillich said, "One cannot command the courage to be and one cannot gain it by obeying a command. Religiously speaking, it is a matter of grace." And grace was by no means "merely spiritual." Christian dualism had for too long divided experience into "bloodless spirituality and mindless vitality." In fact the two were joined in the state of grace.[84]

Tillich's emphasis on the healing powers of grace led some critics (including his former sponsor Reinhold Niebuhr) to deride him as the prophet of a therapeutic Christianity. There were certainly times when Tillich sounded like a psychotherapist in the pulpit—and a guilt-ridden one at that. But Tillich's yearning for wholeness, for the reunion of body and soul, was not far from the traditional meaning of grace as a form of *mana*. And his reverence for "holy waste" put him even closer to the insights at the heart of the culture of chance.

The idea of holy waste embodied a critique of utilitarian ethics—one with occasionally disturbing implications. "There is no creativity, divine or human, without the holy waste which comes out of the creative abundance of the heart and does not ask, 'what use is this?'" Tillich wrote. Yet mainstream Protestantism no longer sanctioned the "wasteful self-surrender" of mystics and saints. "In many people there has been an abundance of the heart. But laws, conventions, and a rigid self-control have repressed it and it has died."[85] Tillich put his finger on the confining aspects of conventional Christianity, but failed to realize that the impulse to "self-surrender" could be manipulated to sinister ends—undermining independent thought, indoctrinating ideologues, raising armies. The holy waste of mystics could become the unholy waste of young lives on the battlefield.

Still, Tillich had recaptured a key element in the religion of Jesus (as opposed to official Christianity). The idea of holy waste expressed the Christian drama of sacrifice and redemption—God's willingness to give up his son, and the son's willingness to suffer and die, so that humanity might be redeemed from sin and enjoy eternal life. Jesus' death on the cross was "the most complete and the most holy waste," Tillich wrote. It was God's gift of grace to the world. Holy waste revealed the sacred significance of reckless generosity—the heart of the culture of chance.[86]

In the end, though, neither Tillich nor Cage created a satisfying synthesis from the traditions of the culture of chance. Their yearnings for grace led to self-absorbed spiritual odysseys, designed for the unattached individual. They revealed little sensitivity to the social meanings of the culture of chance—its ethic of fortune, its moral economy, its capacity to fuse connections between people. This was partly because, like other accidentalists, they paid little attention to the vernacular rituals of the random. A dense cloud of signs and portents, omens and premonitions and coincidences, lay beneath the rarefied world inhabited by midcentury artists and intellectuals. The aesthetes of accident, the philosophers of

play, the theologians of grace—nearly all, despite their reverence for
chance, lived in a universe apart from the gamblers on the street. But not
Ralph Ellison.

AN ENDURING SYNTHESIS

Ralph Ellison may have been the only American modernist literally to
bridge the gap between numbers running and philosophical debate. In *Invisible Man* (1952), Ellison caught some of the largest significance of the
vernacular culture of chance. The narrator has moved from the rural
South to Harlem in the 1930s; it is a world where little old ladies keep
their dream books next to their Bibles so they will know what number
to play, where streetcorner crapshooters affect a grand insouciance even
as they bend their knees to Fortune. Ellison had been a participant in that
world: years later he recalled that as a young boy in Oklahoma he had
bought Freud's *Interpretation of Dreams* on the assumption that it would
help him win the lottery.[87]

But as an educated young black man he was expected to put such
vestiges of superstition behind him. He did, as a student at Tuskegee and
an aspiring writer in New York, on the literary left in the 1930s. But by
the time he started writing *Invisible Man* in 1945 he had developed a nu-
anced appreciation for his own vernacular culture of chance. "I knew that
I was composing a work of fiction," he recalled. "One that would allow
me to take advantage of the novel's capacity for telling the truth while actually telling a 'lie,' which is the Afro-American folk term for an improvised story. Having worked in barbershops where that form of oral art
flourished, I knew that I could draw upon the rich culture of the folk tale
as well as that of the novel, and that uncertain of my skill, I would have
to improvise upon my materials in the manner of a jazz musician putting
a musical theme through a wild star-burst of metamorphosis."[88]

Invisible Man brilliantly reverses the trajectory of the bildungsroman,
or novel of initiation into manhood, by revealing its narrator's disillusionment with definitions of adult identity—or at least the ones available
to him as a black man. Ultimately he rejects the ethic of mastery and the
cultures of control (religious or secular) that sanction it. But for most of
the novel the narrator resists the vernacular culture of chance as a relic of
his rural past. Instead he works his way through two philosophies of his-

tory that emphasize human mastery over fate: first liberal individualism, then Soviet-style collectivism. Both eventually seem hollow, fundamentally flawed in their dependence on a simpleminded notion of history as linear progress and their falure to grant sufficient power to luck. The narrator's rationalism yields to respect for randomness as he learns to emulate local tricksters and finally becomes one. His best trick is to become an invisible man. The performance creates a new universe of possibilities for himself and for his audience.

The narrator begins in a cocoon of evangelical rationality (though an autumnal version of it)—the blend of Providence, individualism, and philanthropy that pervades his college, a thinly veiled version of Tuskegee. On Founder's Day, he is assigned to drive a car fror Mr. Norton, a Brahmin benefactor who insists that his "pleasant fate" is to be tied to the college—his "real life's work," he says, "is "not my banking or my researches, but my first-hand organizing of human life." But at Norton's insistence the narrator foolishly drives him past the cabin of Jim Trueblood, a black farmer who conceived a child with his daughter. Jim's account of the incest scene is too much for Norton, who harbors incestuous longings for his own prematurely deceased daughter. In search of whiskey to revive the fading philanthropist, the narrator drags him to a local bar that is full of black inmates from the local asylum. One, who had been a U.S. Army physician in France during World War I, challenges Norton's moral pretensions, and the philanthropist faints dead away. The college's president Bledsoe hears about the escapade and is furious: "'My God, boy! You're black and livin' in the South! Did you forget how to lie?'"[89]

Expelled from school, the boy begins to wonder whether the fit between merit and reward was as tight as he had been told. "I had kept unswervingly to the path before me, had tried to be exactly what I expected to be," he complains, yet plodding diligence had brought him nowhere. On the bus out of town he runs into the crazy veteran being transferred to another hospital for insulting Norton. "'Play the game, but don't believe in it,'" he advises the narrator. But it will be a long time before the narrator comes to that conclusion on his own. On the bus to New York, his only solace is the packet of letters Bledsoe has given him, supposedly sealed introductions to potential employers in New York. He arrives in the city and takes a room. "I spread the letters upon the dresser like a hand of high trump cards," resolving to embrace the necessary ethos of self-control. "I would have to get a watch. I would do everything to schedule," he vows, imagining himself as a black version of "the junior executive types in *Esquire*" or the actor Ronald Colman.[90]

Such fantasies quickly founder, as the narrator discovers that Bledsoe's letters are damning accounts of his demerits. Evangelical rationality ends in treachery; so much for Protestant Providence. Reeling in ontological confusion, the narrator takes a job at Liberty Paints, but quickly becomes enmeshed in a violent scuffle with white union workers, who resent the company's hiring black nonunion replacements. He awakens from a brawl to confront another culture of control: it is the world of impersonal, managerial technique. White-coated psychiatrists administer electroshock therapy, the purpose of which (one claims) is to lobotomize the patient without scars. In the midst of his ordeal the narrator sees the psychiatrists scribble strange questions, such as "WHO WAS BUCKEYE THE RABBIT?" Or he thinks he sees this. In any case, as his normal waking identity is fragmented, he is reminded of "an old identity"—the trickster Buckeye the Rabbit. The reference is fleeting but foreshadows more tricksters to come. Meanwhile, when he is pronounced "cured," the narrator stares at the head psychiatrist: "I looked at his lined face. Was he doctor, factory official or both?" The healer and the manager came together in the blank, impersonal face of modern authority.[91]

Feeling disconnected from any coherent sense of self, the narrator gropes temporarily toward connection with the African American vernacular. He is taken in by Mary Rambo, the welcoming embodiment of black maternal nurturance. She gives him soup and a room. Stumbling into the street in search of work, he takes in the syncretist culture of chance. In a store window he sees "two brashly painted images of Mary and Jesus surrounded by dream books, love powders, God-Is-Love signs, money-drawing oil and plastic dice." He is overwhelmed by the smell of sweet, hot yams from a vendor's cart, buys one, and begins eating it. After a rush of nostalgia he is "just as suddenly overcome by an intense feeling of freedom—simply because I was eating while walking in the street." Yams, he tells the vendor, are "my birthmark. I yam what I yam!" His "old identity" is again reasserting itself.[92]

When the narrator sees an old couple being evicted from their apartment, he joins the growing crowd at the scene. Their furniture and belongings are scattered on the pavement. On an old chiffonier he spots "nuggets of High John the Conquerer, the lucky stone"—probably an urban adaptation of the root. He is moved to address the crowd, which he does to extraordinary effect. All their long lives and hard work, he says, and this is what this old couple has to show for it—not much. He inspires the crowd to chase off the marshal and carry the furniture back upstairs. In the mêlée that follows he eventually encounters Brother Jack, a leading white official in the communist-style Brotherhood. Brother Jack is impressed and tries to recruit the narrator as a local organizer, but the young black orator is put off by Jack's dismissal of the old couple as dispensable to the struggle, "because they're incapable of rising to the historical situation." "'But I *like* them,' I said. 'I like them, they reminded me of folks I knew down South.'" That, Jack says, is because he has not completely jettisoned his "old agrarian self"—but he will. "*History* has been born in your brain."[93]

Another version of Providence is about to take over the narrator's life. In spite of his misgivings he joins the Brotherhood, mostly for the sixty dollars a week that will allow him to pay off all he owes Mary. When he does, she thinks he's dreamed a lucky number. His skepticism about such matters makes him susceptible to the appeal of Brotherhood: as he tells the crowd at the eviction scene, "these old folks had a dream book, but the pages went blank and failed to give them the number." The alternative to superstition and resignation, he begins to believe, is collective action in the service of deterministic historical laws—Providence and Will united under "scientific" rather than religious auspices. He gets a new salary, a new suit, and a new name. It is a secular rebirth. For a while he is secure in his new identity. He searches for signs of a meaningful universe as avidly as any Christian—or any compulsive gambler. "I lived with the intensity displayed by those chronic numbers players who see clues to their future in the most minute and insignificant phenomena: on passing trucks and subway cars, in dreams, comic strips, the shape of dog-luck fouled on the pavement. I was dominated by the all-embracing ideal of Brotherhood."[94]

But gradually the strains begin to show. Within weeks after he has become a spellbinding street organizer the narrator receives an anonymous note warning him to "go slow," to avoid arousing the racial anxiety of the white leadership. He begins haltingly to recover some of his cultural past: Brother Tarp, the old janitor in his Harlem office, had years before filed through a section of leg-iron to escape a chain gang down South; the old man gives the filed shaving to the narrator as "a kind of lucky piece" and the narrator keeps it on his desk, even though the Brotherhood's leadership disapproves. Unlike the piece of leg-iron on President Bledsoe's desk, Brother Tarp's is not a relic of sufferings endured under slavery, but an emblem of escape—the trickster springing the trap of unjust authority.[95]

Even as the narrator still strives to conform to movement discipline ("Brother, I shall always try to be on time"), he also begins to discover more flexible contemporary options to the Brotherhood's rationalist worldview. One possibility is embodied in Tod Clifton, a brilliant, charismatic organizer: "a hipster, a zoot suiter, a sharpie—except his head of Persian lamb's wool had never known a straightener." Together they confront the black nationalist, Ras the Exhorter; Clifton comes away strangely disturbed—maybe Ras is "unscientific," as the Brotherhood claims, but "sometimes a man *has* to plunge outside history," he says. For the narrator the alternative to purposeful, linear History is chaos, but he is haunted by Clifton's words even as he gives thanks for Brotherhood.[96]

When he is removed from Harlem at the height of his success, his anger flares: "For a moment I had almost allowed an old southern backwardness which I had thought dead to wreck my career." Meanwhile, Clifton disappears, resurfacing as a street vendor, selling dancing Sambo dolls, working without a license, one step ahead of the police. The narrator is enraged, then appalled, as he sees Clifton gunned down in a pointless confrontation with a pursuing cop.[97]

"Why should a man deliberately plunge outside of history and peddle an obscenity"—a dancing Sambo, an emblem of black degradation? the narrator wonders. Why should Clifton abandon the orderly, progressive world picture provided by the Brotherhood? Maybe for some of the same reasons William James rejected the "block universe" of mechanical determinism. And maybe for some different ones.[98]

The complexity of Ellison's philosophical position becomes apparent as the narrator descends underground to the subway. As he watches a group of black boys, recently arrived in Harlem from the Deep South, standing self-absorbed and stiff in their suits on a subway platform, the narrator feels an odd but fundamental kinship with them. They look like him. They remind him of what one of his teachers said to him: "'You're like one of those African sculptures, distorted in the interests of design.' Well, what design and whose?" What was their common bond with him, their common role in history? How could these "birds of passage who were too obscure for learned classification" fit into any linear scheme of progress?

What if history was a gambler, instead of a force in a laboratory experiment, and the boys his ace in the hole? What if history was not a reasonable citizen, but a madman full of paranoid guile, and these boys his agents, his big surprise! His own revenge? For they were outside, in the dark with Sambo, the dancing paper doll; taking it on the lambo with my fallen brother Tod Clifton (Tod, Tod) running and dodging the forces of history instead of making a dominating stand.[99]

The passage suggests a wide range of interpretations. At the most basic level it is part of a plea to include the historically voiceless in history—a task taken up by historians in the decades since Ellison published *Invisible Man*. It could also be constructed as a warning that "the third world is just around the corner"—the forgotten people of the world, the "people without history" are beginning to stir. But far more challenging are the philosophical and ethical textures in the passage. History is unmanageable, it suggests; the dream of technical mastery is an illusion. The acceptance of arbitrary fate is the beginning of wisdom.

This outlook is not mere passivity. It is a different way of inhabiting the world, outside the triumphalist blarings of will and choice. But it is not a prescription for ethical or even political quiescence. It is the way of the trickster, exercising the powers of the powerless, and of the artist, embracing what Joyce called "silence, exile, cunning."[100] It is the way of Ellison's narrator, who retreats to his underground lair and lights it with electricity purloined from Monopolated Power & Light—who embraces "invisibility" as a performance of emotional truth.

He discovers the stance of invisibility by chance. Fleeing Ras, he dons dark glasses to escape detection and discovers that everyone on the street starts mistaking him for Rinehart, a local trickster and confidence man. Men joke with him over drinks; a girl wants to set a date for later; a woman with a shopping bag wants to know "the final figger" (the winning number for that day); some old ladies rhapsodize about his preaching. Like Bledsoe, Rinehart is a black culture hero; both men drive Cadillacs, manipulate appearances, inspire fascination and respect. But Rinehart's identity is fluid and boundaryless. Through a simple disguise the narrator "becomes" Rinehart the lover, the pimp, the numbers runner, the preacher. "You could actually make yourself anew," he concludes. "All boundaries down, freedom was not only the recognition of necessity, it was the recognition of possibility."[101]

The improvised life threatens devotees of control. Through repeated disappointments the narrator discovers that the Brotherhood cannot tolerate improvisation—his style of public speech, which he makes up as he goes along in response to the calls of the crowd; or the improvised funeral procession for Tod Clifton, which turns into a spontaneous mass protest. When Brother Jack tells him that they evaluate strategy on the basis of "scientific objectivity," the narrator feels as if he is again being strapped down for electroshock by impersonal scientists. "'Don't kid yourself,'" he tells Jack, "'the only scientific objectivity is a machine.'" It is the characteristic cri de coeur of the midtwentieth-century humanist, but it leads in uncharacteristic directions.[102]

By unwittingly posing as Rinehart, the narrator dicovers he can escape from polarity to inclusiveness, from "either-or" to "both-and." "'Well, I *was* and yet I was invisible, that was the fundamental contradiction. I was and yet I was unseen,'" he marvels. Instead of the conventional path of success, a steady rise upward, he imagines a new world of possible trajectories: "up *and* down, in retreat as well as advance, crabways and crossways and around in a circle, meeting your old selves coming and going and perhaps all at the same time." But he cannot realize this vision until he falls, quite by accident, through an open manhole (another portal of discovery) into a labyrinth of coal bins and storage areas. Wandering about in the dark, he burns all the old proofs of his identity that he is carrying in his briefcase, beginning with his high school diploma.[103]

It is another rebirth—but not, as it first seems, into solipsism. In his underground retreat, he ponders his grandfather's advice—"Yes 'em to death"—which has been haunting him throughout the novel. He decides it is not merely a tricksters' tactic of deceit, but also a subtler form of affirmation, a recognition that blacks and whites share a common fate, even in a society that insisted on their separateness. As a striving self-made man he was "for" society, as a communist "against" it; but as an invisible man he could both "condemn and affirm, say no and say yes, say yes and say no." The trick was to cultivate a sense of unpredictable possibilities. "Step outside the narrow borders of what men call reality and you step into chaos—ask Rinehart, he's a master of it—or imagination." The process of play was what mattered, not the final result. "It's 'winner take nothing' that is the great truth of our country or of any country. Life is to be lived, not controlled, and humanity is won by continuing to play in the face of certain defeat." So the invisible man decides that "The hibernation is over. I must shake off the old skin and come up for breath."[104]

This is a crucial choice, reflecting its author's own. Unlike some of the other artists who responded to the allure of accident, Ellison neither mocked his audience nor abandoned his attempt to communicate with it. On the contrary, the famous last words of the novel are a direct address: "Who knows but that, on the lower frequencies, I speak for you?"[105] This question concluded the supreme achievement of the mid-century aesthetic of accident—an idiosyncratic synthesis of high and vernacular cultures of chance. *Invisible Man* was a sustained performance by a trickster who opened the portals of chance to unfolding discoveries, and who won his humanity by continuing to play in the face of certain defeat.

{EPILOGUE}

During the last third of the twentieth century, risk-taking became more respectable than it had been for decades. After the centrist managerial synthesis failed to bring victory in Vietnam or sustain prosperity at home, Ronald Reagan's presidency returned free-market fundamentalism to the center of political debate. Neoconservative intellectuals identified "life's lottery" as the guarantor of material progress and class mobility under "democratic capitalism."[1] But the most prominent celebrants of economic uncertainty were safely insulated from it themselves. The new rhetoric of risk concealed the extension of managerial control, embedded in powerful institutions and habits of mind. Real risk was transfered to workers at all levels, and the most interesting homage to Fortuna remained the least visible to free-market ideologues.

By the early 1970s, the midcentury synthesis was crumbling. Fault lines appeared in its base: a comparatively well-paid, economically secure working population. Complaining of pressure from overseas competition, American management withdrew from the midcentury bargain with employees and began to look for cheap labor abroad. Job security disappeared as corporations aimed to "reinvent" themselves for a new era of globalization. Meanwhile, as public revenues declined along with popular tolerance for taxes, state governments turned to legalized gambling as a means of raising money—first lotteries, then casinos, beginning with their return to Atlantic City in 1978.

By the 1980s, a new style of managerial thought had emerged. In business mythology, the new entrepreneur was cooler by far than his gray-flannel predecessors; he incorporated hip styles and even hip metaphysics—a metaphysics that not only drew on the cult of dynamism ("WE EAT CHANGE FOR BREAKFAST!") but that also celebrated spontaneity and chance, using catchphrases culled from Zen masters and quantum physicists. The management guru Tom Peters compared the new entrepreneurship's crusade against Taylorized scientific management with the triumph of quantum physics, which (he said) "has trumped Newtonian physics." Bill Boisvert wittily summarizes Peters's argument: "Newton's orderly, calculable landscape of billiard balls and tidily orbiting satellites has given way to the misty flickering world of wave-particle duality, where companies are both solvent and bankrupt until you do an audit. Thus, any attempt to plan and stabilize the corporate world defies the laws of nature *at the subatomic level*."[2]

Peters's bizarre formulations were a sign of things to come. During the protracted bull market of the 1990s, a maniacal babble swept through management literature and eventually dominated much of public discourse. "Breaking the rules" and "reengineering the corporation" became the slogans of executives posing as countercultural rebels. Plain talk about money and power was drowned out by a din of upbeat banality, most of it centering on the allegedly liberating powers of the Internet. Bill Gates typified the Orwellian pattern, redefining job insecurity as Web-based freedom. Like Gates, legions of corporate apologists reduced positive thinking to absurdity, playing endless variations on the theme of unlimited choice.

At first glance, the new rhetoric of risk appeared to dispense altogether with providentialist frameworks. But in fact, despite their endless talk of choice, Gates and his contemporaries remained wedded to a vision of inevitable progress powered by technology. Like Rockefeller and their other predecessors of a century before, the new breed of managers had the same old goals in mind. They wanted to minimize risk and to control a steady stream of profitability, to ensure that the company was "MAKING AN INVESTMENT, NOT RELYING ON LUCK" (in Gates's words). And as with Rockefeller, the drive for control extended to the details of everyday life. Gates's description of a hyperorganized "Web lifestyle" captures the dream. "When you leave the office for the day, your personal digital companion will download your e-mail, which might include a grocery list from your spouse. At the store, you can download a new recipe from a kiosk, which adds to your grocery list all the items you would need to use the recipe. . . ."[3] And so on. For all its apparent novelty, the description recalled the enduring managerial faith—a secular version of Rockefeller's Protestant self-discipline—that everyday life can be systematically controlled through technology.

The dream of systematic control remained very much alive in the late-twentieth-century United States, at least in the corporate-sponsored mainstream culture of *USA Today,* the *New York Times, CNN,* and National Public Radio. Technophilia ran rampant, rewritten in the idioms of management and money worship. A positivist faith in numbers as precise descriptions of reality sustained huge swaths of daily news: economic reports, epidemiological studies, opinion polls. Reductionist biologism reappeared in respectable places: the *New York Times* reported research that traced lucky hunches to particular kinds of brain chemistry.[4] Even the old pseudo-Darwinian creed of inevitable progress resurfaced in the vogue of "evolutionary psychology."

It was left for Robert Wright to merge technological and biological determinism in *Nonzero: The Logic of Human Destiny.* Wright asserted that evolution always selected for cooperative behavior, putting us all on a purposeful path toward world unity: the latest expression of this directionality in nature was the Internet. It would be hard to find a more muddled attempt to resurrect a providentialist theory of the universe.[5] Yet while scientists dismissed *Nonzero,* journalists treated it with amazing seriousness. Wright was the John Fiske of the 1990s, and he won a comparable audience among the comfortable.

Among the makers of "responsible opinion," determinisms proliferated, confusing freedom and fate, insisting that we were all choosing to do what we had to do, anyway. This melding of progress and will was perfectly compatible with rhetorical commitments to risk, especially among people who were insulated from the vagaries of chance by economic privilege. The new rhetoricians of progress believed that their success was the product of a meritocratic process, that they were the type who took chances successfully, that their superior skill and drive allowed them to make their own luck—and that history was on their side. This is a fair summary of the dominant mood within managerial professional elites, amid the triumphalist atmosphere of the American fin de siècle.

It is still an open question whether that mood altered significantly as the air began to escape from the New Economy balloon—or whether it "changed forever" (as so many commentators claimed) after the terrorist attacks of September 11, 2001. Nearly all Americans, including the most privileged and insulated from risk, were no doubt profoundly shaken by the sight of the World Trade Center turned into a crematorium. One could hardly ask for a more convincing reminder of the arbitrary cruelties of fate. Yet among elites, the tendency to reassert the claims of managerial control survived and even intensified. Politicians and pundits reaffirmed America's providential role as the savior of the world; American technological know-how and moral determination, our president told us, would track evil-doers to their lairs and eliminate them from the face of the earth. No one would deny the need to find and punish the terrorists, but Bush's Manichaean rhetoric divided the world into darkness and light, revealing the dualism that had always plagued the providentialist creed. The forces of modernity would flatten the fundamentalist challenge, from the providentialist view, and the forward march of progress would continue inexorably.

Yet amid the official pieties, more thoughtful responses surfaced. The legal scholar Jeffrey Rosen, noting the attempts to control or compensate for unpredictable menace in the months following the attacks, observed that "contemporary Americans, in particular, are not well equipped to deal with arbitrary threats because, in so many realms of life, we refuse to accept the role of chance." Nineteenth-century legal doctrines such as the assumption of risk had given way to a twentieth-century expectation of "total justice"—the expectation that all victims of all calamities will be compensated, provided they are not solely at fault. Hence, we had the egregious spectacle of personal injury lawyers threatening to sue the architects of the World Trade Center on the grounds that design flaws impeded the victims' escape. If the attack "helps teach Americans how to live with risk," Rosen concluded, "then perhaps we can emerge from this ordeal a stronger society as well as a stronger nation."[6]

Whatever the public consequences of the catastrophe, it resurrected (at least temporarily) the American imagination of disaster. It embodied the eruption of "the cataclysmic in everyday life," as the historian Hendrik Hartog observed. Like the Holocaust and other natural or man-made disasters, the terrorist attacks taught "that everyday life—including its routine, its safety, its security and its freedom—was a momentary accident likely to disappear."[7] Whether that sharp awareness of ultimate contingency would survive, especially among official thought-leaders, remained to be seen. The power of providentialist thinking remained strong.

Outside opinion-making circles, though, many ordinary Americans

had probably not needed the terrorist attacks to remind them of the precariousness of apparent security. Even at the high tide of the bull market,
few reasonably intelligent people could have accepted the nonsense being
served up to them by media elites. Certainly among the less affluent two-
thirds of the population—the part whose income declined or stagnated
during the 1990s—the revival of secular providentialism must have rung
particularly hollow. By the end of the century, their lives were more vulnerable to hazard than most Americans' had been for several decades. Secure jobs with benefits disappeared, as corporations cut labor costs by
turning to temporary and part-time workers. An injury on the job, an
unexpected layoff, a catastrophic illness—all these disasters loomed larger.
As the welfare state shrank, the middle class did, too.

The emerging business model demanded a contingent labor force,
mobile, malleable, assemblable, and dispersable in accordance with management's ever-shifting needs—"just in time" workers to complement
the "just in time" shipments of goods that managers embraced as the key
to the vaunted "flexibility." Unlike long-term employment, contingent
work could not give purpose and direction to life. It became harder to
believe that one's experience is "more than a series of random events,"
observed Richard Sennett. This change in perception may have promoted the spread of gambling, according to Robert Goodman in *The
Business of Luck.* "Legalized gambling," he wrote, "seizes on the public
desire to get ahead through enterprises of chance in a world where work
no longer seems reliable." Political leaders have protected state revenues
through lotteries—essentially a regressive "hope-maintenance tax," (in
Edward Tenner's phrase). Citing the sources of the luck business, Goodman and other critics invoked a familiar litany: the decline of a work
ethic and of opportunities for decent work, the disappearance of family
farms and savings accounts, the rise of a speculative spirit that bet on
everything from pork bellies to baseball cards as a path to quick profits.[8]

Unlike Victorian moralists or Freudian psychoanalysts, Goodman did
not wag his finger at the individual gambler. He was more concerned
with gambling as a symptom of broader social maladies—in particular,
the speculative spirit released by the decline of long-term employment.
But neither Goodman nor other critics of gambling paid much attention
to the vernacular culture of chance.

Among those who did were the civic leaders of Las Vegas, who sanitized the city's recent history as they courted the tourist trade. Consider

the whitewash of Benny Binion (1904–1989), who came to town from Dallas in 1947 after illegal casinos were shut down, opened the Golden Horseshoe casino downtown, and started the World Series of Poker. True to the "big man" tradition, he threw generous parties for hundreds of sycophantic friends, purchased influence deftly from public officials, and resorted to violence to protect his interests. (He was occasionally accused of murder but never convicted.) Binion's eighty-third birthday celebration was held at the University of Nevada–Las Vegas, with entertainment provided by Willie Nelson and Hank Williams, Jr., among others. The Las Vegas *Review-Journal* ran a lengthy tribute to this "unique pioneer in the gaming industry" who came to Las Vegas "as others did and will continue to do as long as this town offers opportunities . . . to get away from the past and start anew." When he died, the city erected a statue of him in a prominent public square, a monument to the American dream of reinventing the self.[9]

This sort of mythmaking overlooked the dark side of gambling—not only the greed and corruption of operators like Binion but the destructive psychological appeal of the games themselves, the mysterious and powerful attraction that led critics to warn of addiction. Certainly there was evidence for their concern, even if their language of pathology oversimplified the reasons for gambling's popularity. Despite its limitations, the diagnosis of addiction at least focused on the frisson that kept gamblers coming back. Video poker was especially seductive. "Sitting at that [video poker] machine was the only time I was happy," said Rose Hosty, a Louisiana mother of eight and owner of a Sno-cone shop, interviewed in 1998. "I didn't have to be a wife, a lover, or a mommy. It was like I went into a trance." Other addicted gamblers told therapists "they feel smarter, sexier, even taller" while they're playing. Feelings of intense experience may be related to the sublime blend of pleasure and danger, or the fleeting sense of immersion in pure possibility, that gambling conveys—especially to people enmeshed in the tedium of routine work for most of the rest of their lives. "What are the odds on 8-to-5?" asks Charles Bishop, historian and gambler. Sometimes, the man who never gambles can lose, too.[10]

Yet gambling remains more than a titillating escape from boredom. It can still ritually enact a philosophical alternative to dominant managerial ideals of control and accumulation. It can still constitute a worldview with ethical and even religious significance. The key to that significance is the gambler's disregard of money—the sacred coin of the realm. Champion poker players, who can calculate the odds for almost any hand in any situation, disdain limited stakes poker as "an unimaginative mechanical game." It is merely "a disciplined job," said Jack Straus, a winner of the World Series of Poker. "Anybody who wants to work out the mathematics can be a limit player and chisel out an existence." But high-stakes poker brought out the bluffer, the feinter, the player in gamblers such as Straus. "If there's no risk in losing, there's no high in winning," Straus said.[11] That was why, just after he had won forty thousand dollars at poker, he was willing to wager it all on whether or not Jack Nicklaus would make his next putt.

This was the quest for intense experience, but something more: a fine, careless disregard for utilitarian standards. The test of the true gambler remains insouciance toward money—handling big losses nonchalantly. Damon Runyon and the Barthelme brothers would agree. The gambler's willingness to reduce (or raise) money to the status of mere counter in a game returns us to the games' largest significance. Despite all the efforts to assimilate contemporary casinos to middle-class mores, the gambler still inhabits a world where prudential economic values have been inverted. Recall the advice of Harlem Pete: "If you want to be rich, Give!" This advocacy of "holy waste" underscores the connections between gambling and the broader values embedded in cultures of chance.

In the United States, the vernacular culture of chance has constantly been depleted by the assimilation of immigrants and replenished by the arrival of new ones. Just as younger American Catholics slipped away from their parents' devotional practices, younger Chinese women viewed their mothers' luck rituals as an oppressive inheritance from a life of patriarchal constraint.[12] Those rituals lacked the capacity to perform emotional truth, at least for the Americanized generation. But at the same time, Mexican and Central American immigrants sustained the magical elements of Catholic tradition, and Haitian immigrants used sorcery to protect undocumented workers from the slings and arrows of American union members. Haitian sorcerers filled a bottle with a mix of graveyard dirt, skull shavings from *nkisi* (intermediate spiritual beings), and other threshold detritus to "put good luck in it [the bottle]." To put good luck in it is to consecrate it, to infuse it with spirit, to make it alive. In New York and other Haitian communities, voodoo lives.[13]

The high culture of chance has survived as well, in both academic and avant-garde versions. During the 1980s and 1990s, the postmodern condition descended on the intelligentsia. In most disciplines (except architecture), the coming of postmodernity simply involved accentuating the modernist delight in fragmentation and ignoring the countercurrents of longing for cosmic order. Chance and play—or more fashionably, *jouissance*—became ends in themselves.

For postmodern philosophers in the pragmatic tradition, the new hegemony of chance was especially striking. In Richard Rorty's *Contingency, Irony, and Solidarity* (1989), he assumed that the task of the social democratic moral philosopher was to show how we could remain committed to humane social values in a postmodern era, when belief in universals is dead and "we treat *everything*—our language, our conscience, our community—as a product of time and chance."[14] Rorty's "we" was largely confined to secular intellectuals in the humanities. He did not acknowledge the widespread persistence of belief in various versions of Providence among Protestants, Catholics, and Jews in the late twentieth century, or the other ideas of cosmic order (orthodox or syncretist) that still commanded respect from a sizable portion of the world's population. But he did describe an important and unprecedented awareness of chance among the Western intelligentsia.

One consequence of that awareness was the debate over "moral luck" led by Bernard Williams, Thomas Nagel, and some other academic philosophers.[15] Most participants seemed to want to challenge the basic assumption of Kantian morality—that intentions are more important than outcomes. Their strategy was to stress outcomes as well as intentions. The degree of our moral responsibility depended not only on our intentions and motives, but also on circumstances and outcomes beyond our control: hence it is a drunk driver's moral luck to hit or not to hit a child when the drunk drives onto the sidewalk. The point of this exercise was not merely to rob Kantian morality of its transcendental authority, but to create a nontranscendental alternative that more accurately reflected everyday practice. By emphasizing the inadequacy of focusing on intentions alone, the idea of moral luck aimed to accommodate the role of contingency in determining our notions of personal responsibility—to meld morality with the caprice of fate.

Other experiments with accident continued to flourish outside the academy. Some were embedded in the performative conception of truth that pervaded the cultures of chance, both high and vernacular. Within the aesthetic of accident, the rituals for conjuring *mana*—or performing truth—were playful and provisional. Consider the career of the architect Frank Gehry. Born Frank Goldberg, the only Jewish kid in an Ontario mining town, growing up in the 1930s and 1940s, Gehry was steeped in the vernacular culture of chance. His grandmother was deeply religious and almost shamanistic ("Whenever someone looked at me funny," Gehry remembers, "she would lick my face"); his father was a slot and pinball machine supplier for local restaurants and bars. When slots were declared illegal in the 1940s, Frankie's dad put his money into a furniture business and went busto; he was a beaten man. The family moved to L.A., and Frankie drove a truck to put himself through USC. When Gehry arrived at the Harvard Graduate School of Design, Le Corbusier was god; Gehry didn't understand why until he discovered that Corbusier's "stunningly original" forms came from his paintings. "That's when I broke through," he told an interviewer. "That's when I threw away the grid system and just said, 'man, there's another freedom out there, and it comes from somewhere else, and that somewhere else is the place I'm interested in.'"[16]

Gehry's discovery of "somewhere else" involved fantasy, playfulness, and a willingness to work with accidents. He was making little boxes of plastic laminate using a material called Color Core, and it looked too much, Gehry thought, like lamps that had already been made famous by Noguchi. So he "sort of accidentally" knocked one to the floor; its frag-

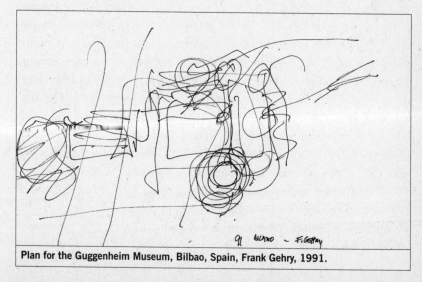

Plan for the Guggenheim Museum, Bilbao, Spain, Frank Gehry, 1991.

ments looked like fish scales so he made it into a fish lamp. Then he made some more. This was neither the first nor last time Gehry would use chance as a method. His working drawings for the Guggenheim Bilbao Museum looked like chaotic doodles, which in a sense they were. "It's just the way I draw when I'm thinking," he said. "I think that way. I'm thinking about what I'm doing, but I'm sort of not thinking about my hands." Gehry's approach recalled Roland Barthes's description of automatic writing: "entrusting the hand with the task of writing as quickly as possible what the head itself is unaware of." After the automatic drawing was "done," Gehry looked within the tangle for random images and accidental forms that might help him solve problems or answer questions that had arisen at the stage of the project.[17]

Leaving (a few) things to chance was a way of preventing repetition and fixation on conventions—keeping improvisation alive in the design process. And improvisation preserved a spirit of play. Gehry's habit of incorporating fugitive materials gathered on the premises into his designs originated in his own childhood, when he would sit on the floor with his grandmother and build makeshift cities with little boxes and trash and leftover pieces of wood. Here as elsewhere, the aesthetic of accident kept the play-sphere of childhood alive.

Gehry became a postmodernist trickster. He refused to aim for unity, assuming that fragmented design embodied broader feelings of cultural fragmentation. In the California Aerospace Museum, he created what he ironically called a "village of forms"—jumbling together dissimilar materials and shapes that don't cohere to express the confusion of contemporary life. This idea is utterly banal, and threatens to leave the trickster on the threshold of the marvelous, beckoning but refusing to take us across. The social significance of Gehry's achievement is difficult to address amid the current din of praise for him. Certainly there is nothing "democratic" about corporate specatacles designed to evoke tourist awe, as Hal Foster has recently observed.[18] But there remans the vexed question of beauty. If Gehry, like Motherwell, puts chance in the service of aesthetic pleasure, then maybe there is something behind the curtain after all.

The idea that beauty is intimately connected with chance brings the aesthetic of accident within range of a notion of grace. Elaine Scarry has written: "The surfaces of the world are aesthetically uneven. You come around a bend in the road, and the world suddenly falls open. When we

come upon beautiful things . . . they act like small tears in the surface of
the world that pull us through to some vaster space." Like pagan gods and
goddesses, flashes of beauty appear and disappear quickly—especially in
nature. Caprice is of their essence.

> . . . you may be sweeping the garden bricks at home, attending
> with full scrutiny to each square inch of their mauve-orange-blue
> surfaces (for how else can you sweep them clean?); then suddenly a
> tiny mauve-orange-blue triangle, with a silver sheen, lifts off from
> the sand between the bricks where it had been sleepily camouflaged
> until the air currents disturbed it. It flutters in the air, then settles
> back down on the brick, a triangle this big: ▲ Why should this tiny
> fragment of flying brick-color stop your heart?

Scarry's question has no clear answer, but it points to the place where
aesthetics and politics meet. "At the moment we see something beautiful," Scarry writes, "we undergo a radical decentering." Beauty demands
that we "give up our imaginary position at the center," according to Simone Weil.[19] This is a move with political implications, especially for
ecological debate.

The environmental movement has been criticized for its preoccupation with "mere" aesthetic concerns—a supposed mark of its "elitism" in
a utilitarian democracy. But what Rachel Carson, Joseph Wood Krutch,
and other environmentalists knew was that the protection of natural
beauty required an altered philosophical outlook: a questioning of human centrality, a rejection of rigid dualism, a disavowal of the ethic of
mastery. Saving natural beauty required a willingness to leave things to
chance, an openness to the experiences of grace that nature gives. This in
turn ironically demanded a conscious effort to resist the managerial
agenda of control. The preservation of a place of grace could be a profoundly political act.

Even at this political juncture, the aesthetic of accident could veer
toward solipsism. The trick to avoiding it was to recognize the role of
other people in the creation of grace. The philosopher Emmanuel Levinas has argued that the essence of morality is a gratuitous moment of
generosity—in which we look a powerless other in the face and acknowledge his or her claims. This is a game in which "someone plays
without winning. . . . Something that one does gratuitously, that is

grace. . . ." It is expressed in "gratuitous love, the conduct of a gratuitous act." In short, there is an ethic as well as a theology of grace.[20]

The passages from Levinas are quoted in Zygmunt Bauman's *Modernity and the Holocaust,* which argues that the destruction of the European Jews was, in effect, the product of specialization, rationalization, and depersonalization, the ultimate expression of the managerial culture of control. Levinas's ethic of grace, in Bauman's view, is the most potent resistance available against the enormity of total evil. We could look further and find worse.

The longing for grace remains at the heart of the culture of chance. What I have tried to do here is reconstruct that culture, revealing its centrality to the American experience of history. The pursuit of grace in what often seems a graceless world has created a powerful alternative tradition, a countervailing force against the dominant American ethos of control.

Gambling ritualizes the yearning for grace and underwrites its unfashionable truth. By taking a chance, by giving up the drive for perfect mastery of fate, gamblers recognize what contemporary prophets of progress so often forget—that the pursuit of happiness defies the attempt to organize it. They sense that happiness is something like the experience Eudora Welty describes: "Something that appears to you suddenly, that is meant for you, a thing that you reach for and pick up and hide at your breast, a shiny thing that reminds you of something alive and leaping."[21] Not unlike those tears in the curtain of the everyday, where the light of less imperfect possibilities shines through.

Like aleatory artists and idiosyncratic believers, gamblers implicitly acknowledge that fortune is best courted obliquely rather than confronted directly and that the willingness to experience chance creates the possibility of grace. This was what William James realized when he said that chance was a kind of gift, "something on which we have no effective claim"—something for nothing. This perspective challenged the ideal of a systematically controlled life and opened portals of possibility undreamed of by utilitarian rationalists.

Now, nearly a century after James's death, the drive for systematic control is still laying claim to everything under the sun. Maybe this shallow utopianism provides ontological reassurance to investors floating in the ether of the New Economy. Maybe it provides comfort and certainty to people who cannot bear the inconclusiveness and complexity of human affairs. Maybe it is just another transitional phase in our ever-transitional contemporary culture. Who knows? New prophets (or antiprophets) may arise—to puncture the pretensions of their time, to cultivate chance as something more than a hot stock tip, to remind us that happiness is "something alive and leaping." Maybe we'll get lucky.

NOTES

[INTRODUCTION: GAMBLING FOR GRACE]

1. "Gamblers Leave Child in Car," *Washington Post*, 1 December 1996, p. A21; "Kids in Casinos? You Bet," *Newsweek*, 21 October 1996, p. 72; Blaine Harden and Anne Swardson, "Addiction: Are States Preying on the Vulnerable?" *Washington Post*, 4 March 1996, p. A8.

2. Walter Cronkite, "The Dice Are Loaded," Discovery Channel special, 12 November 1994; Thomas Grey cited in Margot Hornblower, "No Dice: The Backlash Against Gambling," *Time*, 1 April 1996, p. 29.

3. Michael Walzer, *Revolution of the Saints* (Cambridge, Mass., 1965).

4. William Safire, "Now: Bet While You Booze," *New York Times*, 11 January 1993, p. A17.

5. Alexis de Tocqueville, *Democracy in America* [1835], 2 vols., ed. and trans. Phillips Bradley; Vintage Books ed. (New York, 1960), vol. 2, pp. 164–65.

6. Michel Marriott, "Fervid Debate on Gambling: Disease or Moral Weakness?" *New York Times*, 21 November 1992, p. A1.

7. Johan Huizinga, *Homo Ludens: A Study of the Play Element in Culture* [1938] (Boston, 1955). Other essential works in this tradition are Roger Caillois, *Man, Play, and Games*, trans. Meyer Barash (Glencoe, Ill., 1961), and Clifford Geertz, "Deep Play: Notes on the Balinese Cockfight," in his *The Interpretation of Cultures* (New York, 1973), pp. 412–53.

8. Peter Carey, *Oscar and Lucinda*, Vintage Books ed. (New York, 1988), p. 189.

9. Theodor Reik, "The Study in Dostoyevsky," in his *From Thirty Years with Freud* (New York, 1940), p. 170.

10. Ted Sickinger, "History Shows Attitudes Toward Gambling Change with Times," *Kansas City Star*, 11 March 1997, p. A–11. I am indebted to Charles Bishop for sending me this reference.

11. Norman O. Brown, *Hermes the Thief* (Madison, Wis., 1947), pp. 35–45.

12. I use the translation by Lewis Hyde, "The Homeric Hymn to Hermes," in his *Trickster Makes This World* (New York, 1998), pp. 317–31. Quotations at 330.

13. *Ibid.*

14. Brown, *Hermes*, p. 102.

15. On *mana*, see W. R. Halliday, *Greek Divination* (Oxford, 1913), pp. 101ff; E. A. Wallis Budge, *Amulets and Talismans* (New York, 1970), pp. 24ff.

16. This paragraph and the next summarize a half century or more of debate among anthropologists. For the older but still influential evolutionary view, see Bronislaw Malinowski, "Magic, Science and Religion," in J. Needham, ed., *Science, Religion and Reality* (London, 1925); and Lucien Lévy–Bruhl, *L'Ame primitive* (Paris, 1927). The philosophical basis for the newer view was provided in part by J. L. Austin, *How to Do Things with Words* (Cambridge, Mass., 1962).

17. E. E. Evans–Pritchard began to question the empiricist view in his classic *Witchcraft, Oracles, and Magic Among the Azande* (Oxford, 1937). A more philosophically sophisticated critique is in S. N. Tambiah, "Form and Meaning of Magical Acts: A Point of

View," in Robin Horton and Ruth Finnegan, eds., *Modes of Thought: Essays on Thinking in Western and Non–Western Societies* (London, 1973), pp. 199–229. A contemporary application of Tambiah's views is Mary Nooter Roberts and Allen F. Roberts, "Memory in Motion," in *idem.*, eds., *Memory: Luba Art and the Making of History* (New York, 1996), pp. 177–82.

18. Hyde, *Trickster,* pp. 125–27, 288–89, quotation at p. 126; F. H. Ehmcke, *Graphic Trade Symbols by German Designers from the 1907 Klingspor Catalogue* (New York, 1974), p. 29, #248. I'm indebted to my colleague Belinda Davis for this reference.

19. Victor Turner, *Revelation and Divination in Ndembu Ritual* (Ithaca, N.Y., and London, 1975), p. 200. On the persistence of doubt, see, for example, Evans–Pritchard, *Witchcraft,* p. 251; Roberts and Roberts, "Memory," p. 194; and Rosalind Shaw, "Splitting Truths from Darkness: Epistemological Aspects of Temne Divination," in Philip Peek, ed., *African Divination Systems: Ways of Knowing* (Bloomington, Ind., 1991), pp. 141–44.

20. Roberts and Roberts, "Memory," p. 206. See also Turner, *Revelation and Divination,* p. 221, and Elizabeth McAlister, "A Sorcerer's Bottle: The Visual Art of Magic in Haiti," in Donald J. Cosentino, ed., *Sacred Arts of Haitian Vodou* (Los Angeles, 1995).

21. On this uncertainty principle in divination, see Andrew Karp, "Prophecy and Divination in Ancient Greek Literature," in Robert M. Berchman, *Mediators of the Divine: Horizons of Prophecy, Divination, Dreams, and Theurgy in Mediterranean Antiquity* (Atlanta, 1998), pp. 11–12. See also William James, "Radical Empiricism" [1897], in John J. McDermott, ed., *The Writings of William James* (New York, 1967), p. 135.

22. Robert Farris Thompson, *Flash of the Spirit: African and Afro–American Art and Philosophy* (New York, 1983), pp. 221–22; Hyde, *Trickster,* pp. 125–26.

23. Sophocles, *Antigone,* line 996, translated and cited in Martha Nussbaum, *The Fragility of Goodness* (New York, 1986), pp. 81, 89.

24. Karl Kerenyi, "The Trickster in Relation to Greek Mythology," in Paul Radin, *The Trickster: A Study in American Indian Mythology* (New York, 1955), p. 190; Turner, *Revelation and Divination,* p. 37; Hyde, *Trickster,* pp. 21–22, 116–17, 215.

25. E. C. Devereux, "Gambling and the Social Structure," Unpublished Ph.D. dissertation, Harvard University, 1949, pp. 781–82.

26. On the concepts of continuous and discontinuous revelation, see the lucid discussion in John Thornton, *Africa and Africans in the Making of the Atlantic World* (New York and London, 1992), chap. 9.

27. Max Weber, *The Protestant Ethic and Spirit of Capitalism* [1904], trans. Talcott Parsons (New York, 1958); William James, "The Sentiment of Rationality" [1897], reprinted in John J. McDermott, ed., *The Writings of William James* (New York, 1966), pp. 317–45.

28. David Thomson, *In Nevada* (New York, 1999), pp. 289, 291.

29. Jack Richardson, *Memoir of a Gambler* (New York, 1979), p. 15.

30. Frederick and Steven Barthelme, *Double Down: Reflections on Gambling and Loss* (New York, 1999), pp. 75, 95.

[CHAPTER 1: THE DANCE OF DIVINATION]

1. Chrestien LeClercq, *New Relation of Gaspesia, with the Customs and Religion of the Gaspesian Indians* [1691], ed. and trans. William F. Ganong (Toronto, 1910), pp. 208–13. See also Robert Moss, "Missionaries and Magicians: The Jesuit Encounter with Native American Shamans on New England's Colonial Frontier," in Peter Benes and Jane Montague Benes, eds., *Wonders of the Invisible World* (Boston, 1995), p. 30.

2. Trudie Lamb, "Games of Chance and Their Religious Significance Among Native Americans," *Artifacts* 8 (Spring 1980); 1, 10–11.

3. W. R. Halliday, *Greek Divination* [1913] (Chicago, 1967), pp. 101ff.; E. A. Wallis Budge, *Amulets and Talismans* (New York, 1970), pp. 24ff.

4. Dutch trader quoted in William Bascom, *Ifa Divination* (Bloomington, Ind., 1969), p. 5; M. Drake Patten, "African–American Spiritual Beliefs: An Archaeological Testimony from the Slave Quarters," in Benes and Benes, eds., *Wonders,* p. 51; John Pemberton III, "Divination in Sub-Saharan Africa," in Alisa Lagamma, *Art and Oracle: African Art and Rituals of Divination* (New York, 2000), pp. 10–22; Robert Farris Thompson, *Flash of the Spirit: African and Afro-American Art and Philosophy* (New York, 1983), p. 34.

5. Patten, "African–American Spiritual Beliefs," pp. 46ff.

6. William D. Piersen, "Black Arts and Black Magic: Yankee Accommodations to African Religion," in Benes and Benes, *Wonders,* p. 42.

7. Nicholas Purcell, "Literate Games: Roman Urban Society and the Game of *Alea,*" *Past & Present* #147 (May, 1995): 26–27; Aristotle, *Nicomachean Ethics,* book III, 3; Sallust, Speech to Caesar in the Senate, section I; Marcus Tullus Cicero, *On Divination* [44 B.C.E.], trans. Herbert Poteat (Chicago, 1950); Valerie Flint, *The Rise of Magic in Early Medieval Europe* (Princeton, 1991), pp. 22–24.

8. Cornelius Van Dam, *Urim and Thummim: A Means of Revelation in Ancient Israel* (Winona Lake, Ill., 1997), esp. pp. 37, 203, 229–30; Halliday, *Greek Divination,* p. 205. It may be that the Urim solicited inspiration from Yahweh, while the Thummim interpreted legal disputes. The distinction between inspiration and interpretation parallels Plato's differentiation between *mania* (prophetic madness or frenzy) and *mantike* (divination of signs). Plato, like the ancient Hebrews, elevated the former over the latter. See Gregory Shaw, "Divination in the Neoplatonism of Lamblichus," in Robert Berchman, ed., *Mediators of the Divine: Horizons of Prophecy, Divination, Dreams, and Theurgy in Mediterranean Antiquity,* p. 234.

9. Shaw in Berchman, *Mediators,* p. 227; Flint, *Rise of Magic,* pp. 102–6.

10. Boethius, *The Consolation of Philosophy* [c. 524], trans. Richard Green (Indianapolis and New York, 1962), book I, pp. 14–15; book III, p. 71; book IV, pp. 92, 94.

11. *Ibid.,* book IV, p. 96; book V, p. 101.

12. Keith Thomas, *Religion and the Decline of Magic* (London, 1971), pp. 40–44; Flint, *Rise of Magic,* pp. 286–87.

13. Flint, *Rise,* pp. 94–97, 218–26.

14. *Ibid.,* pp. 274ff., 400–401.

15. Thomas, *Religion and the Decline of Magic* offers a brilliant assessment of this farrago.

16. Here I follow the provocative and persuasive argument of Norman O. Brown in *Life Against Death* (Middletown, Conn., 1959), chap. 14.

17. John Bunyan, *Grace Abounding to the Chief of Sinners and the Life and Death of Mr. Badman* [1666] (New York and London, 1928), pp. 22, 59, 72, 78.

18. Peter Fuller, "Introduction," in Jon Halliday and Peter Fuller, eds., *The Psychology of Gambling* (New York, 1974), pp. 62–63. Unfortunately, Fuller ultimately reduces both gambling and religion to "unsatisfactory attempts to exert and impose control"—a mechanistic formulation that does insufficient justice to the multiple meanings of both activities.

19. John Cotton, *A Practical Commentary, or an Exposition with Observations, Reasons, and Uses upon the First Epistle of John* (London, 1656), pp. 126–27.

20. John Calvin, *Institutes of the Christian Religion* [1561], trans. Ford Lewis Battles, ed. John T. McNeill (Philadelphia, 1956), vol. XX, book I, chap. 16, p. 197. Emphasis in original.

21. Jacob Viner, *The Role of Providence in the Social Order* (Philadelphia, 1972); Thomas, *Religion and the Decline of Magic,* p. 88.

22. Max Weber, *The Protestant Ethic and the Spirit of Capitalism* [1904], trans. Talcott Parsons (New York, 1958).

23. F. J. Snell, *The Chronicles of Twyford* (Tiverton, c. 1893), quoted in Thomas, *Religion*, p. 16.

24. William Shakespeare, *King Lear*, IV, i, 36.

25. Newbell Niles Puckett, *Folk Beliefs of the Southern Negro* (Chapel Hill, 1926), pp. 313ff.

26. Thompson, *Flash of the Spirit*, pp. 221–22; Sally Kevill–Davies, *Yesterday's Children* (Woodbridge, Suffolk, UK, 1992), pp. 56–58, 300ff.; James MacKay, *Childhood Antiques* (New York, 1976), pp. 107–8.

27. Richard Godbeer, *The Devil's Dominion: Magic and Religion in Early New England* (New York, 1992), p. 29.

28. Perry Miller, *The New England Mind: From Colony to Province*. (Cambridge, Mass., 1953), pp. 55–57.

29. Robert Herrick, "The Coming of Good Luck," in James Reeves, ed., *The Cassell Book of English Poetry* (New York, 1965), #346.

30. Robert M. Adams, "Robert Herrick," in *The Norton Anthology of English Literature*, 4th ed., 2 vols. (New York, 1979), I, pp. 1315–16.

31. T. F. Hoad, ed., *The Concise Oxford Dictionary of English Etymology* (Oxford, 1986), pp. 209–10.

32. Moss, "Missionaries and Magicians," pp. 19–20; J. N. B. Hewitt, "The Iroquoian Concept of the Soul," *Journal of American Folklore* 3 (1895): 111.

33. Moss, "Missionaries and Magicians," p. 23.

34. Lalemant quoted in Stewart Culin, *Games of the North American Indians* [1906] (New York, 1975), pp. 109–10.

35. *Ibid.*, p. 110; George Eisen, "Voyageurs, Black–Robes, Saints, and Indians," *Ethnohistory* 24/3 (Summer, 1977): 199.

36. Culin, *Games*, p. 110.

37. Kathryn Gabriel, *Gambler Way: Indian Gaming in Mythology, History, and Archaeology in North America* (Boulder, 1996), esp. pp. 6–11.

38. Eisen, "Voyageurs," pp. 193–94, 200–201.

39. *Ibid.*, p. 194.

40. Culin, *Games*, p. 45. See also M. R. Harrington, *Sacred Bundles of the Sac and Fox Indians* (Philadelphia, 1914).

41. Godbeer, *Devil's Dominion*, p. 56.

42. Mather on dreams cited in Merle Curti, "The American Exploration of Dreams and Dreamers," *Journal of the History of Ideas*, 27 July-Sept (1966): 394–95.

43. Richard Warch, *School of the Prophets: Yale College, 1701–1740* (New Haven and London, 1973).

44. John Dane cited in Michael P. Winship, *Seers of God: Puritan Providentialism in the Reformation and the Early Enlightenment* (Baltimore and London, 1996): p. 1; Mary Rowlandson, *The Sovereignty and Goodness of God, Together With the Faithfulness of His Promises Displayed, a Narrative of the Captivity, Sufferings, and Removes, of Mrs. Mary Rowlandson* [1682] (Boston, 1791).

45. Rowlandson, *Sovereignty and Goodness*, pp. 119, 121.

46. Increase Mather, *Essay for the Recording of Illustrious Providences* (Boston, 1684), p. 261.

47. Godbeer, *Devil's Dominion*, pp. 44, 56.

48. Karin Calvert, *Children in the House: The Material Culture of Early Childhood, 1600–1900* (Boston, 1992), pp. 50–51; Godbeer, *Devil's Dominion*, pp. 9, 84.

49. Increase Mather, *A Testimony Against Several Prophane and Superstitious Customs Now Practiced in New England* (London, 1687), p. 13; John Hervey, *Racing in America, 1665–1865* (New York, 1944), p. 12; Richard P. Gildrie, *The Profane, the Civil, and the Godly* (University Park, Pa., 1994), pp. 74–75; Bruce Daniels, "Sober Mirth and Pleasant Poisons: Puritan Ambivalence Toward Leisure and Recreation," *American Studies* (1993): 127; John S. Ezell, *Fortune's Merry Wheel: The Lottery in America* (Cambridge, Mass., 1960), pp. 12–20.

50. Calvert, *Children in the House,* p. 48.
51. *Ibid.,* pp. 110–11.
52. Edwin Fogel, *Beliefs and Superstitions of the Pennsylvania Germans* (Philadelphia, 1915), pp. 14–18, 98–113; Frederick Weiser, *Fraktur: Pennsylvania German Folk Art* (Lancaster, Pa., 1973); David Freeman Hawke, *Everyday Life in Early America* (New York, 1988), pp. 157–59.
53. Edmund Morgan, "The Labor Problem at Jamestown, 1607–18," *American Historical Review,* 76 (June 1971): 595–611.
54. Jeremy Collier, "An Essay Upon Gaming in a Dialogue," in John and Constance Masefield, *Essays Moral and Polite, 1660–1714* (London, 1906), p. 11.
55. William G. Stanard, "Racing in Colonial Virginia," *Virginia Magazine of History and Biography* 2 (January 1895): 293–94; Timothy H. Breen, "Horses and Gentlemen: The Cultural Significance of Gambling Among the Gentry of Virginia," *William & Mary Quarterly,* 3rd. ser. 34 (April 1977): 239–57.
56. David Hackett Fischer, *Albion's Seed: Four British Folkways in America* (New York, 1989), pp. 342–43; Johan Huizinga, *Homo Ludens, A Study of the Play Element in Culture* [1938] (Boston, 1955) p. 56. I am indebted to the probing observations of Bertram Wyatt–Brown, *Southern Honor* (New York, 1982), p. 344.
57. Richard Beale Davis, "The Devil in Virginia in the Seventeenth Century," *Virginia Magazine of History and Biography* 65 (April 1957): 131–49.
58. Fischer, *Albion's Seed,* p. 343.
59. William Byrd, *The London Diary (1717–1721), and Other Writings of William Byrd of Virginia,* ed. Louis B. Wright and Marion Tining (New York, 1958), pp. 78, 102, 115.
60. Piersen, "Black Arts and Black Magic," p. 43. See also Mechal Sobel, *The World They Made Together* (Princeton, 1987), pp. 72–77, 84–85; Philip D. Morgan, *Slave Counterpoint: Black Culture in the Eighteenth-Century Chesapeake and Lowcountry* (Chapel Hill, N.C., and London, 1998), pp. 610–57; and Paul Gilroy, *The Black Atlantic: Modernity and Double Consciousness* (Cambridge, Mass., and London, 1993), which argues provocatively that Black Atlantic culture constituted "a counterculture of modernity."
61. Melville J. Herskovits, *The Myth of the Negro Past* [1941] (Boston, 1958), pp. 242–44; Newbell Niles Puckett, *Folk Beliefs of the Southern Negro* (Chapel Hill, 1926), pp. 108–11; Michael A. Gomez, *Exchanging Our Country Marks: The Transformation of African Identities in the Colonial and Antebellum South* (Chapel Hill, 1998).
62. Gomez, *Exchanging Our Country Marks,* pp. 128–31.
63. *Ibid.,* pp. 110–11.
64. Puckett, *Folk Beliefs,* pp. 108–9, 496ff.
65. Gomez, *Country Marks,* chap. 3.
66. Thompson, *Flash of the Spirit,* pp. 5, 17.
67. Gomez, *Country Marks,* p. 254. The estimate is controversial and challenges Jon Butler, *Awash in a Sea of Faith: Christianizing the American People* (Cambridge, Mass., and London, 1990), chap. 5, which argues that slavery destroyed indigenous systems of belief and collective practices in an "African spiritual holocaust."
68. Patten, "African–American Spiritual Beliefs," pp. 47–48; Gomez, *Country Marks,* pp. 282–86; Puckett, *Folk Beliefs,* p. 218.
69. B. A. Botkin, *Lay My Burden Down* [1945] (Chicago, 1969), p. 29; Puckett, *Folk Beliefs,* p. 218.
70. Carl A. Brasseaux, "The Moral Climate of French Colonial Louisiana, 1699–1763," *Louisiana History* 27 (Winter, 1986): 27–41; Piersen, "Black Arts and Black Magic," pp. 39–41.
71. Herskovits, *Negro Past,* p. 237; Puckett, *Folk Beliefs,* p. 319.
72. Patten, "African–American Spiritual Beliefs," p. 48; Puckett, *Folk Beliefs,* p. 494.
73. Puckett, *Folk Beliefs,* pp. 264ff.
74. *Ibid.,* p. 163.

75. The phrase is the title of chapter 1 in Claude Lévi-Strauss *The Savage Mind* (Chicago, 1969).
76. Piersen, "Black Magic and Black Arts," pp. 39–40.
77. John Greenleaf Whittier, *The Supernaturalism of New England* [1847], ed. Edward Wagenknecht (Norman, Okla., 1969), p. 102.

[CHAPTER 2: THE AMUSEMENTS OF THE ALEHOUSE]

1. Peter Benes, "Fortune-tellers, Wise Men, and Magical Healers in New England, 1644–1850," in Peter Benes and Jane Montague Benes, eds., *Wonders of the Invisible World, 1600–1900* (Boston, 1995), p. 137.
2. W. J. Rorabaugh, *The Alcoholic Republic: An American Tradition* (New York, 1979), pp. 27–28.
3. Tavern game, "Bell at the Bar," Accession #59.1943, Winterthur Museum, Winterthur, Delaware.
4. *The Histories of Herodotus,* book I, chap. 32.
5. Miguel de Cervantes, *Don Quixote de la Mancha* [1605–1615], trans. Peter Anthony Motteux, Modern Library ed. (New York, 1949), part II, book III, ch. 23, p. 592; Martin Buber, quoted in Julius Lester, "Growing Down," *Change* 11 (October, 1979): 37. For examples of Cervantes's aphorism in English, see John Bartlett, *Familiar Quotations* [1855] ed. Emily Morison Beck, 15th ed. (Boston, 1980), p. 170n.
6. The classic work is Joseph Haroutunian, *From Piety to Moralism* (New Haven, 1932), but the conceptual framework pervades Perry Miller, *The New England Mind: From Colony to Province* (Cambridge, Mass., 1953), and the entire tradition inspired by his work.
7. Jon Pahl, *Paradox Lost: Free Will and Political Liberty in American Culture, 1630–1760* (Baltimore and London, 1992), pp. 94ff. discusses the rhetoric of fortune. The literature on revivalism is immense, but see especially Nathan Hatch, *The Democratization of American Christianity, 1800–1860* (New Haven, 1989), and Christine Leigh Heyrman, *Southern Cross: The Beginnings of the Bible Belt* (New York, 1997).
8. Henry St. John, Viscount Bolingbroke, *Historical Writings,* ed. Isaac Kramnick (Chicago, 1972), pp. 18, 21, 22, quoted in Gordon Wood, "Conspiracy and the Paranoid Style: Causality and Deceit in the Eighteenth Century," *William & Mary Quarterly,* 3rd. Ser. 39 (1982): 415.
9. Washington quoted in Paul Nagel, *One Nation Indivisible: The Union in American Thought* (New York, 1964), p. 149. On the importance of Bolingbroke and other Whig historians to the Revolution, see Trevor Colbourn, *The Lamp of Experience: Whig History and the Origins of the American Revolution* (Baltimore and London, 1965).
10. Thomas Kavanagh, *Enlightenment in the Shadow of Chance* (Baltimore and London, 1993); Lorraine Daston, *Classical Probability in the Enlightenment* (Princeton, 1988).
11. Unidentified Charlestown, Massachusetts, newspaper dated 14 February 1795, reprinted in *Litchfield Monitor,* 4 March 1795, and quoted by Benes, "Fortune-tellers, Wise Men, and Magical Healers," p. 127.
12. Benes, "Fortunetellers, Wise Men, and Magical Healers," pp. 127–28.
13. James Garvin and Donna-Belle Garvin, *On the Road North of Boston: New Hampshire Taverns and Turnpikes, 1700–1900* (Concord, N.H., 1988), p. 103.
14. Judge Martin Smith, "Old Slave Days in Connecticut," *Connecticut Magazine* 1 (1801): 330–31.
15. Alice Morse Earle, *In Old Narragansett* (New York, 1898), pp. 70–74.
16. Coral objects: Child's rattle (c. 1750), Acc. #56.0560; Beads (c. 1725–1800), Acc. #58.0139; Rattle (c. 1770–1800), Acc. #64.0060, Winterthur Museum; Coffin spoons: Mary N. Cole, "Some Hitherto Unpublished Traditions," *Antiques* 13 (October 1925): 207; Walter C. Hunter, "The Spoon as a Funerary Souvenir," *Antiques*

19 (April, 1931): 302–3; Serving spoons (c. 1790–1830), Acc. #62.240. 1185, 1224, 1242, Winterthur Museum; Ceramic°cradle (c. 1760), Acc. #59.2145, Winterthur Museum; Piersen, "Black Arts and Black Magic: Yankee Accommodations to African Religion," in Benes and Benes, *Wonders,* p. 40.

17. Benes, "Fortune-tellers," p. 132–33.

18. Harry B. Weiss, "Oneirocritica Americana," *Bulletin of the New York Public Library* 48 (June 1944): 525–30; Advertisement for Madam Connoisseur, *The Complete Fortune Teller, and Dream Book,* Haverhill, Massachusetts, *Merrimack Intelligencer,* 1816, American Antiquarian Society, reprinted in Benes and Benes, *Wonders,* p. 148. See also S. R. F. Price, "The Future of Dreams: From Freud to Artemidorus," *Past & Present* #113 (November 1986): 3–37; and Merle Curti, "The American Exploration of Dreams and Dreamers," *Journal of the History of Ideas* 27 (1966): 391–416.

19. Entry for 9 April 1813 in Edward Savage, *Police Records and Recollections* (Boston, 1873), n.p.

20. Keith Thomas, *Religion and the Decline of Magic* (London, 1971), pp. 110–11.

21. Letter, James City Parish, Virginia, to Society for the Propagation of the Gospel in Foreign Parts (1724), in William S. Perry, ed., *Historical Collections Relating to the American Church* (n.p., 1840), I, pp. 264–65.

22. Charles Ball, *Slavery in the United States* [1837] (New York, 1969), pp. 164–65.

23. Michael Gomez, *Exchanging Our Country Marks* (Chapel Hill, N.C., and London, 1998), esp. chaps. 2, 3, 9. See also Charles Joyner, *Down by the Riverside: A South Carolina Slave Community* (Urbana and Chicago, 1984).

24. Lathan Windley, *Runaway Slave Advertisements: A Documentary History from the 1730s to 1790,* 4 vols. (Westport, Conn., 1983), 4, p. 160.

25. Gomez, *Exchanging Our Country Marks,* chap. 1; Newbell Niles Puckett, *Folk Beliefs of the Southern Negro* (Chapel Hill, N.C.,1926), p. 284.

26. Winslow C. Watson, ed., *Men and Times of the Revolution; or, Memoirs of Elkanah Watson, including Journals of Travels in Europe and America, from 1777 to 1842,* pp. 261–62. See also Jane Carson, *Colonial Virginians at Play* (Charlottesville, Va. 1965), pp. 160–61.

27. Watson, *Travels,* II, 28–32, quoted in Carson, *Colonial Virginians at Play,* p. 160.

28. Paton Yoder, "Tavern Regulation in Virginia: Rationale and Reality," *Virginia Magazine of History and Biography* 87 (July 1979): 267; Louis Morton, *Robert Carter of Nomini Hall* (Williamsburg, 1941), p. 46; Michael Oriard, *Sporting with the Gods* (New York, 1991), p. 84. The pioneering cultural inquiry into gentry gambling is Timothy Breen, "Horses and Gentlemen: The Cultural Significance of Gambling Among the Gentry of Virginia," *William & Mary Quarterly,* 3rd. Ser. (1977): 239–57.

29. Carson, *Virginians at Play,* pp. 110, 118, 130–31; Patricia Click, "The Ruling Passion: Gambling and Sport in Antebellum Baltimore, Norfolk, and Richmond," *Virginia Cavalcade* 39 (Winter 1990): 64–66; Allen Eustis Begnaud, "Hoofbeats in Colonial Maryland," *Maryland Historical Magazine* 65 (Fall 1970): 207–38; David K. Wiggins, "Leisure Time on the Southern Plantation: The Slaves' Respite from Constant Toil," in Donald Spivey, ed., *Sport in America* (Westport, Conn., 1985), pp. 36–37.

30. Alan D. Watson, "The Lottery in Early North Carolina," *North Carolina Historical Review* 69 (October 1992): 368.

31. Entry for 4 November 1768 in Donald Jackson, ed., *The Diaries of George Washington* (Charlottesville, Va., 1976), II, p. 106. See also John Ezell, *Fortune's Merry Wheel: The Lottery in America* (Cambridge, Mass., 1960), p. 87 *et passim;* and John Findlay, *People of Chance* (New York, 1986), pp. 22–38.

32. Findlay, *People,* p. 31; Ezell, *Fortune's Merry Wheel,* esp. chaps. 3, 6; Watson, "Lottery," p. 377.

33. John Hervey, *Racing in America* (New York, 1944), pp. 40–45.

34. Findlay, *People,* p. 33.

35. Frederick Weiser, *Fraktur: Pennsylvania German Folk Art* (Lancaster, Pa., 1973).

36. "On Good and Bad Fortune," *American Magazine* 2 (September 1745): 397–98.
37. "Cursory Thoughts on the Fickle Goddess, Shewing with What Injustice She Usually Dispenses Her Favours," *New York Weekly Magazine* 2 (July 1796): 30. See also "Reflections on the Mutability of Fortune," *American Magazine* 2 (July 1745): 299–302; "On the mutability of fortune," *Philadelphia Minerva* 2 (10 September 1776; n.p.); "Miscellanea," *Polyanthos* 2 (June 1813): 133.
38. "The Power of Fortune," *Olio* 1 (24 July 1813): 205.
39. "The Gifts of Fortune Incapable of Making Us Happy,"*American Magazine* 2 (September 1745): 398; "A Wise and Good Man is a Proof Against All Accidents of Fate," *New Hampshire Magazine* 1 (June 1793): 50–52.
40. Ross W. Beales, Jr., "The Smiles and Frowns of Providence," in Benes and Benes, *Wonders,* pp. 86–96. Quotation at p. 91.
41. Elisabeth Sommer, "Gambling with God: The Use of the Lot by the Moravian Brethren in the Eighteenth Century," *Journal of the History of Ideas* 59 (April 1998): 269–71.
42. *Ibid.*: 272.
43. "On Making a Lottery Book of the Bible," *The Panoplist, and Missionary Magazine* 12 (March 1816): 109–11.
44. Pahl, *Paradox Lost,* pp. 94–97. Edwards quoted on p. 98.
45. Gomez, *Exchanging Our Country Marks,* pp. 251–54; Melville J. Herskovits, *The Myth of the Negro Past* [1941] (Boston, 1958), p. 234; Eugene Genovese, *Roll, Jordan, Roll: The World the Slaves Made* (New York, 1974), pp. 209–49; Joyner, *Down by the Riverside,* pp. 144–63.
46. Juventus, "A Practical Illustration of the Doctrines of Grace," *Panoplist* 13 (January 1817): 8–16.
47. For a representative selection, see Leonard Labaree, ed., *The Papers of Benjamin Franklin* (New Haven and London, 1959), 36 vols., pp. 2, 3–11, 136–44, 162–72, 90–97; 3, pp. 3–8, 60–66, 100–106.
48. "The Methodist Episcopal Church . . . Vindicated," *Evangelical Record* 1 (November 1812): 350–58.
49. Whitney R. Cross, *The Burned-Over District* (New York, 1950) is the classic account.
50. Max Weber, *The Protestant Ethic and the Spirit of Capitalism* [1904], trans. Talcott Parsons (New York, 1958), pp. 95–98.
51. "On Restraining Grace," *The Adviser, or Vermont Evangelical Magazine* 2 (March 1810): 72–76.
52. Sommer, "Gambling with God," p. 283.
53. David Hackett Fischer, *The Revolution in American Conservatism: The Federalist Party in the Age of Jeffersonian Democracy* (New York, 1965), pp. 24, 25n71. Hillhouse's speech was published in *The American Register, or General Repository of History, Politics, and Science,* (Philadelphia, 1809), pt. I, vol. V, pp. 15–29. I am indebted to my research assistant Neil Miller for bringing the Hillhouse proposal to my attention.
54. "On Making a Lottery–Book of the Bible," pp. 109–11.
55. "On Chance," *Philadelphia Repository and Weekly Register* 3 (1 January 1803): 4.
56. Jonathan Edwards, "The Latter-Day Glory Is Probably to Begin in America," reprinted in Conrad Cherry, ed. *God's New Israel: Religious Interpretations of American Destiny* (Englewood Cliffs, N.J., 1971), pp. 55–60.
57. "The Follies of Superstition," *The Rural Magazine, or Vermont Repository* 1 (July 1795): 348–50.
58. Thomas Paine, quoted in Curti, "Dreams and Dreamers," p. 397.
59. "Superstition," *Literary Tablet* 3 (3 July 1806): 98; for a citation of Hume see "Superstition Defined," *Christian Telescope* 3 (7 November 1823): 52.
60. "A Parallel Between Superstition and Enthusiasm, Commonly Mistaken for Reli-

gion," *American Magazine* 1 (December 1743): 157–59; "Superstition and Enthusiasm," *Sentimental and Literary Magazine* 7 (19 July 1797): 1.

61. "On the Doctrine of Chance: Containing remarks on Ethan Allen's Oracles of Reason—supposed to have been written by the rev. Mr. Dwight, author of the Conquest of Canaan," *American Museum* 2 (October 1787): 408–10.

62. *Ibid.:* 408.

63. Peter Bernstein, *Against the Gods: The Remarkable Story of Risk* (New York, 1996), pp. 105–26, 159; Daston, *Classical Probability,* esp. ch. 3; Ian Hacking, *The Emergence of Probability* (New York, 1985); Kavanagh, *Enlightenment,* ch. 1.

64. Helen Epstein, "The Mysterious Miss Nightingale," *New York Review of Books* 48 (8 March 2001), p. 19. For the idea of statistics as a modern form of numerology, I am indebted to Karen Parker Lears.

65. Theodore Porter, "Statistical Subjects," in Thomas Kavanagh, ed., *Chance, Culture, and the Literary Text* (Ann Arbor, 1994), pp. 49–53; Bernstein, *Against the Gods,* p. 126.

66. Quoted in Bernstein, *Against the Gods,* p. 113.

67. Adam Smith, *An Inquiry into the Nature and Causes of the Wealth of Nations* [1776] Modern Library ed. (New York, 1994), pp. 125–26.

68. Ezell, *Fortune's Merry Wheel,* p. 16.

69. Daniel Defoe, *The English Tradesman* (1732), I, xxv, p. 360, cited in *Oxford English Dictionary,* q.v. "Grace"; Jacob Joder, earthenware plate (c. 1800) Acc. #60.0688, Winterthur Museum.

70. On this general issue, see the thoughtful discussion in Kavanagh, *Enlightenment,* ch. 3.

71. On the persistence of Scottish common sense philosophy, see D. H. Meyer, *The Instructed Conscience: The Shaping of the American National Ethic* (Philadelphia, 1972) and Henry May, *The American Enlightenment* (New York, 1980).

72. Philip D. Jordan, "Lady Luck and Her Knights of the Royal Flush," *Southwestern Historical Quarterly* 72 (1969): 295–96; Watson, "Lottery in North Carolina," 366–68; Carl Brasseaux, "The Moral Climate of French Colonial Louisiana, 1699–1763," *Louisiana History* 27 (1986): 38–39; Yoder, "Tavern Regulation in Virginia," 265–67.

73. William Stith, *The Sinfulness of Gaming* (Williamsburg, 1752), p. 7; Landon Carter, Diary Entry for 9 October 1774, in Jack Greene, ed., *The Diary of Colonel Landon Carter,* 2 vols. (Charlottesville, 1965), vol. I, p. 870.

74. Stith, *Sinfulness,* pp. 11–12.

75. *Ibid.,* p. 13.

76. *Ibid.,* p. 14.

77. *Ibid.,* p. 20.

78. Timothy Breen, "'Baubles of Britain': The American and Consumer Revolutions of the Eighteenth Century," in Cary Carson et al., eds., *Of Consuming Interests: The Style of Life in Eighteenth-Century Virginia* (Charlottesville, Va. 1994), pp. 444–82; Rhys Isaac, *The Transformation of Virginia, 1740–1790* (New York, 1982), p. 247.

79. Yoder, "Tavern Regulation in Virginia," pp. 267–68.

80. Richard Gaskins, "Changes in the Criminal Law in Eighteenth-Century Connecticut," *American Journal of Legal History* 25 (1981): 309–42.

81. Benjamin Austin, reprinted in Gordon Wood, ed. *The Rising Glory of America 1760–1820* rev. ed. (Boston, 1990), p. 151; Thomas Cooper, *Political Arithmetic* (Philadelphia, 1798), pp. 14–15. See the illuminating discussion of these issues by Karen A. Weyler, "'A Speculating Spirit': Trade, Speculation, and Gambling in Early American Fiction," *Early American Literature* 31 (1996): 207–42.

82. *Red and Black; or, the Fates at Faro* (Philadelphia, 1796), pp. 13–14.

83. L. M. Stretch, *The Beauties of History; or, Pictures of Virtue and Vice, Drawn from Real Life; Designed for the Instruction and Edification of Youth* (London, 1777), pp. 299–302.

84. *Red and Black,* p. 14.

85. Gerald W. R. Ward, "Avarice and Conviviality: Card Playing in Federal America," in Benjamin A. Hewitt, Patricia Kane, and Gerald Ward, eds., *The Work of Many Hands: Card Tables in Federal America* (New Haven, 1982), pp. 15–38; Frank A. Wrensch, *Harness Horseracing in the United States and Canada* (New York, 1951), p. 12; Steven A. Riess, *City Games: The Evolution of American Urban Society and the Rise of Sport* (Urbana and Chicago, 1989), p. 24.
86. "Gambling—an Extract," *Boston Weekly Magazine* 2 (9 June 1804): 130.
87. Eli Hyde, A. M., *A Sermon; in which the Doctrine of the Lot is Stated, and Applied to Lotteries, Gambling, and Card-playing, for Amusement* (Oxford, N.Y., 1812), p. 16.
88. *Ibid.*, p. 37.
89. *Ibid.*, pp. 39, 41.
90. Andrew Delbanco, *The Death of Satan: How Americans Have Lost the Sense of Evil* (New York, 1996), p. 144.
91. M. L. Weems, *Anecdotes of Gamblers, Extracted from a Work on Gamblers* (Philadelphia,1816), p. 2.
92. *Ibid.*, p. 5; Weems, *God's Revenge Against Gambling* (Augusta, Ga., 1810), p. 34, cited in Weyler, "A Speculating Spirit," p. 217. For similar views, see "Gambling and Dissipation—an Allegory," *The Port-Folio* 5 (February 1815): 162–65; and [Rees Lloyd,] *The Richmond Alarm; A Plain and Familiar Discourse in the Form of a Dialogue Between a Father and his Son* (Philadelphia, 1814).
93. St. Denis Le Cadet, *The Lottery: A Poem* (Baltimore, 1815), p. 15.
94. "Gambling," *Saturday Evening Post* 1 (25 August 1821): 8.

[CHAPTER 3: CONFIDENCE GAMES]

1. Frederick Douglass, *The Life and Times of Frederick Douglass* [1892] Collier Books ed. (New York, 1962), pp. 115–44. I am indebted to the useful discussion in Lawrence Levine, *Black Culture and Black Consciousness* (New York, 1977), pp. 68–69.
2. Johan Huizinga, *Homo Ludens: A Study of the Play Element in Culture* [1938] (Boston, 1955), p. 23.
3. On the Americanization of poker, see John Findlay, *People of Chance* (New York, 1986), p. 48.
4. John Morris [John J. O'Connor], ed., *Wanderings of a Vagabond* (New York, 1873), pp. 180–87, provides an astute set of rankings from a self-professedly honest gambler's point of view.
5. The classic work on the subject is Bertram Wyatt-Brown, *Southern Honor* (New York, 1982).
6. "Days of Grace," *DeBow's Review* 6 (August 1848): 154.
7. Morris, *Wanderings*, p. 465; Herbert Asbury, *Suckers' Progress* (New York, 1938), pp. 131–32ff.
8. *The Life and Adventures of Robert Bailey* (Richmond, 1822), pp. 14–15, 44.
9. *Ibid.*, pp. 15, 17, 44.
10. John Browne Cutting, *Argument Delivered Before the Judges of the Court of Appeals, in Richmond, Virginia, in the Case of Carter's Executors—Appellants, Against Cutting and Others—Appellees* (Fredericksburg, Va., 1817).
11. Bailey, *Life and Adventures*, pp. 44–45.
12. *Ibid.*, p. 45.
13. *Ibid.*, pp. 61ff.
14. *Ibid.*
15. *Ibid.*, pp. 64–66.
16. *Ibid.*, p. 67.
17. *Ibid.*, p. 66.
18. *Ibid*, pp. 234–35, 304–5.

19. *Ibid.*, pp. 108, 139.
20. *Ibid.*, pp. 304–6.
21. *Ibid.*, pp. 347–48.
22. Alexis de Tocqueville, *Democracy in America* [1835] 2 vols., ed. and trans. Philip Bradley (New York, 1945), I, p. 305; II, pp. 165, 248–49.
23. Greele & Willis, *Specimens of Printing Types and Metal Ornaments, Cast at the New England Type Foundry* (Boston, 1831), n.p.; Hobart & Robbins, *Specimens of Printing Types* (Boston, 1851), Winterthur Library.
24. Board game, "The Sybil's Leaves," (n.p., 1835), Winterthur Archives.
25. Frederick Marryat, *Second Series of a Diary in America* (Philadelphia, 1840), pp. 141–42; Findlay, *People of Chance*, p. 51.
26. Wyatt-Brown, *Southern Honor*, pp. 339–50; Kenneth Greenberg, *Honor and Slavery* (Princeton, 1996), pp. 135–45.
27. Harriet Martineau, *Society in America*, London, 1837, I, p. 157; William Grayson, "The Character of a Gentleman," *Southern Quarterly Review* 7 (January 1853): 59. See also Frederick Law Olmsted, *A Journey Through the Southern Seaboard States in the years 1853–1854, with remarks on their economy*, 2 vols. (New York, 1904), vol. II, pp. 209, 268, 304; and Wyatt-Brown, *Southern Honor*, (New York, 1982), p. 346.
28. John Hervey, *Racing in America* (New York, 1944), pp. 71–88, 99; Elbert Chance, "Fast Horses and Sporting Blood," *Delaware History* 11 (October 1964): 148–81; John Dizikes, *Sportsmen and Gamesmen* (Boston, 1981), pp. 34–43.
29. Rhys Isaac, *The Transformation of Virginia, 1740–1790*, (Chapel Hill, N.C., 1982), p. 102.
30. Grady McWhiney, *Cracker Culture* (Tuscaloosa, Ala., and London, 1988), pp. 105, 256; C. G. Parsons, *An Inside View of Slavery* [1855] (Savannah, 1974), p. 93.
31. Findlay, *People of Chance*, pp. 53–55; William C. Hall, "Reminiscence of Natchez 'Under the Hill,'" *Spirit of the Times* 13 (11 December 1843): 523, reprinted in John Francis McDermott, ed. *Before Mark Twain* (Carbondale, Ill., 1968), pp.196–99.
32. Joseph L. Cowell, *Thirty Years Among the Players in England and America,* (New York, 1853), pp. 91–95, excerpted in McDermott, *Before Mark Twain,* pp. 58–69. Quotation at p. 61. Emphasis in original.
33. *Ibid.*, pp. 61–62; Findlay, *People of Chance*, pp. 60–61.
34. Hubert Howe Bancroft, *California Inter Pocula*, in *The Works of Hubert Howe Bancroft* 39 vols. (San Francisco, 1888), vol. 35, p. 702. The literature on the gold rush is immense. Two of the best recent works are Brian Roberts, *American Alchemy: The California Gold Rush and Middle-Class Culture* (Chapel Hill, N.C., and London, 1999), and Susan Lee Johnson, *Roaring Camp: The Social World of the California Gold Rush* (New York, 1999).
35. Bancroft, *California Inter Pocula*, p. 699.
36. *Ibid.*, p. 709.
37. Morris, ed., *Wanderings*, pp. 27–30; Jonathan Greene, *The Secret Band of Brothers* (Philadelphia, 1847), pp. 9–15.
38. Bancroft, *California Inter Pocula*, pp. 300, 310.
39. Findlay, *People of Chance*, pp. 63, 70ff.; Johnson, *Roaring Camp*, pp. 176–80.
40. Bancroft, *California Inter Pocula*, p. 716; Carl Sifakis, *Encyclopedia of Gambling* (New York, 1990), p. 192.
41. Morris, ed., *Wanderings*, pp. 212, 217.
42. Asbury, *Suckers' Progress*, pp. 149ff.
43. Irvin Anthony, *Paddle Wheels and Pistols* (Philadelphia, 1929), pp. 260ff.; "Gambling on the Western Waters," *Niles National Register* 54 (18 August 1838): 388; Findlay, *People of Chance*, pp. 74–75; Mary N. Ganter, "'You Must Risque to Win': America at Odds with Fortune," *Early American Homes* (April, 1997), p. 44; Sifakis, *Gambling*, pp. 6–7.
44. Anthony, *Paddle Wheels and Pistols*, p. 273.

45. George H. Devol, *Forty Years a Gambler on the Mississippi* (New York, 1926), pp. 185, 276; Cafakis, *Gambling*, pp. 170–71.

46. Devol, *Forty Years*, p. 9.

47. *Ibid.*, p. 13.

48. *Ibid.*, p. 22.

49. *Ibid.*, pp. 28–29, 56, 284.

50. *Ibid.*, p. 184.

51. *Ibid.*, pp. 58–59, 64–65, 101, 116–17.

52. *Ibid.*, pp. 40–42, 158–59.

53. *Ibid.*, p. 285.

54. *Ibid.*, pp. 285, 287.

55. *Ibid.*, p. 282.

56. *Ibid.*, p. 273.

57. Morris, *Wanderings*, pp. 9–18.

58. *Ibid.*, p. 21. For two among many references to "castles in the air," see "The Lottery," *Ladies' Companion* 7 (1837): 81–84; Solomon Nunes Carvalho, *Incidents of Travel and Adventure in the Far West* (New York, 1857), p. 311. On the general tendency to connect unbridled fantasy with masturbation, see Ronald Walters, ed., *Primers for Prudery* (New York, 1974), especially his introduction.

59. *Ibid.*, pp. 27ff.

60. *Ibid.*, p. 295.

61. *Ibid.*, pp. 329ff.

62. *Ibid.*, pp. 180–181, 327, 349.

63. *Ibid.*, pp. 218–19, 259.

64. *Ibid.*, p. 219.

65. Bancroft, *California Inter Pocula*, pp. 698, 710; Devol, *Forty Years*, pp. 232–33.

66. Morris, *Wanderings*, pp. 90–91.

67. Ann Fabian, *Card Sharps and Bucket Shops: Gambling in 19th-Century America* 2nd ed. (New York, 1999), p. 91.

68. Morris, *Wanderings*, pp. 335, 346–49.

69. H. S. Fulkerson, *Random Recollections of Early Days in Mississippi* (Vicksburg, Miss., 1885), pp. 95–97.

70. "Fluctuations of Fortune," *Boston Weekly Magazine* 2 (26 October 1839): 63.

71. Josiah M. Graves, *A Phrenological Chart: Presenting a Synopsis of the Doctrine of Phrenology* (Hartford, 1839), n.p., American Antiquarian Society. I am indebted to Scott Sandage for bringing this reference to my attention. On the connection between "castles in the air" and masturbation, see Walters, ed., *Primers for Prudery*, pp. 56–57; and Stephen Nissenbaum, *Sex, Diet, and Debility in Jacksonian America: Sylvester Graham and Health Reform* (Westport, Conn., 1980). On the gambler's manic–depressive tendencies, see, for example, Morris, *Wanderings*, p. 74, and "The Fickleness of Fortune," *The Christian Journal* (1827).

72. "Effects of Gambling," *Dollar Magazine* 2 (April 1842): 127; "The Freaks of Fortune, and Their Lesson," *Harper's New Monthly Magazine* 17 (August 1858): 344–49.

73. "Freaks of Fortune," pp. 348–49. For examples of continued suspicion of speculators through the 1850s, see the dismissal of "lucky traders" on holiday in John Fanning Watson, "Travel diary, trip to Cape Island Surf, 1856," in Watson Family Papers, Box 2, Winterthur Archives; President James Buchanan's attack on "gambling in stocks" in 1857, quoted in Ron Chernow, *Titan: The Life of John D. Rockefeller* (New York, 1999), p. 57; and Freeman Hunt's assaults on "the licensed gambling of the stock exchange" in his *Worth and Wealth* (New York, 1857), pp. 49, 72, 252, 256, 396–97.

74. "Gambling," *The American Expositor* 1 (May 1850): 6. Board games: *The Reward of Merit* (London, 1801); *The New Game of Virtue Rewarded and Vice Punished* (Boston, 1818); *Smith's Pictorial Parlor Oracle* (Pittsburgh, n.d.[c. 1860]), Winterthur Archives.

75. *The Lotterry Ticket: An American Tale* (Cambridge, Mass., 1822), pp. 17, 19.

76. *Ibid.,* p. 45. For a parallel view, see "On the Morality and Public Tendency of Lotteries," *Christian Spectator* 7 (February 1827): 71–79 and 8. (March 1827): 121–25; also John S. Ezell, *Fortune's Merry Wheel: The Lottery in America* (Cambridge, Mass., 1960), chaps. 10 and 11.

77. "Gambling, or Rain and Sunshine," *Religious Intelligencer* 12 (25 August 1827): 200–201.

78. William J. Snelling, *Expose of the Vice of Gambling, as it Lately Existed in Massachusetts* (Boston, 1833), pp. 5–9.

79. Timothy Flint, *The Ruinous Consequences of Gambling* (New York, 1827), pp. 6, 8, 14, 32.

80. *Ibid.,* p. 6.

81. Reverend John Richards, *Discourse on Gambling Delivered in the Congregational Meeting House at Dartmouth College, November 7, 1852* (Hanover, N.H., 1852), n.p.

82. "On Lucky and Unlucky Days," *Genessee Farmer* 5 (24 January 1835): 25–26; "Good and Bad Luck," *Michigan Farmer* 7 (15 November 1849): 340. See also "The True System—Every Man the Architect of his Own Fortune," *Genessee Farmer* 4 (20 December 1834): 103.

83. Richard Hildreth, *Banks, Banking, and Paper Currencies, in Three Parts* (New York, 1840), p. 150.

84. "Nothing Occurs By Chance," *The Herald of Truth* 2 (July 1847): 37. On the providential plan directing American history, see the views collected in Conrad Cherry, *God's New Israel: Religious Interpretations of American Destiny* (Englewood Cliffs, N.J., 1971), and interpreted in Ernest Tuveson, *Redeemer Nation* (New York, 1968).

85. Newbell Niles Puckett, *Folk Beliefs of the Southern Negro* (Chapel Hill, N.C., 1926), p. 172.

86. Ann Taves, *The Household of Faith* (South Bend, Ind., 1986), p. 48; "Popular Superstitions," *North American Review* 34 (January 1832): 198–220. See also Jay Dolan, *Catholic Revivalism: The American Experience, 1830–1900* (South Bend, Ind., 1978).

87. Taves, *Household,* pp. 47, 56–57. See also Peter Brown, *Society and the Holy in Late Antiquity* (Berkeley, 1982), for the origins of "invisible companions," such as patron saints and guardian angels.

88. Taves, *Household,* p. 57; Dolan, *Revivalism,* p. 108.

89. Taves, *Household,* pp. 49, 59.

90. Charles C. Jones, *The Religious Instruction of Negroes in the United States* [1842] (New York, 1969), pp. 127–28; Olmsted, *Seaboard,* pp. 114–15; Levine, *Black Culture,* pp. 61ff.

91. David H. Brown, "Conjure/Doctors: An Exploration of a Black Discourse in America, Antebellum to 1940," *Folklore Forum* 23 (1990): 3–46.

92. Timothy L. Smith, "Slavery and Theology: The Emergence of Black Christian Consciousness in Nineteenth-Century America," *Church History* 41 (1972): 497–512, is a fine discussion of these issues.

93. "Evidences of Grace," *Religious Intelligencer* 13 (14 February 1829): 60.

94. "Chance," *Atheneum* 4 (15 November 1825): 164 65.

95. "The Head of the Church, Head Over All Things," *American Biblical Repository* 12 (July 1838): 22–46. For background on the gradualist melding of Providence and Progress, see Herbert Hovenkamp, *Science and Religion in America, 1800–1860* (Philadelphia, 1978). I am indebted to Neil Miller for helping to clarify my understanding of "rational religion."

96. Walter Cannon, "The Problem of Miracles in the 1830s," *Victorian Studies* (September 1960): 5–32.

97. Hovenkamp, *Science and Religion,* pp. 20–23, 79–95.

98. For a typical example of evangelical–rationalist thinking on these issues, see Raymond M. Bost, "John Bachman, Man of Faith, Man of Science," *Lutheran Quarterly* 2 (Summer, 1988): 209–26. For an excellent summary of one key denomination's

emerging synthesis, see Theodore Bozeman, "Inductive and Deductive Politics: Science and Society in Antebellum Presbyterian Thought," *Journal of American History* 64 (1977): 704–22.

99. Thomas Boucher, "Divine Providence," *Herald of Truth* 1 (May 1847): 350–53; "Chance or Luck," *American Agriculturalist* 7 (November 1848): 354. Emphasis in original.

100. Nathaniel L. Dayton, *The Young Man* (Lowell, Mass., 1845): pp. 44–49.

101. Ralph Waldo Emerson, "Self-reliance" [1841] in Stephen Whicher, ed., *Emerson: A Selection* (Cambridge, Mass., 1951), pp. 147–68; Walt Whitman, "Song of the Open Road," l, l. 4.

102. Emerson, "Fate" [1852], in Whicher, ed., *Emerson*, p. 340.

103. *Ibid.*, p. 344.

104. *Ibid.*

105. Huizinga, *Homo Ludens*, chap. 5. See also Robert M. Weir, "The South Carolinian as Extremist," *South Atlantic Quarterly* 74 (Winter 1975): 86–103.

106. Lewis O. Saum, *The Popular Mood of America, 1860–1890* (Lincoln, Neb., 1990), pp. 21, 29, emphasis mine.

107. Taves, *Household of Faith*, p. 54.

108. Andrew Delbanco, *The Death of Satan* (New York, 1996), p. 145.

109. Lincoln's Second Inaugural Address [1865] is reprinted in Henry Steele Commager, ed., *Documents of American History* (New York, 1965), p. 347. For a brilliant dissection of "The Battle Hymn of the Republic," see Edmund Wilson, *Patriotic Gore* (New York, 1962), pp. 176–77.

[CHAPTER 4: THE WANING OF PROVIDENCE]

1. Charles A. Mabie, Diary, 30 January 1866, Winterthur Archives, Winterthur Museum.

2. *Ibid.*, 31 January 1866.

3. *Ibid.*, 7 March and 9 March 1866.

4. *Ibid.*

5. William Dean Howells, *The World of Chance* (New York, 1893).

6. J. F. Clark, *The Society in Search of Truth; or, Stock Gambling in San Francisco* (Oakland, 1878), p. 49. For more on the equation of gambling and speculation in the post–Civil War economy, see *Land-gambling versus Mining-gambling* (San Francisco, 1879); Dillon O'Brien, *Dead Broke: A Western Tale* (St. Paul, 1873); and R. Heber Newton, *The Morals of Trade* (New York, 1876), esp. pp. 30, 32, 61–63. I am indebted to Scott Sandage for the latter reference.

7. Clark, *Society in Search of Truth*, pp. 92, 234–35.

8. Alexander Gardiner, *Canfield: The True Story of the Greatest Gambler* (Garden City, N.Y., 1930), documents Canfield's comparative respectability among the New York business elite.

9. Herbert Asbury, *Suckers' Progress: A History of Gambling in America, from the Colonies to Canfield* (New York, 1938), pp. 382–83; Hank Messick and Burt Goldblatt, *The Only Game in Town* (New York, 1976), pp. 72–78. See also C. W. Kennedy, "Gambling on Ocean Steamers," *North American Review* 150 (June 1890): 780–82; H. Parsell, "Another View of Gambling at Sea," *ibid.* 151 (July 1890): 121–22; *Charter, Constitution, Rules, Officers, and Members, Newport Casino* (Newport, R.I., 1881), in Gambling, Box 1, Warshaw Collection, National Museum of American History, Smithsonian Institution, lists among the officers Pierre Lorillard, August Belmont, Levi P. Morton, and Nathaniel Thayer—a roster of ruling-class notables.

10. Parker Morell, *Diamond Jim: The Life and Times of James Buchanan Brady* (Garden City, N.Y., 1934), pp. 7–26ff. Quotation at p. 21.

11. *Ibid.*, pp. 40, 182–83, 200–201.

12. *Ibid.*, p. 209.

13. John F. B. Lillard, *Poker Stories* (New York, 1896), pp. 88–90.

14. George C. Tyler, *Whatever Goes Up: the Hazardous Fortunes of a Natural Born Gambler* (Indianapolis, 1934), pp. 38–39, 44–45, 52–53, 56–57.

15. *Ibid.*, pp. 78, 100.

16. *Ibid.*, pp. 144, 150, 206.

17. Louis Hartz, *The Liberal Tradition in America* (New York, 1955), p. 224. I am indebted to Gadi Taub for bringing this passage to my attention.

18. R.K.M., "Good Luck and Good Acts," *Puck* (New York) 12 (27 September 1882): 54.

19. Hartz, *Liberal Tradition*, p. 224.

20. Flavel Scott Mine, "The Study of a Pool–Room," *Harper's Weekly* 36 (17 December 1892): 319. See also Steven Reiss, *City Games* (Chicago, 1989), pt. 2.

21. In New York City, where an underground lottery persisted after the Civil War, policy players bet on the lottery numbers but did not officially enter the lottery itself; in other cities, where there was no lottery, policy flourished on its own.

22. Samuel Canby Rutherford, "Life Along the Brandywine, 1880–1895," pp. 26–27, unpublished memoir in Winterthur Archives, Winterthur Museum.

23. *Ibid.*; Ted Ownby, *Subduing Satan: Religion, Recreation, and Manhood in the Rural South* (Chapel Hill, N.C., and London, 1990), pp. 76ff. See also *Red Cuban Games, as Bred by George W. Means, Concord, N.C,* catalog in Sports, Box 4, Warshaw Collection.

24. Ownby, *Subduing Satan,* pp. 76–81.

25. Elijah L. Shettles, *Recollections of a Long Life* (n.p., 1973), pp. 89–93; Joseph J. Rosa and Waldo E. Koop, *Rowdy Joe Lowe: Gambler with a Gun* (Norman, Okla., and London, 1989), pp. 46–49; Gary L. Cunningham, "Chance, Culture, and Compulsion: the Gambling Games of the Kansas Cow Towns," *Southwestern Historical Quarterly* (1981): 255–71.

26. Karen Holliday Tanner, *Doc Holliday: A Family Portrait* (Norman, Okla., 1998), pp. 24, 26, 58–59.

27. *Ibid.*, pp. 90ff.

28. *Ibid.*, pp. 109–126ff.

29. Nolie Mumey, *Poker Alice: History of a Woman Gambler in the West* (Denver, 1951); Cynthia Rose, *Lottie Deno: Gambling Queen of Hearts* (Santa Fe, 1994); Stephen Longstreet, *Win or Lose: A Social History of Gambling in America* (Indianapolis and New York, 1977), chap. 6.

30. Carl Sifakis, *Encyclopedia of Gambling* (New York, 1990), pp. 132–33.

31. Tyler, *Whatever,* pp. 77–78.

32. *Ibid.*, pp. 77, 198; John Dizikes, *Yankee Doodle Dandy: The Life and Times of Tod Sloan* (New Haven and London, 2000), pp. 89–90, 119–20. For another example of the calculation involved in training horses for the track, see Charles Marvin, *The Trotting Horse* (New York, 1891).

33. Cunningham, "Chance, Culture, and Compulsion," p. 263; Edward Crapsey, *The Nether Side of New York* [1873] (Paterson, N.J., 1969), p. 97; James D. McCabe, *Lights and Shadows of New York Life* [1872] (New York, 1970), pp. 718–19.

34. McCabe, *Lights and Shadows,* p. 719.

35. Anthony Comstock, *Traps for the Young* [1883] (Cambridge, Mass., 1967), p. 77. For more on the culture of policy, see "Do You Play Policy?" (New York, 1869), unidentified clipping in Gambling, Box 1, Warshaw Collection.

36. McCabe, *Lights and Shadows,* p. 728–29; Crapsey, *Nether Side,* pp. 101–2.

37. Sandy Lydon, *Chinese Gold: The Chinese in the Monterey Bay Region* (Capitola, Calif., 1985), p. 204. See also Ramon Chacon, "The Beginning of Racial Segregation: The Chinese in Fresno and Chinatown's Role as Red Light District, 1870s–1920s," *Southern California Quarterly* 70 (1988): 371–98.

38. For some of the best of the newer scholarship, see John Bodnar, *The Transplanted: A History of Immigrants in Urban America* (Bloomington, Ind., 1985) and Virginia Yans-McLaughlin, ed., *Immigration Reconsidered: History, Sociology, and Politics* (New York, 1990).

39. Cheveux Gris, "The Negro in His Religious Aspect," *Southern Magazine* 17 (1875): 498–502; Joseph LeConte, *The Autobiography of Joseph LeConte* (New York, 1903), pp. 234–35. see also Michael Gomez, *Exchanging Our Country Marks* (Chapel Hill, N.C., and London, 1998), p. 262.

40. Thaddeus Norris, "Negro Superstitions," *Lippincott's* 6 (July 1870): 90–95; Patsy Moses, quoted in David H. Brown, "Conjure/Doctors: An Exploration of a Black Discourse in America, Antebellum to 1840," *Folklore Forum* 23 (1990): 9.

41. Quoted in Brown, "Conjure/Doctors," p. 9.

42. Sara M. Handy, "Negro Superstitions," *Lippincott's* 48 (June 1894): 738.

43. *Atlanta Constitution,* quoted in Stewart Culin, "Concerning Negro Sorcery in the United States," *Journal of America Folklore* 3 (1890): 281; Harry Middleton Hyatt, *Hoodoo-Conjuration-Witchcraft-Rootwork,* 5 vols. (Washington, D.C., 1970), vol. I, p. 1163.

44. Newbell Niles Puckett, *Folk Beliefs of the Southern Negro* (Chapel Hill, N.C., 1926), p. 228; Brown, "Conjure/Doctors," pp. 18–25; Claude Lévi–Strauss, *The Savage Mind* [1962] (English translation, Chicago, 1966), esp. chap. 1.

45. Jaramillo artifacts in Religion Collection, Accession #1991.0741, National Museum of American History, Smithsonian Institution, Washington, D.C.

46. *New York World,* 14 November 1901, p. 14. I am indebted to Scott Sandage for bringing this article to my attention.

47. Carolyn Morrow Long, "John the Conquerer: From Root–Charm to Commercial Product," *Pharmacy in History* 39 (1997): 51.

48. Brown, "Conjure/Doctors," p. 19; George Boddison, quoted in *ibid.,* p. 23.

49. Andrew Delbanco, *The Death of Satan* (New York, 1995), p. 101.

50. P. T. Barnum, *Dollars and Sense* (Chicago and New York, 1890), p. 67.

51. Comstock, *Traps,* pp. 60, 93, 130.

52. *Ibid.,* p. 126. For a similar stress on the need for character armor against hereditary weakness and environmental seduction, see John Phillip Quinn, *Fools of Fortune* (Chicago, 1890), p. 33. For continued emphasis on the gambler's tendency to suicide, see Samuel Irenaeus Prime, "The Gamblers at Monaco," in his *Irenaeus Letters* (New York, 1885), pp. 329–33.

53. Ownby, *Subduing Satan,* esp. chap. 9.

54. Adolph Hefner, *Gambling Communities* (St. Louis, 1894), p. 12.

55. *John B. Stone, et al., vs. the State of Mississippi,* 101 U.S. 814 (1879), quoted in Comstock, *Traps,* p. 62.

56. Bret Harte, "The Luck of Roaring Camp" [1868] in his *The Luck of Roaring Camp and Other Tales* (Boston and New York, 1902), p. 4. I am indebted to the thoughtful interpretation by Susan Lee Johnson in *Roaring Camp: The Social World of the California Gold Rush* (New York, 2000), pp. 337–40.

57. Harte, "Roaring Camp," p. 12.

58. *Ibid.,* p. 13.

59. Reverend C. H. Hamlin, *et al.,* "Gambling and Speculation: A Symposium," *Arena* 11 (1891): 421.

60. John Ezell, *Fortune's Merry Wheel: The Lottery in America* (Cambridge, Mass., 1960), p. 243; Crapsey, *Nether Side,* p. 108.

61. O. B. Frothingham, "The Ethics of Gambling," *North American Review* 135 (August 1882): 164.

62. *Ibid.,* pp. 164–66.

63. *Ibid.*, p. 168. For an argument similar to Frothingham's, see W. D. Mackenzie, "Ethics of Gambling," *Contemporary Review* 60 (August 1891): 220–33.

64. Frothingham, "Gambling," p. 169.

65. *Ibid.*, pp. 170–71. For examples of fetishlike slot machines, see "Slot Machines," *Colophon*, #5 (July–August, 1982): 84–98. On the spider in African divination, see Philip Peek, "African Divination Systems: Non-Normal Modes of Cognition," in *idem.*, ed., *African Divination Systems* (Bloomington, Ind., 1991): pp. 197–98.

66. Barnum, *Dollars and Sense,* p. 67; Henry Ward Beecher, *Lectures to Young Men* (New York, 1886), p. 13. On the prevalence of such views, see Michael Oriard, *Sporting with the Gods* (New York, 1991), pp. 189–90.

67. Gail Hamilton, "The Inequalities of Fortune," *Young Folks* (1866).

68. Bion, in *Diogenes Laertius: Lives of Eminent Philosophers,* book IV, section 50, cited in John Bartlett, *Familiar Quotations* [1855], 15th ed. (New York, 1980), p. 92; Lew Wallace, *Ben-Hur* (1880) book V, chap. 7.

69. Lily Rice Foxcroft, "Superstition in the Bud," *Outlook* (21 September 1895): 466–67. For similar views, see "Superstition," *Scientific American* 65 (22 August 1891): 117; and the Reverend H. N. Brown, "Modern Superstition," *Unitarian Review* 3 (January 1875): 50–59.

70. John Fiske, "Editor's Table," *Popular Science Monthly* 2 (January 1873): 376; Thomas Henry Huxley, *Introductory Science Primer.* I am indebted to Sam Elworthy for bringing these references to my attention.

71. "Chance," *Hours at Home* 11 (October 1870): 522–24; "Gambling for the Sake of Christ," *Unitarian Review* 21 (January 1884): 65–67.

72. John Bigelow, "What Is Gambling?" *Harper's Monthly* 90 (February 1895): 470–80.

73. Jean Strouse, *J. P. Morgan: American Financier* (New York, 1999), pp. 176, 258–59.

74. Bigelow, "What Is Gambling?" p. 470; Howells, *World of Chance,* p. 339.

75. Washington Gladden, "Three Dangers," *The Century,* n.s. 6 (August 1884): 625.

76. *Ibid.*

77. George Levine, *Darwin and the Novelists* (Cambridge, Mass., 1988), p. 30.

78. *Ibid.*, p. 93; Ernest Mayr, *Evolution and the Diversity of Life* (Cambridge, Mass., 1976), p. 33.

79. Chauncey Wright, "Spencer's Biology," *The Nation* 2 (7 June 1866): 725; Louis Menand, "The Socrates of Cambridge," *New York Review of Books* 48 (26 April 2001): 52–55.

80. Chauncey Wright, "The Winds and the Weather," *Atlantic Monthly* 1 (January 1858): 273; Menand, "Socrates," 53.

81. Menand, "Socrates," 54–55.

82. N. S. Shaler, "Chance or Design," *Andover Review* 12 (August 1889): 118–33.

83. John Fiske, *Through Nature to God* (Boston, 1899), excerpted in R. Jackson Wilson, ed., *Darwinism and the American Intellectual* (Homewood, Ill., 1967), pp. 121–22.

84. Quoted in Adam Phillips, "Darwin Turns the Worm," in his *Darwin's Worms: On Life Stories and Death Stories* (New York, 2000), p. 40.

85. *Ibid.*, pp. 40, 42.

86. *Ibid.*, p. 59.

87. Justin Kaplan, *Mr. Clemens and Mark Twain* (New York, 1966), p. 335.

88. Mark Twain, letter to William Dean Howells (22 January 1898), in Frederick Anderson *et al.,* eds., *Selected Mark Twain–Howells Letters* (Cambridge, Mass., 1967), p. 317.

89. Oxford English Dictionary, *q.v.* "Sport." On the changing meanings of sport, see Delbanco, *Death of Satan,* pp. 146ff., and Oriard, *Sporting with the Gods,* pp. 192–249.

90. Theodore Dreiser, *Sister Carrie* (New York, 1900), p. 83; Frank Norris, *McTeague* [1899] (Garden City, N.Y., 1928), p. 78. See also Oriard, *Sporting with the Gods,* pp. 240, 244.

[CHAPTER 5: THE INCOMPLETE TAMING OF CHANCE]

1. I owe this phrase to Ian Hacking, *The Taming of Chance* (New York and London, 1990).
2. The literature on Progressivism is immense. See especially Robert Wiebe, *The Search for Order, 1877–1920* (New York, 1967); Jean Quandt, "Religion and Social Thought: The Secularization of Postmillennialism," *American Quarterly,* 1972, and Daniel T. Rodgers, *Atlantic Crossings* (Cambridge, Mass., and London, 1998).
3. Inglis, quoted in Ron Chernow, *Titan: The Life of John D. Rockefeller* (New York, 1998), pp. 492–93.
4. *Ibid.,* pp. 48ff.
5. *Ibid.,* p. 250.
6. *Ibid.,* pp. 80–81, 169.
7. *Ibid.,* p. 82.
8. *Ibid.,* pp. 100, 54.
9. Carnegie, quoted in Jean Strouse, *J. P. Morgan: American Financier* (New York, 1999), p. 446.
10. Tarbell, quoted in *ibid.,* pp. 452–53.
11. Charles Péguy, ch. on "Old France" from his *Men and Saints* (New York: 1944), trans. Anne and Julian Green, p. 65. The French original (*ibid.,* p. 64) reads: "Ils ne pouvaient pas soupçonner qu'un temps venant . . . ou celui que ne jouerait pas perdrait tout le temps, et encore plus sûrement que celui qui joue."
12. Alfred, Lord Tennyson, "In Memoriam" [1850], Conclusion, st. 36.
13. Robert Bannister, *Social Darwinism* (Philadelphia, 1978), esp. chap. 1; Irwin Wyllie, *The Self–Made Man in America* (New York, 1956).
14. Rodgers, *Atlantic Crossings,* pp. 141, 168.
15. Washington Gladden, "Three Dangers," *The Century,* n.s. 6 (August 1884): 625.
16. Andrew Delbanco, *The Death of Satan* (New York, 1995), p. 151; Michael Oriard, *Sporting with the Gods* (New York, 1991), chap. 5.
17. John Bigelow, "What Is Gambling?" *Harper's Monthly* 90 (February 1895): 470–80.
18. H. C. Vrooman, "Gambling and Speculation: A Symposium," *Arena* (1891): 426.
19. Frank N. Freeman, "The Ethics of Gambling," *International Journal of Ethics* 18 (October 1907): 76–91.
20. Alexis de Tocqueville, *Democracy in America* [1835], ed. and trans. Phillips Bradley (New York, 1960), vol. 2, p. 106.
21. Herbert Asbury, *Suckers' Progress* (New York, 1938), p. 51; Elizabeth Eliot, *Portrait of a Sport: The Story of Steeplechasing in Great Britain and the United States* (Woodstock, Vt., 1957), p. 114; Barton Wood Currie, "The Transformation of the Southwest Through the Legal Abolition of Gambling," *The Century* 89 (April 1909): 905–10. For more examples of the crackdown on gambling at the turn of the century, see "The Issue in New Jersey," *Outlook* 48 (4 November 1893): 798–99; Ridley Wills II, "The Eclipse of the Thoroughbred Horse Industry in Tennessee," *Tennessee Historical Quarterly* 46 (1987): 157–71; Diane B. Haser-Harris, "Horse Racing in Early Oklahoma," *Chronicles of Oklahoma* 64 (1986): 4–17; William Howard Moore, "Progressivism and the Social Gospel in Wyoming: The Antigambling Act of 1901 as a Test Case," *Western Historical Quarterly* 15 (July 1984): 299–316; H. K. James, *The Destruction of Mephisto's Greatest Web* (Salt Lake City, 1914), pp. 67, 136–42, 237–40.
22. William T. Stead, *If Christ Came to Chicago* [1894] (New York,1964), pp. 189, 369, 371, and chap. 12, *passim.*
23. W. I. Thomas, "The Gaming Instinct," *American Journal of Sociology* 6 (1900): 760. See also Freeman, "Ethics of Gambling," p. 90.
24. Walter Lippmann, *Drift and Mastery* [1914] (Englewood Cliffs, N. J., 1961), p. 98.
25. William Graebner, *The Engineering of Consent* (Madison, Wis., 1987); Delbanco, *Death of Satan,* pp. 178–82.

26. John Dewey, "The Influence of Darwinism on Philosophy," in *The Influence of Darwinism on Philosophy and Other Essays in Contemporary Thought* (New York, 1910), pp. 1–19. Morton White applies the "antiformalist" label to a whole generation of thinkers in his influential *Social Thought in America: The Revolt Against Formalism,* 2nd ed. (New York, 1957). For an example, see Thorstein Veblen, "Why Is Economics Not an Evolutionary Science?" *Quarterly Journal of Economics* 12 (1898): 373–97.

27. Albert J. Beveridge, "The Star of Empire" [1900], reprinted in Conrad Cherry, ed., *God's New Israel: Religious Interpretations of American Destiny* (Englewood Cliffs, N.J., 1971), p. 146.

28. W. F. Ogburn, *Social Change* (New York, 1924); Thorstein Veblen, "The Discipline of the Machine," excerpted from *The Theory of Business Enterprise* [1904], in Max Lerner, ed., *The Portable Veblen* (New York, 1948), pp. 335–48. On the connections between technological determinism and imperialism, see Michael Adas, *Machines as the Measure of Men* (Ithaca, N.Y., and London, 1990).

29. Thorstein Veblen, *The Theory of the Leisure Class* [1899], New American Library ed. [New York, 1953), chap. 11: "The Belief in Luck." Quotation at p. 186.

30. *Ibid.*, pp. 187, 193.

31. Bigelow, "What Is Gambling?" p. 80.

32. Charles E. Buell, "How to Counteract Chance," *The Nationalist* 3 (January 1891): 376–79; Rodgers, *Atlantic Crossings,* pp. 217, 235, 245.

33. [H. W. Mabie,] "The Reading Public," *Outlook* 49 (23 June 1894): 1141–42.

34. [Hammond Lamont,] "Fondness for Old Follies," *The Nation* 81 (14 September 1905): 215–16. For examples, see Monroe B. Snyder, "Survivals of Astrology," *Journal of American Folklore* 3 (April 1890): 127–31; J. D. Jerrold Kelley, "Superstitions of the Sea," *The Century* 48 (July 1894): 418–26; Lucy C. Lillie, "Ghostly Premonitions," *Harper's Monthly* 90 (April 1895): 675–79. For an overview of the recovery of superstition, see T. J. Jackson Lears, *No Place of Grace: Antimodernism and the Transformation of American Culture* (Chicago and London, 1994), chap. 4.

35. For the importance of the recapitulation theory, see Lears, *No Place of Grace,* pp. 144–49. The gender dimensions of "race suicide" are discussed in Gail Bederman, *Manliness and Civilization* (Chicago, 1996). On the link between belief in progress and nostalgia, see Christopher Lasch, *The True and Only Heaven: Progress and Its Critics* (New York, 1991), chap. 3.

36. Fanny D. Bergen, "Preface" to W. W. Newell, ed., *Current Superstitions* (Cambridge, Mass., 1896), n.p.; Bronislaw Malinowski, "Magic, Science, and Religion" [1925], in his *Magic, Science, and Religion and Other Essays* Anchor Books ed. (New York, 1954), pp. 17–92.

37. Mark Twain [Samuel L. Clemens], *The Adventures of Tom Sawyer* [1876], Penguin Classics ed. (New York, 1986), pp. 48, 107, 62.

38. *Ibid.*, pp. 14–15.

39. Joe Newman, *Shootin' Craps* (Chicago, 1893); Mathews & Bulger and Maurice Levi, *My Love's a Gamblin' Man* (New York, 1897), Dave Marion, *The Fortune Teller* (Chicago, 1896); Monroe H. Rosenfeld and Alfred Solman, *"Trust Him Not,"* the *Fortune Teller Said* (Chicago, 1899); William Jerome and Jean Schwartz, *The Gambling Man* (San Francisco, 1902); Edgar Leslie, Al Piantodosi, and Murray Bloom, *The Million Dollar Gambler from the West* (New York, 1913), all in DeVincent Collection, National Museum of American History, Smithsonian Institution, Washington, D.C.

40. James H. Dorman, "Shaping the Popular Image of Post-Reconstruction American Blacks: The Coon Song Phenomenon of the Gilded Age," *American Quarterly* 40 (1988): 458.

41. *Ibid.*, pp. 451–56. For later examples of the urbanized Sambo figure and his crossover appeal, see *Rollin' de Bones at Coblenz-on-the-Rhine* (1917) and Clarence A. Stout, *O Death Where is Thy Sting* (New York, 1920), DeVincent Collection.

42. I use Charles W. Chesnutt, *The Conjure Woman and Other Tales* [1899], ed., Richard H. Brodhead (Durham, N.C., and London, 1993).

43. For Chesnutt at his most skeptical, see his "Superstitions and Folklore of the South," [1901] in Alan Dundes, ed., *Mother Wit from the Laughing Barrel* (New York and London, 1981), pp. 369–76.

44. Chesnutt, "Sis' Becky's Pickaninny," in his *Conjure Woman*, pp. 82–93. Quotations at pp. 82–83.

45. *Ibid.*, pp. 83–84.

46. *Ibid.* Quotations at pp. 87, 89, 91.

47. *Ibid.*, pp. 92–93.

48. *Ibid.*, p. 93; Souvenir Coffee Spoons, Acc. #71.1067, Ineson Bissell Collection, Winterthur Museum.

49. G. Laurence Gomme, "Other People's Superstitions," *The Athenaeum* 105 (30 March 1895): 409; Lucy M. J. Garnet, "Other People's Superstitions," *ibid.* (6 April 1895): 443; Ernst Riess, "Other People's Superstitions," *ibid.* (11 May 1895): 477. For similar views, see H. F. L., "A Plea for Superstition," *The Spectator* 74 (23 March 1895): 391–92; and F. Alexander MacDermott, "Popular Superstitions," *Outlook* 99 (21 October 1911): 437.

50. H. F. L., "A Plea for Superstition," p. 392.

51. William Wells Newell, "Introduction," in Fanny D. Bergen, ed., *Current Superstitions,* p. 5; M. J. Gorton, "Premonitions, Coincidences, and Superstitions," *Scientific American* 64 (4 April 1891): 212.

52. Daniel G. Brinton, M.D., "Popular Superstitions of Europe," *The Century* 56 (September, 1898): 643–55.

53. *Ibid.*: 653.

54. Charles S. Peirce, "The Architecture of Theories," *Monist* (January 1891): 161–76, reprinted in Philip S. Wiener, ed., *Values in a Universe of Chance* (Stanford, 1958), pp. 142–59, quotation at 148.

55. Hacking, *Taming of Chance*, p. 200; Henry Adams, *The Education of Henry Adams* [1907] (New York, 1918), esp. chaps. 25–31. For a superb account of the popular revolt against positivism, see Samuel Elworthy, "The Social Origins of Uncertainty," unpublished Ph.D. dissertation, Rutgers University, 1999.

56. D. H. Lawrence, *Studies in Classic American Literature* [1923] (New York, 1972), p. 29. See also Lears, *No Place of Grace,* chaps. 3, 4.

57. H. Addington Bruce, "Our Superstitions," *Outlook* 98 (26 August 1911): 1005–6.

58. William James, *The Varieties of Religious Experience* [1902], Collier Books ed. (New York, 1961), pp. 89–113, quotation at p. 102; Annie Payson Call, *Power Through Repose* (New York, 1906); Gustav Stickley, "Waste: Our Heaviest National Liability," *Craftsman* 20 (July 1911): 344–48. The classic work on mind-cure is Donald Meyer, *The Positivist Thinkers* 2nd ed. (New York, 1980). For a more sympathetic view, which takes the role of gender tensions into account, see Beryl Satter, *In the Kingdom of the Mind* (Berkeley and London, 1998).

59. John F. W. Ware, *The Gambling Element in Life* (Boston, 1871), pp. 3–9.

60. *Ibid.*, pp. 18–21.

61. W. B. Curtis, "The Increase of Gambling and Its Forms," *Forum* 12 (October 1891): 281–92. See also Lawrence Irwell, "Gambling as It Was, and Is," *New Century Review* 4 (July 1899): 33–38. For a spirited but idiosyncratic defense of gambling, based on cultural relativism, hereditarian psychology, and libertarian politics, see James Harold Romain, *Gambling, or Fortuna, Her Temple and Shrine* (Chicago, 1891).

62. Thomas, "Gaming Instinct," p. 760.

63. J. W. von Goethe, *Faust* [1808, 1832], Anchor Books ed., trans. and ed. Walter Kaufmann (New York, 1963), ll. 1700, 11936–37. The relevant lines read, in the German original: *"Verweile doch! Du bist so schon!"* and *" 'Wer immer strebend sich bemuht, / Den konnen wir erlosen.' "*

64. Alfred, Lord Tennyson, "Ulysses," [1833] ll. 22–23; Theodore Roosevelt, *The Stren-uous Life* (New York, 1900), frontispiece.

65. Eugene Edwards, *Jack Pots* (Chicago, 1900), p. 16.

66. "A Divergence of Views Concerning 'Luck,'" *Century* 82 (September 1911): 785–86. For similar views, see "Destiny," *Harper's Weekly* 56 (10 February 1912): 6; and Lester Frank Ward, *Glimpses of the Cosmos* (New York, 1918).

67. Frank Norris, *The Octopus* (New York, 1901), p. 185, and *The Pit* (New York, 1903), pp. 86–87. See also the helpful discussion by Michael Oriard, *Sporting With the Gods* (New York, 1991), pp. 209–15.

68. A. H. Lewis, *Wolfville Days* (New York, 1902), p. 224.

69. A. H. Lewis, *Wolfville* (New York, 1897), p. 6.

70. William James, "The Moral Equivalent of War" [1910] in John J. Mcdermott, ed., *The Writings of William James* (New York, 1967), pp. 660–71. Quotation at p. 664.

71. William James, "Percept and Concept—The Import of Concepts," in *Some Problems of Philosophy* (New York, 1911), pp. 47–74, reprinted in McDermott, *Writings,* pp. 232–43. Quotation at p. 233.

72. For useful background on how issues of chance became central to James's conscious-ness, see Paul Jerome Croce, "From History of Science to Intellectual History: The Probabilistic Revolution and the Chance–filled Universe of William James," *Intellec-tual History Newsletter* 13 (1991): 11–32; and Croce, *Science and Religion in the Era of William James,* vol. 1, *The Eclipse of Certainty* (Chapel Hill, N.C., and London, 1995).

73. William James, "The Sentiment of Rationality" [1880, 1897] in McDermott, ed., *Writings,* pp. 317–43; James, "The Dilemma of Determinism," [1884] in *ibid.,* pp. 587–610. Quotations at pp. 588, 589.

74. *Ibid.,* p. 592.

75. *Ibid.,* p. 593.

76. *Ibid.,* p. 595.

77. *Ibid.,* p. 607.

78. *Ibid.,* pp. 608–10.

79. William James, "The Will to Believe" [1896] in McDermott, *Writings,* pp. 717–35, quotation at p. 720; Fyodor Dostoevsky, *The Brothers Karamazov* [1880], trans. Con-stance Garnett (New York, 1931), pp. 69, 72.

80. William James, "Radical Empiricism," [1897] in McDermott, ed., *Writings,* p. 135.

81. William James, "A Pluralistic Mystic," *Hibbert Journal* 8 (1910): 739–59.

82. James, *Some Problems,* p. 46.

83. William James, *The Principles of Psychology,* 2 vols. (New York, 1890), chap. 9. James's fascination with fringe states of consciousness pervades *Varieties of Religious Experience* as well as his investigations in "psychical research."

84. On the Bergson vogue, see Tom Quirk, *Bergson and American Culture* (Chapel Hill, N.C., and London, 1990), chap. 1. For sympathetic discussions of chance, see Henri Poincaré, "Chance," *Monist* 22 (January 1912): 31–52; and "Chance and Faith" *Liv-ing Age* 280 (14 March 1914): 698–700.

85. John Burroughs, "Life and Chance," *North American Review* 202 (August 1915): 226–38.

86. [A. G. Keller,] "Luck and Primitive Religion" *Literary Digest* 54 (24 February 1917): 464–65.

87. G. Stanley Hall, *Adolescence* (Boston, 1904); Luther Gulick, *The Philosophy of Play* (New York, 1920); Johan Huizinga, *Homo Ludens* [1938] (Boston, 1955).

88. "Io Fortuna!" *Atlantic Monthly* 119 (January 1917): 141–42.

[CHAPTER 6: THE UNCERTAIN TRIUMPH OF MANAGEMENT]

1. "Amulets," *The New Statesman* 11 (8 June 1918): 187–88.
2. Simon Nelson Patten, *The New Basis of Civilization* [1907] (Cambridge, Mass., 1968), esp. pp. 139–41; Talcott Parsons, *The Social System* (Glencoe, Ill., 1951). Also see Jackson Lears, *Fables of Abundance,* (New York, 1994) pp. 113–17.
3. John Dewey, *Experience and Nature* [1925] (New York, 1958), p. 44.
4. *Ibid.,* pp. 53, 68, 70.
5. William James, "The Ph.D. Octopus" [1903], *Essays, Comments, and Reviews* (Cambridge, Mass., and London, 1987), pp. 67–73; David J. Depew, "Philosophy," in Stanley Kutler *et al.,* eds., *Encyclopedia of the United States in the Twentieth Century,* 4 vols. (New York, 1996), vol. 4, p. 1639.
6. Edward Berkowitz and Kim McQuaid, *Creating the Welfare State* (New York, 1988), chap. 1.
7. A. Philip Randolph, "Dialogues of the Old and New Porter" [1927] in Alan Dundes, ed., *Mother Wit from the Laughing Barrel* (New York and London, 1981), pp. 199–205.
8. Studs Terkel, *Hard Times* (New York, 1970), p. 426. Warren Susman, *Culture as History* (New York, 1984), pp. 150–210, offers a brilliant emotional history of the Great Depression.
9. Dale Carnegie, *How to Win Friends and Influence People* (New York, 1936), title page; Pearl London, "Ringing Doorbells with a Gallup Reporter," *New York Times Magazine,* (1 September 1940), p. 9. On the importance of polls and survey research in constructing a homogenous national identity, see Sarah Igo, "America Surveyed: The Making of a Social Scientific Public," Ph.D. dissertation, Princeton University, 2001.
10. Susman, *Culture as History,* pp. 150–210; Igo, "America Surveyed," chaps. 1–4.
11. John Maynard Keynes, *The General Theory of Employment, Interest, and Money* [1936], Harvest Books ed. (New York, 1964), pp. 157, 159. I am indebted to Christine Skwiot for bringing these passages to my attention.
12. *Ibid.,* p. 381.
13. J. M. Keynes, "The General Theory," *Quarterly Journal of Economics* 51 (1937): 209–33.
14. Catalog, Art Directors' 18th Annual Exhibit of Advertising Art (New York, 1939), in N. W. Ayer Collection, National Museum of American History, Smithsonian Institution, Washington, D.C. On the revival of managerial rhetoric among corporate leaders, see William L. Bird, *Better Living: Advertising, Media, and the New Vocabulary of Business Leadership, 1935–1955* (Evanston, Ill., 1999).
15. I have discussed these developments in T. J. Jackson Lears, "A Matter of Taste: Corporate Cultural Hegemony in a Mass Consumption Society," Lary May, ed., *Recasting America: Culture and Politics in the Age of Cold War* (Chicago, 1989): pp. 38–57.
16. Truman quoted in Eric Goldman, *The Crucial Decade—and After* (New York, 1960), pp. 59–60.
17. Eisenhower's First Inaugural Address, quoted in Conrad Cherry, ed., *God's New Israel: Religious Interpretations of American Destiny* (Englewood Cliffs, N.J., 1971), p. 311.
18. Parsons, The *Social System,* pp. 203–4. In "The Concept of Cultural Hegemony: Problems and Possibilities," *American Historical Review* 90 (1985): 567–93, I argue that hegemony should be distinguished from social control. The phrase "hegemony of the normal" is not meant to suggest that ordinary people were brainwashed into accepting experts' definitions of normality, but that those definitions were the only ones that possessed the imprimatur of "responsible opinion." Vernacular alternatives existed, but they were rarely if ever admitted into public discourse.
19. C. Wright Mills, *White Collar: The American Middle Classes* (New York, 1951), p. viii; David Riesman, with Nathan Glazer and Reuel Denney, *The Lonely Crowd: A Study*

in the Changing American Character (New Haven, 1950); William Whyte, *The Organization Man* (New York, 1956).

20. Alexis de Tocqueville, *Democracy in America,* 2 vols., ed. and trans. Phillips Bradley, Vintage Books ed. (New York, 1960), pp. 2, 141. On the preoccupation with conformity, see Lears, "A Matter of Taste," pp. 38–57.

21. Victor Klemperer, *I Will Bear Witness,* trans. Martin Chalmers (New York, 1998), entries for 2 February 1935, 13 February 1945, 22–24 February 1945.

22. Edward R. Murrow, "Edward R. Murrow With the News," CBS Broadcast, 5 November 1952, 7:45–8:00 P.M., quoted in Igo, "America Surveyed," chap. 4, pp. 41–42.

23. Dashiell Hammett, *The Maltese Falcon* [1929], Vintage Books ed. (New York, 1992), p. 64. On the "culture of contingency" embodied in film noir and other midcentury forms, see William Graebner, *The Age of Doubt* (Prospect Heights, Ill., 1998), chap. 2.

24. J. D. Salinger, *The Catcher in the Rye* (New York, 1951), p. 137.

25. Oscar Handlin, *Chance or Destiny?* (Boston, 1955), esp. pp. 191–212.

26. Quoted in Finis Dunaway, "Remembering Nature: Environmental Images and the Search for American Renewal, 1890–1970," Ph.D. dissertation, Rutgers University, 2001, p. 323. I am indebted to Dunaway's insights into the relationship between environmental consciousness and chance.

27. Kurt Gigerenzer, *et al., The Empire of Chance* (New York, 1988), esp. pp. 255–88.

28. Roper quoted in Igo, "America Surveyed," chap. 4, p. 48. For two among many critiques of statistical research, see Peter Bernstein, *Against the Gods: The Remarkable Story of Risk* (New York, 1996), pp. 334–35 (on financial forecasting); and R. C. Lewontin, *It Ain't Necessarily So* (New York, 2000), esp. chap. 7 (on sex surveys).

29. John McDonald, *Strategy in Poker, Business, and War* (New York, 1953), p. 81. On game theory, see Richard Duke, *Gaming: The Future's Language* (New York, 1974); John MacMillan, *Games, Strategies, and Managers* (New York, 1992); and Bernstein, *Against the Gods,* p. 235. Philip Dick, *Solar Lottery* (New York, 1955) is an interesting science fiction application of game theory to a dystopian future.

30. I. Nelson Rose, *Gambling and the Law* (Hollywood, 1986), chap. 1.

31. John McDonald, "Sport of Kings, Bums, and Businessmen," *Fortune,* August 1960, reprinted in Robert Herman, *Gambling* (New York, 1967), pp. 53–69.

32. William Rose Benét, "Mr. Moon's Notebook," *Saturday Review of Literature* 4 (21 April 1928): 781.

33. Warden Lawes, "Gambler's Hell," *True Story* (November 1938): 24–27, 45–50. I owe this reference to Jill Fields.

34. Commission on the Review of the National Policy Toward Gambling, *Moral Views on Gambling Promulgated by Major American Religious Bodies* (Washington, D.C., 1974), pp. 17, 20, 57.

35. "Possible Harm," *America* 98 (5 October 1957): 9. See also John S. Ezell, *Fortune's Merry Wheel* (Cambridge, Mass., 1960), pp. 270–71, and Clyde Brion Davis, *Something for Nothing* (Philadelphia and New York, 1956), p. 170.

36. Lycurgus M. Starkey, Jr., "Christians and the Gambling Mania," *Christian Century* 53 (27 February 1963): 267–70.

37. In the United States, this hardening was encouraged by the influence of positivistic, medical models on psychoanalytic thought: see Nathan Hale, *The Rise and Crisis of Psychoanalysis in the United States* (New York, 1995), esp. chaps. 5, 7, 9, 14.

38. Sigmund Freud, "Dostoevsky and Parricide" [1928], trans. D. F. Tait and James Strachey, *International Journal of Psycho-analysis* 26 (1945): 1–19. For a contemporary nonpsychoanalytic effort to pathologize gambling, see James Hunter and Arthur Brunner, "The Emotional Outlets of Gamblers," *Journal of Abnormal and Social Psychology* 23 (April 1928): 38–39.

39. Edmund Bergler, M.D., *The Psychology of Gambling* (New York, 1958), pp. 58, 64. For

a similar argument, see Robert M. Lindner, "The Psychodynamics of Gambling," *Annals of the American Academy of Political and Social Science* 269 (May 1950): 93–107.

40. *Ibid.,* pp. 56–57.

41. For other examples posing female gambling against domesticity, see Don Robertson and Jack Rollins, "The Queen of Draw Poker Town," and "Gambella (the Gamblin' Lady)," Box 7, Folder D, DeVincent Sheet Music Collection, National Museum of American History, Smithsonian Institution, Washington, D.C.

42. E. Franklin Frazier, "Playing Seriously," excerpt from *Black Bourgeoisie* (Glencoe, Ill., 1957), in Herman, ed., *Gambling,* pp. 32–39. Quotation at p. 33.

43. *Ibid.,* p. 37.

44. Letter, Joseph Carlino to David Levy, 16 December 1963, in "Gambling," Box 1, Warshaw Collection of Business Americana, National Museum of American History, Smithsonian Institution, Washington, D.C.

45. Robert F. Kennedy, "The Baleful Influence of Gambling," *Atlantic Monthly* (1962), reprinted in Herman, *Gambling,* pp. 169–76.

46. Judge John M. Murtagh, "Gambling and Police Corruption," *Atlantic Monthly* 206 (November 1960): 49–53; Davis, *Something,* pp. 108ff; McDonald, "Sport of Kings," *passim.*

47. "'Uncle Syndicate,'" *Newsweek* 38 (12 December 1951): 25; Norton Mockridge and Robert S. Prall, *The Big Fix* (New York, 1954), esp. pp. 35–38; Davis, *Something,* p. 92.

48. Irving Kenneth Zola, "Observations on Gambling in a Lower-Class Setting," *Social Problems* 10 (Spring 1963): 353–61. For a parallel argument, see "In Britain, Gambling Is a Growth Industry," *Business Week* (14 September 1963): 29–31. For arguments viewing gambling as calculation, see Robert Herman, "Gambling as Work: A Sociological Study of the Race Track," in Herman, ed., *Gambling,* pp. 87–104; and Davis, *Something,* pp. 88, 126, 130–31. The most successful sociological effort to depathologize gambling in this era was Erving Goffmann, *Interaction Ritual* (New York, 1967), esp. pp. 39–58.

49. Zola, "Observations," p. 361.

50. G. K. Chesterton, "On Evolutionary Educators," in his *All I Survey* [1933] (Freeport, N.Y., 1967), pp. 156–57.

51. Robert Lynd, "A Defense of Superstition," in his *Solomon in All His Glory* [1923] (Freeport, N.Y., 1969), pp. 156–64.

52. Elsie Clews Parsons, "Anthropology and Prediction," *American Anthropologist,* n.s., 44 (July–September 1942): 337–38.

53. John Ciardi, *Saipan,* p. 64, and Ciardi's interview with Studs Terkel, in Terkel, *The Good War: An Oral History of World War II* (New York, 1984), pp. 194–99. For most of the information in the paragraph, I am indebted to Ann Pfau, "Love and the Machinery of War," unpublished paper presented at the American Historical Association Annual Meeting, Seattle, 1998.

54. For examples of these attitudes, see Charles W. Glover, "Be Watchful and Beware: The Song of the Gypsy" (New York and New Orleans), n.d., and Dave Marion, "The Fortune Teller," (Chicago, 1896), in DeVincent Collection; Lee McCann, "The Fortune Teller's Deck," *Survey Graphic* 1 (October 1927); and Frank Wadleigh Chandler, "Gypsydom from the Literature of Roguery," typescript dated 1907, both in Box 2, Wendler-Funaro Collection, National Museum of American History, Smithsonian Institution, Washington, D.C.

55. Joseph Mitchell, "The King of the Gypsies" [1942] in his *Up in the Old Hotel* (New York, 1993), p. 159.

56. Mitchell, "The Gypsy Women," in *ibid.,* p. 197.

57. *Ibid.,* pp. 195–96.

58. Gypsy child's protective vest, Accession #1996.0568.05, National Museum of American History, Smithsonian Institution, Washington, D.C.; Isabel Fonseca, *Bury Me Standing: The Gypsies and Their Journey,* Vintage Books ed. (New York, 1996), pp. 241–43.

59. Harry Middleton Hyatt, *Hoodoo-Conjuration-Witchcraft-Rootwork,* 5 vols. (Washington, D.C., 1970), vol. 1, pp. ii–iii, 104ff.; Norman E. Whitten, Jr., "Contemporary Patterns of Malign Occultism Among Negroes in North Carolina," *Journal of American Folklore* 75 (1962): 311–25; Carolyn Morrow Long, *Spiritual Merchants: Religion, Magic, and Commerce* (Knoxville, 2001), esp. chaps. 5, 6, 8. Long's book is a superb exploration of the subject.

60. Hyatt, *Hoodoo,* pp. 2, 619ff., 606–7; Whitten, "Contemporary Patterns," pp. 320–25; Lyle Saxon, *et al.,* eds., *Gumbo Ya-Ya: A Collection of Louisiana Folk Tales* (Boston, 1945), p. 67.

61. Hyatt, *Hoodoo,* pp. 2, 628; Frazier, "Serious Play," p. 37; J. Mason Brewer, "Old-Time Negro Proverbs" [1933], in Dundes, ed., *Mother Wit,* pp. 246–50.

62. Ruth Bass, "Mojo" [1930] and "The Little Man" [1935], in *ibid.,* pp. 380–87, 388–96.

63. Hyatt, *Hoodoo,* pp. 1, 222.

64. Mark Haller, "Policy Gambling, Entertainment, and the Emergence of Black Politics: Chicago from 1900 to 1940," *Journal of Social History* 24 (1991): 721–32.

65. Saxon, *et al., Gumbo Ya–Ya,* p. 132.

66. George McCall, "Symbiosis: the Case of Hoodoo and the Numbers Racket," in Dundes, *Mother Wit,* pp. 419–27.

67. *Ibid.,* p. 136; Paul Oliver, *Blues Fell This Morning: Meaning in the Blues,* 2nd ed. (Cambridge, Mass., 1990), p. 127.

68. Saxon, *et al., Gumbo Ya-Ya,* pp. 104–5; McCall, "Symbiosis," 427.

69. Hyatt, *Hoodoo,* pp. 2, 722.

70. Ivan R. Light, "Numbers Gambling Among Blacks: A Financial Institution," *American Sociological Review* 42 (1977): 892–904.

71. Claude McKay, *Harlem: Negro Metropolis* (New York, 1931), pp. 106–11.

72. McCall, "Symbiosis," pp. 421–24; Haller, "Policy Gambling," p. 730.

73. McCall, "Symbiosis," p. 421.

74. *Ibid.*

75. *Ibid.,* p. 125; Light, "Numbers Gambling," p. 896–97.

76. Marty Moss-Coane, "Radio Times," WHYY-FM Radio, 12 February 2001; Victoria Wolcott, "The Culture of the Informal Economy: Numbers Runners in Interwar Detroit," *Radical History Review* 69 (1997): 46–75; Haller, "Policy Gambling," p. 727.

77. McKay, *Harlem,* pp. 106–11; Wolcott, "Informal Economy," pp. 62–63.

78. John Dollard, "The Dozens: Dialectic of Insult," *American Imago* 1 (1939): 3–25; Roger Abrahams, "Playing the Dozens," *Journal of American Folklore* 75 (1962): 209–19; Harry G. Lefever, "'Playing the Dozens': A Mechanism for Social Control," *Phylon* 42 (1981): 73–85; Thurmon Garner, "Playing the Dozens: Folklore as Strategies for Living," *Quarterly Journal of Speech* 69 (1983): 47–57; Oliver, *Blues Fell,* p. 114–16.

79. Oliver, *Blues Fell,* pp. 114–16, 149; Robert Johnson, "Crossroads Blues," recorded 27 November 1936, San Antonio, Tex., rereleased on *Robert Johnson: King of the Delta Blues Singers* (Columbia Records, 1965).

80. W. H. Knickerbocker, *Riley Grannan's Funeral* [1908] (Reno, 1928), p. 14.

81. James Schwock, "The Influence of Local History on Popular Fiction: Gambling Ships in Los Angeles, 1933," *Journal of Popular Culture* 20 (Spring 1987): 103–12; Mockridge and Prall, *The Big Fix,* pp. 33–34.

82. McKay, *Harlem,* pp. 112–14; Carl Sifakis, *Encyclopedia of Gambling* (New York, 1990), pp. 23–24.

83. University of Nevada Oral History Program, *Always Bet on the Butcher: Warren Nelson and Casino Gambling* (Reno, 1994), chap. 6; Davis, *Something,* pp. 156–61.

84. Robert H. Williams, "Spoiled Fruit," *Washington Post,* 15 September 1996, pp. F1, F8.

85. Sifakis, *Encyclopedia,* p. 194; Leo Rosten, "The Adoration of the Nag," in Herman, *Gambling,* pp. 39–49.

86. Carlton Stowers, *The Unsinkable Titanic Thompson* (Burnet, Tex., 1982), pp. 38–44.
87. *Ibid.,* pp. 44–56.
88. *Ibid.,* pp. 56–57.
89. Stephen Longstreet, *Win or Lose: A Social History of Gambling,* (Indianapolis, 1977), pp. 234–38; Stowers, *Thompson,* p. 141; Sifakis, *Encyclopedia,* p. 207.
90. Damon Runyon, "The Idyll of Miss Sarah Brown" [1932], in *Runyon à la Carte* (New York, 1946), p. 92; Stowers, *Thompson,* pp. 144ff.
91. Stowers, *Thompson,* p. 141.
92. Tom Clark, *The World of Damon Runyon* (New York, 1978), p. 192. For another revealing expression of the gamblers' ethos, see *Diamond Spike, Playing the Field: The Autobiography of an American Racketeer* (Sacramento, 1944).
93. Clark, *Runyon,* pp. 175–79.
94. Runyon, "Sarah Brown," pp. 89–91, 94.
95. *Ibid.,* p. 96.
96. *Ibid.,* pp. 103–4.
97. Paul Tillich, "Holy Waste," in his *The New Being* (New York, 1955), p. 47.
98. *Watch Your Dreams With Harlem Pete Dream Book 967* (Philadelphia, 1949), p. 2, in Special Collections, University of Michigan Library, Ann Arbor, Mich. I am grateful to Ann Fabian for bringing Harlem Pete to my attention in her superb book, *Card Sharps, Dream Books, and Bucket Shops: Gambling in Nineteenth-Century America* (Ithaca, N.Y., and London, 1990), p. 152.

[CHAPTER 7: THE PERSISTENT ALLURE OF ACCIDENT]

1. Virginia Woolf, "Mr. Bennett and Mrs. Brown" [1924], in *The Captain's Deathbed and Other Essays* (New York, 1956), pp. 96, 115–17.
2. Quoted in Richard Rorty, *Contingency, Irony, and Solidarity* (New York and London, 1989), p. 31.
3. Quoted in Robert Hughes, *The Shock of the New* (New York, 1981), p. 225.
4. Daniel Belgrad, *The Culture of Spontaneity: Improvisation and the Arts in Postwar America* (Chicago and London, 1998). Belgrad's illuminating work has been enormously helpful to me.
5. William James, *The Principles of Psychology,* 2 vols. [1890] (New York, 1950), vol. 1, p. 240; Horace Kallen, *William James and Henri Bergson* (Chicago, 1914), p. 105. I am indebted to the penetrating discussion of positive negative space in Stephen Kern, *The Culture of Time and Space* (Cambridge, Mass., 1983), pp. 175–80.
6. James, *Principles,* pp. 1, 239, 245, emphasis in original; William James, "A World of Pure Experience" in his *Essays in Radical Empiricism* [1912], ed. Ralph Barton Perry (New York, 1939), pp. 39–91.
7. Kern, *Culture,* pp. 11–16.
8. Marcel Proust, *Remembrance of Things Past* [1913], trans. C. K. Scott–Moncrieff and Terence Kilmartin, 3 vols. (New York, 1981), vol. 1, pp. 47–48.
9. James Joyce, *Ulysses* [1914–1921], Vintage Books ed. (New York, 1961), pp. 421–22, 377.
10. James Joyce, *Stephen Hero* (New York, 1944), p. 211.
11. Kern, *Culture,* p. 30; Charles Musser, "Archeology of the Cinema: 8," *Framework* 22/23 (Autumn 1983): 4–11; Miriam Hansen, *Babel and Babylon: Spectatorship and American Silent Film* (Cambridge, Mass., and London, 1991), chap.1.
12. H. Stuart Hughes, *Consciousness and Society, 1890–1930* (New York, 1958), pt. 1; T. J. Jackson Lears, *No Place of Grace: Antimodernism and the Transformation of American Culture, 1880–1920* (New York, 1981), chaps. 1, 3, 4; Kern, *Culture,* chaps. 6, 7.
13. Ernst Mach, *The Science of Mechanics* [1883] (New York, 1919), p. 223; Albert Einstein, *Relativity: The Special and General Theory* [1916] (New York, 1952), p. 26; Al-

bert Einstein and Leopold Infeld, *The Evolution of Physics* (New York, 1938), p. 181. I am indebted to the lucid discussion of these issues in Kern, *Culture,* pp. 18–19.

14. Herman Melville, *Moby-Dick* [1851], Signet Classics ed. (New York, 1961), pp. 413–14.

15. Joyce, *Ulysses,* p. 190.

16. Lears, *No Place of Grace,* chap. 4; Robert Goldwater, *Primitivism and Modern Art* (New York, 1964).

17. Jorge Luis Borges, "The Lottery in Babylon" [1944], trans. John M. Fein, in Borges, *Labyrinths* (New York, 1964), pp. 30–35.

18. Walker Percy, *The Last Gentleman* (New York, 1966), p. 280. See the intelligent discussion in Andrew Delbanco, *The Death of Satan* (New York, 1995), chap. 6.

19. Lionel Trilling, "On the Teaching of Modern Literature" [1962] in his *Beyond Culture* (New York, 1979), p. 30.

20. Charles Baudelaire, "Le Jeu" in *Les Fleurs du Mal* (Paris, 1857), excerpted and translated in Walter Benjamin, "On Some Motifs in Baudelaire," in his *Illuminations,* trans. Harry Zohn (New York, 1968), p. 180. The French original reads:

> *Et mon coeur s'effraya d'envier maint pauvre homme*
> *Courant avec ferveur à l'abîme béant,*
> *Et qui, soûl de son sang, préférerait en somme*
> *La douleur à la mort et l'enfer au néant!*

21. Fyodor Dostoevsky, *The Gambler* [1866], trans. Jessie Coulson, Penguin Books ed. (New York, 1966), p. 39.

22. Walter Benjamin, *The Arcades Project* [1935–40], trans. Kevin McLaughlin and Howard Eiland (Cambridge, Mass., and London, 1999), p. 513. I am indebted to Leon Wieseltier for bringing Benjamin's remarks to my attention.

23. *Ibid.,* p. 498, quoting Anatole France, *Le Jardin d'Epicure* (Paris, 1895), pp. 15–18.

24. Marcel Raymond, *From Baudelaire to Surrealism,* cited in George Brecht, *Chance-Imagery* (New York, 1966), p. 3.

25. André Breton, "First Surrealist Manifesto" [1924], quoted in Alfred Barr, ed., *Fantastic Art, Dada, Surrealism* (New York, 1947), p. 87; Tristan Tzara, "Lecture on Dada" [1922] in *The Dada Painters and Poets: An Anthology,* ed. Robert Motherwell (New York, 1951), p. 248, reprinted as epigraph to Brecht, *Chance-Imagery,* n.p.

26. Hughes, *Shock of the New,* p. 161.

27. Hans Arp, "Dada Was Not a Farce" [1949] in Motherwell, ed., *Dada,* p. 294.

28. Tzara, "Lecture," p. 247; Daisetz Suzuki, "The Zen Sect of Buddhism" (1906) in his *Studies in Zen* (New York, 1955), p. 28.

29. Werner Heisenberg, *Physics and Philosophy* (New York, 1956), esp. chaps. 2, 3; P. C. W. Davies and J. R. Brown, *The Ghost in the Atom* (Cambridge, UK, 1986), esp. chap. 1.

30. I. J. Good, "Changing Concepts of Chance," *Nature* 332 (31 March 1988): 405–6.

31. Brecht, *Chance–Imagery,* pp. 7–11.

32. Quoted in Eliza Jane Reilly, "Pragmatism, Cubism, Modernism: William James and the Transatlantic Avant Garde, 1905–1925," Ph.D. dissertation, Rutgers University, 2000, p. 182.

33. Kenneth Burke, "Dada, Dead or Alive," *Aesthete 1925* (February 1925): 23–26.

34. Lynda Roscoe Hartigan, "Joseph Cornell: A Biography," in *Joseph Cornell,* ed. Kynaston McShine (New York, 1981), p. 104. Diary entries dated 2 July 1949, 19 April 1954, reel 1059; 1 October 1956, reel 1315, Joseph Cornell Collection, Archives of American Art, National Museum of American Art, Washington, D.C.

35. Cornell diary, 28 May 1955, 3 September 1949, reel 1059, Cornell Collection.

36. Gottlieb quoted in Irving Sandler, *The Triumph of American Painting* (New York, 1970), p. 31. I am indebted to Sandler's superb account of the genesis of abstract expressionism.

37. Edward Renouf, "On Certain Functions of Modern Painting," *Dyn* 2 (July–August 1942): 20.
38. Besides Sandler, two excellent general treatments of abstract expressionism are Michael Leja, *Reframing Abstract Expressionism: Subjectivity and Painting in the 1940s* (New Haven and London, 1993), and Stephen Polcari, *Abstract Expressionism and the Modern Experience* (New York, 1990).
39. Adolph Gottlieb, unpublished transcript of interview with Martin Friedman, p. 24, at Adolph and Esther Gottlieb Foundation, New York, N.Y.; Jackson Pollock, interview with William Wright, 1950, in Ellen H. Johnson, ed. *American Artists on Art, from 1940 to 1980* (New York, 1982), pp. 6–7.
40. Dorothy Gees Seckler, "Start of the Season—New York," *Art in America*, #3 (1961): 85–86, 128–29. Quotation at 128. For examples of the later work, see the National Collection of Fine Arts Exhibit Catalogue, *Robert Rauschenberg* (Washington, D.C., 1976).
41. Olson quoted in Daniel Belgrad, "The Social Meanings of Spontaneity in American Arts and Literature, 1940–1960," 2 vols., Ph.D. dissertation, Yale University, 1994, p. 112; DiPrima quoted in Ann Charters, ed., *The Beat Reader* (New York, 1992), p. 335.
42. LeRoi Jones [Amiri Baraka], undated letter to *The Evergreen Review,* reprinted in *The Beat Reader,* pp. 349–53.
43. *Ibid.,* p. 352.
44. Robert Walser, "Out of Notes: Signification, Interpretation, and the Problem of Miles Davis," *The Musical Quarterly* 77 (1993): 343–65, n2, quotations at 355; Albert Murray, "Improvisation and the Creative Process," in *The Jazz Cadence of American Culture* (New York, 1998), pp. 111–13.
45. Toshiko Takaezu, quoted in Belgrad, "Spontaneity," p. 428.
46. Joseph Wood Krutch, "Human Life in the Context of Nature," in David Brower, ed., *Wilderness* (San Francisco, 1961), p. 73; Krutch, "A Little Fishy Friend," *The Nation* 169 (8 October 1949): 350. I owe these references to Finis Dunaway.
47. C. G. Jung, "Synchronicity: An Acausal Connecting Principle," in *The Structure and Dynamics of the Psyche*, vol. 8 of *The Collected Works of C. G. Jung*, trans. R. F. C. Hull (Princeton, 1960), pp. 520ff.; Heisenberg, *Physics and Philosophy*, chap. 3. Here and elsewhere in this chapter, I owe my emphasis on complementarity to conversations with Karen Parker Lears.
48. Burroughs quoted in Warren Motte, "Burroughs Takes a Chance," in Thomas Kavanagh, ed., *Chance, Culture, and the Literary Text* (Ann Arbor, 1990), p. 215.
49. Alan Watts, "Beat Zen, Square Zen, and Zen" [1958], reprinted in Charters, ed., *The Beat Reader,* pp. 607–10.
50. Daisetz Suzuki, "Zen Buddhism" [1938] in *Studies in Zen,* p.5, and "Buddhist Philosophy" [1951] in *ibid.,* pp. 101, 121. See the thoughtful discussion of Suzuki's influence in Kristine Stiles, "Between Water and Stone," in *In the Spirit of Fluxus,* eds. Elizabeth Armstrong and Joan Rothfuss (Minneapolis, 1990), n.p.
51. Norman Mailer, "The White Negro" [1957] in his *Advertisements for Myself* (New York, 1959), p. 313.
52. Jack Kerouac, *The Subterraneans* [1958] (New York, 1971), p. 57.
53. Ginsberg quoted in Charters, ed., The *Beat Reader,* p. 61.
54. "America," in *ibid.,* p. 75.
55. "Song" [1954], in *ibid.,* p. 100.
56. Jack Kerouac, *The Dharma Bums,* quoted in Charters, ed., *The Beat Reader,* p. xxix.
57. Rose Slivka, *Peter Voulkos: A Dialogue with Clay* (Boston, 1978), p. 52; Daisetz T. Suzuki, *Zen and Japanese Culture* (New York, 1959), p. 15. Bracketed phrase in original.
58. Wassily Kandinsky, *Concerning the Spiritual in Art* [1914], quoted in Belgrad, "Spontaneity," p. 105; Ian Buruma, "Back to the Future," *New York Review of Books,* 4 March

1999, pp. 31–33; Charles Olson, "Projective Verse," in Donald Allen, ed., *The New American Poetry* (New York, 1960), pp. 386–99. Quotation at pp. 387–88.

59. Suzuki, "An Interpretation of Zen–Experience" [1939], in *Studies in Zen,* p. 82.

60. Jackson Pollock, interview with William Wright, 1950, in Ellen Johnson, ed., *American Artists on Art* (New York, 1982), p. 8; Motherwell quoted in Hughes, *Shock of the New,* p. 260.

61. Robert Motherwell, interview with Stephen Addiss, 1991, quoted in Addiss, "Provisional Dualism: Robert Motherwell and Zen," in *Robert Motherwell on Paper: Drawings, Prints, Collages,* ed. David Rosand (New York, 1997), p. 59.

62. Hughes, *Shock of the New,* p. 163; E. A. Carmean, Jr., "The Collages of Robert Motherwell," in *The Collages of Robert Motherwell: A Retrospective Exhibition* (Houston, 1972), pp. 11–39; Motherwell, Addiss interview, p. 79. Motherwell's references to "shuddering" and the "multiple pun" of *The French Line* are on pp. 63 and 69 of *Collages.*

63. Louise Nevelson, *Dawns and Dusks* (New York, 1976), pp. 76, 78. I am indebted to Karen Parker Lears for bringing Frankenthaler and Nevelson to my attention.

64. On Cage's influence, see, for example, Douglas Kahn, "The Latest: Fluxus and Music," *In the Spirit of Fluxus,* p. 103, and Marjorie Perloff and Charles Junkerman, eds., *John Cage: Composed in America* (Chicago, 1994), pp. 1–13.

65. Merce Cunningham, *The Dancer and the Dance* (New York and London, 1985), pp. 31–56; Andreas Huyssen, "Back to the Future: Fluxus in Context," in *In the Spirit of Fluxus,* p. 146; Brecht, *Chance–Imagery,* p. 15; Joseph Jacobs, "Crashing New York à la John Cage," in Joan Marter, ed., *Off Limits: Rutgers University and the Avant Garde, 1957–1963* (New Brunswick, 1999), pp. 66–74.

66. Richard Kostelantz, *Conversing with Cage* (New York, 1987), pp. 211–12. Cage's essays explaining his experiments in the 1950s were collected in his *Silence* (Middletown, Conn., 1961). Lewis Hyde, *Trickster Makes This World* (New York, 1999), pp. 141–50, is an intelligent discussion of Cage and chance.

67. Catherine Cameron, *Dialectics in the Arts: The Rise of Experimentalism in Modern Music* (New York, 1996), pp. 40–42; John Cage, *M: Writings, '67–'72* (Middletown, Conn., 1972).

68. John Cage, quoted in Hughes, *Shock of the New,* p. 356.

69. Jed Perl, "The Variety Show," *The New Republic* 23 July 2001: 27–32.

70. Ernest Fenollossa, "The Chinese Written Character as a Medium for Poetry" in Ezra Pound, ed., *Instigations* [1920] (Freeport, N.Y., 1967), p. 371; Olson, quoted in Belgrad, "Spontaneity," p. 112.

71. Noel Carroll, "Cage and Philosophy," *Journal of Aesthetics and Art Criticism* 52 (Winter 1994): 93–99.

72. John Cage, *Empty Words* [1973–1974] (Middletown, Conn., 1979), p. 11; Christopher Shultis, "Silencing the Sounded Self: John Cage and the Intentionality of Non-intention," *The Musical Quarterly* 79 (Summer 1995): 322.

73. John Cage, "Memoir," in Richard Kostelantz, *John Cage* (New York, 1991), p. 77; Shultis, "Silencing the Sounded Self," p. 316.

74. Cage, "Memoir," p. 77.

75. Shultis, "Silencing the Sounded Self," p. 316; Aldous Huxley, *The Perennial Philosophy* (New York, 1945), p. 20.

76. Aldous Huxley, "Grace, Predestination, and Salvation," *The Hibbert Journal* 29 (January 1931): 193–201; Simone Weill, *Gravity and Grace,* trans. Arthur Wills, (New York, 1952), pp. 45–48; Paul Tillich, *The New Being* (New York, 1955), pt. 1.

77. Eugene McCarraher, *Christian Critics: Religion and the Impasse in Modern American Social Thought* (Ithaca, N.Y., and London, 2000), chap. 5. Quotation at p. 122.

78. *Ibid.,* pp. 134–35; Richard Fox, *Reinhold Niebuhr: A Biography* (New York, 1986), p. 257.

79. Paul Tillich, "You Are Accepted," in *The Shaking of the Foundations* (New York, 1948), pp. 154–62.

80. William James, *The Varieties of Religious Experience* [1902], Collier Books ed. (New York, 1961), p. 138. James presents this experience as if it were someone else's, but his biographers have made it clear that it was his own. See, for example, Howard Feinstein, *Becoming William James* (Ithaca, N.Y., and London, 1984).

81. Paul Tillich, *The Courage to Be* (New Haven and London, 1952), p. 35.

82. *Ibid.*, pp. 44–45.

83. Paul Tillich, "Principalities and Powers," in his *The New Being* (New York, 1955), p. 52.

84. Tillich, *Courage,* pp. 82–85.

85. Tillich, "Holy Waste," in *The New Being,* p. 48.

86. *Ibid.*, p. 49.

87. On Ellison's first encounter with Freud's "dream book," see his "Testimonial for John Wright, c. 1979–1981" in John Callahan, ed., "'American Culture is of a Whole': From the Letters of Ralph Ellison," *The New Republic,* 1 March 1999: 44.

88. Ralph Ellison, "Introduction to the Thirtieth–Anniversary Edition of *Invisible Man,*" in John F. Callahan, ed., *The Collected Essays of Ralph Ellison* (New York, 1995), p. 484.

89. Ralph Ellison, *Invisible Man,* Modern Library ed. (New York, 1952), p. 107. Subsequent page references are all to this edition.

90. *Ibid.*, pp. 118, 125.

91. *Ibid.*, pp. 183, 188.

92. *Ibid.*, pp. 198, 200–201.

93. *Ibid.*, pp. 206, 221.

94. *Ibid.*, pp. 212, 288.

95. *Ibid.*, p. 293.

96. *Ibid.*, pp. 277, 285.

97. *Ibid.*, p. 308.

98. *Ibid.*, p. 331.

99. *Ibid.*, p. 333.

100. James Joyce, *Portrait of the Artist as a Young Man* [1916] (New York, 1964), p. 247.

101. Ellison, *Invisible Man,* pp. 371, 377.

102. *Ibid.*, p. 381.

103. *Ibid.*, pp. 381, 385.

104. *Ibid.*, pp. 433–35.

105. *Ibid.*, p. 438.

[EPILOGUE]

1. Peter Burger, quoted in Michael Oriard, *Sporting with the Gods* (New York, 1994), p. 350.

2. Bill Boisvert, "Apostles of the New Entrepreneur," *Baffler* #6: 75–76.

3. Bill Gates, *Business@the Speed of Thought* (New York, 1999), pp. 136–39, 120.

4. Sandra Blakeslee, "In Work on Intuition, Gut Feelings Are Tracked to Source: The Brain," *New York Times,* 4 March 1997, p. C5.

5. For an incisive critique, see Michael Shermer, "We Are the World," review of Robert Wright, *Nonzero: The Logic of Human Destiny* (New York, 1999), *Los Angeles Times Book Review,* 6 February 2000: p. 6.

6. Jeffrey Rosen, "Bad Luck," *The New Republic,* 5 November 2001: 21–23.

7. Hendrik Hartog, "The Cataclysmic in Everyday Life," *New York Times,* 29 September 2001 p. A23.

8. Richard Sennett, quoted in Jean Bethke Elshtain, "Lost City," *The New Republic,* 4 November 1996: 25; Robert Goodman, *The Luck Business* (New York, 1995), pp. 149, 154. See also Sennett, *The Corrosion of Character* (New York, 1998).

9. Steven R. Reed, "Gambling, Killings, and Payoffs: The High-Stakes Life of Benny Binion," *Houston Chronicle,* 14 March 1989: 1, 4.

10. "Addiction: Are States Preying on the Vulnerable?" *Washington Post,* 4 March 1996: A8; Charles Bishop, "What Are the Odds on 8-to-5?" Unpublished seminar paper, National Endowment for the Humanities Summer Seminar on Grace, Luck, and Fortune, New Brunswick, N.J., 1996.

11. A. Alvarez, *The Biggest Game in Town* (Boston, 1983), pp. 29, 113–15, 147.

12. Amy Tan, *The Joy Luck Club* (New York, 1989), p. 159. For a brilliant account of how some younger Catholics preserved idiosyncratic attachments to church traditions, see James T. Fisher, "Clearing the Streets of the Catholic Lost Generation," *South Atlantic Quarterly* 93 (Summer 1994): 603–29.

13. Elizabeth McAlister, "Sacred Stories from the Haitian Diaspora: A Collective Biography of Seven Vodou Priestesses in New York City," *Journal of Caribbean Studies* 9 (1992): 11–27; idem., "A Sorcer's Bottle: The Visual Arts of Magic in Haiti," in Donald Cosentino, ed., *Sacred Arts of Haitian Vodou* (Los Angeles, 1995), chap. 12. I am indebted to Professor McAlister for sending me her superb work.

14. Richard Rorty, *Contingency, Irony, and Solidarity* (Cambridge, Mass., and London, 1989), p. 22.

15. Bernard Williams, *Moral Luck* (Cambridge, UK, 1981); Thomas Nagel, *Mortal Questions* (Cambridge, UK, 1979), chap. 3; and the essays collected in Daniel Statman, ed., *Moral Luck* (Albany, N.Y., 1993).

16. Calvin Tomkins, "The Maverick," *New Yorker,* 7 July 1997: 38–42.

17. Coosje Van Bruggen, *Frank Gehry: Guggenheim Museum Bilbao* (New York, 1999), pp. 37, 72.

18. Hal Foster, "Slouching Toward Bilbao," *Los Angeles Times Book Review,* 14 October 2001: 8.

19. Elaine Scarry, *On Beauty and Being Just* (Princeton, 1999), pp. 110–11.

20. Emmanuel Levinas, quoted in Zygmunt Bauman, *Modernity and the Holocaust* (Ithaca, N.Y., 1989), p. 214.

21. Eudora Welty, "The Key," pp. 29–38, in *The Collected Stories of Eudora Welty* (New York, 1980). I owe this quotation to Karen Parker Lears.

CREDITS

page 7—The "Puritan" slot machine (USA, Mills Novelty Co., c. 1890)—Warshaw Collection of Business Americana, Archives Center, National Museum of American History, Smithsonian Institution, Washington, D.C.

page 8—The "Rol-a-Top" slot machine (USA, Watling Co., 1935)—National Museum of American History, Smithsonian Institution, Washington, D.C.

page 12—"Fortune" and "Misfortune," plates 311 and 312 in George Richardson, *Iconologia* (London, 1779), vol.1, p. LXXXI. Courtesy The Winterthur Library: Printed Book and Periodical Collection, Winterthur, Delaware.

page 13—German lottery sign, 1907, in F. H. Ehmcke, *Graphic Trade Symbols by German Designers from the 1907 Klingspor Catalog* (Dover reprint, New York, 1974).

page 14—African divination gourd and power figure, artist unknown. Wood, gourd, fiber, vegetable matter. Height 6 inches. Courtesy Mead Art Museum, Amherst College, Amherst, Massachusetts. The Barry D. Maure (Class of 1959) Collection of African Art purchased with Amherst College Discretionary Fund and funds from H. Axel Schupf (Class of 1957) Acc. #1999.50.

page 14—Robbie Parker's lucky box, Wilmington, North Carolina, 1996. Photo courtesy Robbie and Rob Parker.

page 15—Yoruba diviner's bag (Nigeria, twentieth century), courtesy, Metropolitan Museum of Art, Gift of Claire and Michael Oliver, 1999.

page 36—Coral rattle, Joseph Richardson, Sr., maker, Philadelphia, circa 1750, courtesy, Winterthur Museum, Winterthur, Delaware.

page 58—Bell at the bar, eighteenth-century tavern game (New England). Courtesy, Winterthur Museum, Winterthur, Delaware.

page 64—coffin spoon, circa 1790, photograph in Walter Hunter, "The Spoon as Funerary Souvenir," *Antiques,* April 1931, p. 301. Courtesy, The Winterthur Library, Printed Book and Periodical Collection, Winterthur, Delaware.

page 84—Jacob Joder, earthenware plate, circa 1800, courtesy, Winterthur Museum, Winterthur, Delaware.

page 110—Lottery advertisement, in Greele & Willis, *Specimens of Printing Types* (Boston, 1831). Courtesy, The Winterthur Library, Printed Book and Periodical Collection, Winterthur, Delaware.

page 110—Lottery advertisement, in Hobart & Robbins, *Specimens of Printing Types* (Boston, 1851). Courtesy, The Winterthur Library, Printed Book and Periodical Collection, Winterthur, Delaware.

page 111—William Sidney Mount, *Dregs in the Cup* (1838). Oil on canvas. Courtesy, Collection of the New-York Historical Society.

page 116—George Caleb Bingham, *Raftsmen Playing Cards* (1847). Oil on canvas. Courtesy, St. Louis Art Museum. Ezra H. Linley Fund.

page 149—Horace Bonham, *Nearing the Issue at the Cock Pit* (1870). Oil on canvas 20¼ × 27⅛ inches. In the collection of the Corcoran Gallery of Art, Washington, D.C., Museum Purchase, Gallery Fund.

page 169—"Luck," P. T. Barnum, *Dollars and Sense, or, How to Get On* (New York, 1890), p. 67.

page 205—Joe Newman, "Shootin' Craps" (1893), DeVincent Collection, Archives Center, National Museum of American History, Smithsonian Institution, Washington, D.C.

page 205—Clarence Stout, "Oh Death Where Is Thy Sting" (circa 1910), DeVincent Collection, Archives Center, National Museum of American History, Smithsonian Institution, Washington, D.C.

page 205—Leighton & Leighton, "There's a Dark Man Coming with a Bundle" (1904), DeVincent Collection, Archives Center, National Museum of American History, Smithsonian Institution, Washington, D.C.

page 205—William Jerome and Jean Schwarz, "The Gambling Man" (1902), DeVincent Collection, Archives Center, National Museum of American History, Smithsonian Institution, Washington, D.C.

page 205—Dave Marion, "The Fortune Teller" (1895), DeVincent Collection, Archives Center, National Museum of American History, Smithsonian Institution, Washington, D.C.

page 253—Gypsy fortune-teller, Mineola, N.Y., 1932, in Wendler-Funaro Collection, Archives Center, National Museum of American History, Smithsonian Institution, Washington, D.C.

page 254—Gypsy child's protective vest, Kansas, 1920s, National Museum of American History, Smithsonian Institution, Washington D.C.

page 286—Kurt Schwitters, *Merz 410: "Irgendsowas"* (1922), collage, copyright © 2002 Artists Rights Society (ARS), New York/VG-Bild-Kunst, Bonn.

page 289—Joseph Cornell, *Hotel Eden* (1945), construction, courtesy National Gallery of Canada, Ottawa, © The Joseph and Robert Cornell Memorial Foundation/Licensed by VAGA, New York, N.Y.

page 291—Adolph Gottlieb, *The Prisoners* (1947). Oil on canvas. Courtesy Adolph and Esther Gottlieb Foundation/Licensed by VAGA, New York, N.Y.

page 292—Jackson Pollock, *Full Fathom Five* (1947). Oil and assorted materials on canvas. Gift of Peggy Guggenheim, Courtesy the Museum of Modern Art, New York, N.Y./Licensed by SCALA/Art Resource, N.Y., © 2002 The Pollack-Krasner Foundation/Artists Rights Society (ARS), New York.

page 293—Robert Rauschenberg, *Collection* (1953-54). Oil, paper, fabric, and metal on wood. Courtesy San Francisco Museum of Modern Art © Robert Rauschenberg/Licensed by VAGA, New York, N.Y.

page 301—Robert Motherwell, *The French Line* (1959). Oil and collage on laminated rag paper. Collection of Mr. and Mrs. Bagley White, Seattle, © Dedalus Foundation, Inc./Licensed by VAGA, New York, N.Y.

page 302—Louise Nevelson, *Moon Spikes IV* (1955). Wood painted black. Collection of Jeremiah W. Russell, © 2002 Estate of Louise Nevelson/Artists Rights Society (ARS), New York.

page 329—Frank Gehry, plan for Guggenheim Museum Bilbao, Spain (1991). Courtesy Gehry and Associates, Santa Monica, California.

INDEX

Page numbers in *italics* refer to illustrations.

Civil War, U.S., 103, 139, 140, 143–45, 189
  postwar period of, 147–86, 221
Clark, James, 190
Clark, Maurice, 190
class conflict, 178, 191–92
Cleveland, Grover, 178–79
cockfights, 56, 68–69, 114, 129, 157, 170
  gamecocks of, 158–59
  revulsion produced by, 133
Coffin, Paul, 64–65
coffin spoons, 64, *64*
coins, crooked, 36, 51–52
Colden, Cadwallader, 113
Cold War, 232, 237–38, 240, 241, 309
collages, 274, 275, 281, 285–86, 301–2, *301*
"Coming of Good Luck, The" (Herrick), 37–38
Commentaries on the English Common Law (Blackstone), 88
commonsense philosophy, 85
communism, 237–38, 240
complementarity, 295, 299, 305
Comstock, Anthony, 162–63, 170, 174, 195, 196, 215
Comte, Auguste, 176
conduct-of-life literature, 150
confidence games, 99, 103, 122, 145, 155, 159, 253
confidence men, 5, 101, 104–5, 108, 126, 189, 191, 206
  corporate, 21
  self-made men vs., 2–3, 4, 6, 100, 109, 152
conformity, 238–40, 247, 297
Congregationalists, 139
Conjure Woman, The (Chesnutt), 206–8
Connecticut, 64, 77–78
  antigambling laws in, 89
consciousness, 80, 224–25, 276–77, 280
conservatives, 194
Consolation of Philosophy, The (Boethius), 29–30
Constitution, U.S., 77–78
Continental Congress, 89
Contingency, Irony, and Solidarity (Rorty), 328
Conwell, Russell, 156

"coon songs," 204–6
Cooper, Thomas, 89–90
coral, as amulet, 36, 45, 51, 64
coral rattles, infants, 36, *36*, 45
Cornell, Joseph, 275, 289–90, *289*
cosmic optimism, 183
Cotton, John, 44
counterfeit money, 121–22
Courage to Be, The (Tillich), 307, 309
covenant of works, 37, 76, 136
Covey, Edward, 97–99
Cowell, Joseph, 115
cowrie shells, 26, 27, 28, 54
Crabtree, Lotta, 153
cradles, ceramic, 64
Crane, Stephen, 212
Crapsey, Edmund, 173
crap shooting, 121, 257
creationism, special, 140
crookedness, 36, 51–52
Crosby, Bing, 266
crossroads, 51, 255, 259
"Crossroads Blues" (Johnson), 262
Cubism, 285
cultural lag, 198–99
cultures of chance, 4–24, 27, 28, 34, 35–36, 38, 50, 52, 53, 55, 220
  African, 47–52
  chance mixed with skill in, 15, 20
  Christian challenge to, 17–19
  European, 18
  indeterminacy of form in, 14–15
  plenitude in, 12, *13*, 20, 110, *110*, 116, 220–21, 275
  pragmatism and, 20–21
  tricksters in, 10–11, 13, 15, 16, 17, 28, 51, 116, 119–20, 121, 159, 223, 252, 267, 275, 282, 297–98
  see also divination; ethic of fortune; gamblers; gambling
cultures of control, 2–10, 16, 17–24, 53, 103, 142, 143, 145, 222–23
  commonsense philosophy in, 85
  development of, 56–57, 59–62, 75–86, 92–95
  evangelicalism and, 60–61
  Fascist, 287–88, 290–91
  feeling of confidence provided by, 99
  mastery of fate in, 7–8, 9, 15, 17, 46, 157, 180, 222

evangelical Protestantism (*cont.*)
    ecstatic conversions in, 74–75, 76, 135,
        139, 147, 256
    grace in, 60, 76, 77, 137–39, 140
    moralism of, 60, 75, 76, 87, 91, 93,
        101, 109, 129–36, 215; *see also*
        antigambling moralism
    Providence as viewed by, 61–62
    reform literature of, 132–33
    revivalism in, 55, 60, 74–75, 76, 80–81,
        131–32, 135, 139, 256
    superstitions of, 256
evangelical rationality, 61–62, 75, 81, 82,
        88, 91, 92–94, 102–3, 128, 150–51,
        187, 214, 230
    ascendancy of, 168–78
    confidence of, 99
    gamblers as viewed by, 128–29, 130,
        246
    grace in, 135–36
    grace as redefined by, 139–40
    manhood redefined by, 129–36, 150
    miracles and, 141
    natural theology and, 180
    perfectionism of, 139, 148
    positivism in, 176–78
    Progressive ideology vs., 193
    Providence and, 135, 140, 147, 200
    scientific authority in, 141, 143
    self-discipline in, 75
    special providences and, 140, 141
    superstition and, 176, 209–10, 211
    waning of, 150–51, 178–86, 211–12
Evangelical Record, 76
"Every Race Has a Flag but the Coon"
        (Heehan), 204–5
evil spirits, 15, 26, 29, 36, 66
evolution, 140–41
    Darwinian, 151, 178, 180–84, 192,
        197–98, 202, 211, 216–17, 226, 279
    divine design in, 151, 182, 184
    gaming instinct and, 216–17
    natural selection in, 182, 183, 184,
        287
    progress in, 151, 180–81, 182–84,
        202
    Progressives and, 197–99
    spiritual, 183
    vitalist view of, 225–26
Ewe, 49

existentialism, 21, 296, 299
    Christian, 139, 274, 308–11

Fabian, Ann, 128
faith healing, 167
family, 94, 112, 131, 132, 133, 171–72
    suburban, 238
Farmington, Conn., 89
faro, 101, 102, 105–6, 114, 119, 120, 121,
        125, 126, 127, 153, 195
    as aleatory game, 157–58, 161, 162
    Bailey's dealing-box for, 103–4, 108
    as banking game, 194
fastidious ropers, 119
fate, 2, 15, 40, 132, 150, 155, 246, 308
    arbitrariness of, 35, 58, 71, 143–44
    mastery of, 7–8, 9, 15, 17, 46, 75–86,
        157, 180, 222
"Fate" (Emerson), 142–43
Faust (Goethe), 217
Federal Writers Project, 165
Fenollossa, Ernest, 304–5
fetish-beliefs, 51–52
fetishes, 7, 16, 26, 27, 40, 41, 229–30,
        250
    African American, 136, 165
    faith in, 214
    of gamblers, 102, 149, 161, 175
    lottery tickets as, 163
    popular Catholic, 30
    West African, 48, 50–51
    of World War II American airmen,
        251
    see also amulets; charms
Finnegans Wake (Joyce), 305
Fischer, David Hackett, 46
Fiske, John, 177, 180–81, 182–84, 186,
        197–98, 222, 323
Fleming, Alexander, 251
Flint, Timothy, 133
Flint, Valerie, 31
Floating Bear, 293
folklore, 201–3, 210, 214
folk remedies, 43
Fonseca, Isabel, 254
Ford, Henry, 230–31, 238
Fortuna, 6, 7, 29, 35, 46, 47, 57, 58–59,
        66, 68, 78, 81, 82, 117, 151, 158,
        162, 163, 174, 179, 215, 275,
        283–84

primal plenitude linked to, 12, *13,* 110,
110
fortune-telling, 10, 47, 55, 56, 65–66, 72,
137, 250, 256, 284
African American, 62–63, 64
gypsy, 204, 252, 253–54, *253*
parlor game for, 111–12
Puritan, 44
reading tea leaves as, 65, 111, 112, *111*
Forum, 216
fossil record, 140–41
Foster, Hal, 330
"4'33"" (Cage), 303
Fox, 41
fraktur pottery, 71–72
Francis, John, 62–63, 64
Frankenthaler, Helen, 302
Franklin, Benjamin, 75
Frazier, Franklin, 247
Freeman, Frank, 195
French Line, The (Motherwell), 301, *301*
Freud, Sigmund, 212–13, 245–46, 273,
274, 281, 291, 300, 309
Freudian slips, 245, 281
Frisians, 31
Frothingham, O.B., 173–75
Fuller, Peter, 33
functionalism, 238
fund-raising, 177
civic, lotteries for, 56, 70, 89

Gallup, George, 235
Gambler, The (Dostoevsky), 2, 283–84
gamblers, 8, 16, 19, 20, 40–41, 59, 63,
83, 92, 99, 100–136, 147, 243–49,
257–71
alternative moral economy of, 33, 34,
40, 257, 267–68
Chinese, 164
compulsive, 6, 114, 120, 215–16
coolness cultivated by, 160, 161
counterfeit money used by, 121–22
devil as image of, 169, *169*
enslavement of, 87, 133–34, 246
ethics of, 112, 121, 123–25, 126, 143
as fastidious ropers, 119
fetishes of, 102, 149, 161, 175
in films, 246–47, 267
as good losers, 124
Hamburg, 92, 130

home and family of, 94, 131, 132, 133,
171–72
honest, 101, 103–9, 125–28
luck beliefs of, 256–57
male camaraderie of, 115–16, 118, 132
masturbators linked with, 125, 130,
134, 171, 245–46
in modernism, 284
nouveau riche, 148–49, 152–53
patron saint of, 256
phrenology of, 130
preachers as, 119, 123, 124
prodigal, 263–64, 267, 270
professional, 69–70, 101, 113, 119–20,
152, 161, 259, 264, 265, 266–67; *see
also* sharpers
promiscuous social mingling of, 56,
68–69, 87, 115, 116–18, 125, 129,
149–50, 157
psalms of, 259
respectable Victorian, double lives led
by, 118
as seeking nervous excitement, 173–74
self-justification of, 103–9, 123–24
Southern planter elite as, 56, 68–70,
86, 87–88, 104–5, 112–13, 129, 143,
217
suicide and, 92, 94, 105, 130, 148
as superstitious, 158, 161, 174–75, 178,
256–57
theater people and, 154–55
as true sportsmen, 69–70, 101, 103,
112–13
unbridled fantasy as tendency of, 125,
130, 134, 150
women as, 68, 90, 91–92, 118–19, 132,
133, 160, 161, 172, 246, 265
as work shirkers, 173
worldview of, 8–9, 22–24, 33, 34,
46–47, 56, 57, 58, 62, 102, 249,
260
see also sporting crowd
gambling, 1–10, 27, 33, 53–54, 57–58,
62, 68–71, 92–94, 109–36, 190–91,
227, 231, 235–36, 244–45
of African Americans, 69, 113–14,
118, 129, 205–6, 247, 259–61, 264
as aristocratic and gentlemanly pastime,
2, 4, 14, 46–47, 69–70, 86, 88–89,
91–92, 112–13, 117, 129